The English Print Trade in the Reign of Edward VI, 1547–1553

Library of the Written Word

VOLUME 115

The Handpress World

Editors-in-Chief

Andrew Pettegree (*University of St Andrews*)
Arthur der Weduwen (*University of St Andrews*)

Editorial Board

Ann Blair (*Harvard University*)
Falk Eisermann (*Staatsbibliothek zu Berlin – Preußischer Kulturbesitz*)
Shanti Graheli (*University of Glasgow*)
Earle Havens (*Johns Hopkins University*)
Ian Maclean (*All Souls College, Oxford*)
Alicia Montoya (*Radboud University*)
Angela Nuovo (*University of Milan*)
Helen Smith (*University of York*)
Mark Towsey (*University of Liverpool*)
Malcolm Walsby (*enssib, Lyon*)

VOLUME 93

The titles published in this series are listed at *brill.com/lww*

The English Print Trade in the Reign of Edward VI, 1547–1553

By

Celyn David Richards

BRILL

LEIDEN | BOSTON

Cover illustration: Fragment of The New Testament title page (Richard Jugge, [1552]). The Huntington Library: 96524; National Library of Scotland: Hax.45.

Library of Congress Cataloging-in-Publication Data

Names: Richards, Celyn David, author.
Title: The English print trade in the reign of Edward VI, 1547-1553 / by Celyn David Richards.
Description: Leiden ; Boston : Brill, [2023] | Series: Library of the written word, 1874-4834 ; volume 115 | Includes bibliographical references and index.
Identifiers: LCCN 2023013632 (print) | LCCN 2023013633 (ebook) | ISBN 9789004510166 (hardback ; acid-free paper) | ISBN 9789004510173 (ebook)
Subjects: LCSH: Book industries and trade—England—History—16th century. | Printing—England—History—16th century. | Printing—Political aspects—England—History—16th century. | Religious literature—Publishing—England—History—16th century. | Great Britain—History—Edward VI, 1547-1553. | England—Intellectual life—16th century. | Censorship—England—History—16th century.
Classification: LCC Z151.3 .R53 2023 (print) | LCC Z151.3 (ebook) | DDC 686.2094209/031—dc23/eng/20230424
LC record available at https://lccn.loc.gov/2023013632
LC ebook record available at https://lccn.loc.gov/2023013633

Typeface for the Latin, Greek, and Cyrillic scripts: "Brill". See and download: brill.com/brill-typeface.

ISSN 1874-4834
ISBN 978-90-04-51016-6 (hardback)
ISBN 978-90-04-51017-3 (e-book)

Copyright 2023 by Koninklijke Brill NV, Leiden, The Netherlands.
Koninklijke Brill NV incorporates the imprints Brill, Brill Nijhoff, Brill Hotei, Brill Schöningh, Brill Fink, Brill mentis, Vandenhoeck & Ruprecht, Böhlau, V&R unipress and Wageningen Academic.
All rights reserved. No part of this publication may be reproduced, translated, stored in a retrieval system, or transmitted in any form or by any means, electronic, mechanical, photocopying, recording or otherwise, without prior written permission from the publisher. Requests for re-use and/or translations must be addressed to Koninklijke Brill NV via brill.com or copyright.com.

This book is printed on acid-free paper and produced in a sustainable manner.

For Chloé

Contents

Acknowledgements IX
List of Figures, Graphs, and Tables XI
Abbreviations XIII

1 Introduction 1

2 The Reign of Edward VI and the English Book World: An Overview 5
   1 The English Print World before 1547 6
   2 The Political Conditions of the Reign of Edward VI 13
   3 Religious Affairs in England and Europe 16
   4 The English Economy 22
   5 The Output of English Printers, 1547–1553 25
   6 Edwardian Historiography 31
   7 Key Questions 33

3 Print and Government 36
   1 Censorship and the Law 36
   2 Resistance and Suppression 57
   3 The Religious and Social Radical Fringe 67

4 Official Offices, Compulsory Provisions and Rival Texts 77
   1 The Canonical Texts of the Edwardian Church 85
   2 State Patronage: Printers' Patents and Privileges 99

5 A Technical and Design Examination 116
   1 The Henrician State of Affairs 119
   2 Design Conventions 122
   3 Technical Improvements 129
   4 Woodcut Title Borders and Initials 141
   5 Stylistic Conventions and Development 157

6 Commercial Networks 178
   1 The Composite Parts of the English Book World 179
   2 Commercial Relationships between Printers and Publishers 204
   3 Partnerships 210
   4 Printers for Hire 218
   5 Publishers 224

7 **The Growth of the Wider English Book World** 232
    1   'Certayne Honest Menne of the Occupacyon Whose Names Be upon Their Bokes': The Paul's Cross Publishing Syndicate 232
    2   'Private' Patronage 241
    3   Patronage Partnerships 247

8 **Conclusion** 254

    Bibliography 259
    Index 277

Acknowledgements

My deepest thanks are due to many people for their help in completing this monograph. Firstly, I owe the Arts and Humanities Research Council a huge debt for funding my doctoral studies at Durham University (2014–2020) and research trip to the Huntington Library, San Marino, California (2016), via the Northern Bridge Doctoral Training Partnership and International Placement Scheme. Alongside their financial support, without which I would not have been able to begin my studies at Durham, the Northern Bridge fellowship provided opportunities to engage with colleagues among my cohort and specialists within and beyond my fields in a vibrant and engaging environment. The International Placement Scheme contributed to my research more directly, providing the opportunity to spend three months in the reading rooms of the Huntington evaluating hundreds of copies of sixteenth-century printed books. This time was fundamental to this book's chapter on technical and stylistic development but the experience, insight and fresh lines of enquiry it provided are found throughout.

This book is the extension of my doctoral research at Durham University. I am enormously grateful to my supervisors, Alec Ryrie and Natalie Mears, whose support throughout this process was invaluable. I also owe a debt of gratitude to Natalie for encouraging me to participate in the National State Prayers Project and Alec for his introduction to the *Journal of Ecclesiastical History*, where I have enjoyed reviewing works since 2018. Alec's constant guidance has been instrumental and without it, this process may never have been completed. My examiners Professors Richard Gameson (Durham University) and Peter Marshall (University of Warwick) provided insightful, challenging and diligent feedback, which have informed my work and brought clarity to my writing and arguments. Beyond my doctoral years, I must also note my gratitude to the Department of Theology and Religion at Durham for continuing to support my research by awarding me an Honorary Fellowship in 2021. I am also grateful for the continued mentorship and guidance of Matthew McLean, who guided me through my MLitt dissertation at St Andrews, and Maurice Whitehead, whose early modern England module at Swansea University pulled me towards a topic I have yet to set aside. Whether introducing me to fascinating books, opportunities or individuals, I have always valued their guidance and insight.

I must also thank the teams at the research libraries I have visited throughout this project, including the Huntington, Durham University's Palace Green special collections and the National Library of Scotland. At the Huntington, the team was so kind throughout my placement and endured my daily requests for more and more books. The staff at the National Library of Scotland and Palace Green Library have also been extremely patient and accommodating, bringing their newest additions and oldest pieces with equal enthusiasm and encouragement. The images used throughout this monograph are reproduced with the kind permission of the Huntington Library, San Marino, California and the National Library of Scotland.

I also owe a considerable debt to the *Universal Short Title Catalogue* (USTC) team at St Andrews, particularly Andrew Pettegree and Graeme Kemp, who facilitated my research by providing the data upon which much of this research rest. This project first came to life during my MLitt studies in St Andrews and I am delighted to have maintained contact with the department.

I have been very fortunate to present my research throughout my studies. These events have provided occasions to learn from others, re-evaluate my findings and sharpen my outputs. In particular, I would like to note the chances to present at the European Reformation Research Group (ERRG) at Birmingham University, The University of St Andrews School of History Seminar Series and the USTC conference. From the latter, I am enormously grateful to Nina Lamal, Helmer Helmers and Jamie Cumby who helped shepherd my 'Printing for the Reformation' article through the press with their invaluable feedback and perseverance.

Beyond the academic world, I would like to thank my friends and family for their support throughout and beyond my research. My parents have encouraged my academic goals throughout my itinerant university career, whether studying nearby or across the Atlantic Ocean. When writing up my doctoral thesis from Edinburgh, my support network was strengthened by an incredible group of individuals and the space they created with 'The Men Who:'. Finally, I give all of my love and thanks to my wife who has been there from the beginning of this project until its submission and publication. I am enormously grateful for your support as you endured every false hope moment and celebrated every milestone success by my side.

> and what does *Doctor Richards* have to say this time?
>
> c.2007, a despairing secondary school history teacher, Gloucestershire, UK

Thank you for the push

CDR
January 2023

Figures, Graphs, and Tables

Figures

2.1	The 1539 Great Bible title-page	10
4.1	The New Testament title-page (Richard Jugge, [1552])	109
5.1	Inverted woodcut: *The New Testament* (Richard Jugge, [1552])	131
5.2	Woodcut initials: Edward Hall, *The Union* (Richard Grafton, 1550)	133
5.3	Head compartment of Grafton's title-page border: *A concordance* (Richard Grafton, 1550)	134
5.4	Edward Hall, *The Union* (Richard Grafton, 1550)	135
5.5	Illustration of 'John Wycliffe'	136
5.6	Illustration of St John: Miles Coverdale (ed.), The Bible (Cologne: [Eucharius Cervicornus and Johann Soter], 1535)	139
5.7	Thucydides, *The hystory of the warre, whiche was betwene the Peloponesians and the Athenyans* ([William Tylle], 1550)	145
5.8	Octavo border, used 1530–1553: Katherine Parr, *The Lamentacion of a Synner* (Edward Whitchurch, 1548)	147
5.9	Quarto border on folio: Geoffrey Chaucer, *The Works* (Nicolas Hill [for the Paul's Cross publishing syndicate], 1550)	149
5.10	Initials from *Book of Common Prayer* (Richard Grafton, 1552)	151
5.11	Giovanni da Vigo, *The most excelent worckes of chirurgery* (Edward Whitchurch, 1550)	153
5.12	23 × 23mm 'I'	154
5.13	23 × 23mm 'T'	155
5.14	*A prayer sayd in the kings chappell in the tyme of hys graces sicknes* (William Copland, [1553])	161
5.15	The Wyer press illustration style: John Coke, *The debate betwene the heraldes of Englande and Fraunce* ([London, Robert Wyer for Richard Wyer, 1550])	163
5.16	John Lydgate, *The Cronycle of all the kynges* (Robert Wyer, 1552)	165
5.17	Wolfe's rotunda and italic fount: Peter Martyr Vermigli, *Tractatio de Sacramento Eucharistæ* (Reyner Wolfe, 1549)	167
5.18	Peter Martyr Vermigli, *A Discourse or traictise of Peter Martyr Vermilla* ([Robert Stoughton [=Edward Whitchurch] for Nicholas Udall, 1550])	169
5.19	Thomas Cranmer, *A Defence of the True and Catholike Doctrine* (Reyner Wolfe, [1550])	170
5.20	Thomas Cranmer, *Defensio* (Reyner Wolfe, 1553)	171

6.1   The commercial networks of Nicolas Hill and Stephen Mierdman   220
7.1   The Paul's Cross publishing syndicate folio bible (Nicolas Hill for Thomas Petyt, 1551)   239

Graphs

2.1   Total titles produced in England, 1480–1550 (cumulative)   7
2.2   Titles produced per annum, 1530–1546   8
2.3   Titles produced per annum, 1530–1556   25
5.1   Format usage in English titles, 1547–1553   123

Tables

2.1   Titles by location, language, genre and format, 1510–1546   12
2.2   Printed output by location, language, genre and format, 1530–1553   27
2.3   Market share of religious titles, 1547–1553   28
3.1   Authors and titles printed, 1547–1553   46
4.1   The canonical church documents, 1547–1553   86
4.2   Edwardian printing patents   100
6.1   Independent printers, 1547–1553   205
6.2   Printers' collaboration, 1547–1553   209
6.3   Prominent partnerships   211
6.4   William Hill and Thomas Raynald's collaborations   214
6.5   Major printers-for-hire   219
6.6   Minor printers-for-hire   222
6.7   Middling publishers   225
7.1   The Paul's Cross syndicate publications   234
7.2   The Paul's Cross syndicate publishers, 1546–1555   236

Abbreviations

APC	Dasent, John Roche, ed., *Acts of the Privy Council of England*, new series, 4 vols (Burlington, Ontario, Canada: Tanner Richie, 2004–2005)
BCP	The *Book of Common Prayer* (various editions)
BL	The British Library
BLDB	British Library Database of Bookbindings at https://www.bl.uk/catalogues/bookbindings/
EEBO	Early English Books Online at https://eebo.chadwyck.com/home
ESTC	English Short Title Catalogue at http://estc.bl.uk
FB	Pettegree, Andrew and Malcolm Walsby, eds., *French Books III & IV. Books published in France before 1601 in Latin and Languages other than French*, 2 vols (Leiden: Brill, 2011)
HEH	Henry E. Huntington Library Catalogue Local Call Number
H&L	Hughes, Paul L., and James F. Larkin, eds., *Tudor Royal Proclamations, Vol. 1: The Early Tudors* (New Haven, CT: Yale University Press, 1964)
M&F	McKerrow, R.B., and F.S. Ferguson, eds., *Title-Page Borders Used in England & Scotland 1485–1640 – Illustrated Monographs* (Oxford: Bibliographical Society at the Oxford University Press, 1932)
P&PD	McKerrow, Ronald B., ed., *Printers' & Publishers' Devices in England & Scotland, 1485–1640* (London: Bibliographical Society, 1949)
NB	Pettegree, Andrew, and Malcolm Walsby, eds., *Netherlandish Books (Books Published in the Low Countries and Dutch Books Printed Abroad before 1601)* 2 vols (Leiden: Brill, 2010)
NLS	National Library of Scotland
ODNB	*Oxford Dictionary of National Biography* at http://oxforddnb.com
OL	Robinson, Hastings, ed., *Original Letters Relative to the English Reformation: Written during the Reigns of King Henry VIII., King Edward VI., and Queen Mary: Chiefly from the Archives of Zurich*, vols 1–2 (Cambridge: Cambridge University Press, 1846–7)
PR Edward VI	*Calendar of the Patent Rolls Preserved in the Public Record Office, Edward VI: Vol. I–IV, AD 1547–1553* (London: H.M. Stationery Office, 1924–1926)
SP	Knighton, C.S., ed., *Calendar of State Papers: Domestic Series of the reign of Edward VI 1547–1553* (London: H.M. Stationery Office, 1992)
SP Foreign	Turnbull, William B., ed., *Calendar of State Papers: Foreign Series of the Reign of Edward VI 1547–1553* (Burlington, Ontario, Canada: Tanner Ritchie, 2005)

SP Ireland	Hamilton, Hans Claude, ed., *Calendar of State Papers relating to Ireland of the reigns of Henry VIII, Edward VI, Mary and Elizabeth 1509–1573* (London: Longman, Green, Longman & Roberts, 1860)
SP Spanish	Hume, Martin A.S., and Royall Tyler, eds., *Calendar of Letters, Despatches and State Papers relating to the negotiations between England and Spain in the Archives of Simancas and Elsewhere*, vols 9–11 (London: H.M. Stationery Office, 1912)
STC	Pollard, A.W., and G.R. Redgrave, eds., *A Short-Title Catalogue of Books Printed in England, Scotland and Ireland, and of English Books Printed Abroad 1475–1640*, 3 vols, 2nd edn revised and enlarged, begun by W.A. Jackson, and F.S. Ferguson, completed by K.F. Pantzer (London: Bibliographical Society, 1987–1991)
USTC	Universal Short Title Catalogue at http://ustc.ac.uk

CHAPTER 1

Introduction

The English Print Trade in the Reign of Edward VI, 1547–1553 explores a turbulent period of religious change. The Edwardian reformation moved hurriedly, and printers quickly drove forward print production to unprecedented levels. Religion and the printing industry were intimately linked, and reformers and printers alike enjoyed a rapid ascendency. However, this excessive growth in printed output and the factors prompting it had yet to be fully explored. The foremost objective of this study is to shed light on how the English print world came to expand so rapidly and significantly between 1547 and 1553. Primarily, therefore, this is a book considering books and society rather than texts.

This book analyses three crucial areas: the role of the government, the design and technical evolution of the print world, and the commercial networks that allowed the industry swiftly to respond to emerging opportunities. Chapters three and four consider the role of the government and show how the protestant establishment encouraged the print trade by creating a climate of evangelical freedom and sponsoring individuals and publications. Thereafter, the fifth chapter demonstrates how skills and resources became more evenly spread throughout the industry, allowing more printers to join the elite of English printing. Finally, this book outlines and investigates the commercial construction of the Edwardian book world in chapters six and seven. Through these chapters, 1547 to 1553 are established as years of increasingly sophisticated commercial collaboration through the growing influence of publishers, printers-for-hire and widening participation in the trade. This study strives to make clear that whilst the change of religious affiliation of the state was critical, other factors contributed to this spike in printed output. The dramatic upsurge was also fuelled by active sponsorship of specific trade spheres, an increase in skilled printers (thus improved quality and productivity) and developing commercial and social networks within the trade and without. The Edwardian years were a time of facilitation and encouragement for England's print world, and under these conditions, English printing flourished.

To consider and reveal these factors, this study relies on the foundational sources available to book historians of the sixteenth century. The *Universal Short Title Catalogue* (USTC), a database of extant and lost sixteenth-century printed material, forms the foundation for each of these explorations.[1] Placing the trends of the book trade into the specific and unique historical contexts of different parts of the reign casts light upon Edwardian society, politics, commerce and religion. These foundations were consolidated with additional databases specific to the English context: The *English Short Title Catalogue* (ESTC) and *Early English Books Online* (EEBO), A.W. Pollard and G.R. Redgrave's *A Short-Title Catalogue of Books Printed in England, Scotland and Ireland* (STC), and R.B. McKerrow's *Title-Page Borders Used in England & Scotland* (M&F).[2]

Many questions persist around the state of religion and the religion of the state in Edwardian England. This book does not seek to solve the puzzle of early modern protestantism in England. Instead, *The English Print Trade in the Reign of Edward VI, 1547–1553* will contribute to existing scholarship by casting further light on the Edwardian reformation and the growing stature and significance of the print world during this short but influential reign. Still, it aims to acknowledge the printing trade's role in promulgating the official reformation and furthering religious discourse in England. It remains true that the reformation was critical to this efflorescence of printing, but this book seeks to advance a more nuanced understanding of how this came to pass. This monograph contends that the English print world progressed so dramatically during this reign due to a coalescence of favourable factors.

The shift in power from the conservative latter days of Henry VIII's reign to the invigorated hard-line reform faction saw printers seize opportunities to print more outwardly reformist tracts. These proceedings opened a new vein of potential religious works to be imported, translated and produced. England's printers could now welcome some of the best-selling authors and publications of the period to their presses. In response, they printed floods of literature to satisfy English readers. English reformers had a voice in this literature, with renewed and new authors contributing works, including Archbishop of Canterbury Thomas Cranmer, John Bale, John Hooper and Hugh Latimer. The output boasted an internationalism, too, with a significant European component, including Martin Luther, Jean Calvin, Heinrich Bullinger, Philipp Melanchthon and many others. Much of this output would

---

1 The *Universal Short Title Catalogue* at https://www.ustc.ac.uk.
2 *English Short Title Catalogue* at http://estc.bl.uk; *Early English Books Online* at https://eebo.chadwyck.com/home; A.W. Pollard and G.R. Redgrave, eds., *A Short-Title Catalogue of Books Printed in England, Scotland and Ireland, and of English Books Printed Abroad 1475–1640*, 3 vols, 2nd edn revised and enlarged, begun by W.A. Jackson, and F.S. Ferguson, completed by K.F. Pantzer (London: Bibliographical Society, 1987–1991); R.B. McKerrow and F.S. Ferguson, eds., *Title-Page Borders Used in England & Scotland 1485–1640 – Illustrated Monographs* (Oxford: Bibliographical Society at the Oxford University Press, 1932).

have been unsaleable before 1547, either directly outlawed by the government or implicitly understood to be too risky by printers. The shift in religious climate under Edward VI made these publications possible. Edwardian reform also required new publications for the Church of England and the church hierarchy's new direction for English evangelicalism. These official works were not produced to placate the curiosity of English readers but to provide for their spiritual needs as decided by the government. The government also made official appointments and granted patents to its favourite printers, helping to boost output and underpin printing enterprises. Through these central areas, print and protestantism walked hand-in-hand and drove forward the trade and the new religion.

Despite the many continuities between late Henrician and Edwardian printed products, English printing advanced in technical and stylistic terms between 1547 and 1553. Print output increased dramatically, but the distribution of skills throughout the industry also improved. Whilst some printers made noteworthy attempts to bring Edwardian printing forward stylistically, its greatest advancement was made as an industry-wide improvement of standards. In the Henrician 1540s, London had only three names of printers in high-quality printed books: Richard Grafton, Edward Whitchurch and Thomas Berthelet. These three printers can be considered the elite of English printing until Edward's reign. By 1553, this number was closer to ten. English readers continued to look to European fairs and importers of books for high-quality Latin works, but finer English works were being produced than ever before and in greater variety. English readers could look to London for high-quality books to adorn their libraries. Whilst certainly still trailing the leading lights of European print centres, London's print trade was able to make up ground in terms of production output, distribution of skills and high-quality products.

Underpinning this improved distribution of skills was a new cooperative commercial spirit through which the trade grew substantially. The flourishing role of non-printing publishers and printers-for-hire drew more individuals and more capital into the trade. The dynamics of printer-and-printer, printer-and-publisher and printer-and-publishing syndicate collaboration brought a new commercial spirit to the print trade which galvanised printers and facilitated growth. The networks of Tudor patronage, too, contributed to the industry as authors, translators, printers, and publishers were supported by patrons. These opportunities saw the ranks of the book world swell, the commercial construction of the trade change and the output of the presses increase. Here, the book trade is demonstrated to be moving towards a more complex and efficiently running industry of collaborating parts.

Advancements in the book trade also impacted society. Through increased output for public and private consumption, print came to hold a more prominent presence in the lives of people in early modern England. Projects directly sponsored by the church and crown brought more books into parish churches, and religious pamphlet material brought more accessibly priced publications to book shops and readers. In this respect, improvements in the print world meant change in people's lives. Printed literature was being placed in the hands of more people more frequently, accelerating the transmission of texts, ideas and learning. This idea was the backbone of a policy to present specific texts before parishioners, but it extends beyond official religious policy to broader society. Whilst this phenomenon cannot guarantee the quality of texts, printed publications became a more meaningful contributor to society. The English book trade made rapid progress between 1547 and 1553, bringing more books into more hands. Driven, such as it was, by religious printed material, the book trade affected the day-to-day devotional lives of Edward's subjects directly and prompted changes in society during this tempestuous episode of English history.

CHAPTER 2

The Reign of Edward VI and the English Book World: An Overview

The accession of Edward VI to the English throne sparked a period of disarray, but also of opportunity. England was amid an incomplete reformation and entering a royal minority: international diplomacy, political stability, and the reformation sat on a knife's edge. Edward's government had to adjust and progress quickly to secure themselves as what would become 'the most powerful Protestant state in Europe'.[1]

The output of the English presses grew rapidly and disproportionately during Edward's reign. The principal concern of this book is how the English print world came to flourish so dramatically in these years.[2] In addition, the study explores the government's role in these developments and the changes in the industrial, technical, and commercial cultures that surrounded English printing. These areas highlight that the disproportionate growth in the industry was caused by active sponsorship and support provided by the government, advancements in skills and resources beyond the uppermost reaches of the English print world, and the development of more sophisticated networks of cooperation. Budding evangelical fervour boosted Edwardian print culture, but the story is more nuanced than this factor alone. The political, religious and economic climate of the Edwardian years played a critical role in how English printing came to flourish so spectacularly. The print trade was a reflection of the favourable alignment of many factors. The economic and religious climate created an opportunity that the establishment supported to create this most dynamic chapter in English printing history.

In order to provide the foundation for this study, it is critical first to understand the state of English printing at Edward's accession. Henry VIII's reign had already seen progress in this sphere, and London's printers had made great strides since the advent of English print. Thereafter, the period's unique

---

1 Alec Ryrie, *Protestants: The Faith that Made the Modern World* (New York: Viking, 2018), p. 75.
2 The term 'print world' will be used throughout this book with the specific meaning of English printing production in its fullest and most inclusive sense. The print world includes publishers, printers, and all of their various employees and partners in associated trades including woodcut artists and binders. The term 'book world' will be used to incorporate a wider span of individuals, including authors, patrons, traders in books and other associated materials, international printers and readers.

national and international religious and political setting must be emphasised, before establishing how the printing industry stood as part of a much broader national economy, with all the benefits and constraints that this brought. The printing trade did not function in isolation; it was enveloped in the economic, political and religious settings of the reign and functioned with these factors in mind.

1 The English Print World before 1547

To understand the significance of the developments in the book trade under Edward VI, we need to appreciate its background. The pre-1547 English book trade was a minor and dependent player in the European context but was already undergoing some significant changes and was more autonomous than is sometimes appreciated. London, like many of the central print hubs in Europe, was increasing its output during the first half of the sixteenth century. From 323 titles in the first decade of the century, English title output had risen to 861 in the 1530s.[3] Year by year, the early sixteenth-century book trade saw undulations in production but overall was a picture of gradual growth from 1500 to 1540.

---

3 The output by decade is as follows: 1500–09: 323 titles; 1510–19: 481 titles; 1520–29: 670 titles; 1530–39: 861 titles. The USTC database is favoured, in part, due to its international focus. This allows for comparisons between print centres all over Europe and enables researchers to consider the English industry as part of a wider European book world. The USTC also provides ESTC (or other national equivalents) citation numbers, links to EEBO digital copies, and known library copies. The figures used in this introduction are derived from the USTC database online (see graph 2.1 notes for further information). The term 'titles' is used throughout this book in accordance with the USTC. A 'title' represents any printed item that varies from another. Phillip Gaskell, *A New Introduction to Bibliography* (Oxford: Clarendon Press, 1972), pp. 313–316 explains: 'An edition, first of all, is all the copies of a book printed at any time (or times) from substantially the same setting of type and includes all the various impressions, issues and states.' Secondly, an impression is defined as 'all the copies of an edition printed at any one time'. One edition will, therefore, comprise one or more impressions. Each edition and impression of a publication is classified as a separate title in the USTC. Furthermore, Gaskell describes an issue as 'all the copies of that part of an edition which is identifiable as a consciously planned printed unit distinct from the basic form of the ideal copy'. Examples from the Edwardian years include those publications printed for a syndicate of publishers bearing variant title-pages, which are classified as separate titles in the USTC. Gaskell describes 'The term state is used to cover all other variants from the basic form of the ideal copy'. The Whitchurch folios of Erasmus' *Paraphrases* in 1548 are often different states, and as such qualify as separate titles.

This pattern of general growth continued into the Henrician 1540s (see graphs 2.1 and 2.2). Across the first seven years of the 1540s, there was an increase against the preceding seven years from 590 titles to 667 titles. Following a spike in production in 1540, with 105 titles, output dipped dramatically to fifty-six titles in 1541, before recovering to between eighty and ninety titles per annum between 1542 and 1544, and 115–120 titles in 1545 and 1546. This low production year of 1541 was the lowest since 1524 and a stark anomaly from the general upward trends in production. A pattern of incremental growth in English printing, then, was the scene set prior to Edward's accession, reaching a new pinnacle of output in 1545.

English printing was on the rise, but it continued to trail its continental counterparts. Andrew Pettegree has placed the sixteenth-century English vernacular market in the third tier of European printing with the Portuguese, Polish

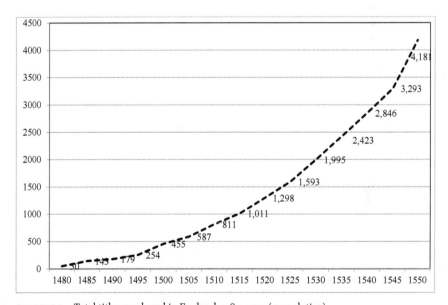

GRAPH 2.1   Total titles produced in England, 1480–1550 (cumulative)
Note: These figures have been gathered from the USTC database available at http://www.ustc.ac.uk. The USTC enables researchers to filter by keyword, author, translator, editor, short title, printer, place of printing, year, year range, country, language, format, digital copies, classification and citation. All statistics used in this book derive, in the first instance, from combinations of these filters. For those works examined at the Huntington Library, additional information and filters were applied to allow exploration by type used, lines of text, page area, the printed area of the page, number of pages, dedications, illustrations, initials and ornament sizes.

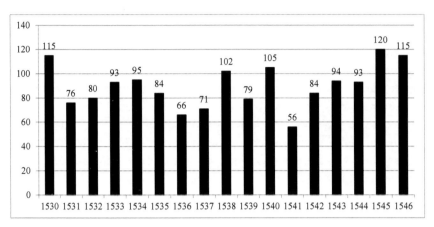

GRAPH 2.2   Titles produced per annum, 1530–1546

and Czech markets.[4] The statistics of the USTC reflect this reality. Between 1530 and 1539, six territories outproduced the English market: France, the Holy Roman Empire, the Italian States, the Low Countries, the Swiss Confederation and Spain. In many of these states, printing was largely centralised. In France, Paris and Lyon out-produced London, alongside Venice, Antwerp and three cities in Germany, too, giving London the eighth largest output of any European city.[5] During the Henrician 1540s, the international scale and standing of the London and English industry remained stable: England retained its position as seventh largest title output by territory, and London the eighth largest output by city.[6]

The English print world was subordinate to the Continent, not only in output but also in skills and resources. Printers in England continued to import raw materials (particularly paper and type) throughout the sixteenth century. Many of England's printers were European émigrés and relied upon the influence and skills of Europeans who worked in English printing houses. In general terms, early printers in England (William Caxton, Wynkyn de Worde,

---

[4] Andrew Pettegree, 'Printing and the Reformation: the English Exception', in *The Beginnings of English Protestantism*, eds. Peter Marshall and Alec Ryrie (Cambridge: Cambridge University Press, 2002), pp. 157–180 (p. 162).

[5] In these statistics, the London borough of Southwark is included as part of London. The figures are 777 for London and an additional sixty-three Southwark imprints. Ahead of London were Paris (4,858), Lyon (2,299), Venice (1,889), Antwerp (1,212), Nuremberg (1,146), Wittenburg (920), Augsburg (848).

[6] 1540–46 by country: France (6,758), Holy Roman Empire (5,316), Italian States (2,903), Low Countries (1,625), Swiss Confederation (1,101), Spain (881), England (667). 1540–46 by city: Paris (4,122), Lyon (2,197), Venice (1,940), Antwerp (1,170), Nuremberg (722), Wittenberg (703), Basel (666), London (662).

Richard Pynson among others) have their names in the annals for being among the first to complete their accomplishments on the isles, rather than for ground-breaking accomplishments in the European context.

The wider English book world also reflected this internationalism. Printers and merchants had forged paths for books printed on the Continent, particularly Antwerp, Basel, Paris, and Venice, to reach English readers. Moreover, the works of continental authors were translated and reprinted in English print houses. However, England's position in the international printing arena was that of an inward-facing peripheral market. Whilst some European printing centres and prestigious printing houses served transnational readerships and targeted the major international book fairs, English printing houses were less ambitious. The vast majority of sixteenth-century English printed output was produced in the vernacular and served a national audience. Of the 1,528 titles produced between 1530 and 1546, seventy-five per cent (1,144 titles) were in the vernacular. By continental standards, this was disproportionately high; Spain had the only larger printing industry with over sixty per cent of output in its native tongue or tongues.[7] A national readership supported the English printing industry, and printers made little effort to challenge their often higher-quality counterparts on the European stage.

The most significant and substantial English projects conducted prior to Edward's accession were the editions of the crown-supported Great Bible, completed in 1539, 1540 and 1541.[8] This project was shepherded through the press by Richard Grafton and Edward Whitchurch, who acted first as publishers when they commissioned the work from the Parisian print house of François Regnault in 1539. The repatriation of the work following a raid in Paris secured Grafton and Whitchurch's places as the elite of English printing.[9] This project was of an unprecedented scale for English print culture. With over one thousand large folio pages (385 × 265mm), adorned with a huge and sophisticated title-page, richly detailed illustrations, woodcut ornaments and initials, and an extensive range of typefaces, the Great Bible was a remarkable

---

7   Between 1540 and 1546, German-language publications made up sixty per cent of Holy Roman Empire titles, Italian-language publications made up fifty-two per cent of titles from the Italian States, and German-language and French-language titles combined made up twenty-six per cent from the Swiss Confederation.

8   These projects are found in the USTC (1539) 182295, 503073; (1540) 503151, 503153, 518561; (1541) 503233, 503234, 502235, 503237, 503272.

9   David Daniell, *The Bible in English: Its History and Influence* (New Haven, CT: Yale University Press, 2003), p. 203. Daniell suggests that there was a transfer not only of resources and material but also of the craftsmen who printed this work.

FIGURE 2.1 The 1539 Great Bible title-page
THE HUNTINGTON LIBRARY: 32897, *USTC* 503272

publication.[10] Moreover, its crown-mandated provision in every parish church ensured this project was the largest of its kind by some distance.[11]

In order to gain a sense of the industry-wide patterns of production in the Henrician book trade, one can turn to the statistics provided by the USTC. Henry VIII's reign was long, and English print culture was not stagnant. A significant evolution within the Henrician print world emerges if we break down printed output into decades (see Table 2.1).

A basic understanding of book construction and the folding of sheets of paper into quires or gatherings is important at this stage. An unfolded sheet of paper is a broadsheet with two sides, therefore offering two potential pages. A single fold in half creates a folio, with four pages, and a second equal fold (creating a quarto) offers eight pages. An octavo is formed by folding the sheet once more in half, creating sixteen pages. Each fold in the sheet of paper makes the sheet proportionally smaller and printers selected their formats carefully for each work. These three formats were the backbone of the Henrician and Edwardian book trades.

Between 1510 and 1529, printers focused upon Latin texts and the dominant format was the quarto. During the 1530s and 1540s, neither continued to be true. English-language publications doubled from thirty-six per cent in the 1520s to seventy-two per cent in the 1530s. The market share of quartos plummeted, meanwhile the octavo rose from an eight per cent market share in the 1520s to fifty per cent between 1530 and 1546. This sea change of design and technical approach to the English print world saw a transformation of the physical products of the press that we continue to handle and read in libraries and archives today.

Between 1500 and 1540, the USTC classifies over one-third of all works printed in England as 'religious' in content.[12] Religious publications were, throughout the period, the driving force of the English industry. This convention is upheld in the years immediately preceding Edward VI's kingship, with thirty-two per cent between 1540 and 1546. In terms of other staple genres, 'educational' works represented over twenty per cent of all publications

---

10   Initials and ornaments in the Great Bible of 1541 included 65 × 65mm, 35 × 35mm, 30 × 30mm, 25 × 25mm, 22 × 22mm, 20 × 20mm, 17 × 17mm, 12 × 12mm. The type of the body of the text was a 102mm textura. Lotte Hellinga, 'Printing', in *The Cambridge History of the Book in Britain, Vol. III: 1400–1557*, eds. Lotte Hellinga and J.B. Trapp (Cambridge: Cambridge University Press, 1999), pp. 65–108 (pp. 105–106).
11   *H&L*, 1, pp. 296–298 – 6 May 1541.
12   From the 2,411 publications in total, 858 are considered primarily religious in genre, with fifty listed in a sub-section 'Bibles (including parts)'.

TABLE 2.1   Titles by location, language, genre and format, 1510–1546

	1510–1519 Total	1510–1519 Percentage	1520–1529 Total	1520–1529 Percentage	1530–1539 Total	1530–1539 Percentage	1540–1546 Total	1540–1546 Percentage
USTC Total Titles	553		670		861		667	
London & Southwark	515	93	651	97	838	97	662	99
USTC Language[a]								
Latin	290	52	338	50	186	21	101	15
English	206	37	244	36	624	72	520	78
USTC Genre[b]								
Religious	174	31	183	27	352	40	215	32
Educational	117	21	150	22	71	8		
Jurisprudence	59	11	126	19	160	19	170	25
USTC Format								
Folio	102	18	147	22	142	16	124	19
Quarto	346	63	397	59	234	27	102	15
Octavo	24	4	52	8	421	49	348	52

a   'Language' categorisations by the USTC are, in areas, incomplete. Only a small minority of the titles classified as neither English nor Latin can be accounted for by publications attributed to another language. 'Law French' is a masked listing in the USTC database not available to access via the website. For the years 1547 to 1553, Law French accounts for 34 titles, whereas on the online database, only 12 titles are categorised as French. 'Law French' therefore likely makes up a significant portion of the between five and fifteen per cent of the unaccounted titles in these Henrician decades.

b   'Genres' will be discussed throughout this book. Without reading every text produced in the period, reclassifying these works independently would be too open to misappropriation. The genres used in this book are derived from the USTC database and are used only as a guide. Whilst this opens up the listed genres of particular publications to dispute, the remit of this study prevents any further reclassification at present. Further information on these genres can be found at http://eeb.chadwyck.com/help/subj_class_help.jsp. 'Religious' works, for example, make up a huge portion of the market and encompass a wide range of texts, though the boundaries between 'religious' and 'educational', for example, are difficult to define and would require further scrutiny to be used as the centre piece of scholarship on this period. The natural progression of this project would see the religious publications categorised into smaller sub-categories.

between 1509 and 1520. Thereafter, the market share of 'educational' publications declined as 'jurisprudence' became the second most prominent genre. In the Henrician 1540s, 'medical texts' and 'ordinance & edicts' each rose to gain a market share of eight per cent of all titles produced.[13]

There was also a fundamental change in the presentation of publications between 1510–1529 and 1530–1546. In the first of these periods, the quarto was the leading format of choice for England's printers, accounting for sixty-one per cent of all titles. In the 1530s, quarto production halved as the octavo began to dominate the market. After accounting for fewer than seven per cent of publications between 1510 and 1529, octavos accounted for half of all English printed output between 1530 and Edward's accession. We can only highlight this significant shift of publication patterns once we deconstruct the Henrician years into separate decades, but the indications are there: the English book world was already changing before Edward's accession.

By the end of the reign of Henry VIII, the print world was developing to become more insular, providing a greater proportion of works in its native tongue. Its focus on religious literature fluctuated but remained around one-third of all titles produced. The inherited position of the English print world coming into the reign of Edward VI was one of stable incremental growth, accommodating the needs of the domestic market alone.

2   The Political Conditions of the Reign of Edward VI

The death of the notorious Tudor patriarch Henry VIII on 28 January 1547 left the religious change of his reign at a critical juncture. In order to begin to understand the role of the government in promoting and controlling print, we need to be aware of the specific religious and political conditions of Edward's reign.

Henry VIII surrounded the soon-to-be boy-king by a family, council and educators of broadly reformed persuasion, designed to secure an 'unassailable position to take over at his death'. Diarmaid MacCulloch's seminal monograph *The Tudor Church Militant* christened this scholarly, political, and religious sodality 'the evangelical establishment'.[14]

---

13   The genres of 'medical works' and 'ordinances & edicts' account for a combined total of fifty-one titles in these years, accounting for eight per cent of output.
14   Diarmaid MacCulloch, *Tudor Church Militant: Edward VI and the Protestant Reformation* (London: Allen Lane, 1999), p. 7; Alec Ryrie, *The Age of Reformation: The Tudor and Stewart*

In its first manifestation, the emergent government became the protectorate of Edward Seymour, duke of Somerset. The regent's tenure, characterised by an unsuccessful military campaign in Scotland, 'popularity' politics, personal ambition, and a radical religious trajectory interrupted by rebellion, has created rich historiography.[15] The arrest of the duke brought this political period to a swift close in October 1549, owing to the ineffective repression of rebellion, poor financial stewardship and personal grievances.

One of the policies so costly for Somerset was warfare in Scotland. This latest stage of the 'Rough Wooing' to wed Mary Queen of Scots to Edward VI, and the topic of William Patten's *The Expedicion into Scotlande of the most woorthely fortunate prince Edward, Duke of Soomerset* in 1548, saw 'the most sustained and brutal Anglo-Scottish warfare since the 1330s'.[16] Somerset's campaign began with a spectacular victory at the Battle of Pinkie before it 'lost momentum and direction' hindered by the 'hugely, ruinously, expensive' policies of the duke of Somerset.[17] The early victory did little to aid Somerset's reputation in light of the campaign's 'spectacular failure' and 'humiliating defeat', which finally led to peace following Somerset's fall.[18]

In 1549, peace in England was shattered. The multifaceted rebellions of 1549 have been touted as 'the most dangerous episode of civil unrest in England in the entire sixteenth century'.[19] Alongside various other popular risings spanning March to August, The Western Rising, or 'Prayer Book' rebellion saw thousands of rebels from Cornwall and Devon besiege Exeter for thirty-five

---

Realms 1485–1603, 2nd edn (Abingdon: Routledge, 2017), pp. 136–137; John Strype, ed., *Ecclesiastical Memorials, relating chiefly to Religion, and the reformation of it, and the emergencies of the Church of England, under King Henry VIII, King Edward VI and Queen Mary I, with large appendixes, containing original papers, records, &c.*, 2, 1 (Oxford: Clarendon Press, 1822), pp. 13–14.

15 *SP Spanish*, 9, pp. 90–93: 29 May 1547 – van der Delft to the Emperor; Catharine Davies, *A Religion of the Word: The defence of the reformation in the reign of Edward VI* (Manchester: Manchester University Press, 2002), p. 10; MacCulloch, *Tudor Church Militant*, p. 74; Ethan H. Shagan, *Popular Politics and the English Reformation* (Cambridge: Cambridge University Press, 2003), p. 275; Barrett Beer, 'Seymour, Edward, duke of Somerset [known as Protector Somerset] c.1500–1552', *ODNB*; Jennifer Loach, *Edward VI*, eds. George Bernard and Penry Williams (New Haven, CT: Yale University Press, 1999), pp. 89–93.

16 USTC 504112; Ryrie, *The Age of Reformation*, pp. 144–145.

17 Peter Marshall, *Heretics and Believers: A History of the English Reformation* (New Haven, CT: Yale University Press, 2017), p. 314.

18 MacCulloch, *Tudor Church Militant*, p. 11; Ryrie, *The Age of Reformation*, pp. 193–194.

19 Ryrie, *The Age of Reformation*, pp. 145–146.

days and during Kett's rebellion, rebel forces sixteen-thousand strong rose in Norfolk and seized the city of Norwich. Disruption spanned large swathes of the country throughout the spring and summer of 1549.[20] The Western Rising seems to have been an uprising with religion at its heart, though anti-gentry sentiment and enclosure commissions certainly contributed to these widespread risings and the precarious political and economic situation.

Jennifer Loach contended that even alongside Somerset's inability to deal with the 1549 uprisings, 'most of the difficulty lay in the protector's personality'.[21] Somerset was soon surrounded by enemies, blamed for stirring up popular discontent, anti-landlordism and conservative opposition.[22] Somerset was perceived to have ruled beyond his brief as lord protector and spent too heavily on vanity projects. The protectorate's fate was sealed in 1549 with Somerset's arrest, bringing the first stage of Edwardian government to a close.

Somerset's successor in influence, if not in official title and power, was John Dudley, earl of Warwick, elevated to lord president of the council on 2 February 1550, and duke of Northumberland on 11 October 1551.[23] Northumberland's tenure was less popular but more diplomatically and economically sound than the Somerset protectorate.[24] MacCulloch bestows upon Northumberland 'idealism without fireworks', whilst David Loades prefers a 'pragmatic realism' which brought about stability and restored normality.[25] Loach contended that Northumberland held closer control over the king than Somerset before him but his tenure as lord president endured poor harvests, crown finance difficulties, popular discontent, religious tension and enduring factionalism.[26] Northumberland brought about peace with France and Scotland (March 1550) and ended the debasement period which had cost the crown purse profoundly under Henry VIII and Somerset.

---

20 Loach, *Edward VI*, pp. 71–72, 78, 85.
21 Loach, *Edward VI*, p. 89.
22 Marshall, *Heretics and Believers*, pp. 335–336.
23 David Loades, 'Dudley, John, duke of Northumberland, (1504–1553)', *ODNB*.
24 Davies, *A Religion of the Word*, pp. 10–12.
25 MacCulloch, *Tudor Church Militant*, pp. 17, 52–56; Loades, 'Dudley, John, duke of Northumberland'.
26 Loach, *Edward VI*, pp. 96–98, 109, 112.

Whilst Diarmaid MacCulloch has effectively argued an 'essential continuity of purpose in a graduated series of religious changes', this factionalism and the two-phase construction of Edwardian rule had repercussions for politics and printing.[27] The Edwardian establishment had many influential voices; each was distinct and motivated by different priorities. The character of works encouraged by the regime, therefore, reflected the priorities of these empowered nobles and their allies at any given time. In equal measure, this is true also of the works that these ruling parties condemned. The distribution of official offices and patents to England's printers, too, was enveloped in the world of patronage that surrounded the English political elites. This created varying political, economic and religious landscapes as even crown patronage lay in the hands of two very different men.

3   Religious Affairs in England and Europe

In England, the reformation was the product of a small clique of the landed and learned, who wrested control from their conservative counterparts. The religious climate of the reign was one of faction and confessional variety. England's episcopate and religious elite represented an uneasy coalition of reformers with diverse theological outlooks and besieged conservatives. This collective had an inherently international and eclectic complexion, and the balance of power between factions was ever changing.[28] This spectrum of religious division and debate fuelled the presses.

Lutheranism had initially won supporters in England, but its influence waned, and what developed among England's hierarchy was an assortment of variant theological outlooks.[29] This internationalism and confessional variety

---

27   Diarmaid MacCulloch, *Thomas Cranmer: A life* (New Haven, CT: Yale University Press, 1996), pp. 365–366.
28   MacCulloch, *Tudor Church Militant*, pp. 7–8; Stephen Alford, *Kingship and Politics in the reign of Edward VI* (Cambridge: Cambridge University Press, 2002), pp. 18–19; Carl R. Trueman, 'Early English Evangelicals: Three examples', in *Sister Reformations: The Reformation in Germany and in England*, ed. Dorothea Wendebourg (Tübingen: Mohr Siebeck, 2010), pp. 15–28 (p. 28).
29   Alec Ryrie, 'The Strange Death of Lutheran England', *Journal of Ecclesiastical History*, 53 (2002), pp. 64–92. For Zurich and Bullinger, see W.J. Torrance Kirby, *The Zurich Connection and Tudor Political Theology* (Leiden: Brill, 2007), pp. 1–2, 5, 25–26; John Craig, 'Erasmus or Calvin? The Politics of Book Purchase in the Early Modern English Parish', in *The Reception of Continental Reformation in Britain*, eds. Polly Ha and Patrick Collinson (Oxford: Oxford University Press, 2010), pp. 39–62 (pp. 54–55). For Melanchthon, see John Schofield, *Philip*

saw England's evangelicals engage closely with their European counterparts.[30] During the Edwardian years, a resurgent reforming faction aligned with reformed thought in the Zurich (or Tigurine) tradition came to hold significant influence and impact upon religious policy. Returning Henrician religious refugees, whose 'presence on the religious battlefield was worth thousands' along with new religious émigrés were swiftly absorbed into the establishment as preachers, scholars and bishops.[31] Even as the reformed faction seized control, episodes including the 1549 and 1552 *Books of Common Prayer* and the Vestment Controversy of 1550–1551 highlight that no singular theological tradition was able to entirely dominate religious affairs.

The English religious landscape lacked a defined religious trajectory when Edward acceded to the throne, but it was not without a commanding voice. The theological lynchpin of the reformation was the Archbishop of Canterbury, Thomas Cranmer. The Archbishop's contemporaries and historians have debated his theological evolution and alignment; however, under his stewardship, the church was incrementally shepherded further into the reformed camp with no small level of diligence and assuredness.[32] Beyond Cranmer, the Edwardian episcopacy was in a constant state of flux. A flurry of deprivations expelled the conservative remnants of Henry VIII's final years and many key

---

Melanchthon and the English Reformation (Aldershot: Ashgate, 2006); Andrew Pettegree, 'The Reception of Calvinism in Britain', in *Calvinus Sincerioris Religionis Vindex: Calvin as Protector of the Purer Religion*, eds. Wilhelm H. Neuser and Brian G. Armstrong (Kirksville, MO: Sixteenth Century Journal Publishers, 1997), pp. 267–290 (pp. 276–279) Pettegree notes sixty-one copies of Melanchthon's works in Cambridge wills during the 1540s, and forty-one in the 1550s, far exceeding any continental theologian aside from Erasmus. For Bucer, see N. Scott Amos, 'Protestant Exiles in England. Martin Bucer, the Measured Approach to Reform, and the Elizabethan Settlement – "Eine gute, leidliche Reformation"', in *Sister Reformations: The Reformation in Germany and in England*, ed. Dorothea Wendebourg (Tübingen: Mohr Siebeck, 2010), pp. 151–174 (pp. 162–163).

30 Andrew Pettegree, *Marian Protestantism: Six Studies* (Aldershot: Scolar Press, 1996), pp. vii, 126.

31 Alec Ryrie, *The Gospel and Henry VIII: Evangelicals in the Early English Reformation* (Cambridge: Cambridge University Press, 2003), chapter 3, p. 96; Bruce Gordon, *The Swiss Reformation* (Manchester: Manchester University Press, 2002), pp. 283, 300–302; W.J. Torrance Kirby, *The Zurich Connection*, pp. 1–5; returning exiles included Miles Coverdale (almoner to Katherine Parr, bishop of Exeter) and John Hooper (bishop of Gloucester and Worcester).

32 Andrew Pettegree, *Foreign Protestant Communities in Sixteenth Century London* (Oxford: Clarendon Press, 1986), pp. 25, 29; MacCulloch, *Tudor Church Militant*, pp. 89, 172; MacCulloch, *Thomas Cranmer*, p. 353; Ashley Null, 'Princely Marital Problems and the Reformers' Solutions', in *Sister Reformations: The Reformation in Germany and in England*, ed. Dorothea Wendebourg (Tübingen: Mohr Siebeck, 2010), pp. 133–149 (p. 136).

conservatives, including Stephen Gardiner (Winchester) and Edmund Bonner (London), saw their offices granted to prominent evangelicals. The regime also supported a stream of reformed theologians and preachers who held great influence without holding bishoprics or significant offices in the Church of England. There were many ways the regime could support protestant theologians, biblical scholars, churchmen, preachers and polemicists to forge paths to prominence.

The passage of Edwardian religion was incremental but consistent. From the onset of the reign, the reformers were on the ascendency. With Somerset at the helm of state and Cranmer steering the church, the reformers grew bold. The *Homilies*, twelve sermons to be given in the absence of an appropriate preacher, were introduced into every parish church in 1547 and in January 1548, the Council abolished many of the Roman Catholic remains of Henry VIII's evangelicalism, before issuing a ban on church imagery the following month. The dissolution of the chantries in 1548 and the ban on preaching by anyone other than the eighty or so individuals with a license solidified the reformers' grip.[33] Following this incremental programme of reform, the next stage of the English reformation was coming: the 1549 *Book of Common Prayer*. The Act of Uniformity made the 1549 *Book of Common Prayer* compulsory in England and promoted significant steps towards a protestant Church of England. In Cranmer's ambition to ensure that 'the curates shall need none other books for their public service but this book & the Bible', the *Book of Common Prayer* provided a *lectio continua*, which would guide services through the year.[34] The *Book of Common Prayer* was a radical change in English devotional lives. The 1549 edition, however, received little encouragement from either side of the religious divide, with conservatives lamenting the removal of old orders and the reformers seeing stunted progress.

Following the fall of Somerset, efforts continued to bring uniformity to the religious landscape. The first *Book of Common Prayer* was superseded by the 1552 *Book of Common Prayer*, which further advanced the cause of reformed protestantism in England. Eamon Duffy has proclaimed that 'the difference between the two books provide a telling index of the distance which the reform had travelled in just three years'. The eucharistic debate was settled, with the communion service of remembrance firmly established, prayers for the dead removed and anointings at baptisms and ordination withdrawn.[35] Again, the

---

33 Marshall, *Heretics and Believers*, pp. 314–315.
34 Eyal Poleg, *A Material History of the Bible, England 1200–1553* (Oxford: Oxford University Press for The British Academy, 2020), pp. 175–176.
35 Eamon Duffy, *The Stripping of the Altars: Traditional Religion in England 1400–1580*, 2nd edn (New Haven, CT: Yale University Press, 2005), pp. 472–473.

Book of Common Prayer was the product of coalition, compromise and contest between competing factions, famously shown by the 'black rubric' which justified kneeling at communion against criticism from a budding protégé of Northumberland, John Knox.[36] This was a significant step towards outlining a decidedly reformed protestant church.

The progress of religious reform was stunted when Archbishop Cranmer's proposed revision of canon law was blocked in the House of Lords, but in spite of persistent internal divisions an authoritative statement of the reformed protestant Church of England, The Forty-Two Articles, was delivered in June in 1553.[37] The Forty-Two Articles did not solve the question of religion in Edwardian England but they were a landmark statement in promoting uniformity and are considered foundational for the course of the Elizabethan church and its settlement of religion in 1559.[38]

Elements of legislation and religion will be discussed further in chapter three, particularly direct interventions by the authorities and how this changing religious landscape guided printers' self-censorship, but it is important to set out with an understanding of the undulating religious landscape during these years. These factors are critical to any consideration of English printing. Religious publications were the mainstay of early modern printing in England and elsewhere. The new direction of the church was forged hand-in-hand with official church publications, and the ruling powers disseminated polemic and rhetoric via print. The evolving nature of Edwardian religious policy meant that printers had to decide, at any given moment, how potential publications would sit within the religious and political landscape. Printing religious works was not as simple as producing works of prominent theologians; as we shall see, an understanding of the religious trajectory of the reign at any time was crucial.

Internationally, too, the continental movement for reform was splintered geographically, socially and theologically. The reformers were a faith under siege.[39] Attempts to settle the deepening divisions and reconcile the different confessional alignments were orchestrated but ultimately had failed.[40]

---

36   MacCulloch, *Thomas Cranmer*, pp. 525–529.
37   Ryrie, *The Age of Reformation*, pp. 154–156.
38   John N. King, 'Paul's Cross and the Implementation of Protestant Reforms under Edward VI', in *Paul's Cross and the Culture of Persuasion in England, 1520–1640*, Studies in the History of Christian Traditions, 171 eds. Torrance Kirby and P.G. Stanwood (Leiden: Brill, 2013), pp. 141–150 (p. 142).
39   Pettegree, *Foreign Protestant Communities*, p. 23.
40   These efforts included the Marburg Colloquy (1 and 4 October 1529) and the Wittenberg Concord (29 May 1536). The Consensus Tigurinus was signed in 1549 by Jean Calvin and Heinrich Bullinger but failed to bring widespread accord. Missing from negotiations were Basel, Berne and any English or Lutheran participants. Peter Stephens, 'The Sacraments

The 1540s ushered in a period of renewed persecution of evangelicals in France and the Netherlands and the commencement of a Roman Catholic counter-reformation with the Council of Trent. The eponymous hero for many reformers and the most printed author of the period, Martin Luther, succumbed to illness less than a year before Edward became King of England. Whilst polarising in the extreme, Luther was a captivating orator and prolific author; this loss was profound. Moreover, not three months after Edward's accession, the Lutheran Schmalkaldic League were defeated at Mühlberg, and catholic forces entered the heart of the Lutheran reformation: Wittenberg.[41]

The cause of the reformation, however, was not without hope. Lutheranism had spread throughout Germany and into Northern Europe and the Baltic.[42] The reformed faith under the banner of Huldrych Zwingli in Zurich established religiously autonomous cantons in the Swiss Confederation. Basel, Berne and Zurich shared an emphasis upon the ancient languages and education, but their theological outlooks remained independent.[43] Jean Calvin's rise in Geneva began during the Edwardian years, but he was not without opposition and he did not yet hold the esteem and profile that we attribute to him in hindsight.[44] Attempts to unite the continental movements for reform ensured

---

in the Confessions of 1536, 1549, and 1566 – Bullinger's Understanding in the Light of Zwingli's', *Zwingliana*, 33 (2006), pp. 51–76 (p. 62); Mark Greengrass, 'The theology and liturgy of Reformed Christianity', in *Cambridge History of Christianity, Vol 6: Reform and Expansion 1500–1660*, ed. R. Po-chia Hsia (Cambridge: Cambridge University Press, 2007), pp. 104–124 (pp. 117–118); J. Wayne Baker, 'Christian Discipline, Church and State, and Toleration: Bullinger, Calvin and Basle 1530–1555', *Zwingliana*, 19, 1 (1992), pp. 35–48 (p. 38); Glenn Ehrstine, *Theatre, Culture and Community in Reformation Bern, 1523–1555* (Leiden: Brill, 2002), p. 57.

41   These measures included the Edict of Châteaubriant (27 June 1551), see Malcolm Smith, *Montaigne and Religious Freedom: The Dawn of Pluralism* (Geneva, 1991), pp. 13–16; Pettegree, *Europe in the Sixteenth Century*, pp. 112–113, 134; Ryrie, *The Age of Reformation*, p. 140.

42   Denmark and Norway had declared for Lutheranism in the 1520s and 1530s.

43   Gordon, *The Swiss Reformation*; Stephen G. Burnett, *Christian Hebraism in the Reformation Era 1500–1660: Authors, Books and the Transmission of Jewish Learning* (Leiden: Brill, 2012), p. 57; Matthew McLean, 'Between Basel and Zurich: Humanist Rivalries and the works of Sebastian Münster', in *The Book Triumphant. Print in Transition in the Sixteenth and Seventeenth Centuries*, eds. Malcolm Walsby and Graeme Kemp (Leiden: Brill, 2011), pp. 270–291 (p. 278); Roland Diethelm, 'Bullinger and Worship: "Thereby Does One Plant, and Sow the True Faith"', in *Architect of Reformation: An introduction to Heinrich Bullinger, 1504–1575*, eds. Bruce Gordon and Emidio Campi (Grand Rapids, MI: Baker Academic, 2004), pp. 135–158 (p. 139).

44   Gordon, *The Swiss Reformation*, pp. 312–313; Bruce Gordon, *Calvin* (New Haven, CT: Yale University Press, 2009), pp. 253–257.

that many of the leading minds of the reformation maintained an international outlook. Archbishop Cranmer took up the mantle as one of the premier conciliatory forces for international evangelicalism.[45] England became a centre of protestant exile as Oxford and Cambridge universities bolstered their ranks with leading European scholars and theologians, and prominent European reformers came to England with the establishment of the stranger churches of London in 1550.[46]

This international religious climate was also pivotal for the ascent of English print. Andrew Pettegree and Elizabeth Evenden have uncovered swathes of émigrés who flooded into London, many of whom worked in England's printing houses.[47] This migration channel brought skilled workers into the printing industry and authors whose work the printers could reproduce. From an

---

[45] Ryrie, *Protestants*, pp. 75–76; MacCulloch, *Tudor Church Militant*, pp. 99–100.

[46] For England's Universities, see Bruce Gordon, 'The Authority of Antiquity: England and the Protestant Latin Bible', in *The Reception of Continental Reformation in Britain*, eds. Polly Ha and Patrick Collinson (Oxford: Oxford University Press, 2010), pp. 1–22 (pp. 2–6); these scholars included Paul Fagius and Immanuel Tremellius (successive Regius Professors of Hebrew at Cambridge), Martin Bucer (Regius Professor of Divinity, Cambridge) and Peter Martyr Vermigli (Regius Professor of Divinity, Oxford). For London and the stranger churches, see Pettegree, *Foreign Protestant Communities*, pp. 35–36. A patent awarded to Jan a Lasco's granted a substantial salary of £100 per annum and the Stranger communities were grant of the church of Austin Friars; the stranger churches also brought Jan Utenhove (pp. 54–55), Martin Micronius (pp. 49–50), Richard Vauville (p. 53) and Francis Perussel (p. 52) to England. Susan Brigden, *London and the Reformation* (Oxford: Clarendon Press, 1989), p. 459; W.K. Jordan, *Edward VI: The Young King* (Cambridge, MA: Harvard University Press, 1974), p. 190. N. Scott Amos includes in his list of émigrés Bernardino Ochino; Immanuel Tremellius; Francis Dryander; Jan à Lasco; Pierre Alexander; John Ab Ulmis; Paul Fagius; and Vallerand Poullain in N. Scott Amos, 'Strangers in a Strange Land: The English Correspondence of Martin Bucer and Peter Martyr Vermigli', in *Peter Martyr Vermigli and the European Reformations: Semper Reformanda*, ed. Frank A. James III (Leiden: Brill, 2004), pp. 26–46 (p. 21n.); Dirk J. Rodgers, 'À Lasco [Laski], John (1499–1560)', ODNB. Bernardino Ochino was made Prebendary of Canterbury Cathedral.

[47] Peter W.M. Blayney, *The Bookshops in Paul's Cross Churchyard* (London: Bibliographical Society, 1990), pp. 18–19; David Loades, 'Books and the English Reformation prior to 1558', in *The Reformation and the Book*, ed. Jean-Francois Gilmont, trans. Karin Maag (Aldershot: Ashgate, 1998), pp. 264–291 (p. 273); Elizabeth Evenden, 'The Fleeing Dutchmen? The Influence of Dutch Immigrants upon the Print Shop of John Day', in *John Foxe at Home and Abroad*, ed. David Loades (Aldershot: Ashgate, 2004), pp. 63–78 (p. 65); Pettegree, *Foreign Protestant Communities*, pp. 91–92; Davies, *A Religion of the Word*, pp. x–xi; Evenden, 'The Fleeing Dutchmen?', pp. 64–65, 69–70; Robert J. Milevski, 'A Primer on Signed Bindings', in *Suave Mechanicals. Essays on the History of Bookbinding Volume 1*, ed. Julia Miller (Ann Arbor, MI: Legacy Press, 2013), pp. 165–179 (pp. 176–178). Milevski notes Garret Godfrey, Nicholas Spiernick and John Siberch as binders in England pre-1550.

international standpoint, Edwardian England became a beacon of hope for the reformers when 'much of the optimism of the movement had evaporated'.[48] Only with an understanding of this specific international religious landscape can we fully appreciate the remarkable growth of England's printed output, particularly when the printed output in the majority of reforming cities stagnated or fell.

This fractured atmosphere for the reformation is key to understanding changes in printing, and texts, during Edward's reign. In the face of clampdowns across Europe, those at the heart of the Edwardian reformation knew that they had to act quickly. Moreover, for the first time, England was at the forefront of the European reformation and seen as a haven for those fleeing persecution. This situation prompted the arrival of prominent theologians to English universities and London and many individuals who found work in printing houses. English printing had always been disproportionately dependent on international workers, and the Edwardian years represented a short period when England became a desirable refuge for continental evangelicals.

4   The English Economy

Understanding the specific economic context of mid-Tudor England is a vital precondition for any understanding of the book trade. Tudor England inherited much of its economic structure from its medieval past.[49] London was the only English city of international significance, and England's power, wealth and trade were heavily centralised. By 1540, London was the sixth-largest city in Europe, and by 1600 it was only smaller than Paris and Naples.[50] The capital was the fulcrum of England's international trade and boasted the highest concentration of literacy and middle-class merchants.[51] Books were tradable goods. In this respect, they were part of the same national and international landscape of English trade and economy. With printing and continental importation overwhelmingly concentrated in the capital, London was the

---

48   Andrew Pettegree, *Europe in the Sixteenth Century* (Oxford: Blackwell Publishing, 2002), p. 140.
49   Patrick Wallis, Justin Colson and David Chilosi, 'Structural change and economic growth in the British Economy before the Industrial Revolution, 1500–1800', *Journal of Economic History*, 78 (2018), pp. 862–903 (p. 864).
50   Pettegree, *Europe in the Sixteenth Century*, pp. 72–74; Jeremy Boulton, 'London 1540–1700', in *The Cambridge Urban History of Britain, Vol. 2: 1540–1840*, ed. Peter Clarke (Cambridge: Cambridge University Press, 2000), p. 314.
51   Robert Tittler, *Townspeople and Nation: English Urban Experiences 1540–1640* (Stanford, CA: Stanford University Press, 2001), pp. 19–22, 30.

indisputable hub of the English book world and, therefore, is the principal concern of this study.

Whilst commerce was increasingly centralised, the links between London and the wider country were also improving. These distribution networks were crucial for national trade, and the English book world abided by the same commercial pathways as any other industry. Jeremy Boulton has termed London a 'revolving door', which acted as a centre point for the urban and rural exchange of 'capital, information, cultural contacts, goods and services'.[52] The production and trade of printed matter relied upon a healthy exchange of all of these things, so it is of little surprise that the English print world had come to be centralised so heavily in the capital. Nonetheless, on a continental scale, this level of centralisation was unusual. During Edward's reign, Venice produced two-thirds of titles emanating from Italian states, Paris accounted for only half of French output owing to the competing industry in Lyon. In the Holy Roman Empire territories, meanwhile, print production was far more dispersed, with no city producing more than fourteen per cent of total output. In England, London accounted for ninety-five per cent.

Nonetheless, English printers had to serve the wider population. With this in mind, the Edwardian years saw the reestablishment of provincial printing in 1548, an enterprise abandoned since the late 1530s.[53] Provincial printing occurred in four locations: Ipswich, Canterbury, Worcester and Dublin. These provincial enterprises were facing significant challenges, limited as they were by smaller potential markets, far from the capital and yet still challenging London's established printers. There were limitations on the level of success and output one might expect of these ventures under the conditions they faced. Whilst these provincial ventures represented small enterprises, expansion beyond the boundaries of the capital highlights the increasing confidence of printers. Initially, the forty-nine titles they produced appear to be only a footnote in the history of English printing; however, these short-lived enterprises represent commercial entrepreneurialism and reveal print as an instrument of Edwardian religious policy. The English print world was on the rise, and confidence in the industry was building.

No discussion of the Edwardian economy could avoid consideration of the government's policies of the debasement of the coinage, which tested the economic robustness of the Crown and the country in the 1540s. Governmental

---

52   Boulton, 'London 1540–1700', p. 345.
53   These dates are marked from the USTC database listings for each location. For further considerations of provincial printing in Henrician England, see Peter Blayney, *The Stationers' Company and the Printers of London, 1501–1557*, 2 vols (Cambridge: Cambridge University Press, 2013), pp. 133, 194–196, 289, 429–436, 506–510.

interference with the coinage during 'the Tudor debasement period' between 1542 and 1560 were severe.[54] Estimates suggest that the bullion content in the English coinage was reduced by twenty-five per cent in gold and eighty-three per cent in silver between 1542 and 1551.[55] This economic tampering resulted in dramatic price rises, with Susan Brigden postulating that prices in the capital rose by eighty-nine per cent between 1544 and 1551.[56] Whilst the debasement raised exorbitant sums of money for the Crown, it weakened the value and international buying power of English coinage and proved detrimental to many of the realm's subjects.[57]

The English printing industry was primarily inward-facing; the overwhelming majority of works were printed in English and designed exclusively for an English audience. Nonetheless, English printing remained reliant upon the Continent for certain workers, skills, and products (most notably for its supply of paper), so in affecting international trade, the debasement policies directly influenced the book world. Many of the requisite goods for completing a book project, particularly a new prestige volume, continued to be imported and as the value of English coinage fell, these prices rose.

Just as printed works were goods, print production was a craft. The collective that made up the English print world included manual labourers, skilled artisans, and merchants. Once removed from the creative practices of authorship, printing was a trade, craft and industry like many others. This book seeks to treat the English printing and book world in such terms, exploring and understanding the economic underpinnings of a trade, rather than focusing upon the literary and cultural merit of authors, texts and readers.

---

54 Nuno Palma, 'Reconstruction of annual money supply over the long run: The case of England, 1279–1870', *European Historical Economics Society Working Papers In Economic History*, 94 (2016), pp. 10–11.

55 Li Ling-Fan, 'Bullion, bills and arbitrage: exchange markets in fourteenth- to seventeenth-century Europe' (unpublished doctoral thesis, London School of Economics, 2012), pp. 75, 88.

56 Brigden, *London and the Reformation*, p. 490.

57 Ling-Fan, 'Bullion, bills and arbitrage', pp. 115, 118, (n. 228); Palma, 'Reconstruction of annual money supply', pp. 10–11; MacCulloch, *Tudor Church Militant*, p. 55. Christopher Challis estimates that almost 1.3 million pounds sterling was raised between 1542 and 1551, a figure just shy of the notoriously high military expenditure of the first five years of Edward's reign, Christopher E. Challis, 'The Debasement of the Coinage, 1542–1551', *Economic History Review*, New Series, 20 (1967), pp. 441–466 cited in John H. Munro, 'The Coinages and Monetary Policies of Henry VIII (r. 1509–1547): Contrasts between Defensive and Aggressive Debasements', *University of Toronto Working Paper*, 417 (2010), p. 33.

5 The Output of English Printers, 1547–1553

Edward VI's accession to the throne in 1547 welcomed a period of prosperity for English printing. A tally of titles during the reign shows the production of a staggering 1,212 titles. Every year during Edward's reign outproduced any year of the preceding reign. The Edwardian figure almost doubled the equivalent preceding seven-year period (1540–1546: 667 titles) and outproduced the following (1554–1560) by over three hundred titles. The second year of Edward's reign, 1548, was a watershed year for English print production: the 246 titles produced more than doubled the most prolific Henrician year and would not be matched for thirty years. This disproportionate and spectacular growth far exceeded the general trending pattern of the period.

Between 1547 and 1553, English output surpassed Spain and the Swiss Confederation States to become the fifth largest in Europe. London's output rose disproportionately against all surrounding markets, with only Paris, Lyon and Venice producing more titles. Print production declined in Basel, Nuremberg, Wittenberg and, in particular, Antwerp, which saw a thirty per cent decline.[58] The reduction in output in the protestant centres of Wittenberg and Nuremberg was a natural result of diplomatic and military troubles

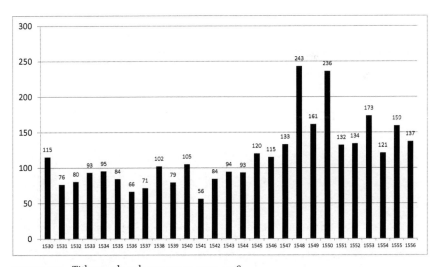

GRAPH 2.3   Titles produced per annum, 1530–1556

---

58   These figures are taken from the USTC, comparing 1540 to 1546 and 1547 to 1553: Antwerp 1,170:833; Basel 666:596; Nuremberg 722:614; Wittenberg 703:655.

occurring in the Holy Roman Empire in the 1540s, where political pressures upon protestants were increasing, and the output of reform-minded printers fell significantly.[59] Basel's renown as a printing centre in Europe relied upon its significant output in Latin biblical and scholarly works. These works were the foundation of its reputation and the city's printers produced religious works at a four-to-one ratio of scholarly languages against the vernacular.[60] When short (and quick to print) vernacular religious polemic dominated the printed output of many of the cities declared for the reformation, it is not surprising that the Basel industry failed to keep pace with the spike in publications.

The Edwardian period was undeniably one of dramatic growth in English printing. This story, however, was not one of exponential growth. Despite initial rapid expansion, there were undulations in production levels. The developments in the industry and the upheavals of these pivotal years of the reformation were intimately connected. Edward's accession was the catalyst for 'an explosion of Protestant print', which created an upsurge disproportionate to a natural outgrowth of the Henrician industry.[61] Seminal examinations of English protestantism, European publishing, and English publishing have all highlighted the period as one in which political and religious conditions proved conducive to market prosperity.[62]

Religious publications comprised the majority of the English market in the sixteenth century. The Edwardian reformation saw this market dominance increase still further. The USTC classifies fifty-six per cent of titles produced between 1547 and 1553 as 'religious' and the undulations in the production of these publications shaped the peaks and troughs of the Edwardian trade. The two years in which Edwardian production amounted to over 200 titles, 1548 and 1550, were the only two years before 1579 that English

---

59   Evenden, 'The Fleeing Dutchmen?', pp. 65–67; Diarmaid MacCulloch, *Reformation: Europe's House Divided 1490–1700* (London: Allen Lane, 2003), pp. 134–135, 211, 256–299.
60   Celyn David Richards, 'Print and Faith in the Swiss Reformation, 1517–1575' (unpublished master's thesis, University of St Andrews, 2013), p. 13.
61   Pettegree, 'Printing and the Reformation', p. 172; Elizabeth Evenden, *Patents, Pictures and Patronage: John Day and the Tudor Book Trade* (Aldershot: Ashgate, 2006), pp. 47–48; Loades, 'Books and the English Reformation', pp. 282–283.
62   Andrew Pettegree, *The Book in the Renaissance* (New Haven, CT: Yale University Press, 2010), pp. 127–128; Brigden, *London and the Reformation*, p. 430; Ian Green, *Print and Protestantism in Early Modern England* (Oxford: Oxford University Press, 2000), p. 12.

TABLE 2.2 Printed output by location, language, genre and format, 1530–1553

	1530–1539		1540–1546		1547–1553	
	Number	Percentage	Number	Percentage	Number	Percentage
Total titles	861		667		1,212	
London and Southwark	838	97	662	99	1,152	95
Language[a]						
Latin	186	21	101	15	71	6
English	624	72	520	78	1,069	88
Genre[b]						
Religious	352	40	215	32	683	56
Of which Bibles (incl. parts)	33	4	25	4	109	9
Jurisprudence	160	19	170	25	115	9
Format[c]						
Folio	142	16	124	19	208	17
Quarto	234	27	102	15	172	14
Octavo	421	49	348	52	695	57

a The remaining languages for publications between 1547 and 1553 include Law French (thirty-six), Dutch (sixteen), French (twelve), Welsh (two), multilingual (two), English/Welsh (one), Italian (one), English/Italian (one); the two multilingual listings are both dictionaries.
b Between 1547 and 1553, fifteen genres which contributed fewer than ten titles, the remaining are as follows 'adages, aphorisms emblem books' (fifteen), agriculture (fourteen), calendars, almanacs, prognostics (thirty-one), classical authors (seventeen), dictionaries (ten), economics (thirteen), educations books (fifteen), history and chronicles (eighteen), literature (twenty), medical texts (forty-three), ordinances (seventy-nine), philosophy and morality (thirteen), poetry (twenty-seven), political tracts (fourteen), science and mathematics (thirteen).
c The remaining format listings in the year 1547 to 1553 include duodecimo (one), trigsecundo (two), Broadsheet (thirty-four) and unclassified listings (100). It is important to note that works that survive only as fragments are classified as broadsheet, from the Huntington sample these include USTC 504199, 504180, 504176.

presses exceeded 100 religious titles. Such was the religious output in 1548 that it would remain unmatched even throughout the reign of Elizabeth I, with forty-four religious titles more than the 138 produced in 1581, the highest output of Elizabeth I's reign.[63]

---

63 The statistics for the Elizabethan period are taken from the USTC.

TABLE 2.3   Market share of religious titles, 1547–1553

	Total titles	Religious titles	Percentage
1547	133	69	52
1548	243	182	75
1549	161	99	61
1550	236	118	50
1551	132	75	57
1552	134	63	47
1553	173	77	45

The correlation between the reformation and printed material is proven. When administered by the government, changes in religious policy required the press as a central vehicle for the dissemination of new works and the creation of uniformity. The successful religious reformations of the sixteenth century demanded that printers produce the bible in the vernacular, new prayer books, and new official church works. Moreover, continent-wide, whether successful or suppressed, the reformation caused an enormous influx of writing, printing and reading. The ability of print to deliver ideas to such a broad audience so effectively and efficiently ensured its importance in the European movements for religious reform.

Historians widely accept that the reformers typically secured the upper hand in many of the polemical exchanges of the reign and were certainly the more active. The protestant ascendancy brought a new wave of engagement with religious publications as evangelicals of every level in society engaged with books, thus fuelling demand, sales, profits and reinvestment. Through this engagement, the religious reformation under Edward VI facilitated and actively stimulated growth in the English print world, creating an opportunity for rapid progress.

A significant characteristic of the Edwardian reformation was the official publications that it required. Chapter four, 'Official offices, compulsory provisions and rival texts', will examine the canonical documents of the Edwardian church and the vast quantities of work that the regime's key religious policies initiated. The state was a leading patron for the English print world; many of the members of the religious-political sodality that made up the English hierarchy during these years also patronised (or became) authors and funded printers directly. With the bible in the vernacular as its standard, the establishment of the 'new religion' also led to new prayer books, official church works, and academic discourses. An official reformation required new books, and the discourse of the reformation had to reach its audience.

Whilst the English reformation under Henry VIII and Edward VI was not driven by popular dissent, printers printed polemic widely. This literature sought to incite interest, persuade the population, and defend the burgeoning church. Catharine Davies adeptly analysed the key themes of the evangelical literature of this reign in her invaluable *A religion of the Word*.[64] Pro-reform literature of this nature was often inherently anti-catholic or anti-radical in its message and often outstripped the official lines of religious change. Andrew Pettegree's assessment that the regime 'deliberately fostered a Protestant publishing offensive' is crucial: most of the evangelical polemic of Edward's reign was not born of the establishment, but it was sheltered and protected, at least for a time, nonetheless.[65] The regime created a climate of protestant freedom, which inspired the creation of swathes of religious works before strides to bring uniformity created a climate of increasing conformity. Existing scholarship attributes a large proportion of the growth of Edwardian publishing to the increased output of this polemical religious literature.[66] Inexpensive religious pamphlet literature enabled many inexperienced or under-capitalised printers to grow their businesses.[67] However, it was not solely through pamphlet literature that market share for religious works expanded. The historiography of the period refers to the increased breadth of evangelical works available to English readers during the reign.[68]

In keeping with the movement towards a more defined protestant state, English-language publications dominated the English religious book world. With Latin service books rendered redundant, and catholic prayer books outlawed, their production ceased on home shores. The USTC classifies 683 English titles printed between 1547 and 1553 as 'religious' in genre. Of these titles, a total of 616 (over ninety per cent) were English-language works, with the remaining parts composed of Latin (thirty-six titles), Dutch (seventeen)

---

[64] Davies, *A Religion of the Word*.
[65] Pettegree, 'Printing and the Reformation', p. 173.
[66] John N. King, 'The Book trade under Edward VI and Mary I', in *The Cambridge History of the Book in Britain, Vol II: 1400–1557*, eds. Lotte Hellinga and J.B. Trapp (Cambridge: Cambridge University Press, 1999), pp. 164–178 (pp. 164–167); Brigden, *London and the Reformation*, pp. 436–440; Ryan M. Reeves, *English Evangelicals and Tudor Obedience, c.1527–1570* (Leiden: Brill, 2014), pp. 99–100.
[67] John N. King, 'John Day: master printer of the English Reformation', in *The Beginnings of English Protestantism*, eds. Peter Marshall and Alec Ryrie (Cambridge: Cambridge University Press, 2002), pp. 180–208 (p. 183); Catharine Davies, *A Religion of the Word*, p. xi.
[68] Pettegree, *The Book in the Renaissance*, p. 127; Catharine Davies, *A Religion of the Word*, p. xv.

and French (twelve). The market continued to be primarily inward-facing, serving the local populations of English-speaking natives. This vernacular focus reflects the aspirations of printers, who chose not to seek out the major international markets in scholarly texts, but also of authors, publishers and patrons who were more concerned with the national market. The authority of the continental reformed faiths against catholicism was rooted in the classical and biblical languages, but protestant printed output in England was almost exclusively in the vernacular.[69]

Alongside the market dominance of religious works and bibles, the other leading USTC genres in Edwardian publishing were 'jurisprudence' and 'ordinances'. Between 1547 and 1553, works of jurisprudence accounted for 122 titles, while ordinances totalled seventy-nine.[70] An array of yearbooks, supplemented by official statutes, made up the majority of these jurisprudence works. For the genre of ordinances and edicts, we see a large number of acts and proclamations emphasising that the Edwardian government valued print as a vehicle to disseminate its messages. The majority was printed or published by Richard Grafton (appointed King's Printer of all books of statutes, acts, proclamations, injunctions and other volumes issued by the king on 20 April 1547), though Grafton's predecessor Thomas Berthelet and successor John Cawood each printed a small number.[71] It is noteworthy that despite their significance in terms of the number of titles produced, neither genre significantly affected market trends. Jurisprudence texts were at their height in the two accession years (1547 and 1553), whilst ordinances saw their highest output in 1549 and 1551. These genres, therefore, were not the driving force behind the most prosperous years for the Edwardian industry (1548 and 1550).

In personnel terms, the Edwardian print world was constructed of a large number of individuals though much of the trade's power resided with a select few. Over seventy names were listed in colophons of Edwardian printed books, and thirty-five of these individuals are known printers of books, rather than publishers or funding parties receiving colophon credits. This number of active printers expanded beyond the Henrician years, but England's printers' proficiency and productivity varied enormously. England's output was centralised within a small number of print houses. Only Richard Grafton and John Day can be directly linked to over 150 titles, while Edward

---

69 Alec Ryrie, *Being Protestant in Reformation Britain* (Oxford: Oxford University Press, 2013), pp. 259–264.
70 See Tables 2.1 and 2.2.
71 USTC (William Powell) 504745, (Robert Wyer) 504821, (Edward Whitchurch) 504402, and (Nicolas Hill) 505413 all appear under this genre.

Whitchurch, William Seres and Dutch immigrants Nicolas Hill and Stephen Mierdman were each involved in over eighty. These six men were all at the forefront of Edwardian print culture by their production levels but tiers within the trade can also be established in terms of capital, productivity, proficiency, patronage and commercial role (see chapter six). As we shall see, different Edwardian print houses enjoyed periods of ascendancy and endured periods of decline but by the end of the reign Grafton, Day, Whitchurch, Hill and Mierdman could all boast a sufficient combination of these factors to divide themselves as the elite of English printing.

The Edwardian industry, then, was centred on religious publications. Table 2.3 highlights that the octavo gained a heavier dominance over other alternative formats, whilst the dominance of vernacular titles highlights an inward-facing national industry. The Edwardian print world appears to have flourished by reinforcing its commitment to publishing in English for its population and inciting readers' interest in religious topics.

6   Edwardian Historiography

Despite focusing upon the print trade, this book owes a debt to a wide range of historical disciplines. The Tudor years have rich historiography where governance and rebellion often feature as principal concerns. W.K. Jordan's two-part study had long stood as an informative and comprehensive account of Edward's reign, though a series of later studies have gradually undermined its authority.[72] In more recent years, the Edwardian period has received more attention, principally through Diarmaid MacCulloch's *Tudor Church Militant* and *Thomas Cranmer: A Life*, Jennifer Loach's *Edward VI*, and Stephen Alford's *Kingship and Politics in the reign of Edward VI*.[73]

A second critical theme in wider Tudor and Edwardian historiography is the role of religion in society. In this area, broader studies and biographies alike have explored Edward's reign within their remits. Eamon Duffy's monumental *The Stripping of the Altars* champions a significant degree of continuity between England's medieval and early modern past for the conservative majority, wherein the reformation was a devastating force.[74] This perspective,

---

72 Jordan, *Edward VI: The Young King*; W.K. Jordan, *Edward VI: The Threshold of power. The Dominance of the Duke of Northumberland* (Cambridge, MA: Harvard University Press, 1970).
73 Alford, *Kingship and Politics in the reign of Edward VI*; Loach, *Edward VI*, MacCulloch, *Tudor Church Militant*; MacCulloch, *Thomas Cranmer*.
74 Duffy, *Stripping of the Altars*, pp. 448–454.

however, is at loggerheads with the work of Andrew Pettegree and Diarmaid MacCulloch, among others, for whom the rise of protestantism and the reformation in England is seen less as a destructive process. Alongside investments in churches, hospitals and schools, Edward's reign has built a positive reputation for its unusual tolerance, which was particularly notable in the light of increasing persecution on the Continent and the authoritarianism and oppression of reformers shown in the previous and subsequent reigns of Henry VIII and Mary I.[75] The level of popular support for protestant reform in Tudor England continues to be an area hotly debated. Scholars including Peter Marshall, Alec Ryrie and Ethan Shagan have made valuable contributions to our understanding of how high-politics and daily religious life intersected and our understanding of life as an evangelical in the Tudor years.[76]

The matter of print and publications is touched on more directly by textual scholars of the period. Here, historians often analyse Edwardian books from the standpoint of texts and images rather than workers and industry. At the forefront of this field has been John N. King, whose *English Reformation Literature: The Tudor Origins of the Protestant Tradition* offered tantalising glimpses into the world of Tudor patronage.[77] Many of King's links, however, too readily overextend brief associations in an attempt to discover more meaningful networks. Many Tudor patronage networks may have been lost only due to the lack of archival documents, but King's claims often remain unsubstantiated. In 2002, Catharine Davies' *A Religion of the Word* highlighted the range of topics explored by Edwardian religious authors, though as a literary study focused upon texts and the rather than print production.[78] David Daniell considered *The Bible in English: Its History and Influence*, which provided information critical to reconstructing the Tudor printing world.[79] The Great

---

75   Pettegree, *Foreign Protestant Communities*, chapter 2; Brigden, *London and the Reformation*, pp. 477–480; Luc Borot, 'The Bible and Protestant Inculturation in the Homilies of the Church of England', in *The Bible in the Renaissance: Essays on Biblical Commentary and Translation in the Fifteenth and Sixteenth Centuries*, ed. Richard Griffiths (Aldershot: Ashgate, 2001), pp. 150–175 (p. 161); Jordan, *Edward VI: The threshold of power*, p. 347; John N. King, *English Reformation Literature: The Tudor Origins of the Protestant Tradition* (Princeton, NJ, Princeton University Press, 1982), p. 76; MacCulloch, *Tudor Church Militant*, pp. 7, 179–181; Pettegree, *Foreign Protestant Communities*, p. 20; Ryrie, 'The Strange Death of Lutheran England', p. 91; Marshall, *Heretics and Believers*, p. xiii.
76   Marshall, *Heretics and Believers*; Ryrie, *Being Protestant in Reformation Britain*; Shagan, *Popular Politics and the English Reformation*.
77   King, *English Reformation Literature*.
78   Davies, *A Religion of the Word*.
79   Daniell, *The Bible in English*.

Bible's position in the history of English printing is, of course, hugely significant, but Daniell's work also casts light upon the development of preceding and subsequent translations making their way into the hands of early modern English readers.

In recent years, direct explorations of the print world and printers have also come to the fore. Andrew Pettegree's *The Book in the Renaissance* has brought clarity to a field long guided by Elizabeth Eisenstein's *The Printing Press as an Agent of Change*.[80] Spearheading this movement in the English context has been Ian Green's *Print and Protestantism in Early Modern England* and the painstaking research of Peter Blayney, which culminated in 2013 with *The Stationers' Company and the Printers of London 1501–1557*.[81] This monumental study will be a critical reference point for scholars of Tudor printing for many years to come. Blayney's research is authoritative and detailed, though the chronological breadth of his project and exclusive focus upon the industry and dynamics within it allows less time for placing that industry within its historical setting. Elizabeth Evenden's *Patents, Pictures and Patronage*, too, is an influential work on English printing despite focusing upon the career of one individual: John Day.[82] The premier Tudor printer's career extended well beyond the Edwardian period, as has Evenden's research. In order to contribute to the growing body of scholarship on sixteenth-century English printing, this study focuses upon one reign and attempts to frame the occurrences in the print trade within their historical setting.

7 Key Questions

This overview of the Edwardian print world highlights the excessive growth in printed output and confirms that the subject requires more critical analysis and detailed examination. The contributing factors to this growth and how these factors affected the industry and the material output of the reign remain unclear. In order to answer these questions, this study builds upon the data collected by the British Library *English Short Title Catalogue*, which the USTC

---

80   Elizabeth L. Eisenstein, *The Printing Press as an Agent of Change: Communications and Cultural Transformations in Early-Modern Europe*, 2 vols (Cambridge: Cambridge University Press, 1979).
     Pettegree, *The Book in the Renaissance*.
81   Ian Green, *Print and Protestantism in Early Modern England* (Oxford, Oxford University Press, 2000); Blayney, *The Stationers' Company*.
82   Evenden, *Patents, Pictures and Patronage*.

have linked to their database and supplemented. These catalogues provide data on every sixteenth-century English imprint, which underpins the statistical analyses conducted throughout this project. In addition, USTC listings provide, where possible, links to digital copies of publications found at EEBO, which were foundational in the commencement of this project. Chapter five is also built upon a sample of 298 books examined at the Henry E. Huntington Library in San Marino, California.[83] This sample includes a large proportion of the Huntington Library's Edwardian holdings, which has been supplemented by digital examinations of *Early English Books Online* copies.

This first core consideration of *The English Print Trade in the Reign of Edward VI, 1547–1553* is the role of the government and its effect upon the industry. Previous research has cited sweeping changes in legislation and the deregulation of the trade as fundamental in creating this dramatic increase in output. In order to test this narrative, firstly, we must explore the regulations and this bureaucratic legislative framework before placing this letter of the law in the reign's unique political and religious surroundings. Individuals broke the law under Henry VIII, Edward VI and Mary I, just as individuals break the law today. The letter of the law alone cannot account entirely for which laws are broken, or when, or by whom. Thereafter, chapter four, 'Official offices, compulsory provisions and rival texts' seeks to identify and consolidate the extent to which the regime played an active role in promoting and facilitating English printers by examining the official offices to which prominent individuals were appointed, the patents issued to printers, and the publications they sponsored.

Chapter five, 'A technical and design examination', explores Edwardian print from the material products it produced. As we have already seen, the Edwardian printing industry had more in common with the late Henrician industry than many historians suggest. Edwardian printing, particularly in the boom year of 1548, is portrayed as part of a carnival-style outpouring of anticlericalism and reforming zeal that arrived with Edward's accession. Books, however, have meaning above and beyond the texts that they contain. The way a printer chose to produce a publication was meaningful: costs were borne to create a fine edition or saved by printing a cheaper one. This chapter examines the

---

83 This sample was constructed using the Huntington library catalogue (at: https://catalog.huntington.org/search) using the search parameters of 1547 and 1553 and 'London' in the first instance to gather as many titles as possible into the database. There are currently 323 items listed in the Huntington catalogue for works printed in London during these years. Regrettably, due to time constraints, not all the Huntington holdings could be examined, but a suitably large and representative sample has been gathered through these 298 works, from which broader findings on the trade can be inferred with a degree of caution.

design conventions within English printing and how some printers attempted to challenge these expectations. Thereafter, this chapter explores the distribution of resources evident within English printed books. Illustrative materials, including woodcut title-page borders, initials, and type, can tell us a great deal about which printers were investing in new or second-hand materials and how this influenced their products.

The final two core chapters explore the individuals involved in the industry and how they fit into the surrounding commercial and religious backdrop of the reign. Chapter six, 'Commercial networks', identifies and explores the number of individuals involved in the English book world and the many roles they fulfilled. Any publication, particularly any large book, required the efforts of many people before, during and after printing. This reality is often hidden when we discuss the printers of the period, where a single name might be attached to the monumental efforts of many individuals that any major project represented. Thereafter, 'The growth of the wider English book world' demonstrates the divergent commercial approaches taken by individuals in the print trade during these years to explore the evolution and expansion of the trade towards a wider functioning and multifaceted industry.

Through these core themes, this study seeks to expand our understanding of the significance and influence of printing in a turbulent period of English history. This study contests the notion that the improvements in the book trade were due to the change in religious affiliation alone and seeks to emphasise that a range of religious, governmental, commercial, industrial and personnel factors coalesced to drive forward English print during the young king's tenure.

CHAPTER 3

Print and Government

With the accession of Edward VI, opportunity dawned for the embattled reforming faction of England's 1540s. In one fell swoop, they seized control, inciting a flurry of official injunctions and proclamations targeting the conservative remnants of the Henrician church.[1] Individuals in the uppermost echelons of the English polity orchestrated the Edwardian reformation, and they aimed to mobilise print to aid their cause.[2]

The short reign of Edward VI saw an extraordinary increase in the output of printed material. The English book world developed a discernible character marked by the texts it produced and those individuals involved. Within this process, the ruling powers played a formative role, facilitating a social climate that liberated printers from specific restrictions of the final years of the Henrician kingship. The trajectory of religious change represented a significant opportunity for printers as new areas of religious discussions were unlocked and encouraged. 'Print and government' first examines Henrician and Edwardian statutes, proclamations and edicts to challenge the historiographical narrative of a deconstruction of censorship, establishing a new narrative of an implicit climate of protestant freedom and printers' self-censorship. Thereafter, new light is cast upon the discordant voices who opposed England's religious path in print. The Edwardian years are traditionally depicted as a time of press liberation, but influential boundaries were established to guide religious discourse in line with the government's ambitions.

1   Censorship and the Law

Whilst the religious policies of the Edwardian regime were defiantly evangelical, England's presses were not merely vehicles of state. On the contrary, the printed output of the reign included a broader spectrum of theological texts

---

1   Eamon Duffy, *Stripping of the Altars: Traditional Religion in England 1400–1580*, 2nd edn (New Haven, CT: Yale University Press, 2005), pp. 450–465; Diarmaid MacCulloch, *Tudor Church Militant: Edward VI and the Protestant Reformation* (London: Allen Lane, 1999), pp. 8–9, 57.
2   Alec Ryrie, 'Counting sheep, counting shepherds: the problem of allegiance in the English Reformation', in *The beginnings of English Protestantism*, eds. Peter Marshall and Alec Ryrie (Cambridge: Cambridge University Press 2002), pp. 84–110 (p. 99); Diarmaid MacCulloch, *A History of Christianity. The First Three Thousand Years* (London: Allen Lane, 2009), p. 622.

than ever before: conservatives, catholic reformers, evangelicals of every gradation, and radicals used English presses to disseminate their theologies.

The religious and legislative changes following Edward's accession shifted the landscape of religious discussion, prompting a period of great opportunity for England's printers. For over thirty years, presses at Antwerp, Basel, Wittenberg and Zurich had been spreading the word of the reformation, making its chief protagonists some of the best-selling authors of the age.[3] During the Henrician 1540s, only three of England's ten most-printed authors wrote primarily religious works: Thomas Becon, Desiderius Erasmus, and the conservative martyr John Fisher.[4] Edwardian England brought the reformation to the fore. Nine of the top ten authors were religious writers, including six English evangelicals (Becon, Thomas Cranmer, John Hooper, John Bale, Hugh Latimer, and the late William Tyndale), two continental evangelicals (Heinrich Bullinger and Jean Calvin) and one conservative humanist (Erasmus).

The foundational narrative of Edwardian printing is built upon the notion of a collapse of censorship in 1547.[5] Cyndia Susan Clegg states that the press 'enjoyed extraordinary freedom' for five years, the like of which John N. King has asserted 'would not be exceeded until 1640'.[6] Catharine Davies advances that the policy 'enabled protestants to print without fear of reprisal'.[7] In order to determine how central legislative changes were, we must establish a coherent picture of Henrician censorship. A series of official edicts, proclamations and statutes restricted scripture reading and religious discussion, threatening and, at times, implementing harsh penalties. Historians have focused upon the Act of Six Articles (1539) and the Act for the Advancement of True Religion (1543) as the crucial decrees establishing an unforgiving state of control.[8]

---

3 Between 1518 and 1547, Martin Luther is listed as an author of 3,404 titles; Desiderius Erasmus is the second most printed, with 2,174; Philipp Melanchthon is the fourth with 908.
4 Andrew Pettegree, *The Book in the Renaissance* (New Haven, CT: Yale University Press, 2010), p. 107.
5 Ryan M. Reeves, *English Evangelicals and Tudor Obedience, c.1527–1570* (Leiden: Brill, 2014), p. x; John N. King, *English Reformation Literature: The Tudor Origins of the Protestant Tradition* (Princeton, NJ: Princeton University Press, 1982), pp. 77, 85.
6 John N. King, 'The Book trade under Edward VI and Mary I', in *The Cambridge History of the Book in Britain, Vol II: 1400–1557*, eds. Lotte Hellinga and J.B. Trapp (Cambridge: Cambridge University Press, 1999), pp. 164–178 (p. 133); Cyndia Susan Clegg, *Press Censorship in Elizabethan England* (Cambridge: Cambridge University Press, 1997), p. 27; in response, see Peter Blayney, *The Stationers' Company and the Printers of London, 1501–1557*, 2 vols (Cambridge: Cambridge University Press, 2013), pp. 601–604.
7 Catharine Davies, *A Religion of the Word: The defence of the reformation in the reign of Edward VI* (Manchester: Manchester University Press, 2002), p. x.
8 Clegg, *Press Censorship*, p. 26; David Loades, 'Books and the English Reformation prior to 1558', in *The Reformation and the Book*, ed. Jean-Francois Gilmont, trans. Karin Maag

The Act of Six Articles stated that any person proclaiming that communion was necessary in both kinds, 'by worde writitng printinge ciphringe or otherwise', was subject to forfeit all goods and be imprisoned for a first offence, and be adjudged a felon and executed for a second.[9] Four years later, relating directly to printing and reading, the Act for the Advancement of True Religion outlined three months' imprisonment, forfeiture of all offending books and a fine of ten pounds per book as first-offence penalties. Thereafter, a second offence would evoke the forfeiture of all goods and perpetual imprisonment.[10] We ought not to underestimate these sanctions. Although likely only an illustration of the perceived severity of the crime, the financial penalty for any industry-standard print run would have devastated any English print house.

English legislation also restricted the production and ownership of publications opposing Henry VIII's church. Henry's enduring condemnation of the Tyndale and Coverdale biblical translations betray his fear that his subjects' were susceptible to 'erroneous' translations that 'corrupted' the bible.[11] Regulations ordered the burning of these translations until his death, restricted lay scripture reading and ordered the removal or defacement of all accompanying commentaries and preambles.[12] Henry expected his subjects to approach the Great Bible 'humbly, meekly, reverently, and obediently' without engaging in 'common disputation, argument or exposition'.[13]

The regime also prohibited specific books: they named fifteen in 1530 proclamations, thirty-eight in Bishop Bonner's 1542 Register, and burned ninety-two at St Paul's Cross in 1546.[14] Furthermore, Henrician censorship installed pre-publication licensing from 22 June 1530, further reinforced by proclamation in 1538.[15] The Act for the Advancement of True Religion and proclamation

---

(Aldershot: Ashgate, 1998), pp. 264–291 (pp. 271–272); Alec Ryrie, 'The Strange Death of Lutheran England', *Journal of Ecclesiastical History*, 53 (2002), pp. 64–92 (pp. 85–86, 89).
9   31 Henry VIII, *c.*12.
10 34 & 35 Henry VIII, *c.*1.
11 *H&L*, 1, pp. 193–197 – 22 June 1530; *H&L*, 1, pp. 373–376 – 8 July 1546; 34 & 35 Henry VIII, *c.*1.
12 *H&L*, 1, pp. 296 – 6 May 1541; 34 & 35 Henry VIII *c.*1; Alec Ryrie, *The Gospel and Henry VIII: Evangelicals in the Early English Reformation* (Cambridge: Cambridge University Press, 2003), p. 47.
13 Gilbert Burnet, *History of the Reformation of the Church of England*, 1, 2 (London: Richard Priestley, 1820), p. 364.
14 R.W. Heinz, *The Proclamations of the Tudor Kings* (Cambridge: Cambridge University Press, 1976), pp. 132–133; Dorothy Auchter, *Dictionary of Literary and Dramatic Censorship in Tudor and Stuart England* (Westport, CT: Greenwood Press, 2001), p. xiv; Ryrie, *The Gospel and Henry VIII*, pp. 104–105.
15 Clegg, *Press Censorship*, pp. 26–27; Auchter, *Literary and Dramatic Censorship*, p. xiv.

of 8 July 1546 reinforced printers' accountability, demanding the statement of printers' names and publication dates on all English publications.[16]

Henrician controls intensified during the conservative ascendancy that concluded the reign.[17] Alec Ryrie has identified seven printers and two booksellers imprisoned and over twenty-five questioned by the Privy Council concerning publishing and book-related infringements in this period of suppression.[18] These investigations highlight a reality of which England's printers were acutely aware: official punishments could be swift and severe.

Richard Grafton, who became the leading printer of the Edwardian regime, was reprimanded three times during Henry's rule. First, in 1540, he was one of the hundreds rounded up in an ambitious, albeit impracticable, attempt to purge London of its protestants under the Act of Six Articles.[19] In 1541, he was brought before the Privy Council under suspicion of unlawful printing, though no record of further proceedings is known. Despite this, Grafton received a patent for service books in January 1543, only to be incarcerated once more before the authorities released him in May, ten days prior to the institution of the Act for the Advancement of True Religion.[20] According to these events, Grafton's actions had prompted investigation and imprisonment and yet he retained his service book patent and was appointed printer to Edward, the Prince of Wales in 1545.[21] These were unpredictable times for printers.

Henrician legislation also attempted to curtail the flourishing clandestine export trade from continental print houses. In early 1534, legislation prohibited the import of pre-bound books, restricted continental imprints to wholesale purchases, and prevented non-denizen strangers from selling books, each at the penalty of forfeiture and a 6s. 8d. fine per book.[22] Later, a proclamation of 8 July 1546 forbade subjects:

> to bring any manner of English book concerning any matter of Christian religion printed in the parts of beyond the seas, into this realm, or sell, give, or distribute any English book, printed in outwards parts.[23]

---

16 *H&L*, 1, pp. 373–376.
17 Loades, 'Books and the English Reformation', p. 281.
18 *Ibid.*; Ryrie, 'Strange Death of Lutheran England', p. 87; *APC*, 1, p. 107 – 8 April 1543.
19 Alec Ryrie, 'Edward Whitchurch (d.1562)', *ODNB*; Meraud Grant Ferguson, 'Grafton, Richard (1506/7–1573)', *ODNB*.
20 *APC*, 1, p. 107 – 8 April 1543; *APC*, 1, p. 125 – 2 April [May] 1543.
21 Ferguson, 'Grafton, Richard'; *USTC* 503615.
22 25 Henry VIII, c.15.
23 *H&L*, 1, pp. 373–376 – 8 July 1546.

Henry's regime nonetheless struggled to quell imports. Between the passage of the Act of Six Articles (1539) and Edward's accession, sixty-three English-language titles were produced abroad for clandestine import.[24] Stemming from protestant strongholds, particularly Antwerp (fifty-two), these publications were dominated by religious themes and authored by English and continental reformers, many of whom the 1546 proclamation targeted.[25]

Henrician law on censorship was clear. Its implementation, however, was not so precise. These laws were the framework of a particularly bureaucratic state aware of the threat that printing posed, which took strides to suppress recalcitrant printers both at home and abroad. Nonetheless, the legislation did not necessarily determine the penalties enforced.

Edwardian England's presses produced floods of polemical literature. With Henrician regulations in mind, the historiographical narrative for this growth is a collapse of censorship.[26] Previous studies compartmentalise Edward's reign into three periods of press censorship: freedom (1547–1548), returning regulation (1549–1550) and control secured (1551–1553).[27] These phases follow legislative changes and inspired a historical narrative that attempted to account for both political developments and fluctuations in production.[28] However, this letter of the law model is too neat for a period of such political and religious transition and requires revision. Peter Blayney's discerning eye for the intricacies of law has caught issues that many have overlooked, including that regulations passed by proclamation, particularly those before the 1539 Statute of Proclamations, would cease to function unless re-issued by the new king.[29] Further scrutiny upon the proclamations of the reign and the works printed, both in England and abroad between 1540 and 1553, highlights that evading

---

24 USTC statistics show that seventeen came from the Holy Roman Empire, and eight from Swiss Confederation; but nine of seventeen Holy Roman Empire titles and seven of eight Swiss titles are false imprints now inferred to Antwerp.

25 H&L, 1, p. 373 prohibited specific authors '[John] Frith, [William] Tyndale, [John] Wycliff, [George] Joy, [William] Roy, Basille [Thomas Becon], [John] Bale, [Robert] Barnes, [Miles] Coverdale, [William] Turner, [Richard] Tracy'. The English authors from Antwerp imprints included Bale, Henry Brinklow, Coverdale, Frith, Joye, Thomas Some, Tracey, Turner, William Barlow, and Europeans Bullinger, Bibliander, Melanchthon, Zwingli.

26 MacCulloch, *Tudor Church Militant*, p. 84; Reeves, *English Evangelicals and Tudor Obedience*, pp. 97–99; Davies, *Religion of the Word*, p. 19; King, 'The Book Trade under Edward VI and Mary I', pp. 164–165.

27 MacCulloch, *Tudor Church Militant*, p. 141; Pamela Neville-Sington, 'Press, politics and religion', in *The Cambridge History of the Book in Britain Vol. III: 1400–1557*, eds. Lotte Hellinga and J.B. Trapp (Cambridge, 1999), pp. 576–607 (p. 601); Davies, *A Religion of the Word*, p. x.

28 The significant declines in production between 1548 and 1549, and then 1551 and 1552 have both been attributed to the re-imposition of legal controls.

29 31 Henry VIII, c.8; Blayney, *The Stationers' Company*, pp. 602–603.

censorship required a tacit understanding of the regime's religious trajectory and considerable tact.

This historiographical notion of press freedom and lack of controls stems from two regulations: the 1547 royal injunctions and the Act for the Repeale of Certaine Statutes covering Treasons, Felonyes, &c. (November 1547).[30] In the first instance, both the official line and the ramifications have been over-stated. Concerning the Great Bible and Erasmus' *Paraphrases*, the 31 July 1547 injunction read:

> the same set up in some convenient place within the said church ... their parishioners may most commodiously resort unto the same and read the same ... they [the clergy] shall discourage no man (authorised and licensed thereto) from the reading of any part of the Bible, either in Latin or in English, but shall rather conform and exhort every person to read the same as the very lively word of God.[31]

John N. King's reading that the establishment "authorised and licensed" all men to read and interpret the bible and related writings' has guided the historiography but is a misinterpretation.[32] This injunction reaffirmed permission for anyone already authorised and licensed to read the bible to do so in parish churches; it did not authorise and license all subjects to read the bible. This proclamation withdrew no restrictions upon the reading of scripture. It also attempted to create a uniform paraphrase and commentary to replace those 'blotted out' and 'utterly extinguished' under the Act for the Advancement of True Religion. Moreover, this freedom was constrained to the Great Bible and Erasmus' *Paraphrases*, books printed (or forthcoming) under royal license and patent, and only included reading within churches. The government had already mandated the Great Bible's provision in parish churches through multiple proclamations.[33] This injunction set a precedent for the coming environment of reform and scripture reading, but, in its strictest terms, it simply laid the foundation for the literary foundations of Edward VI's church.

The Act for the Repeale of Certaine Statutes coveringe Treasons, Felonyes, &c. (November 1547) is widely considered the critical prompt for an outpouring of evangelical polemic in 1548. The terms of this act abolished many

---

30   *H&L*, 1, pp. 393–403 – 31 July 1547; *USTC* 515355.
31   *H&L*, 1, pp. 393–403 – 31 July 1547.
32   King, *English Reformation Literature*, p. 85.
33   Heinz, *The Proclamations of the Tudor Kings*, p. 188.

controls instituted by Henry VIII, and thus their restrictions upon matters of religion and punishments for heresy:

> all Actes of plament and Estatutes towchinge mencyoninge or in anny wise concernynge Religion or opinyons ... shall fromhensfurthe be repealed and utterlie voyde and of none effecte.[34]

Paul Whitfield White asserts that the Act of Repeal's effect upon the world of English drama was 'immediate and far-reaching' as evangelical, anti-papal plays were written, performed and enjoyed in the earliest years of Edward's reign.[35] Whilst it is tempting to assert the same for the print world, we are constrained by a lack of specificity. Sixteenth-century colophons typically provide only a publication year, so it remains difficult to assert immediate effects. Nonetheless, studies have credited the act with enabling hitherto prohibited religious discussion. The act repealed the Six Articles, which had outlined the church and state's position on the Eucharist, prompting Catharine Davies to assert that the Act of Repeal 'in combination with Somerset's relaxation of censorship, allowed discussion in print of these issues for the first time'.[36] In making the Act of Repeal the centrepiece of the narrative of Edwardian censorship, several official proclamations have been marginalised or simply ignored. The Edwardian authorities did not stand idle. Proclamations issued on 24 May 1547, 27 December 1547, 24 April 1548 and 23 September 1548 all restricted religious discussion. These acts did not all explicitly prohibit the printing of similar material, but there was an implicit link between the pulpit and the presses even in this bureaucratic state. The repeal of existing legislation created an atmosphere of freedom, but government policy never permitted the printing of inflammatory polemic.

The statements of Davies and many others on Eucharistic polemic also fail to consider the Act Silencing Disputes on the Eucharist, 25 December 1547.[37] This act forbade subjects to 'argue, dispute, reason, preach, or teach affirming

---

34   1 Edw. VI, c.12; USTC 515355; Donald Carl Bracco, 'The Influence of King Edward VI (1547–1553) on English Ecclesiastical History' (unpublished doctoral thesis, Wisconsin State University, 1968), pp. 42–43.

35   Paul Whitfield White, *Theatre and Reformation: Protestantism, Patronage, and Playing in Tudor England* (Cambridge: Cambridge University Press, 1993), p. 56.

36   Davies, *Religion of the Word*, pp. 18–19, 53; Antoinina Bevan Zlatar, *Reformation Fictions: Polemical Protestant Dialogues in Elizabethan England* (Oxford: Oxford University Press, 2011), pp. 41–42 also states 'it was only afterwards that the issue of the Eucharist could be addressed in print'.

37   1 Edw. VI, c.1; USTC 515353.

any more terms of the said Blessed Sacrament' and was supported by the *Order of the Communion*, printed the following year. The Act of Repeal only legalised discussion of the Eucharist for a matter of days. The authors and printers of Eucharistic tracts in 1548 produced their works no more legally than if they had produced the same works in 1547, or indeed under Henry VIII's kingship. The Imperial Ambassador Van der Delft wrote to the emperor on 22 January 1548 that the regime had published its Eucharist statement and that 'They prohibit under very heavy punishment all disputes or discussions questioning these decisions'.[38] Therein lay the importance of understanding the religious trajectory of the regime: the threat of punishment is only significant alongside an expectation of implementation. For those with elite connections, who understood this trajectory, the opportunity to outstrip the official line of the reformation without reprimand was tempting. Elizabeth Evenden has highlighted that fifty per cent of the John Day and William Seres partnership output in 1548 denounced the Eucharistic doctrine.[39] These printers had influential patrons who would have known which publications the regime would appreciate, once they set a precedent, others could follow.

The Act of Repeal did mobilise certain readers. The 1543 act had threatened purchasers, readers and owners of Tyndale's translations with confiscation and a £5 fine per book and maintained specific prohibitions upon scripture reading. Thus, the repeal amendments had a marked impact upon biblical printing. In 1547, Edward Whitchurch produced the only small-format English New Testament. Following the Act of Repeal, English printers produced five small-format New Testaments in 1548 (two quartos, one octavo, and two sextodecimos) before innovating and expanding the market in 1549 (a quarto bible, two quarto New Testaments, and three octavo new testaments) and 1550 (two quartos, three octavos, one duodecimo, and two sextodecimos).[40] Buoyed by legislative changes, printers explored new markets, generating growth in this sphere.

These proclamations undermine the notion of the complete removal of controls. The repeal of Henrician statutes, which had allowed the institutional punishment of heretics, was a signal of great significance, but it is worth remembering that no printers were ever proceeded against beyond the preliminary stages of these statutes. These years saw a reduction in the

---

38   SP *Spanish*, 9, pp. 243–246 – 22 January 1548.
39   Elizabeth Evenden, *Patents, Pictures and Patronage: John Day and the Tudor Book Trade* (Aldershot, Ashgate, 2008), pp. 12–13.
40   USTC (1549) 504170, 504200, 504320, 504321, 504322, 504323; (1550) 504405, 504521, 504532, 515397, 516485, 516495, 516499, 677208.

implementation of censorship legislation, providing the publications aligned with the trajectory of English religious reform. They did not, however, allow the unbridled discussion of religious controversy.

Despite their proclamations, the government feared they were losing control. In December 1548, comptroller of the King's household William Paget wrote to Lord Protector Somerset: 'now every man hath liberty to do and speak at liberty without danger'.[41] Political and religious contention alike came to mar the Somerset protectorate, and the outbreak of rebellion changed the political landscape. In light of the Western Rising in Devon and Cornwall (June–August 1549) and Kett's rebellion in Norfolk (July–August 1549), cementing political and religious obedience became a principal concern. On 13 August 1549, the Privy Council heard a case of subversive printing which led to repercussions for the wider print trade. This case, against a clerk of the royal mint, John Mardeley, commanded the following recognisance:

> do not any tyme herafter publishe or set foorth in writing or print, or cause to be published or set foorth in writing in print, any boke, ballet or other work then siche as he or they shalbe licensed to sett forth by my Lord Protectour and the rest of the Kinges Majestes Counssile, the same woorke or workes to be first subscribed with the hand of William Cicill, esquire; that then, &c.[42]

In isolation, this reprimand appears in line with the prohibition of preaching orders issued throughout the reign. However, the critical importance lies with the note:

> An Ordre was taken that from hensforth no prenter sholde prente or putt to ventre any Englisshe books butt such as sholde first be examined by Mr. Secretary Peter, Mr. Secretary Smith, and Mr. Cicill, or the one of them, and allowed by the same, undre payne.

This regulation, had it been fully implemented, would have caused a sea change in Edwardian censorship. The appointment of three high-profile censors to pre-license publications reinstituted the procedures of Henry VIII's reign. Implementation of this policy, though, was far from seamless. Due to their associations with Somerset, both Thomas Smith and William Cecil found

---

41　Barrett L. Beer, 'A Critique of the Protectorate: An Unpublished Letter of Sir William Paget to the Duke of Somerset', *Huntington Library Quarterly*, 34 (1971), pp. 277–283 (p. 280).

42　*APC*, 2, p. 312 – 13 August 1549.

themselves incarcerated within two months, serving a term of 10 October to 25 January.[43] These proceedings left William Petre as the sole licensor for at least three of the first five months. Given the date of this policy's institution and the political turmoil following Somerset's fall, it is unfeasible that this policy was genuinely effective.

Nevertheless, religious titles fell dramatically from 182 in 1548 to ninety-nine in 1549: a decline of forty-six per cent, albeit there was a partial recovery to 118 religious titles in 1550. The historiographical convention that 1549 saw a 'reinstitution of censorship' enacted when 'immediately after taking power, Dudley re-imposed prior censorship and abrogated Seymour's "libertarian" policy' clearly overstates the influence of this order.[44] It is important to remember that the Edwardian reformation developed throughout the reign. 1548 was a year of opportunity for printers and authors prior to the 1549 Act of Uniformity and the increasing definition of this reformation. Considering Table 3.1 below, it is highlighted that whilst the printed output of some of the more controversial authors of 1548 fell in the following year, an impracticable introduction of pre-licensing of publications fails to account for the decline in this area of the trade. We have already seen that the letter of the law alone did not shape printed output; it was also printers' tacit understanding of which works aligned with official religious proceedings. 1549 was a period of significant political instability and civil unrest. Widespread popular uprisings, some with significant religious components others with commonwealth narratives, threatened the political order. Following some faltering starts and indecision from Somerset's government, the earl of Warwick, soon to be Duke of Northumberland, suppressed these uprisings with severity. Furthermore, in January 1549, the institution of the first *Book of Common Prayer* shored up the religious direction of the regime. This atmosphere of uncertainty and the production of a key statement of orthodoxy more reasonably account for the decline in controversial literature than the introduction of three censors three-quarters of the way through the year, particularly when two of the censors were swiftly imprisoned.

---

43 Peter Blayney, 'William Cecil and the Stationers', in *The Stationers' Company and the Book Trade 1550–1990*, eds. Robin Myers and Michael Harris (Winchester: St Paul's Bibliographies, 1997), pp. 11–34 (pp. 11–12).

44 Neville Sington, 'Press, politics and religion', p. 601; Andrew Pettegree, 'Printing and the Reformation: the English Exception', in *The Beginnings of English Protestantism*, eds. Peter Marshall and Alec Ryrie (Cambridge: Cambridge University Press, 2002), pp. 157–180 (p. 172); King, *English Reformation Literature*, p. 86, 88; Stephen Alford, *Kingship and Politics in the reign of Edward VI* (Cambridge: Cambridge University Press, 2002), p. 117.

TABLE 3.1 Authors and titles printed, 1547–1553

English reformers	Pre-1547 in England	Pre-1547 outside England	1547	1548	1549	1550	1551	1552	1553	Edwardian total
Thomas Cranmer	8		11	4	4	3	4	1	1	28
John Ponet					3	1			6	10
Miles Coverdale	30	18	3	10	9	5		7	1	35
William Tyndale	29	31	4	15	12	7	11	4	2	55
John Hooper					3	11	2	1	2	19
John Bale	1	12	5	6	2	3	3	4	5	28
Luke Shepherd				9						9
John Frith	6	7		8	1	2				11
Henry Hart				1	3					4
John Mardeley				4						4
Hugh Latimer	3	1		2	8	2			1	13
Thomas Becon	22	1	1	3	4	8	3		2	21
Anthony Gilby	1			1			4		1	6
Edmund Allen				2	2	1	3			8
George Joye	8	23	3	2	2	1				8
Thomas Lever						5	5			10
Religious émigrés										
Bernardino Ochino		44		2	2	2				6
Peter Martyr Vermigli		2			1	2				3
Jan Laski		22					4	1	3	8
Jan Utenhove							2	1	2	5
Martin Micronius	1							2	3	5
Michelangelo Florio									2	2
Martin Bucer	3	183	1	2	1					4
Continental reformers and scholars										
Martin Luther	15	4,547	1	7	1	1				10
Jean Calvin		86		8	2	5	1	2	1	19
Huldrych Zwingli	2	211		2		3				5
Heinrich Bullinger	4	93	1	4	1	1	3	6		16
Philipp Melanchthon	5	1,714	2	5		3			1	11
Johannes Oecolampadius		264		1						1

TABLE 3.1   Authors and titles printed, 1547–1553 (*cont.*)

Continental reformers and scholars	Pre-1547 in England	Pre-1547 outside England	1547	1548	1549	1550	1551	1552	1553	Edwardian total
Desiderius Erasmus	77	3,510	3	10	6	11	1	4	9	44
Sebastian Munster		41						1		1
Antoine de Marcourt	1	10	4	2						6
Andreas Osiander	3	156		1						1
Hans Sachs		205		2						2
Urbanus Rhegius	3	288		6						6
Erasmus Sarcerius	2	65						4		4

The next instance of increased control occurred on 28 April 1551, when a proclamation announced:

> that from henceforth no printer or other person do print nor sell within this realm ... any matter in the English tongue ... unless the same be first allowed by his majesty or his Privy Council in writing signed with his majesty's most gracious hand or the hands of six of his said Privy Council.[45]

This expansion of pre-publication licensing extended censorship beyond Henrician precedents and the order of August 1549. This proclamation has been seen throughout the historiography as 'sweeping moral and theological press censorship' and a 're-imposition of controls' spearheaded by recently elevated duke of Northumberland, who was 'particularly concerned to suppress criticism of the government'.[46] Debora Shuger notes that the proclamation did not take root, but that had it done so, it would have represented censorship comparable to continental reformed cities, particularly Jean Calvin's Geneva.[47] The successful implementation and impact of the 1551 proclamation have often been taken as a given. Cyndia Susan Clegg asserted that the 1551 proclamation initiated 'press licensing far more intrusive than any

---

[45] *H&L*, 1, p. 517.
[46] Davies, *A religion of the Word*, p. x; King, *English Reformation Literature*, p. 86; Loades, 'Books and the English Reformation', p. 284; MacCulloch, *Tudor Church Militant*, p. 141.
[47] Debora Shuger, *Censorship and Cultural Sensibility: The Regulation of Language in Tudor-Stuart England* (Philadelphia, PA: University of Pennsylvania Press, 2006), pp. 64–65.

Henry had instituted', whilst John N. King stated 'The sharp drop in the number of titles during Dudley's last three years in power, after Seymour's final imprisonment, is consistent with Dudley's re-imposition of controls'.[48] Religious publications accounted for 118 titles in 1550, seventy-five titles in 1551, and sixty-three the following year. Moreover, the variety of theological outlooks coming forth from England's presses during the Northumberland years reduced. This consistent recession, more gradual than between 1548 and 1549, is significant and highlights an increasing consciousness that the establishment was casting a watchful eye over the English print world. It is true that the duke of Northumberland reinstated control but, as we shall see, this downturn was enveloped in the religious and political world around the trade and about more than the letter of the law.

The Edwardian regime did not officially withdraw censorship in 1547, nor did it allow the unbridled discussion of the Eucharist from 1548 onwards. The government implemented further controls as the reign progressed but not merely as an attempt to backpedal. The dominant historiographical narrative attempted to use legal indicators to explain print production trends. The following section will advance a new three-stage theory founded on the development of a more defined protestant identity of the regime which seeks to better accounts for the production trends of the period.

Table 3.1 highlights the array of influential and prolific religious authors of the Edwardian print world. Emergent patterns of production offer another explanation for the types and quantities of publications printed during the reign. This new three-stage model separates 1547 from 1548, and 1548 from the remainder of the reign and, in the absence of defined legislation, employs the notion of printers' self-censorship according to developments in the religious outlook of the regime.

This first stage is characterised by the uncertainty of the direction of religious reform. In spite of the fleet-footed political manoeuvrings of the protestants to secure power early in the year, 1547 saw the narrowest range of evangelical authors. The English authors printed in these years were already established, and largely of episcopal, or pseudo-episcopal, status: Archbishop Cranmer, Miles Coverdale, William Tyndale, John Bale, George Joye and Thomas Becon. These individuals had all already authored works in England or as part of the clandestine import trade into Henrician England. This first year was a time of trepidation for new authors and printers: Edwardian evangelicalism was yet to find its voice.

Reformation polemic in England, as elsewhere in Europe, arrived in small books, quick to write and to print. Relating to a spate of anti-mass tracts in

---

48 Clegg, *Press Censorship*, p. 27; King, *English Reformation Literature*, p. 88.

1548, John N. King states that 'the impetus for this actively came from English authors, printers, stationers and readers'.[49] If we are to accept this notion, it must be asked: amongst an atmosphere of iconoclasm and protestant ascendency, why did this eleven-month delay occur, and what made 1548 so different?

Whilst authorial delays might well have played a role in the delay between the Edwardian reformation's iconoclastic dawn and the controversial works historians have so long associated with it, there was no shortage of existing protestant texts. Scholarship upon the underlying trajectories of late-Henrician and Edwardian evangelicalism has offered insight into these foundational influences, theologies, and texts.[50] Many English reformers had already hoisted their colours by 1547 and the Henrician exiles' polemic was at the disposal of willing printers and yet few printers took up the mantle. In reality, it was the reintegration of these exiles into the new regime that revived their influence. Printers self-censored, they printed the works of those adopted by the regime, so not to risk investigation or censorship. The same caution cannot be ascribed to England's clergymen, who were often far more confrontational in their public orations than their writing. Susan Wabuda has argued that court sermons were a dubious distinction, as 'preachers might hope to interest the king and sway him to a particular policy, but there was also a serious danger that they would inadvertently give offence, with disastrous results'.[51] Printers faced the same problem and, whilst they could use sermons as barometers of popularity and royal favour, caution often outweighed courage in 1547.

The leading authors among the clandestine protestant import book trade of Henry's reign were John Bale (twelve titles) and George Joye (eleven), who each saw an upturn in production during the first year of Edward's reign, with five and three titles respectively. The Henrician proclamation of 8 July 1546 prohibited ten specific authors '[John] Frith, [William] Tyndale, [John] Wycliff, [George] Joy, [William] Roy, Basille [Thomas Becon], [John] Bale, [Robert] Barnes, [Miles] Coverdale, [William] Turner, [Richard] Tracy'. From this list, English printers produced works by five authors during Edward's first year on the throne, five more returned to the English book world in 1548, and another

---

49 King, 'The Book trade under Edward VI and Mary I', p. 166.
50 Ryrie, 'Strange Death of Lutheran England'; Bryan D. Spinks, 'German Influence on Edwardian Liturgies', in *Sister Reformations: The Reformation in Germany and in England*, ed. Dorothea Wendebourg (Tübingen: Mohr Siebeck, 2010), pp. 170–181 (pp. 175–177); Carl R. Trueman and Carrie Euler, 'The Reception of Martin Luther in Sixteenth- and Seventeenth-Century England', in *The Reception of Continental Reformation in Britain*, eds. Polly Ha and Patrick Collinson (Oxford: Oxford University Press, 2010), pp. 63–81 (pp. 63, 68).
51 Susan Wabuda, 'Hugh Latimer', *ODNB*; MacCulloch, *Tudor Church Militant*, p. 22.

in 1550.[52] England's printers largely overlooked the early opportunity to reproduce these publications. Thus, we see the continuation of the trade of continental imports to provide English readers with these works, spearheaded by Stephen Mierdman (Antwerp), Derick van der Straten (Wesel) and Augustin Fries (Zurich).[53]

John Bale established himself as a prolific evangelical polemicist during his exile. Printers from the three principal printing centres serving underground English reformers printed his works: Antwerp, Wesel and Zurich. Derick van der Straten produced The *first examinacyon of Anne Askewe* in late 1546 and *The lattre examinacyon of Anne Askewe* from his Wesel print house in early 1547.[54] In November 1547, Dutchman Nicolas Hill printed an edition of the *First examinacyon* in England, highlighting that printers could reclaim these texts even if the author had yet to return from exile.[55] The Imperial ambassador's letter to the emperor (24 June 1547) allayed previous fears that the publication was 'issued by the consent of the present rulers of England', when discussing the Wesel imprint, but the London edition followed just five months later.[56] Another to repatriate John Bale's work was John Day, with *A brife and faythfull declaration of the true fayth of Christ* (1547). This publication skews preliminary statistics as it accounts for four titles due to variant imprints. Bale's five titles in 1547, therefore, exaggerate the repatriation process, which included only two texts. The most famous work of Bale's exile, *The Image of Both Churches*, succinctly summarises printers' reticence to prematurely adopt English protestant literature. Despite Stephen Mierdman publishing the second part in Antwerp in 1545, which made the work available for English printers to reproduce, it was not until after Bale's reintegration into the English religious landscape in 1548 that Richard Jugge published the first part in London.

English printers' approach to continental theologians in 1547, too, was less than daring. Martin Bucer, Heinrich Bullinger, Philipp Melanchthon (two titles each) and Erasmus (three) each had works produced, whilst Antoine de Marcourt's *Boke of Marchauntes* (previously printed in England prior to Edward's accession) (four titles) and Martin Luther's *The dysclosing of the*

---

52   1547: Bale, Becon, Coverdale, Tyndale, Joy; 1548: Barnes, Frith, Tracy, Turner and Wycliffe; 1550: William Roy.
53   USTC (Wesel) 659959, 503826, 503830, 503988, 699335, 670730; (Antwerp) 441423, 441424; (Zurich) 632072, 632074, 611799; Three 1547–1548 Wyer publications have false imprints: 'Zurich' 690537, 690538, 'Wesel': 516453; Carrie Euler, *Couriers of the Gospel: England and Zurich, 1531–1558* (Zurich, 2006), p. 312.
54   USTC 657517, 670730.
55   USTC 503834.
56   SP Spanish, 9, pp. 110–111: 24 June 1547 – Van der Delft to the Emperor.

canon of the popysh masse were both printed under pseudonym.[57] The use of pseudonyms suggests the printer was aware they might be overstepping the mark of official legislation but considered the risk worthwhile as a commercial enterprise, but few publications bore pseudonyms in this year.

For printers, the question remained whether they would find an active protestant audience. The reformation mobilised populist readerships across Europe, but the equivalent English market was by no means guaranteed.[58] England had low literacy levels and, aside from London, a sparse, rural population totalling three million, many of whom remained committed to Roman Catholicism and conservative theologies.[59] Sustaining an English pro-reform book market to uphold the small-scale Henrician clandestine import trade was a very different prospect to providing the core of the national market as it came to in the coming years. England's reformation was spearheaded by a portion of the country's political and religious elites, not widespread popular protestant zeal. In 1547, it was difficult to know whether English readers had interest and appetite for controversial and pro-reform literature to match printers' production capabilities. As such pamphlet and protestant literature did not necessarily appeal to printers as we assume in hindsight. English printers, it seems, were not prepared to mortgage their liberty on sensitive works that may or may not be worth the risk during the earliest stages of the reign. Motivated by self-preservation and commercial potential, printers measured the regime's religious policies and self-censored accordingly.[60]

The Edwardian outburst of protestant print occurred in 1548 rather than immediately following Edward's accession.[61] Despite legislation to curtail theological discussion, printers reached unprecedented levels of output –

---

57 W.J. Torrance Kirby, 'Wholesale or Retail? Antoine de Marcourt's *The Boke of Marchauntes* and Tudor Political Theology', *Renaissance and Reformation / Renaissance et Réforme*, 28 (2004), pp. 37–60; W.J. Torrance Kirby, 'Religion and Propaganda: Thomas Cromwell's Use of Antoine de Marcourt's Livre des Marchans', in *Persuasion and Conversion: Essays on Religion, Politics and the Public Sphere in Early Modern England*, ed. W.J. Torrance Kirby (Leiden: Brill, 2013), pp. 37–52 (pp. 39, 45); USTC 515262.

58 Alec Ryrie, 'Paths not taken in the British Reformations', *Historical Journal*, 52 (2009), pp. 1–22 (p. 21); Luc Borot, 'The Bible and Protestant Inculturation in the Homilies of the Church of England', in *The Bible in the Renaissance: Essays on Biblical Commentary and Translation in the Fifteenth and Sixteenth Centuries*, ed. Richard Griffiths (Aldershot: Ashgate, 2001), pp. 150–175 (p. 152).

59 Keith Wrightson, *Early Necessities: Economic Lives in Early Modern Britain, 1470–1750* (New Haven, CT: Yale University Press, 2000), p. 122.

60 Ryrie, Alec, 'The slow death of a tyrant: learning to live without Henry VIII, 1547–1563', in *Henry VIII and his afterlives: literature, politics and art*, eds. Mark Rankin, Christopher Highley and John N. King (Cambridge: Cambridge University Press, 2009), pp. 75–93 (p. 75).

61 Pettegree, 'Printing and the Reformation', p. 172.

243 titles in total, 110 more than in any prior year in English history. The overwhelming majority of these works was protestant. Susan Brigden asserts that eighty per cent of the increased output can be accounted for by evangelical polemic, whilst David Loades describes a 'major explosion of pastoral and polemical works'.[62] 1548 was also the daring year of the Edwardian print world: printers produced a broader spectrum of evangelical theology and controversial literature as the Edwardian reformation forged its direction and English reformers found their voices.

Antoinina Bevan Zlatar is correct to assert that the 'evangelical tenor of the regime became more audible' and cite preaching and printing as vehicles of this movement.[63] Of course, legislative proceedings highlighted this trajectory, but censorship legislation alone cannot account for this phenomenon. The lack of printing suppressions and the confessional alignment of the preachers the regime patronised encouraged the ascent of reformers and created an environment of enablement. Most of the 1548 publications that contributed to the outpouring were not officially endorsed, funded or supported, and reflected less the voice of the regime than that of either committed evangelical or entrepreneurial authors and printers. For some historians, polemic and iconoclasm have come to define the nature of the Edwardian reformation as a hostile and destructive movement.[64] It is with great caution, though, that we ought to link individual publications to defining the regime's outlook.

The wide variety of anticlericalism, anti-Roman Catholicism and pro-reform evangelicalism that England's presses produced could not all align with the regime's objective of religious uniformity. Nevertheless, the influential precursors of Edwardian protestantism came from the presses in substantial numbers. This body of work included the repatriation of works by William Tyndale (fifteen titles), John Frith (eight), Henry Brinklow (five) and Robert Barnes (two), and reformers who would be absorbed back into power, including Miles Coverdale (ten) and Hugh Latimer (two). Publications also emerged from the presses from polemicists William Turner (seven) and Richard Tracy (four), and scholars including Thomas Gilby, who contributed to a more academic aspect of the Edwardian reformation. Many of these works were rooted in the

---

62   For Brigden's figures to be correct, a perfectly feasible 88 titles of evangelical propaganda in 1548, would have been required; Susan Brigden, *London and the Reformation* (Oxford: Clarendon Press, 1989), pp. 432–433; Loades, 'Books and the English Reformation', pp. 282–283.
63   Bevan Zlatar, *Reformation Fictions*, pp. 42–43.
64   Duffy, *Stripping of the Altars*, pp. 449–450, 480; MacCulloch, *Tudor Church Militant*, pp. 71–73, 134–135; Peter J. Thuesen, *In Discordance with the Scriptures: American Protestant Battles over Translating the Bible* (Oxford: Oxford University Press, 1999), pp. 21, 24–25.

Henrician exile movement but were among the more restrained publications of 1548.

Just as 1548 saw a spike in the number of prominent English authors adopted by English presses, this was true also of continental authors. There were upturns in output from the conciliatory voices of Martin Bucer, Philipp Melanchthon, Urbanus Rhegius and Heinrich Bullinger, along with the emergence of Jean Calvin (eight), Huldrych Zwingli (two), Johannes Oecolampadius (one) and Bernardino Ochino (two) onto the English scene. Martin Luther's output spiked, too, rising from one title in 1547 to seven in 1548. The second year of Edward's tenure, then, is also a year of significant internationalism for English print culture. Printers looked to reformers from every strand of continental reform, exposing readers to new theological outlooks.

As we shall see, radical polemicists, including Luke Shepherd (nine titles), John Mardeley (four), Henry Harte and John Champneys, contributed to the flood of religious literature. This portion of the 1548 outpouring outstripped the official line, and each author faced legal sanctions. Having not produced any works before 1547, Mardeley and Shepherd accounted for thirteen titles in 1548: more than Bale, Cranmer and Latimer combined. This small number of authors fell afoul of official lines but made plenty of noise before the path of Edward's church was confirmed. It is clear, then, that some of the polemic and rhetoric of the reforming parties outran Edwardian legislation, even if they did not outrun the evolving confessional identity of those at the heart of the regime. This dynamic is symptomatic of the bureaucratic construction of both church and state: official doctrinal statements resulted from time-consuming accords, whereas polemical literature could be penned, printed and released more quickly. Counter-intuitively, the reformers might well have profited from those outstripping the official line as it enabled the Church of England to develop an image of toeing a more moderate line, using anti-catholic and anti-radical rhetoric.[65] From the opposite side, conservative circles and communities challenged the reformers, which centralised the official reformation between traditional conservatism and the radical fringe. Where conservative polemic arose, the reformers sought opportunities to undermine their critics and these publications provided ammunition for the assault upon the conservative remnants of the Henrician church.[66]

The substantial rise in polemic output in 1548 and the lack of official clampdowns emphasise that the self-censoring policy of England's printers in 1547 was over-cautious. Having seen several fervently reformed publications in 1547 go unpunished, and more of the same as 1548 progressed, printers were

---

65 Euler, *Couriers of the Gospel: England and Zurich*, p. 221.
66 Duffy, *Stripping of the Altars*, pp. 457–459.

emboldened by the climate of increased protestant freedom: a climate, which was only partly created by changes to the letter of the law.

Limiting discordant voices was critical as the church and government consolidated the Edwardian reformation and sought to end social friction. The Duke of Northumberland violently suppressed the 'Prayer Book' rebellion in 1549, and soon after the first Edwardian martyr, Joan Bocher, was burned at the stake in May 1550. The centralised print world was easier to control than those dissatisfied conservative rural populations who rose in rebellion in 1549. The printers of England, almost exclusively based in the capital, would have been acutely aware of the increasing scrutiny of dissidents, as would authors.[67] Moreover, gaining an understanding of the direction of the church was significantly easier following the Act of Uniformity church settlement of 1549. A focus upon censorship legislation alone has unreasonably removed the book trade from the world around it. The climate of opportunity and spiralling religious discussion of 1548 ended. In some instances, authorities restricted dissident's access to the press, but some printers simply forfeited these publications. Luke Shepherd's and John Mardeley's presence disappeared completely, John Frith's eight titles in 1548 became one in 1549, and Martin Luther, too, went from seven titles in 1548 to one in 1549. As these authors' output declined, the voice of uniformity and conformity became more pronounced.

The decisions printers and authors made in self-censoring were rooted in the world around them; therefore, it is unsurprising that print culture reflected a climate of increasing control. Authors and printers alike reverted to being averse to publicly outstrip acceptable religious discussion as English protestantism became better defined. Those who held, or had ambitions of holding, significant office within the political or religious establishment took these prohibitions seriously. Even Archbishop Cranmer, for example, requested a waiver of the prohibition on controversial texts for his *Answer to a crafty and sophistical cavillation devised by Stephen Gardiner* (Reyner Wolfe, 1551).[68] Cranmer held the highest religious office in England, and it is no surprise that he was careful not to alienate the regime that had ousted Somerset. English religious printing became increasingly linked to authors whose places in the establishment, or within their good graces, had been secured.

The international voice within English print also reflected a renewed drive for uniformity. In 1549, Martin Luther's output in England was one lone title; a

---

67 MacCulloch, *Tudor Church Militant*, p. 141; Andrew Pettegree, *Foreign Protestant Communities in Sixteenth-Century London* (Oxford: Clarendon Press, 1986), p. 44.

68 Felicity Heal, 'The Bishops and the Printers, from Henry VII to Elizabeth I', in *The Prelate in England and Europe, 1300–1560*, ed. Martin Heale (York: York Medieval Press, 2014), pp. 142–170 (pp. 164–165).

second followed in 1550 before his voice was withdrawn from the print world. In contrast, Edwardian religious émigrés and those closest to the regime's religious outlook became a louder presence. Bernardino Ochino had four titles between 1549 and 1550, along with Peter Martyr Vermigli's three in 1549 and 1550. Thereafter, the voice of the stranger churches developed, admittedly in their native tongues, with Jan a Lasco (eight), Jan Utenhove (five), Martin Micronius (five) and Michelangelo Florio (two) each having works printed. This international element to the English book world overlapped with a landmark policy of the regime and evidently aligned with the authorities' will.

The marked reduction in controversial literature during these years is significant. The Church of England was making strides towards uniformity, and whilst portions of the population had voiced their discontent, the discontented voices in print subsided more readily. Making money in a small inward-facing market directly under the nose of the authorities involved an element of 'toeing-the-line' to remain in favour or, at least, under the radar.

John Hooper, one of the foremost and most volatile exponents of reform in England, published his work at the Zurich press of Augustin Fries throughout his exile.[69] It was only following his return to England and, critically, his assimilation into the Church of England hierarchy that London became the centre for Hooper's publications. During 1547 and 1548, when his place in England's reformation was uncertain, Hooper remained unpublished in England. Once he had returned to England and taken up residence with the duke of Somerset in 1549, his works were printed by two London-based printers. These editions, printed by Stephen Mierdman (for Edward Whitchurch) and John Herford, are almost exact replicas but for variant woodcuts and initials.[70] This is a critical indicator of self-censorship: following the successful printing, marketing and sale of the first edition in London, the second printer could expect to follow without reprisal. It is more likely that the Mierdman publication was the first of these editions; he already held a considerable reputation for producing protestant literature in Antwerp and London. Whilst Herford had been printing in London since the 1530s, his output was low and included leading conservatives, Richard Smith and Stephen Gardiner. Herford, it seems, was testing the waters of reformist literature and entering a field where Mierdman had made his living for some time.

Hooper's ascent survived his association with Somerset, and the Crown invited him to preach the Lenten sermons before the king in 1550.[71] This

---

69   USTC 611799, 632074, 632072.
70   USTC 504305, 504268, 504254.
71   D.G. Newcomb, 'Hooper, John (1495 × 1500–1555)', ODNB.

endorsement provided a green light for England's printers, who responded with eleven Hooper titles within the year, including two collections of the Lenten sermons printed by William Seres and John Day.[72] The topic of these sermons (the oath of the ordinal and clerical vestments) would soon spark international debate.[73] Throughout 1550–1551, this controversy pulled in reformers and influential statesmen of all theological gradations, including Martin Bucer, Henrich Bullinger, Archbishop Cranmer, Jan a Lasco, Thomas Lever and Peter Martyr Vermigli. Hooper fought against clerical vestments ferociously, seeing them as an enduring symbol of Roman Catholic excess, and refused to be ordained wearing them. Finally, in January 1551, the regime's patience for their controversial preacher failed him: he was incarcerated first at Lambeth Palace and subsequently transferred to Fleet Prison. Hooper submitted and he was ordained, wearing clerical vestments, as Bishop of Gloucester and Worcester in March 1551. While Hooper remained prominent, his printed output declined sharply. Only two further titles emerged from English presses: one from John Day – a reprint of a 1550 publication with an inferred date of 1551, due to a December 1550 dedication – and one original text from a press in his new diocese: *Godly and most necessary annotations in ye .xiii. chapyter too the Romaynes* (Worcester, John Oswen, 1551).[74] Hooper's involvement in the book world, therefore, mirrored his prominence and standing with the government rather than the letter of the law on religious discussion. Printers were hesitant to utilise his works before his standing with the regime was known, pounced on the opportunity to produce his works during his prominence and swiftly moved on when contention was rife.

If zealous protestantism alone prompted printers to circumvent the law in 1548, this process would have occurred in 1547 and continued more readily during and beyond 1549. The decision of whether to publish particular works was surrounded by personal relationships and an understanding of the political concerns of the time, not simply the letter of the law. This reality has been hitherto marginalised. The law mattered, but it was not the only factor to consider.

Throughout the historiography, producing a religious work has been presented as printers nailing their colours to the shop sign and whilst this was true in some instances, printing was principally a commercial enterprise.[75]

---

72 USTC 504450, 5151419.
73 Bruce Gordon, *The Swiss Reformation* (Manchester, Manchester University Press, 2002), pp. 301–302; Pettegree, *Foreign Protestant Communities*, pp. 31–32, 39–40; SP Spanish, 10, pp. 261–266 – 9 April 1551: Advices sent by Jehan Scheyfve.
74 USTC 515421, 504629.
75 Susan Powell, 'The Secular Clergy', in *A Companion to the Early Printed Book in Britain, 1476–1558*, eds. Vincent Gillespie and Susan Powell (Cambridge: Brewer, 2014), pp. 150–175

The centralised English print world was one of the easiest in Europe to police: typefaces, illustrations and ornaments could be identified quickly and attempting to subvert the regime was risky.[76] If a publication was censored and confiscated, then prospective profits were lost. Printers and authors knew this and self-censored so their output could run alongside the regime's religious trajectory.

2   Resistance and Suppression

From the earliest stages of Edward's reign, there were attempts to ensure religious conformity and quash dissent. England was a fastidiously bureaucratic state, yet few records remain of book-related prosecutions or confiscations. Despite this, we can discern a three-pronged attack against non-conformists on each side of the theological spectrum. The first was the application of legal and political pressures through imprisonments, forced recantations and deprivations of office. The second restricted press access and censored those setting forth controversial material. The final was to mobilise a printed counterattack founded upon academic disputations, refutations and scathing polemic. This counterattack simultaneously reaffirmed the reformers' position and undermined their opponents, and involved authors acting under various degrees of state protection, sponsorship or facilitation.

Here we tackle the little-discussed printed opposition to the Edwardian reformation. Evangelical polemic authors outproduced their conservative counterparts, but they did not hold a monopoly. Confessional lines are difficult to draw, often formed by perceptions of difference as much as difference itself; thus, texts and authors are rarely conducive to neat categorisation. These confessional boundaries were fluid, but we can explore those falling foul of the regime through case study examples and industry-wide trends to cast light upon printed religious dissent.

Leading members of the new protestant ascendency kept a wary eye on their formerly dominant catholic opponents.

> Such is the maliciousness and wickedness of the bishops, that the godly and learned men who would willingly labour in the Lord's harvest are hindered by them; and they neither preach themselves, nor allow the liberty of preaching to others … a great portion of the kingdom so adheres

---

(p. 173); Brigden, *London and the Reformation*, p. 438; Davies, *A Religion of the Word*, p. x.

76   Pettegree, 'Printing and the Reformation', p. 167.

> to the popish faction, as altogether to set at nought God and the lawful authority of the magistrates...
>
> JOHN HOOPER to Heinrich Bullinger, 25 June 1549.[77]

Hooper's assessment betrays a state of affairs masked by the printed output of the period. The influence of England's conservatives deteriorated during Thomas Cromwell's prominence before a period of recovery and consolidation. At Edward's accession, the conservative faction had prominent bishops, a body of polemical material and powerful rhetoric of continuity during the young king's minority.[78] The conservative faction, however, was quickly quietened. Alec Ryrie labelled Edwardian conservatism 'one of the most mysterious dogs that failed to bark in the English Reformation', whilst Ethan Shagan highlighted 'The ballad of Little John Nobody, who (under that Name) Libels the Reformation under Kind Edward VI' when discussing the conservative resistance.[79] Through intermittent incarcerations, the deprivation of bishoprics and the restriction of access to English presses, the government neutralised the voice of Edwardian conservatives.

Systematic legal and political pressures suppressed Edwardian conservatives. The authorities targeted reluctant conservatives with imprisonments and the deprivation of bishoprics and attempted to quash the import of conservative polemic from Europe. A flurry of deprivations quickly ousted conservatives from power and replaced them with reformers. The foremost conservative opponent, Stephen Gardiner (bishop of Winchester), endured periodic incarceration from mid-1547 and was deprived in 1551.[80] The regime deprived Edmund Bonner (bishop of London) more swiftly, replacing him with the reform-minded Nicholas Ridley in October 1549.[81]

Despite these examples, some resistance to the Edwardian religious trajectory persisted. Jehan Scheyfve, the Imperial ambassador, wrote on 9 April 1551 that the establishment had detained 'several doctors ... among whom is the vicar of suffragan of the old Bishop of Winchester, who had been so bold as

---

77   OL, 1, pp. 65–67 (p. 65).
78   Ryrie, 'Strange Death of Lutheran England', p. 78.
79   Ryrie, 'Paths not taken in the British Reformations', p. 21; Ethan Shagan, 'Confronting compromise: the schism and its legacy in mid-Tudor England' in *Catholics and the 'Protestant nation': Religious politics and identity in early modern England*, ed. Ethan Shagan (Manchester: Manchester University Press, 2005), pp. 49–68 (pp. 59–61).
80   SP Spanish, 9, pp. 242–243 – 22 January 1548: Van der Delft to the Flemish Council of State; APC, 2, pp. 404–405 – 4 March 1549; APC, 3, pp. 46–48 – 14 June 1550; APC, 3, pp. 67–68 – 10 July 1550.
81   Susan Wabuda, 'Ridley, Nicholas (c.1502–1555)', ODNB.

to defend and maintain his master's cause'.[82] Even the pragmatic Cuthbert Tunstall, prince-bishop of Durham, suffered house arrest before being confined to the Tower and finally deprived of his bishopric in October 1552.[83] Other principal catholics fled to Europe where collectives gathered at Louvain, Rouen and Paris.[84]

The conservative branches of Edwardian society were less active in writing and publishing than their reformer counterparts. Knowing that legal and political repercussions could follow, this is not surprising, particularly considering the ease with which authorities could identify dissident printers.[85] Many would-be authors self-censored and most conservative bishops played no part in the Edwardian book world. The acquiescence of England's conservatives in the matter of the royal supremacy spoken more to Henry's authority than the impiety of England's conservatives; however, these actions, combined with the exclusion of this matter from the Act of Repeal, undermined their resistance. Eamon Duffy has claimed that 'Marian apologetic and polemic writing has been seriously underrated', but if this is true, we must acknowledge that the Edwardian years offered few indications that an adequate counterattack was looming.[86] Self-censorship and the watchful eye of the regime ensured that conservative publishing was a muted effort, but even in this time of acquiescence, some cases of defiance emerged as some conservatives turned to presses in England and abroad.

The second tactic of the regime was to deny conservatives access to English presses. In part, this process followed the political sanctions above, but the authorities shored up their position with legislation surrounding printing that created effective self-censorship. The conservative resistance lacked the clandestine import market, which had flourished in Antwerp under Henry VIII and was later cultivated in Emden under Mary I, therefore preventing access to English presses was a critical policy.

Edwardian conservatism was not without texts. Conservatives penned refutations and polemics that remained unpublished.[87] The succession saw a num-

---

[82] *SP Spanish*, 10, pp. 261–266 – 9 April 1551: Advices sent by Jehan Scheyfve.
[83] *SP Spanish*, 10, pp. 424–426 – 27 December 1551: Advices sent by Jehan Scheyfve; *SP Spanish*, 10, pp. 590–591 – 20 November 1552: Advices sent by Jehan Scheyfve.
[84] Brigden, *London and the Reformation*, pp. 427, 453–455; Loades, 'Books and the English Reformation', p. 279.
[85] Pettegree, 'Printing and the Reformation', p. 167.
[86] Eamon Duffy, *Fires of Faith: Catholic England under Mary Tudor* (New Haven, CT: Yale University Press, 2009), p. 78.
[87] Gardiner's unpublished refutations of Peter Martyr Vermigli, John Hooper and Johannes Oecolampadius, Cuthbert Tunstall's *De Veritate* and Miles Huggarde's *Assault of the Sacrament of the Altar* each exemplify this.

ber of these works published, and the 'underrated' nature of Marian apologetic literature bears testament to how the Edwardian authorities discouraged printers from producing conservative material. Ellen Macek has noted nine key works of conservative polemic published in 1554 and six more published in 1555, many of which were completed during the Edwardian years.[88] These works exemplify that the authorities had effectively and systematically denied access to English presses.

The figurehead of late-Henrician and Edwardian conservatism was Stephen Gardiner. The embattled Bishop of Winchester authored fifteen English titles printed between 1530 and 1546, including original polemical tracts in 1546.[89] The USTC lists Gardiner as an author for ten titles between 1547 and 1553; this figure, however, grossly exaggerates his access to the press. Reform-minded print houses produced seven of these titles, and an English protestant in Wesel published another. Many were the work of John Bale (produced in Marian 1553), who translated *De vera obedientia*, wherein Gardiner had upheld the royal supremacy.[90] Gardiner's authorial catalogue over these years included only two publications that would not have caused embarrassment, and both were French imprints. The first, *An explication and assertion of the true catholique fayth*, was printed by Robert Caly at Rouen in 1551.[91] The second, *Confutatio Cavillationum*, printed in Paris by Prevost and De Roigny in 1552, responded to Cranmer's polemical attack.[92]

Whilst imprisoned, Gardiner penned four refutations of prominent protestants – Peter Martyr Vermigli, Martin Bucer, John Hooper, and Johannes Oecolampadius – but his confinement ensured that these went unpublished.[93] The nature of Gardiner's writing in these years, both published and unpublished, communicates conservative priorities. Gardiner sought to undermine the position of prominent evangelicals via academic refutations but was not writing for a popular, or even non-expert, audience. Nonetheless, Gardiner's inability to put them forth in print represented a significant coup by the government; he was one of few English theologians who could attract a widespread international scholarly audience. This low level of output from the leading figure of English conservatism highlights that the regime had limited

---

88   Ellen A. Macek, *The Loyal Opposition: Tudor Traditionalist Polemics, 1535–1558* (New York: Peter Lang, 1996), pp. 1–13.
89   These fifteen titles included six from English presses, two in Louvain, two in Cologne, two in Ingolstadt, and one each from presses in Bonn, Strasbourg and Hamburg.
90   USTC 517667, 517668, 151267.
91   USTC 150736.
92   USTC 151037.
93   C.D.C. Armstrong, 'Gardiner, Stephen, c.1495–1555', ODNB, cites BL Arundel MS 100, fols. 1–182; SP 10/12, fols. 2–68.

Gardiner's access to the press through their policy of incarceration and curtailing continental imports.

Richard Smith was a distinguished religious scholar who had secured the patronage of both Henry VIII and Edmund Bonner and had published widely in 1546 and 1547.[94] Edward's accession brought an emphatic stop to his advancement. The authorities forced public recantations in London and Oxford, both of which incorporated book burnings.[95] The church hierarchy also mobilised printer Reyner Wolfe to use these two recantations as a protestant polemic, and following public disputes with Peter Martyr Vermigli, Smith's position at Oxford quickly became untenable and he fled the country.[96] Thomas Raynald produced Smith's final Edwardian title from an English press in 1548: a sixteen-page octavo *Of unwryten verytyes*.[97] Raynald printed a range of theological works and it is possible he printed this work to spike interest and debate against his other publications by reformers and radicals. *Of unwryten verytyes* was undoubtedly controversial and received responses from England's evangelicals contemporaneously and into Mary I's reign.[98]

Thereafter, Smith absconded to Louvain, but his publications soon returned. In January 1551, the Privy Council wrote to Sir John Masone concerning 'a slanderous book against the Bishop of Canterbury'.[99] This publication, *A confutation of a certen booke* (Paris, Regnault Chaudière, [1550]), was soon followed by two refutations of Peter Martyr Vermigli from Chaudière's press and the Louvain presses of Anthoni-Marie Bergagne and Jan Waen.[100] Between 1547 and 1553, Richard Smith authored ten titles printed across Europe: four in London (three from 1547 and one from 1548), three from Louvain (1550, 1551) and three from Paris (1550, 1551).[101] The authorities discovered a plot to import works via clandestine networks from Paris in 1551.[102] Whilst Smith was protected in exile, the government could only seek to thwart attempts to import his works. Nonetheless, Smith's limited role in the English book world represents another victory for the government. Political pressure had removed Smith

---

94 USTC 503770, 503774, 503785, 503786.
95 J. Andreas Löwe, *Richard Smyth and the Language of Orthodoxy: Re-Imagining Tudor Catholic Polemicism* (Leiden: Brill, 2003), pp. 34–40.
96 USTC 503898; 503900.
97 USTC 504130.
98 Peter Marshall, *Religious Identities in Henry VIII's England* (Aldershot: Ashgate, 2006), pp. 96–98; Ethan Shagan, *Popular Politics and the English Reformation* (Cambridge: Cambridge University Press, 2003), pp. 64–65 (n. 8); USTC 505296.
99 SP 68/9A f.218 – 18 January 1550–1: The Council to Sir John Masone.
100 USTC 139222; 150518, 150849; 400853, 403456.
101 The Parisian imprints are all from the Chaudière press, whilst the three Louvain imprints are produced by one of Anthoni-Marie Bergagne, Jan Waen and/or Hugo Cornwels.
102 *Salisbury MSS*, 1.83 cited in J. Andreas Löwe, 'Smyth, Richard (1499/1500–1563)', ODNB.

from Oxford, and his recantations provided valuable polemic for the regime. His output was limited to a single English imprint and continental products aimed at continental audiences as well as England, the import of which was rooted out in earnest.

Gardiner and Smith had contemporary counterparts in the junior rungs of theological discourse and polemic. The publications making up this section of the conservative resistance were short: ballads and brief polemics. Miles Huggarde, a lay catholic, expounded his Eucharistic doctrine with *An Aunswer to the Ballad called the Abuse of ye Blessed Sacrament* in 1547. Huggarde was quickly summoned by the Privy Council for examination, and they repressed his tract. Neither Huggarde's first or second publication (*The Excellency of Mannes Nature*) has survived.[103] His third polemic, *Assault of the Sacrament of the Altar*, remained unpublished until after Edward's death, ultimately bearing the words: 'Written in the yere of our lorde 1549 by Miles Huggarde dedicated to the Quenes moste excellent maiesty, beyng then ladie Marie: in whiche tyme (heresie then raigning) it could take no place'.[104] Huggarde's reputation now stands as one of the key 'traditionalist polemicists' and 'the best of the Roman Catholic propagandists in the bitter pamphlet war of 1553–1558'.[105] Soon following Mary I's accession, Huggarde's works were circulating, with a favourite printer of the Marian regime, Robert Caly producing *The assault of the sacrament of the altar*, *The path waye to the towre of perfection* and *Howe Christ by perverse preachyng was banished out of this realme* in 1554.[106] The known production of three original Huggarde texts during the Edwardian period, without any Edwardian imprints surviving, suggests again that the authorities were succeeding in their unyielding programme of textual suppression.

John Proctor was a second lay catholic who attempted to undermine the direction of the Church of England. *The Fal of the Late Arrian* (William Powell, 1549) was an anti-radical tract dedicated to Princess Mary, described by Alan Bryson as a 'sly critique of the Protestant reformation'.[107] Proctor's ability to find an accommodating printer may owe something to his outward condemnation of anti-trinitarianism, radicalism and the Somerset protectorate (instead of

---

103   C. Bradshaw, 'Huggarde, Miles (*fl.* 1533–1557)', ODNB.
104   USTC 505012.
105   Macek, *The Loyal Opposition*, pp. 185–188; J.W. Martin, 'Miles Hogarde, Artisan and aspiring Author in Sixteenth century England', *Renaissance Quarterly*, 34 (Chicago, 1981), pp. 359–383 (p. 359).
106   USTC 505012, 505033, 516538.
107   Alan Bryson, 'Order and Disorder: John Proctor's History of Wyatt's Rebellion (1554)', in *The Oxford Handbook of Tudor Literature: 1485–1603*, eds. Michael Pincombe and Cathy Shrank (Oxford: Oxford University Press, 2009), pp. 323–336 (pp. 324–326).

the newly installed political faction governed by the duke of Northumberland) allowing his critique to avoid reprimand. Nonetheless, this was Proctor's single authorial credit of the Edwardian years. Ellen Macek describes Proctor as only a minor polemicist of the traditionalist cause.[108] Unlike Huggarde, his literary career did not expand significantly following Mary I's accession; though he did return to the English book world with the polemical *The History of Wyatt's Rebellion* and a translation of Vincent of Lérins's *Commonitorium* following Mary I's accession.[109] The case of John Proctor suggests that self-censorship worked hand-in-hand with the authorities, alongside the political and religious events of the reign to decide whether a publications was suitable.

The clandestine book import market did not cease entirely in the reign of Edward VI. Between 1547 and 1553, however, these were either small-scale enterprises or English readers represented only a minor portion of their business. Whilst these were not parts of the English print trade, they represent a noteworthy component of the English book world. We can split the thirty-seven English-language titles bearing continental imprints between into two markets: Rouen, Louvain, Paris and Lyon serving the conservatives, and Zurich, Wesel, Strasbourg, Antwerp and Hamburg serving the reformers.

Records remain of only one Englishman to set up a press-in-exile during the Edwardian period: Robert Caly.[110] Some historians have credited Caly's activities at Rouen as an independent exile press; however, Peter Blayney's more recent research has relegated his standing to 'probably printing in Rouen, but only as a journeyman'.[111] The USTC lists only one title by Caly: Stephen Gardiner, *An explication and assertion of the true catholique fayth* (Rouen, 1551).[112] However extensive his activities in Rouen, Roman Catholic loyalists noticed Caly's efforts and following his repatriation in 1553, he assumed control of Richard Grafton's presses and established himself as one of England's premier catholic printers.[113] The legacy of Caly's Rouen enterprise was strong, but his output was more marginal than once believed.

---

108   Macek, *The Loyal Opposition*, p. 35.
109   USTC 505006, 505210; David Loades credits Proctor also with translating *The Way Home to Christ and Truth* in 1554. 'Proctor, John, (1521?–1584)', ODNB; Ryrie, 'Paths not taken in the English Reformation', pp. 7–9; USTC 505043.
110   Jennifer Loach, 'The Marian Establishment and the Printing Press', *The English Historical Review*, 101, 398 (1986), pp. 135–148 (p. 137).
111   Brigden, *London and the Reformation*, pp. 454–455; Loades, 'Books and the English Reformation', p. 272; Blayney, *The Stationers' Company*, p. 605.
112   USTC 105736.
113   Duffy, *Fires of Faith*, p. 58; Valerie Schutte, *Mary I and the Art of Book Dedications: Royal Women, Power and Persuasion* (New York: Palgrave Macmillan, 2015), pp. 72–73; Blayney, *The Stationers' Company*, pp. 762–765, 771–773.

Aside from Caly's, a further eight imprints appear initially to have originated from Rouen, which targeted English readers. In fact, only two can be firmly placed within Edward's reign or even to have originated from Rouen: a bible (Nicholas le Roux for Edward Whitchurch, 1550) and the *Prymer of Salisbury* (Nicholas le Roux, 1551).[114] The quarto bible was published by a favourite of the regime, and decidedly on-brand for Whitchurch, suggesting that this was not a seditious project. The remaining English-language imprints were, in fact, evangelical polemic. John Day's false imprints as 'Michael Wood' from 'Rouen', a mystery solved by Elizabeth Evenden, represent at least three, if not more, of these titles.[115] The two remaining titles, John Bale's *An Admonishion to the bishoppes of Winchester, London and others* and an anti-nicodemite tract attributed to Robert Horne and John Hooper, each represent the evangelical cause.[116] From the preliminary statistical and historiographical image of a conservative press-in-exile, the reality of Caly's small enterprise emerges, and the false imprint 'Rouen' instead becomes a hallmark of subversion against the Marian regime.

Edwardian exiles established another centre of resistance in Louvain. The university city hosted conservatives including John Clement, John Story, and Anthony Bonvisi.[117] There was little to suggest that Louvain would become a thriving clandestine print centre for English conservatism. It was a small book trade in the shadow of Antwerp, producing only 302 titles between 1547 and 1553 (188 of which were in Latin) and only 110 religious titles.[118] Nevertheless, Louvain was the centre for Richard Smith's voice in 1550 and 1551 with three Latin works produced.[119] Anthoni-Marie Bergagne, who printed two Smith publications, also printed two titles of the duke of Northumberland's recantation at the scaffold in 1553 – one in Dutch and one in Latin.[120] Eamon Duffy credits Cardinal Pole with championing this recantation's dissemination around Europe and printers in Antwerp and Vienna also produced editions.[121] Gardiner's *Confutatio cavillationum*, too, was reprinted by Reinerus Velpius

---

114   USTC 206225, 150982.
115   Evenden, *Patents, Pictures and Patronage*, chapter 2 (pp. 29–37).
116   Karl Gunter, *Reformation Unbound: Protestant Visions of Reform in England, 1525–1590* (Cambridge: Cambridge University Press, 2014), p. 112; Felicity Heal, *Reformation in Britain and Ireland* (Oxford: Oxford University Press, 2003), p. 252; USTC 206226, 151402 (FB: 55844, 74376).
117   Brigden, *London and the Reformation*, pp. 427, 453.
118   The USTC lists the languages of Louvain works as Latin (111), French (fifty-five), Dutch (thirty-nine). Religious publications (111) are followed next by music (forty-six).
119   USTC 400853, 403456; 415630.
120   USTC 410940 (NB: 23006); 410943 (NB: 2008).
121   Duffy, *Fires of Faith*, p. 88; USTC (Cawood) 504918; (Louvain) 410940, 410943; (Antwerp) 415879; (Vienna) 667826, 706288.

and Petrus Colonaeus in Louvain in 1554. One of the central characters of conservative printing in Louvain was Scottish: Jan Waen.[122] The Waen press produced eleven titles during Edward's reign, including folio bibles in Dutch and French and six other religious works, including two Latin tracts by Smith, and Hendrick Herp's anti-reformation tract *Den Spiegel der volmaectheyt*.[123] Conservative works may well have aligned with Waen's religious alignment, his daughter married Rutger Velpius (later appointed printer to the catholic court in Brussels), equally the marriage may simply highlight commercial pragmatism.[124]

The exiles in Louvain embarked upon the *Works of Thomas More*, ultimately published in 1557. If Edward's reign had continued, this collection might have come to represent a flagship publication for the conservative resistance. Both More's and Smith's Louvain publications had international appeal. Thomas More was one of few Henrician conservatives with an international reputation, and Smith's tracts addressed themes of international controversies. As a result, these Latin texts of esteemed scholars could target widely dispersed readerships. This is important, as printers were not relying on English readers and the clandestine import market alone, making for more favourable commercial conditions to print.

Louvain represents a more-fruitful symbol of Edwardian conservatism-in-exile and early-Marian internationalism than Rouen despite boasting no English printers and short title catalogue figures showing fewer titles by leading conservative theologians. The ramification of the authorities' policies on the book world spread into wider society. By controlling access to the presses, the reformers strengthened their grip on power and limited discord from conservative sympathisers. As we see in the later reign of Mary I, an engaged subversive printing trade, this time stemming from protestant Europe, could influence society in England. Under Edward, the protestant faction was able to stop literature from gathering momentum and building into more significant social pressures. The Edwardian authorities were engaged with the English book world; whether encouraging or discouraging a specific type of literature, they made their presence felt for their ambitions.

Anti-Roman Catholic publications were a significant component of Edwardian printed output. Publications emanating from the uppermost echelons of church and government, including the archbishop of Canterbury,

---

122 John Durkan, 'Some Scottish Bookmen', *The Innes Review*, 57, 2 (2006), pp. 216–218.
123 USTC 415630, 403456; one of 454 pages, and a second of 152 pages; USTC 407461, NB: 14711; Anna Dlabčová, *Literatuur en observantie: De Spieghel der volcomenheit van Hendrik Herp en de dynamiek van laatmiddeleeuwse tekstverspreiding* (Hilversum, Netherlands: Uitgeverij Verloren, 2014), p. 351.
124 'Velpius, Rutger', CERL *Thesaurus*.

provided the learned refutations, whilst an array of polemicists demonised the conservatives and the papacy. The core of controversial evangelical literature comprised of anti-papal and Eucharistic tracts. The printed counterattack often blurs the lines of state sponsorship, patronage and protection. Particularly during 1548, when this phenomenon reached its zenith, it is difficult to disentangle those publications with official, or pseudo-official, support from those under private evangelical patronage and those taken up as private projects with commercial or theological motivations.

Catharine Davies has adeptly analysed the themes tackled in this printed counterattack, and her authoritative work treats this topic in more detail than can be afforded in this project.[125] The examples of false imprints and subversive publications condemning the nicodemism of conservatives' previous works have been discussed above, as have the publications of the recantations of Richard Smith.[126] These works sat alongside direct disputations penned by Anthony Gilby (*An answer to the devillish detection of Stephane Gardiner, Bishoppe of Wynchester*) and Archbishop Cranmer (*Answer to a crafty and sophistical cavillation devised by Stephen Gardiner*).[127] Huggarde, too, was countered directly by evangelicals, including Robert Crowley (*The confutation of the mishapen aunswer*).[128]

Meanwhile, the battle for England's popular opinion unfolded in short octavo or sextodecimo tracts produced cheaply and aimed at a mass readership. Eucharistic tracts written by laypeople, lower-ranking clergymen and academics had potential to overstep the official lines and stray into the realms of radicalism. The glut of Eucharistic tracts in 1548 included works by continental theologians, but also an increasing range of English evangelicals. These works fuelled the dramatic and disproportionate growth in English printing in 1548. The establishment created an atmosphere of evangelical freedom and the printers reacted by creating a body of literature that criticised conservatives and conservative beliefs. The attack upon, and counterattack against, conservatism inspired a greater response from English presses than the conservatives themselves and became an integral part of the book trade.

The conservative faction failed to mount a consistent opposition to the Edwardian evangelicals. Political pressures scuppered any ambition to lead the resistance as authors, whilst book burnings and the seeking out of imported

---

125 This section, along with the section on the counterattack against radicalism, is indebted to Catharine Davies' *Religion of the Word*.
126 USTC 503898; 503900.
127 USTC 504053, 516505.
128 USTC 504020.

books laid waste to any hope of emulating the clandestine trade of the Henrician evangelicals. Moreover, Edwardian conservatives seemed to show a general disinterest in engaging in public polemic: the authors discussed in this study are the outliers of the conservative faction. Whether English conservatives considered print a valuable tool has been much discussed in the Marian historiography, but it is undeniable that they failed to establish a foothold in the Edwardian book world.[129] Edwardian conservatives were not willing authors, and those who wrote were not prolific authors in the vernacular.

Alongside this conservative inactivity, the evangelicals produced swathes of academic and polemical attacks upon the catholic church and the conservatives. Skirmishes such as those between Gardiner and Cranmer were printed for prearranged evangelical victories and printers produced recantations and previous outputs to undermine and embarrass the esteemed opposition. Much of the wider counterattack polemic can only be described as pseudo-official at best and was born from an environment of opportunity. However, the Edwardian regime facilitated and encouraged these events by creating a political and religious climate of anti-conservativism and reformist zeal.

3 The Religious and Social Radical Fringe

Radicalism in early modern Europe encompassed a wide range of theologies. Location and the authority you were challenging defined the perception of your radicalism. In the Edwardian context, anabaptism, anti-trinitarianism, sacramentarianism, the free-willers and denial of the incarnation represented the radicalism ubiquitously feared by established churches.[130] During Henry's tumultuous final years, reformers and radicals came under intense scrutiny, culminating in a spate of executions.[131] These legal and political pressures continued for radicals during the reign of Edward VI and curtailing their influence occupied the minds of some of England's foremost theologians.[132]

The production of radical works required authors committed to disseminating their theologies and printers willing to risk the wrath of the regime. Radicalism was not a natural bedfellow of educated linguists and scholars; many radical strands focused upon anti-establishment and anti-scholarly

---

129 Loach, 'The Marian Establishment and the Printing Press'; Neville-Sington, 'Press, politics and religion', pp. 605–607; Duffy, *Fires of Faith*, pp. 60–63, 69–78.
130 Brigden, *London and the Reformation*, p. 442, Davies, *Religion of the Word*, p. 77.
131 MacCulloch, *Tudor Church Militant*, p. 63; Ryrie, 'The Strange Death', pp. 83–88, 91.
132 *SP* 10/15, no. 15 – Thomas Cranmer to the Council.

approaches to scripture, which alarmed and alienated many. Even when radical authors emerged, the issue of willing printers remained. Printers not only had to be prepared to outrun the religious trajectory of the regime, but they also had to believe, or hope, that it could be commercially viable.

Peter Marshall identifies the broader English reformation as having been 'unusually and bloodily prolific in its creation of martyrs'.[133] Edward's reign was a short respite with only two radicals martyred: Joan Bocher (2 May 1550) and George van Parris (24 April 1551). Bocher was 'burned for holding that Christ was not incarnate of the Virgin Mary', whilst van Parris was condemned for anti-trinitarianism.[134] Bocher's denial has been labelled by Carrie Euler as a prominent heterodox belief as 'one of the most frequent heretical statements uttered by radicals in England at this time'. David Loewenstein's account of the 'urging of Edward VI's privy council' to condemn Bocher, meanwhile, is in direct contrast to W.K. Jordan's previous assessment that 'Somerset refused to permit Bocher's execution, and that Cranmer declined to conduct any active persecution'.[135] In the case of van Parris, the king's journal for April 1551 records that 'a certain Aryan of the strangers, a Dutchman, being excommunicated by the congregation of his countrymen, was after long disputation condemned to the fire'.[136]

These executions present a crucial reminder about Tudor authority: legislation was only as powerful as its implementation, and restrictions were only as important as the authorities' adherence to them. Neither Bocher nor van Parris committed their theologies to publication, though Joan Bocher's condemnation of Cranmer has survived in Miles Huggarde's later polemical martyrology.[137] For this study, their central importance lies in the printed

---

133 Peter Marshall, *Heretics and Believers: A History of the English Reformation* (New Haven, CT: Yale University Press, 2017), p. xiii.
134 Pettegree, *Foreign Protestant Communities*, p. 65.
135 Euler, *Couriers of the Gospel: England and Zurich*, p. 209; David Loewenstein, *Treacherous Faith: The Spectre of Heresy and Religious Conflict in the English Reformation* (Oxford: Oxford University Press, 2013), p. 132; John N. King, 'Paul's Cross and the implementation of Protestant Reforms under Edward VI', in *Paul's Cross and the culture of persuasion in England, 1520–1640*, eds. W.J. Torrance Kirby and P.G. Stanwood (Leiden: Brill, 2013), pp. 141–159 (pp. 141–142).
136 W.K. Jordan, ed., *The Chronicle and political papers of Edward VI* (Ithaca, NY: Cornell University Press, 1966), pp. 28–29, 58; Jordan's interpretation is that Bocher maintained radical views with a strain of anti-trinitarianism whilst van Parris held unitarian as well as anabaptist views.
137 USTC 505355, 505358, fol. 47v; J.W. Martin, *Religious Radicals in Tudor England* (London: Hambledon Press, 1989), p. 46, highlights that Van Parris spoke no English (Coverdale acted as an interpreter during Cranmer's investigations), so a capable translator would also have been required before his works could reach an English audience.

PRINT AND GOVERNMENT   69

counterattack against radicalism. Andrew Pettegree has asserted that Bocher's execution prompted a renewed 'campaign against sectarian error', perhaps in response to her claims that there were a thousand anabaptists in London before her death.[138] This reactionary campaign took place via political and clerical exclusions, investigations, royal commissions (April 1549 and January 1551) and tribunals and via printed polemic.[139]

The religious proceedings of the Edwardian reign were rife with controversy from within the protestant ranks and without. For centuries, England had taken its religious direction from the Roman Catholic church. Now, fresh from the wrathful final years of Henry VIII's reign, the newly installed reformers needed to consolidate their religious position and control the pace of religious and social change. Controlling the radical fringe was central to establishing uniformity within the Church of England as it attempted to define itself in motion.

Across reformation Europe, few radicals actively attempted to disseminate their theologies via print. In Germany, almost contemporaneous to Edward's reign, the *Schleitheim Articles* – the first confession to come from an anabaptist gathering – came from the press of Philipp I Ulhart in Augsburg.[140] Although marginalised, continental radical authors and social revolutionaries of the period could find patrons and presses who would print their works when commercial and political conditions aligned.[141] In England, chances were more limited. Catharine Davies' *A religion of the Word* highlights only four individuals of radical persuasion in her biographies of authors appendix: Thomas Cole (heterodox), John Champneys (unorthodox), Henry Harte (anti-predestinarian

---

138 Brigden, *London and the Reformation*, p. 444, Brigden cites I.B. Horst, *The Radical Brethren: Anabaptism and the English Reformation to 1558* (Nieuwkoop: B. de Graaf, 1972); see also J.F. Davis, 'Joan of Kent, Lollardy and the English Reformation', *Journal of Ecclesiastical History*, 33 (1982), pp. 225–233 (p. 225); Pettegree, *Foreign Protestant Communities*, p. 44.

139 *APC*, 4, p. 13; Martin, *Religious Radicals*, pp. 46–48; Davies, *A religion of the Word*, p. 68; Euler, *Couriers of the Gospel: England and Zurich*, p. 210.

140 The Schleitheim Confession of 1527 can be found in translation in William R. Estep Jr. (ed.), *Anabaptist Beginnings 1523–1533* (Nieuwkoop: B. de Graaf, 1976), pp. 99–105.

141 Augsburg was a small centre of radical printing in the 1520s and 1530s with printers Philipp I Ulhart and Heinrich von Augsburg Steiner leading the field of spiritualist and radical publishing. Ulhart printed seven titles by Hans Denck, a title by anabaptist martyr Michael Sattler, Melchior Hoffman and the Schleitheim Articles, while Steiner printed works by Sebastian Franck, Denck, Hoffman and Balthasar Hubmaier. Presses in Strasbourg, too, had produced works by authored by radicals in the 1520s and 1530s, particularly the Prüß-Beck press. Pettegree, *The Book in the Renaissance*, p. 86; C. Arnold Snyder and Linda A. Huebert Hecht (eds.) *Profiles of Anabaptist Women: Sixteenth-Century Reforming Pioneers* (Waterloo, Ontario: Wilfred Laurier University Press, 1996) p. 268.

separatist) and John Mardeley.[142] This is in no small part due to the lack of publicity sought by a marginalised and largely underground religious movement. Government initiatives also played a significant part: the authorities sought to deny radicals access to the press and prosecute those who did publish. Few proceedings against radical authors, or printers who produced radical tracts, can be found. Those remaining provide snapshots of the theological convictions of the authorities at specific moments but also of the printers hoping to promote (or profit from) radical publications. Here, we must not devalue the significance of curiosity and notoriety to entice readers. Susan Brigden has argued, relating to anti-papal material produced in 1548, that readers 'could not but be excited by the controversy'.[143] During the outburst of evangelical polemic during 1548, the radical fringe also sought access to English presses. Whether authors or printers drove this process cannot be ascertained, but a concentration of radical works emerged. In order to examine this more thoroughly, this section will examine how far readers' appetite and printers' boldness extended from anti-papal sentiment into religious radicalism. Moreover, it will highlight how authors who faced reprimand can pose as case studies to articulate how the regime denied access to the press.

In 1548, Thomas Raynald printed three octavos authored by John Mardeley.[144] The first two were among the many Eucharistic tracts that violated the proclamation of December 1547. When recommencing pre-publication licensing legislation in August 1549, the authorities named Mardeley's publications directly. Whilst this legislation was unlikely to have been implemented fully, it shows a commitment to quashing printed religious dissent. Mardeley's case is intriguing due to assertions that he was patronised by the duke of Somerset.[145] It is perhaps indicative of Somerset's dissatisfaction that Mardeley's works prompted such sweeping legislative amendments. A connection between the author and the duke is implied in Mardeley's recognisance, which required any subsequent publications to be licensed directly by the duke rather than the newly established censors. John Bale's contemporaneous account links Mardeley to the anonymous *A Ruful Complaynt of the Publyke Weale to Englande*, which echoed the rhetoric of Kett's rebellion (July–August 1549), stating Mardeley 'only evaded death with great difficulty'.[146] The authorities brought Mardeley

---

142 Davies, *A religion of the Word*, Chapter 2 and pp. 235–246.
143 Cyndia Susan Clegg, 'The authority and subversiveness of print', in *The Cambridge Companion to the History of the Book in Britain*, ed. Leslie Howsam (Cambridge: Cambridge University Press, 2015), pp. 125–142 (p. 133); Brigden, *London and the Reformation*, p. 439.
144 USTC 504094 and 515364; 504093; 504104.
145 Davies, *A religion of the Word*, p. 243.
146 USTC 504366; Cathy Shrank, 'Mardeley, John (*fl.* 1548–1558)', ODNB; USTC 692634, 692633.

to heel quickly and there we no further titles of his authorship: both he and the printers of England knew his works were off-limits. This case highlights the importance of placing these books in their historical context. The social spirits of 1548 and 1549 were very different. Whilst 1548 was a climate of stretching religious and social boundaries, 1549 saw widespread social discord, in which these types of publications were liable to thrive or to be repressed more swiftly. John Mardeley was quickly brought before the authorities and silenced.

Later described as 'the principal of all those called free-will men', Henry Harte published four titles between 1548 and 1549.[147] The first title came from the press of peripheral printer Robert Stoughton in 1548, but John Day and William Seres soon replicated Stoughton's work and added *A godlie exhortation to all suche as professe the Gospell*.[148] Another printer aligned with the government, John Oswen, produced *A consultorie for all Christians Most godly and ernestly warynyng al people* in 1549.[149] These four titles, along with another now lost, places Harte among the most prolific radical authors in Edwardian England.[150] Harte's anticlericalism reached beyond the Roman Catholic church and bemoaned the elitism of the episcopacy.[151] Harte was mentioned in depositions during the clampdown upon radicalism in Kent and Essex in 1551.[152] Archbishop Cranmer may have shielded Harte (just as he had when Harte was arrested in 1538), but Harte was nonetheless quickly repressed for his unorthodoxy and dispelled from the English print world.[153]

Luke Shepherd also voiced his discontent in 1548. Through printers Day and Seres, he produced six original anonymous polemical tracts and further titles followed from the presses of Anthony Scoloker, Richard Wyer and William Hill.[154] Shepherd's satires were short and ripe with anticlericalism and attacks upon the papacy.[155] Whilst John Bale's support of Shepherd's prose

---

147 Thomas Betteridge, 'Harte, Henry (*d.* 1557)', ODNB.
148 USTC (Robert Stoughton) 504054; (William Seres and John Day) 515384; 504269.
149 USTC 504255.
150 Betteridge, 'Harte, Henry (*d.* 1557)'; a record remains via John Knox's refutation printed in Geneva in 1560.
151 Patrick Collinson, 'Night schools, conventicles and churches', in *The Beginnings of English Protestantism*, eds. Peter Marshall and Alec Ryrie (Cambridge: Cambridge University Press, 2002), pp. 209–235 (p. 227); Davies, *A religion of the Word*, p. 70.
152 Thomas Freeman, 'Dissenters from a dissenting church: the challenge of the Freewillers, 1550–1558', in *The Beginnings of English Protestantism*, eds. Peter Marshall and Alec Ryrie (Cambridge: Cambridge University Press, 2002), pp. 129–156 (pp. 129–131).
153 Betteridge, 'Harte, Henry (*d.* 1557)'.
154 USTC 504122, 504129, 504143, 504145, 504146, 504149, 504150, 504158, 504136.
155 Evenden, *Patents, Pictures and Patronage*, pp. 12–13.

has been established, this was not the consensus of the authorities.[156] Edward Underhill's contemporaneous account suggests that Shepherd was incarcerated in the Fleet Prison in 1548 and that John Day escaped the same fate only by Underhill's timely intervention.[157] Previous studies have used Shepherd's brief career to highlight how 1548 was a boom year without governmental controls; however, if Underhill's account is to be accepted, it serves better as an example of how easily the authorities could suppress recalcitrant authors.

London radical John Champneys' case provides an explicit record of official proceedings. *The Harvest is at hand* (Humphrey Powell, 1548), a 104-page octavo, was an anticlerical work targeting both Roman Catholic and Edwardian evangelical preachers.[158] A heresy commission summoned Champneys on 28 April 1549 and he was duly convicted.[159] This is Champneys' only surviving publication, and he appears to have been effectively silenced by the regime. Champneys' reintegration, which ultimately led to his ordination, required a public recantation and the recall of his publications.[160] Joseph Walford Martin has postulated that his promise to recall 'as many of his books' as possible suggests that Champneys may have had other titles in print, but this can only be conjecture.[161] Without a definitive date of publication for *The Harvest is at hand*, it is difficult to see how swiftly the establishment responded: publication and conviction could have occurred anything from four to sixteen months apart. Humphrey Powell, who later received a patent from the regime, also produced Bullinger's *An holsome antidotus or counter-poysen, against the pestilent heresye and secte of the Anabaptistes* in 1548, suggesting that he believed profit could be found on either side of the radical debate. It may be, like Wolfe's inclusion of Gardiner's text in his edition of Cranmer's *Answer to a crafty and sophistical cavillation* (1551), that Powell produced this radical material to frame the evangelical counterattack. It is more likely, however, that the government treated this publication as an isolated event, and Powell soon reintegrated with the reformed Church of England mainstream.

---

156 Evenden, *Patents Pictures and Patronage*, p. 12, states that Bale described Shepherd as 'a most elegant poet, not at all inferior to [John] Skelton'.
157 Janice Devereaux, 'Shepherd, Luke (*fl.* 1548)', ODNB; John Gough Nichols, ed., *Narratives of the days of the Reformation, chiefly from the manuscripts of John Foxe the Martyrologist* (London: The Camden Society, 1859), pp. 171–172; Evenden, *Patents, Pictures and Patronage*, pp. 12–13.
158 USTC 503986.
159 Brigden, *London and the Reformation*, pp. 442–443; Thomas Betteridge, 'Champneys, John (d. in or after 1559)', ODNB.
160 Betteridge, 'Champneys, John'; Diarmaid MacCulloch, *Thomas Cranmer: A Life* (New Haven, CT: Yale University Press, 1996), p. 424.
161 Martin, *Religious Radicals*, p. 45.

One of few legal proceedings against both author and printer is the case of John Lawton and William Marten, for the production of a 'seditious ballet' on 7 June 1552.[162] The ballad has not survived so the exact nature of author Lawton's seditiousness is uncertain. Lawton's sanctions included a recognisance of £100, the recall and surrender of his ballads and weekly appearances before the Council. David Loades uncovered that Lawton was pilloried for his crimes, whilst William Marten 'merely had his stock confiscated'.[163] Whilst confiscation did not involve public humiliation or physical torment, it could irreparably damage a business venture. Marten's name is absent from the sixteenth-century short title catalogues until 1561, when his name emerges in a collaborative project with William Copland: John Bradford's *The hurte of hering masse*.[164] Whether this collaboration speaks to a deeper relationship is uncertain, but Copland produced several anti-catholic tracts throughout the reign, some under pseudonyms and others anonymously.[165] Marten's delayed arrival into catalogues may reflect this confiscation and Lawton also cannot be found in the USTC. Ballads are disproportionately unlikely to survive, but this absence also may suggest that the regime achieved its goal of suppressing Lawton's work.

Throughout the reign, works from the radical fringe and works from accepted preachers verged on heretical topics. In the face of an unprecedented output of evangelical tracts in 1548, the establishment targeted those most culpable. As the reign progressed, printers and authors alike learned from these isolated examples of individuals over-stepping the mark and self-censored to avoid reprimand. Political pressures within and outside the English printing industry effectively silenced radical opposition. The suppressions of the authorities ensured that the overall output of religious literature spoke harmoniously with the religious trajectory of the regime. The flood of favourable protestant polemic alongside the swift subdual of discordant voices meant that printed material was a valuable tool in bringing readers towards reformed protestantism, without straying towards ideas too radical for the Church of England.

The printed counterattack against the radicals created a significant number of publications from English presses. Authors from every social and religious gradation admonished the radical threat. Unlike the conservative counterattack, this body of work offered few direct literary responses and focused instead on the threat of radical heresies to law, order, and the church.

---

162 APC, 4, p. 69 – 7 June 1552.
163 Loades, 'Books and the English Reformation', p. 284.
164 USTC 505858.
165 USTC 516471, 503941; 504335, 504339.

One of the leading European anti-radical authorities and polemicists of this cause was Zurich *Antistes*, Heinrich Bullinger, whose publications and correspondence betray concerns of quelling the radical threat.[166] Among his correspondents was John Hooper, who grew alarmed by radicals who interrupted his sermons and claimed that not only were 'heresies reviving that were formerly dead and buried, but new ones are springing up every day'.[167] Humphrey Powell printed Bullinger's *An holsome antidotus or counterpoysen, against the pestilent heresye and secte of the Anabaptistes* in 1548, and John Oswen produced *A most necessary and frutefull dialogue* in 1551.[168] John Day and William Seres printed an anti-anabaptist text authored by Jean Calvin, titled *A short instruction for to arme all good Christian people agaynst the pestiferous errours of the common secte of Anabaptistes*.[169] Catharine Davies has identified these tracts by the Tigurine reformers as some of the most sophisticated refutations of specific doctrinal errors.[170]

The ranks of the English authors writing against the radicals included Edmund Becke, William Turner, and John Hooper.[171] These were inflammatory works, penned by well-known authors demonising the threat of religious radicalism, lending weight to the non-toleration of radicalism and supporting the increasing vehemence with which the regime tackled its opposition. Becke's four-leaf quarto, *A brefe confutatacion of this most detestable, and Anabaptistical opinion, that Christ dyd not take hys flesh of the blessed Vyrgyn Mary*, printed by Day and Seres in 1550, was a direct response to the anabaptist opinions for which Joan Bocher was burned at the stake. This publication aligned directly with Bocher's prosecution and lent timely support to the protestant's anti-radical line established in John Hooper's 1549 *A lesson of the incarnation of Christe* printed by both Stephen Mierdman for Edward Whitchurch and the widow of John Herford in 1549. The following year, William Turner's *A perservative, or triacle, agaynst the poyson of Pelagius* (Stephen Mierdman for Andrew Hester, 1551), a 104-leaf octavo, was a more substantial publication and

---

166   Rainer Henrich, 'Bullinger's Correspondence: An International News Network', in *Architect of Reformation. An Introduction to Heinrich Bullinger, 1504–1575*, eds. Bruce Gordon and Emidio Campi (Grand Rapids, MI: Baker Academic, 2004), pp. 231–241 (p. 233); The University of Zurich have created a database of Bullinger's correspondents, at https://www.irg.uzh.ch/en/hbbw/datenbank.html; J. Wayne Baker, 'Church, State and Dissent, The Crisis of the Swiss Reformation, 1531–1536', *Church History*, 57 (1988), pp. 135–152 (pp. 138, 141, 149–150); Gordon, *The Swiss Reformation*, pp. 210–211.
167   Brigden, *London and the Reformation*, p. 443.
168   USTC 503977, 504582.
169   USTC 504195.
170   Davies, *A religion of the Word*, p. 75.
171   USTC 504387, 504653, 504268, 504305.

its release in the same year as George van Parris became the second Edwardian martyr highlights that the threat of radicalism continued even if radical access to English presses had been systematically denied by successful clampdowns in 1548 and 1549.

The anti-radical counterattack has another key publication aligning with the print strategy against the conservatives. This approach saw regime-favoured printer Reyner Wolfe produce a recantation credited to Thomas Cole in 1553.[172] Historians identify Cole as a heterodox schoolmaster and a leader of free-willers in the conventicle at Kent equal to Henry Harte. As a result, Carrie Euler questioned the relationship between *A godly and frutefull sermon, made at Maydestone in the county of Kent the fyrst sonday in Lent*'s contents and the author's beliefs, though Cole had been investigated and imprisoned in February 1551 and may have been absorbed back into 'religious respectability' as stated by Diarmaid MacCulloch.[173] This recantation would mirror those repentances expected of conservatives in Edward's reign. Once more, the regime sought to utilise this recantation, published as a sermon given before the archbishop to undermine the radical cause, and halt the spread of these ideas.

The radical opposition made little headway in the printing industry. Perhaps motivated by belief or perhaps by entrepreneurial profit-seeking, some printers produced radical works. However, without prolific authors or a unifying voice in the English vernacular and in the face of daunting sanctions for printers and particularly authors, this remained a muted effort. Where we can find evidence, radical printing occurred as part of the octavo pamphlet phenomenon of 1548. The evangelical counterattack represented a more substantial corpus of literature, as authors attempted to demonise radicals and uphold the new direction of religious proceedings. How far radicalism was propped up as a strawman to be blown over by prevailing reformed protestant ideas falls outside the consideration of this study, but it is clear that the printed counterattack was at least in part pre-emptive and attempted to contribute to a debate occurring above and beyond the book world. Many of the radical movements of the sixteenth century were inherently anti-scholarly, and the regime came down heavy-handily upon the radical fringe. In simple commercial terms, radical works was an unenviable field for a printer to try to make money in whereas

---

172 USTC 504807.
173 APC 3, pp. 206–207 – 3 February 1551; Davies, *A Religion of the Word*, pp. 81 n.14; Marshall, *Heretics and Believers*, p. 342; Euler, *Couriers of the Gospel: England and Zurich*, p. 211; MacCulloch, *Tudor Church Militant*, p. 144.

the counterattack, safe in the good graces of the authorities, could provide a steadier stream of publications.

Edward VI expected any 'reasonable person and loyal subject to follow with due obedience the rules laid down by those superior in authority and set aside those opinions that are contrary to divine law'.[174] By the end of his reign, this rang true for the print trade. This feat was accomplished, in part, by silencing critics via political sanctions and denial of access to presses. Moreover, the reformers launched reactionary and pre-emptive counterattacks against dissident conservatives and radicals. This three-pronged attack is an undervalued reason that England's protestants enjoyed such overwhelming success in the war of printed words.

The so-called 'collapse of censorship' occurring early in the reign can now be attributed to the creation of a climate of evangelical freedom rather than amendments to the letter of the law. Restrictions remained in place, and the protestant regime was not above implementing them when it suited them. Publications encouraging evangelical religious change and undermining conservatives went unpunished, and printers who understood the religious trajectory of the new regime printed them widely. This tacit understanding of the religious direction of the Church of England allowed printers to assess which publications to produce and when. As the Edwardian reformation developed, the religious landscape became clearer and this movement brought clearer uniformity to English printing. A new historical narrative must now be employed to reflect the fact that much of the navigation of this reality was the responsibility of printers. Edwardian printers self-censored because whether the regime would implement their censorship regulations mattered more than the letter of the law. Printers' self-censorship went hand-in-hand with the implementation of these regulations in instances of censorship. Religious conservatives and radicals alike were denied access to English presses throughout the reign, and few printers proved willing to incur the wrath of the regime. The government, through these factors, played a significant role in shaping the output of the English printing industry as press freedom was afforded to a particular portion of the religious spectrum, and those falling outside it were quickly quietened.

---

174 *SP Spanish*, 10, pp. 209–210 – 28 January 1551: Edward VI to Lady Mary.

CHAPTER 4

Official Offices, Compulsory Provisions and Rival Texts

> For as the good husbandman makes his ground good and plentiful, so does the true preacher with doctrine and example print and grave in the people's mind the word of God.
>
> EDWARD VI, *Discourse on the Reform of Abuses in Church and State* (1551)[1]

∴

New religious policies demanded the dissemination of new texts as the Church of England encouraged the promulgation of evangelicalism. Andrew Pettegree surmises that the revolution within the industry was 'deliberately encouraged' and 'fostered' by the establishment.[2] Stephen Alford, too, acknowledges the influence of the regime but states: 'This was not necessarily a rigid and inflexible form of "state-sponsored" print'.[3] This chapter explores the significant inducements offered to those printers within the confidence of the regime, alongside the print activity commissioned by the government as it pursued its temporal and spiritual objectives.

Shortly following Edward's accession, the government made two appointments in the print world. On 17 April 1547, Reyner Wolfe was appointed 'King's Typographer and Bookseller for Latin, Greek and Hebrew'; three days later, Richard Grafton was appointed 'King's Printer of all books of statutes, acts, proclamations, injunctions and other volumes issued by the king'.[4] These offices carried the incentives of protection from competition, an annual salary, and distinction above all others in the industry. Whilst the post of King's

---

1   Gilbert Burnet, *History of the Reformation of the Church of England*, 2, 2 (London: Richard Priestley, 1820), pp. 98.
2   Andrew Pettegree, 'Printing and the Reformation: the English Exception', in *The Beginnings of English Protestantism*, eds. Peter Marshall and Alec Ryrie (Cambridge: Cambridge University Press, 2002), pp. 157–180 (pp. 172–173).
3   Stephen Alford, *Kingship and Politics in the reign of Edward VI* (Cambridge: Cambridge University Press, 2002), p. 134.
4   PR *Edward VI*, 1, p. 187.

Printer for statutes &c. had been in use since 1506, Wolfe became the inaugural King's Typographer and Bookseller for the ancient languages.[5] These two appointments highlight from the onset that prominent individuals within the establishment would dictate official involvement with the printing industry and that official support could ensure significant inducements for printers.

Grafton's graduation to the office of King's Printer of statutes &c. followed a career trajectory of increasing alignment with the Tudor establishment. Following their license to print the English bible, Grafton and Whitchurch received patents for church books in 1541 and 1543. Grafton was styled 'Printer to the Princes Grace' from 1545 and secured a patent for the primer in English and Latin in 1546.[6] Grafton's patronage stemmed from Thomas Cromwell, Henry VIII and ultimately Edward VI. The office and patents secured highlight that inducements offered by the establishment could elevate their favourites to the pinnacle of the industry. Grafton's colophons include many recognitions of royal support: 'printer to his princes' grace', 'printer to his moste royall majestie', 'prynter to our souveraigne lorde Kyng Edward VI', 'printer to his kynges maiestie', and 'printer to the kinges highnes'.[7] Grafton also employed Latinised colophons, including 'typographi regii' and 'typographus regius'.[8] These colophons have led to a historiographical misconception. Often, historians have abbreviated Grafton's office to simply 'the King's Printer', which has led to an overstatement of this particular office.[9] Grafton was responsible for printing many official Edwardian church documents, but he secured these projects through a separate patent for 'all service books for the church'. Patronage and support in Edward's reign often overlapped, but we must establish their respective boundaries to comprehend each patent and post awarded.

---

5   Pamela Neville-Sington, 'Pynson, Richard (c.1449–1529/30)', ODNB; K.F. Pantzer, 'Berthelet, Thomas (d. 1555)', ODNB.

6   Tamara Atkin and A.S.G. Edwards, 'Printers, Publishers and Promoters to 1558', in *A Companion to the Early Printed Book in Britain, 1476–1558*, eds. Vincent Gillespie and Susan Powell (Cambridge: Brewer, 2014), pp. 27–44 (p. 39); USTC 503615, 503618.

7   'printer to his princes' grace' (HEH: 62258); 'printer to his moste royall majestie' (HEH: 61530); 'prynter to our souveraigne lorde Kyng Edward VI' (HEH: 243485); 'printer to his kynges maiestie' (HEH: 81920, 47767, 59433); 'printer to the kinges highnes' (HEH: 17348).

8   'typographi regii' (HEH: 31377, 95886); 'typographus regius' (HEH: 20891, 79936).

9   Susan Powell, 'The Secular Clergy', in *A Companion to the Early Printed Book in Britain, 1476–1558*, eds. Vincent Gillespie and Susan Powell (Cambridge: Brewer, 2014), pp. 150–175 (p. 172); Peter Blayney, 'William Cecil and the Stationers', in *The Stationers' Company and the Book Trade 1550–1990*, eds. Robin Myers and Michael Harris (Winchester: St Paul's Bibliographies, 1997), pp. 11–34 (p. 21); Cyndia Susan Clegg, 'The authority and subversiveness of print' in Leslie Howsam (ed.), *The Cambridge Companion to the History of the Book in Britain* (Cambridge: Cambridge University Press, 2015), p. 128, states 'the position of printer to the king or queen was a lucrative office both because anything printed was privileged and because official printing included bibles and liturgies'.

The office of King's printer of statutes &c. provided Grafton with a reliable stream of short publications that became a mainstay of his enterprise. Between 1547 and 1553, the USTC lists seventy-nine English-printed 'ordinances and edicts' (sixty-three by Grafton) and 115 'jurisprudence' works (thirty-two by Grafton). The remit of Grafton's position spans these two classifications, as statutes fall under 'jurisprudence'. Ten additional documents also fall under this appointment, including religious injunctions and visitation articles. The regime likely commissioned these titles in print runs far exceeding industry conventions due to the need to be disseminated so widely. However, the majority of these publications consisted of folios of five leaves or fewer or broadsheet publications.[10] These works were conducive to quick production and dispatch and required little deviation from a standardised template; moreover, they had a guaranteed market, making them an ideal print job. Grafton built his business around this role: 105 of his 210 titles fell under the remit of this office. It is clear from these figures that the position as King's Printer of statutes &c. required a great deal of work, albeit technically straightforward work.

An undeveloped area of Grafton's biography is how the Crown paid him for his work. Statutes, proclamations and acts were to be circulated widely around the country, as the government needed to notify the population of changes in official policy. Print runs, therefore, must have been vast to serve this demand, but the cost must have been borne either by the Crown or readers. Grafton's appointment mentions two sums: 'the fee of 12d. yearly at Easter' and 'an annuity of 4l. after the death of Thomas Bertlet, late printer of Henry VIII ... taking 12d. yearly also'. Berthelet lived until September 1555 and remained in the king's favour, for he was assigned a coat of arms in 1549.[11] Grafton is, therefore, unlikely to have received this additional annuity. This salary of 12d., however, does not reflect the esteem of Grafton's position during Edward's reign, and further evidence can be found. Another indication of payments is located within the Notebook of William Cecil, from July 1552: 'Grafton: to the King. £125 respite till Michaelmas. By the King to him. £410 more'.[12] Payments of this size suggest that Grafton may well have been paid by the project and claimed back expenses from the regime.

Grafton was able to secure other commercial assistance for work in this office. On 18 December 1547, he was permitted to take up 'as manye prynters, composytours and founders as well housholders as prentyces and jornymen'

---

10 Of Grafton's seventy-six ordinances and edicts, ten were broadsheet, forty-one folio, two quarto and ten unlisted; of his thirty-three jurisprudence works, twenty-four were folio, three were octavo, and six are unlisted.
11 K.F. Pantzer, 'Berthelet, Thomas (d. 1555)', ODNB.
12 SP 10/14 no. 53 – July 1552: Notebook of William Cecil.

for the king's works in his office, and also 'paper, ynke, presses and matrices, paying for them immediately at reasonable rate; also to take carriage for the same'.[13] That the regime would make these concessions to aid the smooth running of his operations indicates Grafton's standing and the centrality of print to the regime.

The creation of the office of King's Typographer and Bookseller for the ancient languages represents a bid to develop England as a centre for scholarly printing. Hitherto, England had only marginal influence in this sphere. Reyner Wolfe seemed a sound commercial decision; he was the only living individual in England who had printed in Greek before Edward's accession.[14] Wolfe was well-connected. He had served Henry VIII and Thomas Cranmer in their correspondence with Swiss reformers Simon Grynaeus, Heinrich Bullinger and Zurich's preeminent reformation printer Christopher Froschauer.[15] Wolfe also printed *The late expedicion in Scotlande made by the Kynges hyghnys armye* (1544), which would have endeared him to the expedition's commander: the duke of Somerset.[16] Wolfe had proven his value, and these were precisely the type of men that the Edwardian government favoured.

Between 1547 and 1553, the denizened Dutchman produced thirty-seven titles from his shop at the sign of the brazen serpent in St Paul's churchyard: ten in Latin, two diglot Latin and English, one polyglot dictionary, but none in Greek or Hebrew.[17] Despite his willingness to print Latin works, few of his twelve Latin publications fell under the remit of his office.[18] Chief among his Latin publications were Peter Martyr Vermigli's *Tractatio de sacramento Eucharistiae* (1549), which became the subject of a patent dispute, and four titles of John Ponet's *Catechismus Brevis* (1553).[19] Wolfe's involvement in the

---

13 PR *Edward VI*, 2, pp. 98–99 – 18 December 1547.
14 According to the USTC listings, the only other Greek works printed in England before 1547 were USTC 515127 (Wynkyn de Worde, 1511) and USTC 515135 (Richard Pynson, 1513). Recent scholarship maintains that Wolfe was the first to print in Greek in England, see Andrew Pettegree, *Foreign Protestant Communities in Sixteenth-Century London* (Oxford: Clarendon Press, 1986), p. 93; Pamela Robinson, 'Materials: Paper and Type', in *A companion to the Early Printed Book in Britain, 1476–1558*, eds. Vincent Gillespie and Susan Powell (Cambridge: Brewer, 2014), pp. 61–74 (p. 71).
15 Andrew Pettegree, 'Wolfe, Reyner (*d.* in or before 1574)', ODNB.
16 USTC 503483.
17 USTC 75640 504744; FB: 18854.
18 Which works were produced for this office and which were private projects cannot be deciphered with certainty, but Wolfe's Latin works by Cranmer, Bucer and Peter Martyr, and Somerset (three total) can be agreed with some conviction. Richard Smiths' recantation was an official commission, two titles, but was in English.
19 Peter Martyr's Eucharist Disputation was the subject of a patent request by Nicholas Udall in 1550: PR *Edward VI*, 3, p. 315; Wolfe received the patent for Cranmer's reply to Stephen Gardiner *APC*, 3, p. 375 – 1 October 1551.

trade was built foremostly around scholarly and theological works, including Cranmer's dispute with Gardiner. Thereafter, broadly educational books were central: one 616-page dictionary, three titles for William Lily's grammars, and six titles by Robert Record.[20]

A distinctive feature of Edwardian printing was its overwhelming concentration upon the vernacular.[21] Wolfe's official title allowed him to challenge this distinctively English approach; however, he would have to fly in the face of established market protocols and compete with esteemed European printing houses. Wolfe acquired his greek type from Basel, but there is no evidence he invested in a Hebrew type.[22] Works of Greek and Hebrew scholarship, along with the cartographical works included under his appointment, required three prerequisites: financial investment, technically accomplished printers, and far-reaching distribution networks.[23] Wolfe showed little enthusiasm to compete with presses in Antwerp, Basel and Venice; he focused his official output on English-Latin grammars, and even his Latin works were of specific English interest. Henry VIII had standardised these grammars in a decision upheld by injunction on 31 July 1547, which stated: 'none other grammar shall be taught in any school or other place within the King's realms and dominions'.[24] This proclamation afforded Wolfe security; it allowed him to judge print run sizes more effectively and protected him from competitors. In many respects, Wolfe's appointment granted him the easiest-earned salary of 26s. 8d. per annum in the printing industry, alongside all profits of his office. Wolfe's publications brought a continental style to the English market and he initiated a new stage of European stylistic emulation during the Edwardian years, which was directly linked to his official office.

A final official appointment relating to the book world was the Keeper of the King's Library at Westminster: Bartholomew Traheron.[25] Appointed 14 December 1549, Traheron was another Henrician exile rising through the Edwardian

---

20   One dictionary has two titles: *USTC* 75640, 504744; Grammars: *USTC* (1548) 504045, (1549) 504295, (1553) 516536; Robert Record: *USTC* 503906, 504107, 504286, 504659, 504669, 504764.
21   Andrew Pettegree, 'Afterword', in *The Reception of Continental Reformation in Britain*, eds. Polly Ha and Patrick Collinson (Oxford: Oxford University Press, 2010), pp. 229–236 (p. 231).
22   Whilst England did boast some expert Hebraists, demand was not sufficient to justify casting Hebrew fount. Stephen G. Burnett, *Christian Hebraism in the Reformation Era 1500–1660: Authors, Books and the Transmission of Jewish Learning* (Leiden: Brill, 2012), p. 32; Kenneth Austin, *From Judaism to Calvinism: The Life and Writings of Immanuel Tremellius (c.1510–1580)* (Aldershot: Ashgate, 2007), pp. 61–62.
23   Pettegree, 'Wolfe, Reyner (*d.* in or before 1574)'.
24   *H&L*, 1, pp. 393–403 – 31 July 1547.
25   *PR Edward VI*, 3, pp. 74–75 – 14 December 1549.

ranks. He later secured a range of other offices, including tutor to Henry Brandon (duke of Suffolk), dean of Chichester, and canon of Windsor.[26] Westminster was the most distinguished of the king's libraries; Traheron's role permitted him to 'take books from the king's other libraries to furnish the library or promote the king's studies'. As a result, the British Library records account for a significant centralisation of the royal collections under Traheron's stewardship.[27]

John Roche Dasent has claimed in the Acts of Privy Council calendar that Traheron and the Crown sacrificed the lavish bindings of Edward's library between 1550 and 1552 to save the crown purse. Yet, the account in his work 'the purging of his Highnes Librarie at Westminster of all superstitiouse bookes, as masse bookes, legendes and suche like, and to deliver the garnyture of the same bookes, being either of golde or silver, to Sir Anthony Aucher in the presence of Sir Thomas Darcie, &' discredits this notion.[28] Edward was curtailing the influence of catholicism in the spirit of his reformation; he was excising excess, not pillaging his library. Bartholomew Traheron was a committed evangelical whose letters to Heinrich Bullinger consistently advocated further reform in England along the lines of his former host in Zurich's church.[29] He, too, forged a relationship with a creative force in the book world: Edward Whitchurch. In 1543, Whitchurch printed a folio edition of Giovanni da Vigo's *The most excellent works of chirurgerye*, which Traheron had translated into English and would resurface with an Edwardian edition in 1550.[30] Traheron's motivation to excise the excess in the library went beyond financial gain for the crown purse. Mirjam Foot's research has shown that Edward's library commissioned the 'Medallion binder', who used gold tooling and calf leather bindings, further discrediting Dasent's idea of money-saving tactics.[31] Traheron's position was one of standing and importance considering the young monarch's apparent penchant for learning and Traheron's annuity of twenty marks per annum.

---

26 Brandon had previously been taught with Edward VI, under the royal tutors: Richard Cox, John Cheke and Roger Ascham, between 1550 and 1551. S.J. Gunn, 'Brandon, Charles, first duke of Suffolk (c.1484–1545)', *ODNB*; Carl R. Trueman, 'Traheron, Bartholomew (c.1510–1558?)', *ODNB*.
27 'The Royal Library under the Tudors, Later Acquisitions: Edward VI, Mary I and Elizabeth I', at https://www.bl.uk/catalogues/illuminatedmanuscripts/TourRoyalTudor.asp.
28 James Gardiner, *Lollardy and the Reformation in England: An Historical Survey* (Cambridge: Cambridge University Press, 2010), p. 184, *APC*, 3, pp. xvii, 224 – 25 February 1550.
29 *OL*, 1, pp. 322–323.
30 *USTC* 503456, 504548.
31 Mirjam Foot, 'Bookbinding 1400–1557', in *Cambridge History of the Book in Britain, Vol. III: 1400–1557*, eds. J.B. Trapp and Lotte Hellinga (Cambridge: Cambridge University Press, 1999), pp. 109–127 (p. 127).

This appointment, particularly during a royal minority, had significant implications. At the point of Traheron's appointment, the young king's education would have been expected to impact his capabilities and compassion and as the English monarch for decades to come. Placing the young king's libraries in the hands of Traheron, with the opportunity to instil in the king this spirit of excising excess, was a clear commitment to a protestant education which could further the reformation's cause and inspire further religious change.

The official appointments to printing and book-related positions occurred swiftly and decisively. English religious change was occurring rapidly, and appointing men who would align with the new religious trajectory of the government was crucial. The significance of these appointments is two-fold. First, it offers direct evidence of the types of individuals that the establishment was keen to support at this critical juncture. Moreover, it also speaks to the establishment's commitment to books and print. The appointment of an official King's Typographer and Bookseller for the ancient languages represented an investment in an individual and the power of books in England. The establishment facilitated and encouraged the development of English printing with the direct sponsorship of specific individuals.

The evangelical ascendency saw many prominent offices of the Church of England change hands. The regime deprived a series of conservative bishops and installed evangelicals in their stead. In addition, many authors held, or would later hold, office within the church and state. The critical question relating to these posts is whether the establishment rewarded active authors or whether publishing was an expectation of those appointed. In short, did publications prompt promotions, or did promotions prompt publications?

Preliminary statistics suggest an episcopate keen to publish. Over 130 English titles produced between 1547 and 1553 were authored, edited or translated by individuals who held a bishopric during the reign, eleven of them in total. The foremost authors were Thomas Cranmer (Canterbury, twenty-eight titles); Miles Coverdale (Exeter, thirty-five); John Bale (Ossory, twenty-eight), and John Hooper (Gloucester and Worcester, nineteen). Cranmer was the lead author for twenty-five of his twenty-eight titles: more than any author in the Edwardian years. The USTC credits Coverdale, a prolific biblical translator, with thirty-five authorial acknowledgements between 1547 and 1553. Many of these works were completed before Edward's accession, and at least twenty-eight were produced before his consecration in August 1551. In the same vein, most authorial credits for both John Hooper (fourteen of nineteen) and John Bale (nineteen of twenty-eight) were published before their respective consecrations in March 1551 and October 1552. The broader contribution of the Edwardian episcopacy was modest. John Ponet (Rochester; Winchester), who would later become a prolific author, contributed seven titles, though four are the same Latin catechism commissioned by the duke of Northumberland.[32] Thereafter, only Stephen Gardiner (Winchester; deprived, five titles) and Edmund Bonner (London; deprived, four titles) were linked to more than one publication.[33] Participation within the printing industry, then, was not demanded of Edward's bishops. The king and court scrutinised the episcopate through sermons rather than publications. However, an active and agreeable voice in print was advantageous when deciding whom to prefer. The reputations of Bale, Coverdale and Hooper as both authors and preachers endeared them to the establishment who responded by promoting them to positions of authority.

Many individuals within the Edwardian religious and political hierarchy contributed as authors. After all, there were many reasons why prominent scholars and theologians may not have been awarded a bishopric whilst still receiving patronage and positions. Prominent preacher and former bishop Hugh Latimer enjoyed pseudo-episcopal standing, and his preaching and publication record was undoubtedly a key to this preferment. Thomas Becon (twenty-one) was appointed one of the preachers of Canterbury and chaplain to both Somerset and Cranmer.[34] He was at the heart of the religious establishment, and his publications spanned the reign, spiking in 1550. Bernardino Ochino, the Italian reformer appointed Prebendary of Canterbury Cathedral in May 1548, contributed six titles spread evenly between 1548 and 1550. We can include universities, where Peter Martyr Vermigli (three titles) and Martin Bucer (four) took positions as Regius Professors of Divinity at Oxford and Cambridge respectively, and Thomas Lever (ten) was appointed Master of St John's Cambridge in 1551. During Edward's reign, a 'procession of talented scholars and theologians' were involved in 'counteracting the still conservatism of the university' of Oxford.[35] These individuals played a significant role in accelerating religious change in England, and their publications were influential. There were also the directly patronised communities of the stranger churches to consider. Jan a Lasco (eight), Martin Micronius (five) and Jan Utenhove (five) each emerged later in the reign to contribute to the output of the print world. Michelangelo

---

32 Pamela Neville-Sington, 'Press, politics and religion', in *The Cambridge History of the Book in Britain Vol. III: 1400–1557*, eds. Lotte Hellinga and J.B. Trapp (Cambridge, 1999), pp. 576–607, (p. 601).

33 John Taylor (Lincoln) William Barlow (St. David's; Bath and Wells), Richard Sampson (Coventry and Lichfield) and Robert King (Oxford) each contributed to one title.

34 Jonathan Reimer, 'The Life and Writings of Thomas Becon, 1512–1567' (unpublished doctoral thesis Cambridge University, Pembroke College, 2016), pp. 130–132; Seymour Baker House, 'Becon, Thomas (1512/13–1567)', ODNB.

35 Diarmaid MacCulloch, *Thomas Cromwell: A life* (London: Allen Lane, 2018), p. 229.

Florio (two), who preached for the Italian-speaking communities in England's capital, also secured posts working for William Cecil and Lady Jane Grey.

The lack of specific dates in early modern imprints creates some difficulty in establishing whether publications were produced before or after any given appointment or deprivation. The printed output of England's bishops whilst in office suggests that printing was not part of their remit once holding a diocese. When considering those individuals patronised by the Church of England through the episcopacy, universities and the broader church hierarchy, authorial catalogues were impactful. The establishment promoted authors with high profiles and publication clout, even if they did not demand the continuation of this output.

1 The Canonical Texts of the Edwardian Church

Official publications were a central component of Edwardian religious proceedings. The state and church cooperated to develop five publications which would play a fundamental role in the day-to-day devotional lives in the English population.[36] These authorities leveraged official proclamations to obligate every church and cathedral in the country to purchase a copy of each of these works for use in the services. Through these works, the government created a national subscription of religious works specifically designed to outline an English reformed protestant orthodoxy. To support and supplement the Great Bible, five new works were produced in this programme of national reform: Archbishop Cranmer's *Homilies* and Erasmus' *Paraphrases* (31 July 1547), the *Order of Communion* and the *Catechism* (8 March 1548), and the *Book of Common Prayer* (January 1549 and November 1552).[37]

Rolling out a policy of mandatory publications for churches prompted significant activity in the print world. The Church of England generated thousands of days of presswork for their selected printers. Print runs could extend beyond industry standards to accommodate this vast demand. Moreover, particularly in the cases of Erasmus' *Paraphrases* (600 folio pages) and *Book of Common Prayer* (300 folio pages), these were larger books than industry standards. Peter

---

36 This section summarises arguments brought forward at the USTC summer conference at the University of St Andrews and subsequently published as Celyn Richards, 'Printing for the Reformation: The Canonical Documents of the Edwardian Church of England 1547–1553' in *Print and Power in Early Modern Europe (1500–1800)*, eds. Nina Lamal, Jamie Cumby and Helmer J. Helmers (Leiden: Brill, 2021), pp. 111–133.

37 For the *Homilies* and Erasmus' *Paraphrases*, see *H&L*, 1, pp. 393–403 – 31 July 1547. For the *Order of Communion* and the *Catechism*, see *H&L*, 1, pp. 417–418 – 8 March 1548; For the BCPs, see 2 & 3 Edward VI c.1; 5 & 6 Edward VI, c.1.

TABLE 4.1 The canonical church documents, 1547–1553

	Formats used	Number of titles	Printers	Years printed
Homilies	Quarto	10	Richard Grafton; Edward Whitchurch	1547, 1551
Paraphrases, Vol. I	Folio	8	Edward Whitchurch	1548
Litany	Octavo / Quarto	4	Richard Grafton; John Day; Thomas Raynald and William Hill	1548, 1549
Catechisms	Octavo	4	Nicolas Hill for Gwalter Hill; John Day; Richard Grafton	1548, 1549, 1551
1549 *Book of Common Prayer*	Folio / Quarto	13	Richard Grafton; Edward Whitchurch; John Oswen (Worcester)	1549, 1550
1552 *Book of Common Prayer*	Folio	21	Richard Grafton; Edward Whitchurch; John Oswen (Worcester); Humphrey Powell (Dublin)	1552, 1553

Blayney's probing research has established that the average number of sheets of paper used by an Edwardian publication was 18.5. In comparison, a folio *Book of Common Prayer* required around 150, and the *Paraphrases* required 300 or more sheets.

Alongside generating industry, they generated capital. The first canonical work of the reign, Archbishop Cranmer's *Homilies*, can be found in the churchwardens' accounts in Yatton, Somerset for 2s. between 1547 and 1548, though as low as 16d. in St. Andrew Hubbard, London.[38] The *Paraphrases*, a far more substantial book, include purchase records for 6s. 4d. (Yatton) and 5s. (St Mary's At Hill, Suffolk). Later, and perhaps in response to these varying prices across the kingdom, the *Book of Common Prayer* was set at proclamation-mandated retail

---

38   Clive Burgess, ed., *The Church Records of St Andrew Hubbard, Eastcheap, c1450–c1570* (London: London Record Society, 1999), p. 165; J. Charles Cox, *Churchwardens' Accounts from the fourteenth century to the close of the seventeenth century* (London: Methuen & Co, 1913), pp. 118–119.

prices of 2s. 2d. (unbound), 2s. 10d. (bound in forel), 3s. 3d. (bound in sheepskin) and 4s (bound in calf) – figures which are borne out in churchwardens' accounts in Eastcheap and Devizes for the second *Book of Common Prayer*.[39] These price points broadly align with market forces, where Frances R. Johnson's calculations postulate 0.45d. per printed sheet in the mid-sixteenth century, particularly once considering that these larger works were disproportionately likely to have been bound in fine materials against the wider industry.[40] At these rates outlined by the government, the total gross sales sums could be extraordinary: half the required *Books of Common Prayer* for England's parishes, at the price outlined by the proclamation, could retail for over £480.

The canonical document printing projects were the largest of the Edwardian years; as such, the Church of England and the Crown (albeit via parishioners and churches) became the single largest patrons of the book world. For example, whilst Edward Whitchurch is unlikely to have produced enough copies of the *Paraphrases* to furnish every parish church in England, this project alone at one hundred per cent compliance would have necessitated over 1 million edition sheets to be printed. The multiple titles coming from Whitchurch's press, and the readiness with which the print house took up the second edition, even without canonical church document status, suggests that production and profits balanced favourably.

The canonical works generated a total of sixty titles during the reign, with the lion's share being completed by the two leading printers for the Edwardian church – Richard Grafton and Edward Whitchurch. These two premier official church printers held patents and commissions for church works under Henry VIII and had completed the transition from the publishers of the 'Matthew' Bible (Antwerp: Matthais Crom, 1537) to operating the print houses of the Great Bible projects of the Henrician 1540s.[41] These projects elevated the printers to the top tier of English print history and their official support was renewed for a further seven years following Edward's accession. These two principal printers of the canonical documents (fifty of sixty titles) tailored

---

39 Cox, *Churchwardens' Accounts*, p. 112.
40 Francis R. Johnson, 'Notes on English Book-prices, 1550–1640', *The Library*, 5 (1950), pp. 89–90, cited in Jennifer Winters, 'The English Provincial Book Trade: Booksellers Stock-Lists, c.1520–1640' (unpublished doctoral thesis, University of St Andrews, 2012), p. 90. Archival indications for the *Paraphrases* range from 0.4–0.5d and 0.64–0.7d. for the 1552 BCP.
41 David Daniell, *The Bible in English: Its History and Influence* (New Haven, CT: Yale University Press, 2003), pp. 200–203 suggests that there was a transfer of staff along with materials in this repatriation of the Great Bible projects from Francois Regnault's print house in Paris in the 1540s; USTC 503073, 503272, 503237, 503234, 503235, 503153, 503233, 518561, 503151.

their wider output and other projects to cater for the regime in this mutually beneficial relationship.

Whitchurch contributed five quarto editions of the *Homilies*, eight folios for Erasmus' *Paraphrases*, five 1549 *Book of Common Prayer* folios, and ten 1552 *Books of Common Prayer* (seven folios, two quartos and one octavo). These twenty-eight titles represent one third of Whitchurch's titles between 1547 and 1553. When Whitchurch's presses were occupied with a major canonical publication, his wider output declined; in 1548, amid the *Paraphrases* project, Whitchurch's only other projects each required eighteen sheets or fewer.[42] This signals the intensity of work placed upon his presses in these years. If Whitchurch deployed two presses full-time on the *Paraphrases* project, we could estimate that these presses would be occupied for between 18–24 weeks. Attempting to complete even half of the required copies 9,000 copies over just two presses would occupy these two presses all year.

The second most active printer of the canonical church documents was Richard Grafton. A close associate of Whitchurch's throughout the reign, Grafton also balanced his role as 'King's printer for all books of statutes, acts, proclamations, injunctions and other volumes issued by the king' with his opportunities as a church document patent holder. Securing these roles allowed Grafton's print house to function on a steady diet of official commissions throughout the reign and he remained the leading printing in the output. In the canonical church works context, Grafton produced twenty-two canonical titles: the *Homilies* (three quartos and one octavo), the litany (two quartos), a catechism (quarto), and the two *Book of Common Prayer* (1549 – five folios and one quarto; 1552 – eight folios and one unlisted). Grafton's engagement with the government and circles of power in Edwardian England far outstripped his contemporaries: sixty-four per cent of his output can be covered by his patents, official offices and the canonical works.

These printers of official church works operated in the confidences of the Church of England and the Crown and, by necessity, each had access to draft copies and printers' sheets prior to their release. In 1552, the Council reminded Grafton of his obligations, demanding that he 'stay in any wyse from uttering any of the bookes of the Newe Service and ... not to put any of them abrode untill certaine faultes therein be corrected'.[43] With Edwardian religious change occurring rapidly and being contested consistently – the failed response to the Western Rising following the release of the 1549 *Book of Common Prayer*, after all, had led to the fall of the duke of Somerset – the regime needed printers it could trust and

---

42   In this year, Whitchurch produced psalters, a catechism and Katherine Parr's *Lamentacion of a Synner*; USTC 503922, 503943, 503984, 503996, 504091, 515966, 518560, 504134, 504135.
43   APC, 4, p. 131: 27 September 1552.

depend on. Between 1547 and 1553, Grafton and Whitchurch were the foremost printers of the government and the church and their products and productivity spearheaded the trade and impacted society. In order for the *Homilies* or the *Books of Common Prayer* to contribute meaningfully to the devotional lives of Edward's subjects, a reliable stream of publications needed to come forth from the presses.

The regime supported two provincial printers in an attempt to disseminate official print in areas less readily served by the London industry. A distinctive characteristic of the sixteenth-century English book world was its overwhelmingly centralisation.[44] Despite this, the government granted two patents to provincial printers to contribute to the spread of official church works: John Oswen (Wales and the Marches) and Humphrey Powell (Ireland).

The printing of service books attached a legitimacy and prestige to these provincial printers but did not amount to an official post comparable to the one held by Richard Grafton. For Oswen and Powell, the canonical church documents represented a comparatively small number of works as their total print output remained small. The regime granted them believing in the power of print to expedite religious change in resistant provinces. Both Ireland and the South West had resisted the regime's religious trajectory early in the reign, and the regime supported these ventures to promote evangelical printing.

John Oswen printed defiantly evangelical works. He produced polemic by Jean Calvin, Antoine de Marcourt, and Peter Moone from Ipswich in 1548.[45] Following his relocation to Worcester in 1549, he continued in this vein, producing works by Henry Hart, John Hooper, Thomas Lever, Matteo Gribaldi, and Heinrich Bullinger and Huldrych Zwingli.[46] Oswen's contribution to the production of canonical church documents was far more limited than the central printers, totalling four titles. Oswen produced two folio titles for the 1549 *Book of Common Prayer*, a quarto edition of the *Homilies* and a folio 1552 *Book of Common Prayer* during this brief involvement with official publications which also contributed a psalter and two quarto New Testaments. Whilst this output is small in the national print landscape, the opportunity to print official works and bibles contributed to Oswen's business, representing his four most substantial printing projects in Worcester.

The USTC registers Humphrey Powell's 1552 *Book of Common Prayer* as the first surviving edition from a press in Ireland. Powell was awarded a £20 contribution

---

44 Provincial printing occurred in four locations under Tudor rule during Edward's reign: Ipswich (1548), Canterbury (1549–1553), Worcester (1549–1553) and Dublin (1550).
45 USTC 503961, 503962, 503983, 503994, 504049, 504059, 504092.
46 USTC 504255, 504629, 504912, 504674, 504445, 504577, 504582, 504545. Gribaldi was an anti-trinitarian, but Oswen's publication of Bullinger's anti-radical tracts may have saved his standing with the regime. Clegg, 'The authority and subversiveness of print', p. 133.

towards his relocation costs for the move to the staunchly-conservative Ireland in 1550, to launch a press which could also facilitate the dispersal of official print.[47] Powell was facing a challenge greater even than Oswen's to establish a successful printing enterprise and the venture appears destined for failure. The fact that his relocation costs were subsidised, however, demonstrates that there was official support for print as a vehicle for religious change.

At the onset of the reign, these provincial markets lacked almost all the requisite conditions for a commercial enterprise to be successful. There were few successful precedents in the English context; furthermore, there was no established funding, fewer (if any) experienced specialist workmen, and there were lower levels of literacy and support for the reformation. Nonetheless, there are indicators that the seemingly small total output of Edwardian provincial presses belies their historical significance. Whilst largely unsuccessful, these short-lived enterprises suggest an entrepreneurial spirit and confidence within the book trade, but they also reaffirm our understanding that print was a key instrument of Edwardian religious policy. There were significant limitations to the prospects of provincial printing in England, which Powell was seemingly unable to navigate in Ireland.

Following his short stay in Ipswich (producing twelve titles in a year), Oswen produced sixteen titles from his Worcester press between 1549 and 1551 on a stable output of short religious polemical works and official projects. Whilst the products of his press offered little to challenge or impress the leading printers in the London trade, for a brief moment it appeared that there might be a small but sustainable opportunity. Ultimately, the English print trade was centralised, in part, due to a continued reliance upon the Continent for materials but also due to the economic foundations the capital provided. In the Edwardian years, official support was not enough to support a successful commercial enterprise in the challenging conditions of England's provincial markets.

Between 1547 and 1553, individuals who did not hold official letters patent produced three editions of canonical church titles. There was also competition from other printers to offer bibles, service books and rival publications (both authorised and unauthorised) to usurp market share from the canonical church works and their printers. The Act for the putting away of diverse books and images, 25 December 1549, ought to have ended competition in the sphere of official church works.

> all Books called Antyphon's Myssales Scrayles Pcessionalles Manuelles Legends Pyes Portuyses Prymars in Lattyn or Inlishe Cowchers Journales

---

47   APC, 3 18 July 1550, p. 84.

> Ordinales, or other books or writings whatsoever heretofore used for s'vice of the Churche, written or prynted in the Inglishe or Lattyn tongue, other then suche as are or shalbe settforthe by the Kings Majestie, shal by auctoritie of this p'sent Acte clerelye and utterlye abollished extinguished and forbidden for ever to be used or kepte in this Realme or elles where within any the Kings Dnions.
>
> Act for the putting away of diverse books and images (25 December 1549)[48]

This act made clear that the canonical church works were protected and yet we see three works seemingly impinging on these official appointments. The short canonical documents were the type of works highly coveted by entrepreneurial printers: they required little technical effort and could be printed and disseminated quickly. Early in 1548, Richard Grafton put forth the first quarto edition of the English Litany (the *Order of Communion*), and editions soon followed from John Day (1548) and Thomas Raynald and William Hill (1549).[49] Day also produced a Church of England *Catechism* in 1548. The patentees could confiscate patent-infringing stock and prosecute, and yet this right was not exercised against any of these seemingly 'pirate' printers.

The Edwardian book world was small and governed by close personal and business relationships. By 1548, John Day had hoisted his colours as a reform-minded printer. He gained the confidence and esteem of the regime, and both he and his publishing partner William Seres had secured valuable patronage.[50] Moreover, Day had collaborated with the two primary canonical document printers, each of whom had printed two works published by Day.[51] On more than one occasion in 1548, Day borrowed woodcuts from Grafton, further cementing at least a commercial, if not personal, relationship prior to this publication.[52] It is entirely plausible that he printed the work with their consent, particularly in a year when we know that Whitchurch's print house

---

48 3 & 4 Edward VI, c.10; *H&L*, 1, p. 485 – 25 December 1549.
49 *SP Spanish*, 9, pp. 260–261 – 22 March 1548: Van der Delft to the Emperor; USTC 503974, 503975, 516481.
50 Elizabeth Evenden, 'The Fleeing Dutchmen? The Influence of Dutch Immigrants upon the Print Shop of John Day', in *John Foxe at Home and Abroad*, ed. David Loades (Aldershot: Ashgate, 2004), pp. 63–78 (p. 66); Richard C. Barnett, *Place, Profit, and Power: A Study of the Servants of William Cecil, Elizabethan Statesmen* (Chapel Hill, NC: The University of North Carolina Press, 1969), p. 117.
51 Whitchurch printed: USTC 504134, 504135 (both 1548); Grafton printed: 503862 (1547), 518570 (1548).
52 Alford, *Kingship and Politics in the Reign of Edward VI*, pp. 116–117; Elizabeth Evenden, *Patents, Pictures and Patronage: John Day and the Tudor Book Trade* (Aldershot, Ashgate, 2008), pp. 10–11.

was focusing upon Erasmus' *Paraphrases*, which would explain why the regime and printer waived the opportunity to act upon the infringement.[53]

Between 1548 and 1549, the partnership of Thomas Raynald and William Hill attempted to break into the sphere of official church documents. Their octavo edition of the *Order of Communion* was produced in the same year as a folio edition of the complete 'Matthew' bible – a non-patented predecessor to the Great Bible.[54] These two often-overlooked printers are discussed further below as collaborators (chapter six), but it is sufficient to say, at this point, that they were printers aligned with the reformation, with catalogues of evangelical polemic clear for the regime to see. It is noteworthy that the *Order of the Communion* produced by this printing partnership was an octavo, likely printed for private use, rather than the quarto editions produced by Grafton and Day for use in the church.

Without any indication of the print run size for these two 'pirated' editions of the *Order of the Communion*, it is difficult to assess any commercial impact upon the patent-holding publications that they imitated. The most unambiguous indication that they did little to damage the businesses of the patent holders is that they sparked no legal proceedings. Grafton and Whitchurch held the legal right, official support and commercial motivation to prosecute infringements upon their patent. As the shortest canonical publication, the Grafton edition of the litany was likely produced in a vast print-run in an attempt to cover as much demand of the parish churches as possible in one fell swoop. For Grafton, two pirated editions of a short print job likely made little difference to his commercial activities, and Whitchurch's focus in this year was the *Paraphrases*. Grafton and Whitchurch's collaborations with Day and their preoccupation with other projects suggests that at the least they were unconcerned by this infringement, and it is possible that they outsourced the task.

Edwardian religious change, and the climate of freedom it created, mobilised a wider scripture-reading laity. Printers responded by expanding this market sphere to incorporate a greater variety of texts and formats. Folio Great Bibles were the only canonical and officially mandated bibles, but it was not without critics or competitors. Moreover, the folio Great Bible was the only format and translation covered by the service books patent. In total, forty-one individuals were listed in the colophons of the 111 Edwardian titles classified by the USTC as 'Bibles (incl. parts)'. In order to examine how government initiatives on scripture reading affected bible printing, we must widen our analysis to include these other biblical publications.

---

53 PR *Edward VI*, 1, p. 100 – 22 April 1547.
54 This folio edition employed a title border formerly owned by Froschauer, Nicholson and Petyt/Redman for Thomas Berthelet, and used later by Nicolas Hill.

Biblical printers utilised a variety of translations during the Edwardian years.[55] This panoply of non-patented competing translations provided the opportunity to angle into the market and denied the Great Bible a monopoly. Many of these translations shared a mutual heritage from the English translations of the 1520s to the early 1540s. Translations completed during the Henrician years made up over half of these 111 publications, and over sixty-five per cent if we remove metrical works. The only new translations produced between 1547 and 1553 were Edmund Becke's two revisions of the 'Matthew' bible and the Taverner bible and Richard Jugge's revision of the Tyndale New Testament. Jugge received a patent for his new revision, but the other translations, both new and old, were unprotected and allowed printers to exploit Edwardian evangelicalism's inherent and encouraged focus upon scripture. This opportunity was not overlooked: twenty-nine New Testaments and fifteen complete bibles were printed in England between 1547 and 1553. Of the complete bibles, eleven titles were folios, and four were quartos; meanwhile, of the twenty-nine New Testaments, eight titles were quarto, fifteen were octavos, one was duodecimo, and five were sextodecimos.

Richard Grafton and Edward Whitchurch produced no folio bibles in the Edwardian years. As summarised previously, this is indicative of high levels of Henrician compliance. However, a number of England's printers believed that the market for vernacular folio bibles extended into the private sphere or that the parochial and clerical markets were not saturated. The *USTC* lists a misleading eleven complete folio bibles produced in Edwardian England. The reality of these eleven titles is that they represent only five print runs. The projects were a lavish John Day and William Seres edition of Becke's revision of the 'Matthew' bible (printed by Stephen Mierdman, 1549), a 'Matthew' bible by Thomas Raynald and William Hill (1549); another John Day bible (1551) a Nicolas Hill edition funded by a syndicate of booksellers, and an edition of the Great Bible produced by Stephen Mierdman and Nicolas Hill (1553).

With two superbly executed folio bibles (1549 and 1551), John Day's publications announced that there was a new star on the rise in England's book world.[56] The 1549 folio bore a prefatory dedication to the king and was laden with illustrations. It has been claimed that Stephen Mierdman printed the 1,136-page (284-sheet) bible with Day acting only as a co-printer, or even co-publisher, of the work.[57] Even if Mierdman printed this folio bible, by 1551,

---

55   The *STC*, and thus the *ESTC*, offer additional information on individual translations used in their database listings.
56   *USTC* 504300, 504663.
57   Catalogue information for this publication varies. The *USTC* states '[Stephen Mierdman for] John Day'; *ESTC* states '[Stephen Mierdman for] John Day and William Seres'; the *EEBO* copy has 'John Day and William Seres' but makes no mention of Stephen Mierdman.

Day had printed his own independently, which was a landmark project and symbolised his entry into the elite printers of England. Day's engagement with this sphere was foundational in developing skills for the ambitious projects that define his Elizabethan career. However, at this early stage in his career, these projects were prestige-building exercises targeting profit from the small collective of individuals that could feasibly afford such a publication and future patronage.[58]

Alongside their *Order of Communion*, Thomas Raynald and William Hill also printed a folio bible. The productive first year of their partnership likely provided the confidence to commence this more technically sophisticated and capital-consuming challenge. For each printer, this represented a giant leap from their conventional practices. Hitherto, each printer had produced exclusively in smaller formats with their independent and collaborative projects typically preferring the octavo format.[59] Whilst they completed the mammoth 1,576-page project effectively – the final product is by far Raynald and William Hill's most substantial material product – the partnership did not return to biblical printing, instead choosing to revert to more manageable works. It is likely that this reflects the competitiveness of the biblical market: printing was a commercial venture and, unless underpinned by patronage, the most likely reason for exiting the field was a lack of profits.

Nicolas Hill's 1551 folio bible was the most statistically deceptive printing project of Edward's reign. The title represents seven titles but only one print run. In four of the titles that this project encompasses, Hill shares the colophon with another individual: William Bonham, Richard Kele, Abraham Veale, or Thomas Petyt. Hill's role is masked entirely in the remaining three, presenting John Wyght, Robert Toy or John Walley as the individual responsible for each publication.[60] In reality, this was one edition with matching pagination

---

John N. King has suggested that this was Mierdman's work due to the use of woodcuts he inherited from Matthias Crom, which is far from definitive as they shared resources on numerous occasions. Peter Blayney, *The Stationers' Company and the Printers of London, 1501–1557*, 2 vols (Cambridge: Cambridge University Press, 2013), p. 638, notes that a number of Crowley works by Day are misattributed to Mierdman, and states on p. 674, though makes no mention of Mierdman when expanding on, pp. 676–677.

58 Evenden, 'The Fleeing Dutchmen?', p. 68.
59 Raynald and William Hill produced six publications together in 1548, five were octavo, one was a sextodecimo. Hill produced nineteen titles outside of this partnership in 1548, three were quarto, fourteen were octavos and two were sextodecimos. Raynald produced nine titles outside of this partnership, eight were octavos, and one was a quarto.
60 Nicolas Hill, one print run, 'printing for' or 'at the cost of' William Bonham (*USTC* 518678), Richard Kele (518679), Abraham Veale (518679), Thomas Petyt (504570). Hill's efforts are not credited in those published by John Wyght (504643); Robert Toy (504644) and John Walley (515045).

registers, illustrations, and page breaks but set with unique title-pages (six of seven carry the same date). This edition was the product of a publishing syndicate, discussed further in chapter seven, who collectively underwrote the edition, with each investor receiving a portion of the completed print run. This commercial tactic is challenging for historians: on the one hand, seven individuals all believed that a folio edition printed by Hill could realise profitable or prestigious returns and yet, on the other, no individual was willing to sponsor the project as a whole.

An indication of the commercial success of this project is provided two years later when Stephen Mierdman and Nicolas Hill embarked upon the printing of an 1,160-page folio Great Bible. These printers had each completed high-quality folio bibles on behalf of publishers before the project but, in this instance, self-published. Whilst they both built their presence in the trade around collaborations, it was their only collaboration together. As Hill and Mierdman often worked for external publishers and had completed works of this nature previously, it is impossible to decipher who led the project. Nonetheless, it indicates that both printers' previous editions were commercially successful. These editions occupied presses for months at a time, and neither printer would wish to act as the principal funders unless it was financially viable.

Another factor at play in these years requires exploration to understand how this market was allowed to develop. The Great Bible was the subject of dissatisfaction among England's reformers. Archbishop Cranmer bemoaned the lack of a new translation and enlisted Martin Bucer and Paul Fagius to complete a new Latin translation in May 1549.[61] This translation, it was hoped, would, in turn, provide the foundation for the English bible to be translated afresh. Holding the confidences of the regime, Grafton and Whitchurch would have anticipated being the printers of choice. As businessmen, it made little commercial sense to produce more Great Bibles if they believed that the book could soon be superseded. Whilst the project never neared completion, it is conceivable that the patent holders were aware that a new translation was a priority. Indeed, the pursuit of a new translation continued in exile and at home under Mary I and Elizabeth I as Wittingham's New Testament (1557), the *Geneva Bible* (1560) and the *Bishop's Bible* (1568) vied with later Great Bible editions for primacy and authority; the catholic reaction also prompted the

---

61   Bruce Gordon, 'The Authority of Antiquity: England and the Protestant Latin Bible', in *The Reception of Continental Reformation in Britain*, eds. Polly Ha and Patrick Collinson (Oxford: Oxford University Press, 2010), pp. 1–22 (p. 4).

Rheims-Douai Bible (1582).[62] Grafton and Whitchurch's withdrawal from this area of the trade, then, is not an indication of the lack of a market, but instead of two businessmen weighing up a commercial opportunity and ceasing to produce a product that could soon be superseded.

These projects provide an interesting illustration of affairs in Edwardian English printing. The technical accomplishments of the Day/Mierdman folio bible in 1549, his subsequent printing of another folio bible in 1551, and the Mierdman/Hill 1553 production all indicate that projects of this type could be commercially viable. In contrast, however, Raynald and William Hill's single attempt and the cost-spreading initiatives employed by Hill's publishers suggest that this market was not risk-free. Previous historical accounts have asserted that the publication of a complete bible in folio was an exercise in prestige building, and this is true, to an extent.[63] However, printers were businessmen and would not embark upon such demanding projects without expectations or aspirations of profits. It is in this profit seeking that these folio bibles highlight their true importance: three of these four projects produced non-patented translations and, as such, were targeting audiences not legally obligated to purchase. As objects, these books became increasingly elaborate: the improved technical ability demonstrated (and capital spent on) these projects emphasises that book quality was increasingly important for success in this sphere. The wealthier ranks of English readers were becoming more discerning in their tastes and more demanding in their expectations.

Edward's religious proceedings enabled and encouraged a wider portion of the population actively to engage with scripture. This led to an expansion of the market for small-format bibles designed for personal reference and independent study. During Edward's reign, four complete bibles and eight New Testaments were produced in quarto, and one bible and ten New Testaments in octavo. For the first time, duodecimo and sextodecimo editions of the New Testament also came forth from England's presses. Bibles came to mean a great deal to a widening portion of the population during the reformation. Avner Shamir details an Edwardian councillor using a bible as a stool only for

---

62   Vivienne Westbrook, *Long Travail and Great Paynes, A Politics of Reformation Revision* (Dordrecht: Kluwer Academic Publishers, 2001), pp. 127–142; Daniell, *The Bible in English*; Eamon Duffy, *The Stripping of the Altars: Traditional Religion in England, c.1400–1580*, 2nd edn (New Haven, CT: Yale University Press, 2005), p. 530; Jack P. Lewis, *The Day After Domesday: The Making of the Bishops' Bible* (Eugene, OR: Wipf & Stock, 2016).

63   Elizabeth Evenden and Thomas Freeman, *Religion and the Book in Early Modern England: the making of John Foxe's "Book of Martyrs"* (Cambridge: Cambridge University Press, 2011), p. 15; Evenden, 'The Fleeing Dutchmen?', p. 68.

Edward VI to gather it up, kiss it and lay it back in its rightful place.[64] The bible was also a central component of lay evangelicalism during the sixteenth century.[65] The importance of bibles to evangelicals sparked competition, innovation, and significant growth from Henrician output.

Following a proclamation of 31 July 1547, there was a fresh demand for the clergy to own copies of the New Testament:

> Also, that every parson, vicar, curate, chantry priest, and stipendary, being under the degree of bachelor of divinity shall provide, and have of his own, within three months of the visitation, the New Testament, both in Latin and in English.[66]

Three diglot New Testaments appear to have been designed explicitly for adherence to this proclamation: William Powell's two quarto editions of 1548 and 1549, and Thomas Gaultier's octavo printed for John Cawood in 1550.[67] These publications used parallel columns aligned for comparison. This freshly obligated readership, which D.G. Newcombe's research has suggested could have included well over half of the realm's clergymen, ought to have been substantial enough to ensure the success of these editions.[68] The fact that Powell's 1549 edition was essentially a direct reprint of his 1548 edition suggests, though does not prove, a degree of commercial success. Powell was principally a printer of legal works (thirty-two of his sixty-seven titles), and these two diglots were his only forays into biblical printing. Powell's wider catalogue offers a glimpse of religious motivations. In 1549, he printed conservative John Proctor's *The Fal of the Late Arrian*.[69] This may indicate that Powell was driven to publish in a bid to counteract the movement towards scripture in the vernacular alone. This notion can also be applied to the edition funded by John Cawood, who

---

64 Avner Shamir, *English Bibles on Trial: Bible burning and the desecration of Bibles, 1640–1800* (London: Routledge, 2017), p. 181.
65 Alec Ryrie, *Being Protestant in Reformation Britain* (Oxford: Oxford University Press, 2013), pp. 294–295.
66 *H&L*, 1, pp. 393–403 – 31 July 1547.
67 USTC 504132; 504323; 504532.
68 D.G. Newcombe, 'John Hooper's visitation and examination of the clergy in the diocese of Gloucester, 1551', in *Reformations Old and New: Essays on the Socio-Economic Impact of Religious Change c.1470–1630*, ed. Beat A. Kümin (Aldershot: Scolar Press, 1996), pp. 57–70 (p. 63).
69 Powell was brought before the Privy Council for printing Proctor's work – this experience may have discouraged him from printing anything that could be considered to discourage vernacular scripture.

withdrew from the trade until becoming printer to Mary I.[70] The discontinuation of diglot bibles can be attributed to the improved perception of the authority of vernacular scripture and the growing variety of smaller-format vernacular New Testaments.

The printers of Edward's canonical church documents also realised that the market for English bibles was shifting towards smaller formats. Whitchurch and Grafton each produced quarto Great Bibles (1549 and 1553 respectively), and John Oswen printed a quarto New Testament in 1550.[71] However, it was an entrepreneurial émigré, Stephen Mierdman, who spearheaded innovation in the presentation of scripture. The inaugural printing of the English New Testament in sextodecimo occurred in 1548 as Mierdman produced one for Richard Jugge, and John Herford produced another.[72] Mierdman's subsequent commissions from John Day in 1550 and Richard Jugge in 1552 indicate the commercial success of these works.[73] Mierdman's innovative techniques did not finish here: in 1550, he produced the only duodecimo English New Testament of the sixteenth century.[74] These format innovations were an exercise in cost-saving and increasing accessibility. The financial ramifications ensured that scripture was more affordable and accessible for a wider readership. Printers leveraged another market tactic to accommodate English bible readers: John Day and William Seres produced Becke's revision of the 'Matthew' bible as a printed-in-five-parts octavo edition between 1549 and 1551.[75] These small-format or sale-in-increments approaches were built upon commercial strategies that happily aligned with the government's active encouragement of a wider reading public.

Statistically, biblical printing made up a significant portion of the Edwardian industry. The expansion of both obligated and encouraged readerships prompted competition and technical innovation. Whilst the Edwardian

---

70 Cawood's religious inclinations are uncertain, but his withdrawal from the trade after this diglot edition of the bible, until the accession of catholic Mary I may suggest that this project was, in part at least, an attempt to get Latin translations of the bible into the hands of English conservatives.
71 USTC (Whitchurch) 504170, (Grafton) 504854; (Oswen) 516495, 515397.
72 USTC (Mierdman for Jugge) 504120; (Herford) 516461.
73 USTC (Mierdman for Day) 516499; (Mierdman for Jugge) 515430. In 1550, Day also collaborated with Christopher Froschauer (the leading reformation printer in Zurich) to produce a sextodecimo English New Testament.
74 USTC 504521; this publication will be examined in further detail in chapter five..
75 Evenden, *Patents, Pictures and Patronage*, pp. 15, 21 – claims that these editions were produced in sextodecimo format, but BL and USTC catalogues state octavo. Evenden also states that a number of the parts published in the earlier years were published following the final edition produced in 1551.

Church of England establishment did little to sponsor specific bible projects in comparison to their Henrician predecessors, they did mobilise a lay readership. Without a new official translation to prompt growth, the progress evident in this sphere of the industry was sparked by private businessmen in the name of revenue as much as reformation. Those printers protected by the establishment reduced their output and in the resulting vacuum entrepreneurial printers competed for prestige and profit.

2 State Patronage: Printers' Patents and Privileges

The cooperative networks connecting the elite evangelical sodalities to England's printers were a distinctive feature of the English book world. Intricate webs of patronage 'deliberately fostered' a 'Protestant publishing offensive'.[76] The regime presented financial and political inducements by awarding official patents. The study of Tudor literary patronage owes much to John N. King, Elizabeth Evenden, and Peter Blayney, who have established how the allocation of patents was enveloped in the religious, political and social worlds of the Edwardian hierarchy.[77] Whilst private patronage from the English elite will be discussed in chapter seven, this portion of the book will emphasise the critical importance of the official support of the Crown. The role of the evangelical establishment in this area was two-fold: granting the exclusive right to publish specific works and protection from illegal reproductions. Edwardian patents were on parity with Henrician precedents in both design and implementation but were offered more widely than ever before.

The thirteen individuals who acquired patents include many of the premier names of the English print world. It has been argued that patents and privileges were the keys to success in the Tudor book world, but how far this was the case during the Edwardian reign depends on whether patents were the passage to, or a hallmark of, success within the industry.[78] This chapter also demonstrates that patrons within the evangelical establishment were influential in the establishing preferment in the distribution of patents.

Principally, there were three primary forms of financial inducement offered: patents covering single publications or collections of works, patents protecting individuals from pirate reproductions of their publications, and commercial

---

76 Pettegree, 'Printing and the Reformation', p. 173.
77 Evenden, *Patents, Pictures and Patronage*; John N. King, *English Reformation Literature: The Tudor Origins of the Protestant Tradition* (Princeton, NJ, Princeton University Press, 1982); Blayney, *The Stationers' Company*.
78 Evenden and Freeman, *Religion and the Book in Early Modern England*, p. 14; Evenden, 'The Fleeing Dutchmen?', p. 71.

allowances to aid the smooth running of print houses. The importance of the patents issued varied dramatically. This analysis of patents and privileges broadens our understanding of official sponsorship of print in Edward's reign and emphasises how lucrative it could be to be favoured by the establishment.

TABLE 4.2   Edwardian printing patents

Printer / Publisher	Patented works	Date of patent	Historical record
Richard Grafton	All service books for the Church of England	22 April 1547	PR Edward VI, 1, p. 100
Edward Whitchurch	All service books for the Church of England	22 April 1547	PR Edward VI, 1, p. 100
Gwalter Lynne	*the begynnyng and endyng of all poperey or popishe kyngdom* and all other books 'consonant to godliness'	1 December 1547	PR Edward VI, 1, p. 61
John Oswen	Service books for Wales and the marches	7 January 1549	PR Edward VI, 1, p. 269
Nicholas Udall	Peter Martyr's Eucharist Disputation	[July 1550]	PR Edward VI, 3, p. 315
Humphrey Powell	Service books for Ireland	18 July 1550	APC, 3, p. 84
Stephen Mierdman	All not-previously-printed books at his own expense for five years	26 July 1550	PR Edward VI, 3, p. 314
Richard Jugge	Revision of the New Testament	15 January 1551	PR Edward VI, 3, p. 227
Reyner Wolfe	Thomas Cranmer's reply to Stephen Gardiner	1 October 1551	APC, 3, p. 375
Thomas Gaultier	French service books for the stranger churches	14 December 1552	*Ecclesiastical Memorials*, 2, 2, p. 37
William Seres	Primers and psalters	6 March 1553	PR Edward VI, 5, pp. 50–51
John Day	John Ponet's *ABC with Short Catechism* & works of Thomas Becon	25 March 1553	PR Edward VI, 5, p. 43
Richard Tottell	Common Law Books	12 April 1553	PR, Edward VI, 5, p. 47

The first and most influential Edwardian printing patent was issued to Richard Grafton and Edward Whitchurch on 22 April 1547 for the production of all service books for the Church of England. The new Edwardian patent granted the right to print all books:

> concerning divine service or containing any kind of sermons or exhortations that shall be used, suffered, or authorised in our churches of England and Irelonde or either of them ... in the English or Latin tongue. No other printer is to print such books on pain of forfeiture of the books and imprisonment at the king's will.[79]

This patent covers the canonical documents discussed above but also wider categories of church documents, including primers, psalters, catechisms, and the ordinal.

With Richard Grafton, it is difficult to decipher which works fell under his patent for service books and which fell under his official office. This is likely the reason that the historiographical convention of redacting his title to 'King's Printer' and classifying them all as official documents has endured.[80] Grafton's official office and the canonical church documents, as we have seen, formed the foundation of his business, but this patent covered an additional set: six primers, five psalters, a quarto Great Bible and two *The forme and makyng and consecrating of bishops* (The Ordinal).[81] Grafton received the most significant assignments and most support from the government. The combination of his official office and the work initiated by this patent made him the most decorated and influential printer of the reign.

Whitchurch's output, likewise, reflects the significance of this patent. He produced twenty-eight canonical church documents and an additional six non-canonical service books: three Great Bible psalters and three primers.[82] Whitchurch's patents and privileges became increasingly important. From

---

79 PR *Edward VI*, 1, p. 100.
80 For example, the forty-two articles and *The Ordinal* are difficult to place. Despite the forty-two articles being a uniform outline of the Edwardian church, it was passed as law and therefore is counted under the remit of the King's Printer for Statutes &c. *The Ordinal*, meanwhile, is counted as falling under the patent for service books as it was a book 'concerning divine service'.
81 Primers: USTC (1547) 516030, 518460; (1548) 515368; (1549) 504238; (1551) 504598, 504599; psalters (1548) 504008; (1549) 504198, 504213; ([1552]) 518131; ([1553]) 518161; *The Ordinal* ([1549] in fact 1550) 518564, 518597.
82 Primers: USTC (1548) 503996, (1549) 518640, (1550) 518228; psalters: (1547) 503822, (1548) 504175, (1549) 504230. Whitchurch also produced psalms for private use 504348 and 504354.

1551 onwards, he printed almost exclusively staple works: ten *Books of Common Prayer*; nine of Thomas Sternhold's *Metrical Psalms*; two more titles of Edmund Allen's *Catechism*, two ABCs *with catechism*, and two titles of William Baldwin's *A Treatise of Morall phylosophye*.[83] The Sternhold and Allen publications were not canonical church documents, and there is no evidence of a patent, but Whitchurch nonetheless secured the exclusive printing.[84] This was true also of the second volume of the *Paraphrases* (1549). If we incorporate these three works, which were undoubtedly the subject of patronage if not patents, we reach an output of forty-nine titles (fifty-five per cent of his output) and an even larger proportion of the printing work required. Patents, supported by other patronised projects, were the mainstay of Whitchurch's business.

The equivalent patents procured by John Oswen and Humphrey Powell, too, have been discussed in relation to the canonical documents. Oswen's permitted him to 'print and sell books which have been or shall be set forth by the king for service to be used in churches, sacraments and instruction'. However, Oswen's patent came with a caveat: 'sufficient only for the said principality [Wales] and marches'. Under this patent, Oswen printed four canonical church documents (three *Books of Common Prayer* and one *Homilies*), along with two quarto titles of the New Testament and a psalter.[85] The inclusion of general service books supplemented Oswen's canonical document output, but regional limitations restricted his market, which ultimately prevented his press from becoming more than a small bastion of evangelicalism in the western provinces of England. For Powell, as we have seen above, the rewards of becoming a service book printer for Ireland appear to have been even more limited, ultimately securing the sole Irish imprint of the reign.

These service book patents came from the uppermost echelons of the Edwardian polity. The canonical church document titles and twenty-three additional service books produced establish them as the most impactful patents of the reign. Other members of the trade gradually contested this all-encompassing patent and later patents encroached upon its terms, but this did little to hamper the holders' thriving businesses. The centrality of this patent to two premier Edwardian printers highlights that patents could be the vehicle by which printers achieved and maintained elite status.

---

83 Felicity Heal, 'Allen, Edmund (1510s–1559)', ODNB. Heal asserts that Allen was responsible for a short catechism in 1550 – there appears to be no listing of this in the USTC. Allen's catechism: USTC (1548) 503943, 51860, (1551) 504556, 504558, and ABC *with catechism*: (1551) 504555; 504557 (1551); Metrical psalms: (1549) 504280, 504306, 504314, (1551) 504640, 504651, 516506, (1552) 517828; (1553) 504880, 504887, 504916, 515449, 515454.

84 Patents were issued for the psalms under Elizabeth I: John Day was granted the patent for the psalms with music, William Seres for psalms without music.

85 USTC 515397, 516495, 504235.

Whilst the service book patents were clearly defined, this was not always the case. Two patents awarded to Netherlandish émigrés granted protection covering undefined collections of works. These individuals had very different approaches to the book world, and despite each of their patents having great potential, in reality, each gained little from their issue.

The first, a seven-year patent awarded to Gwalter Lynne on 1 December 1547, poses several interesting questions. The terms of the patent include a single named publication: Joachim of Fiore, *The begynnyng and endyng of all poperey or popishe kyngdom*, but also included 'all other maner of bokes consonant to godliness'.[86] This blanket statement represents a significant show of faith from the Edwardian regime: Lynne had no experience of printing or publishing in England or English. Lynne was an affluent member of the Dutch stranger community in London and linked to three titles published in Antwerp during the 1530s, but these were hardly watertight credentials.[87] It is through the clause 'consonant to godliness' that the regime outlined its expectations. Alarm bells may have rung for the regime with Lynne's choice of printer: John Herford, who had printed pro-mass tracts in 1546 for Robert Toy authored by Gardiner, Richard Smith and William Peryn.[88] However, Lynne repaid his patrons' faith, and Herford repaid Lynne's. The named publication was a 64-page quarto adorned with an elaborate title-page, fifteen woodcut illustrations, intricate ornaments and initials, and a dedication to the king and the Lord Protector.[89]

Lynne plunged into the protestant programme of reform by producing twenty-two titles, nineteen of which the USTC classifies as primarily religious.[90] His catalogue read as a Who's Who of continental reform, including Heinrich Bullinger, Wolfgang Capito, Martin Luther, Bernardino Ochino, Urbanus Rhegius, and a *Catechism* attributed to Archbishop Cranmer.[91] Lynne

---

86   USTC 504066; PR Edward VI, 1, p. 61. This patent is the likely inspiration for Stephen Alford's succinct summary that 'By the late 1540s and early 1550s the evangelical buzzword "godliness" had become a key term in explaining royal favour and support for authors and printers': Alford, *Kingship and Politics in the reign of Edward VI*, p. 117.

87   Andrew Pettegree, 'Lynne, Walter (d. in or before 1571)', ODNB. Pettegree cites R.E.G. Kirk and E.F. Kirk, eds., *Returns of aliens dwelling in the city and suburbs of London, from the reign of Henry VIII to that of James I* (London: Huguenot Society of London, 1900–1902) 10/1, pp. 25, 61, 85, 134, 161, 202, 209–10, 214, 331, 443; 10/2, p. 70.

88   USTC 503726, 503732 503733, 503754, 503785, 515351, 503784.

89   USTC 504066.

90   The remaining three are classified as: 'educational work', 'history and chronicles' and 'women'.

91   This catechism (HEH: 129196, USTC 504011) was an English translation of Andreas Osiander's catechism, translated into Latin by Justus Jonas, and thereafter English in 1548; Diarmaid MacCulloch, *Thomas Cranmer: A Life* (New Haven, CT: Yale University Press, 1996), pp. 386–390; D.G. Selwyn, ed., *A Catechism set forth by Thomas Cranmer From the*

certainly came to curry favour with the regime, but there are no hallmarks of patronage before this patent, making it an unusual case.[92] The 'Cranmer' catechism is the most reasonable motivation for John N. King assigning to Lynne the mistaken title of 'Printer to the Archbishop of Canterbury'. His publications offer indicators of alternative patronage links: he addresses dedications to Anne Seymour (duchess of Somerset), Lord Protector Somerset and the king, though these may simply be acknowledgements of the patent.

A second official patent was issued to Lynne on 21 June 1549, granting a license to import '800 tuns Gascoign wine and Tholoze woad' for sale in England. The significance of this patent is that it was unrelated to the book trade. Lynne published throughout 1549 and 1550, which suggests he made sufficient profits, but also that he supplemented his income with commodity trading even before withdrawing from the book world within eighteen months. This patent highlights that a businessman (even one holding one of the most open patents in England) could be tempted to withdraw from the trade once a more profitable commercial opportunity presented itself. Every ton of Gascon wine was fixed at a maximum sale price of £6 6s. 8d. by a 1552 official proclamation – 800 tons was a potentially handsome payday.[93] Again, printing is shown to be a commercial activity, and seemingly for Lynne, a less profitable one than the import and sale of Gascon wine.

The patent granted to Stephen Mierdman, awarded 26 July 1550, concerned 'various books, hitherto unprinted'.[94] Whilst the terms appear even more open than those issued to Lynne, Mierdman was a known quantity. He had served an English evangelical readership from Antwerp, producing fourteen English works in eight years, including works authored by Andreas Osiander, Philipp Melanchthon, John Frith, William Barlow and John Bale. Following his relocation to London in 1546–47, Mierdman established a substantial printing enterprise, printing eighty-three titles between 1547 and 1553. Prior to his patent, Mierdman had already printed or co-printed at least twenty-eight titles in England, including works by prominent reformers. Mierdman's credentials had been made perfectly clear to the establishment before any official endorsement was conveyed. Unfortunately, there are no definitive hallmarks of patronage of Lynne or Mierdman. This is not to say they were not supported, but it is also possible that Lynne and Mierdman negotiated their patents as

---

Nuremberg Catechism translated into Latin by Justus Jonas (Appleford: Sutton Courtney Press, 1978). USTC 504022, 504023, 504011.
92   Pettegree, 'Lynne, Walter'.
93   *H&L*, 1, pp. 536–537 – 1 February 1552.
94   PR *Edward VI*, 3, p. 314.

private businessmen; Lynne's clause 'consonant to godliness', for example, may well be a reference to assurances he made during an application process.

The undefined nature of these patents makes it unusually difficult to decipher which publications were covered and, thus, how important or lucrative each patent was. The decisive feature of the patent in each instance is whether it was the inaugural publication of any given title, and this was the case for very few titles. Mierdman's market practice also creates further ambiguity, as he was one of the Edwardian industry's leading 'printers-for-hire'. Collaboration was a distinctive feature of Mierdman's career, as we shall see in chapter six, but none of his publications printed for publishers would have been protected under his patent.[95] From a total of eighty-one titles, then, only twenty-three could possibly fall under the terms of his patent and, in fact, only ten were previously unprinted in England, including two Dutch works.[96] Even within these works, Mierdman's patent did not, in practice, secure the exclusive printing of each text. Mierdman's publications in Dutch, for example, soon came under the remit of Nicolas Hill, who assumed the responsibility for printing works for the Dutch stranger church in 1552.

The patents offered to Lynne and Mierdman were distinct from others issued in early modern England; they provided free rein where others were limited. Ultimately, whilst promising much, these patents delivered little commercial protection or advancement. These individuals built a strong business presence from a position of authority but led primarily by their business acumen rather than their patents. James Raven states that 'fortunes beckoned for those securing official patents and orders', but not all patents were made equal, and Lynne and Mierdman made their living beyond the remit of their patents.[97]

For one of two primary reasons, many of the book patents during Edward's tenure had little impact on the industry or even individual patentees. The first reason includes patents issued with restrictions relating to local markets or single publications, including those given to Reyner Wolfe, Thomas Gaultier and Richard Jugge. The second reason is the timing of the patent's issue. This

---

95   John Bale's expostulation is listed as Stephen Mierdman, 1552, consultation with *EEBO*, however, shows 'Imprynted at London, by Jhon Daye, dwelling over Aldersgate' (*USTC* 504712); Joseph Ames, *Typographical antiquities: an historical account of printing in England, Scotland and Ireland*, 1, ed. Thomas Frognall Dibdin (London: William Miller, 1810), p. 167; Mierdman thrived in the industry as a printer-for-hire and, as such, he held little claim to exclusivity, and the level of protection and stimulus to his business offered by his patent reflects that.

96   Evenden, 'The Fleeing Dutchmen?', p. 70 claims Mierdman's umbrella patent was lucrative.

97   James Raven, *The Business of Books: Booksellers and the English Book Trade* (New Haven, CT: Yale University Press, 2007), p. 47.

second category encompasses patents issued in the final year of Edward's reign to John Day, William Seres and Richard Tottell. Ultimately, these seven patents combined resulted in thirty patented titles during Edward's reign.

Reyner Wolfe, as we have seen, worked as King's Typographer and Bookseller for the ancient languages. He was also granted another privilege on 1 October 1551, issuing a license to publish and sell *An answer of Thomas archebishop of Canterburye, unto a crafty cavillation by S. Gardiner*, which appeared as two titles.[98] This publication, a 472-page folio, was an important academic refutation of leading conservatives, typifying the evangelical counterattack discussed above. Wolfe was a central player in this process, having already printed Smith's recantations at Oxford and St Paul's in 1547 and Cranmer's *A defence of the true and Catholic doctrine of the sacrament*.[99] Wolfe was not granted patents for these works, but they likely aided him in securing Cranmer's major publication. Wolfe shared a close personal connection with the archbishop, and while he was only offered the patent to one of Cranmer's works between 1547 and 1553, he was the printer of choice for England's prelate.[100] Wolfe's patent was limited in its scope and reflected his status as an elite printer rather than the patent being the vehicle by which he achieved this standing.

Later, an official patent was issued to Thomas Gaultier (December 1552) to print works for Edward's Channel Islands. Whether the resulting publications were designed purely for this purpose, or also intended to bring the stranger churches into line with the official English Reformation, or be shipped abroad remains unclear. Thomas Gaultier was already the preeminent French-language printer in England: of the eight French-language titles whose printer is known, six came from his press.[101] Gaultier is identified in John Strype's *Ecclesiastical Memorials* as 'King's Printer for the French Language', supported by his colophon: 'Imprimeur du Roy en la langue Francoise, pour les Isles de sa Magesté'.[102] If Strype is correct, it is probable that the four French

---

98   APC, 3, p. 375 – 1 October 1551.
99   USTC 503898; 503900; USTC 504403; 504416; 504417; (504816 was in Latin and printed in 1553).
100 Evenden and Freeman, *Religion and the Book in Early Modern England*, p. 66; Cyndia Susan Clegg, *Press Censorship in Elizabethan England* (Cambridge: Cambridge University Press, 1997), p. 24.
101 Only eight of the twelve French-language publications between 1547 and 1553 have a known printer, four remain unattributed.
102 John Strype, ed., *Ecclesiastical Memorials, relating chiefly to Religion, and the reformation of it, and the emergencies of the Church of England, under King Henry VIII, King Edward VI and Queen Mary I, with large appendixes, containing original papers, records, &c.*, 2, 1 (Oxford: Clarendon Press, 1822), 3, p. 208; Blayney, *The Stationers' Company*, p. 628; no evidence for this official title has been found in the *Patent Rolls* or *Acts of Privy Council* of Edward's reign.

works produced in England in 1552, including Perussel's *Forme des prieres ecclesiastique* and *Doctrine de la penitence publique*, also came from his press or were subcontracted out.[103] The following year, Gaultier was the only confirmed printer to produce works in French: an octavo New Testament and an edition of the *Le livre des Prieres Communes* (*Book of Common Prayer*).[104] It is worth noting that the establishment of the stranger churches of London at Austin Friars in 1550 was a landmark initiative of the regime, designed to ensure refuge for European evangelicals escaping persecution.[105]

An essential prerequisite for these churches was the provision of service books. Historians estimate the total immigrant population of England (of which Dutch and French were believed to comprise less than half) at between five and ten thousand, although they were claimed to be far higher by some contemporaries.[106] Stephen Mierdman, a member of the Dutch stranger church, printed these publications initially, including three for the French strangers and two editions of Jan Utenhove's Dutch *Catechism*.[107] The catechism used by the French stranger church, meanwhile, is believed to have been Jean Calvin's *Le catechisme de Geneve*.[108] Nicolas Hill usurped Mierdman as the leading printer of Dutch-language works in England, producing ten of the thirteen during 1552 and 1553, including all the Dutch catechisms.[109] He may have received some form of official inducement though no record is known to have survived. Gaultier's position may well have brought him into the world of printing for the stranger churches, which would have aided him in these French-language publications that otherwise may have been less than enviable commercial projects. The surviving patent record suggests the official remit included only small potential markets. The patent awarded to Gaultier

---

103 USTC 5203, 5204, 23090 are listed without an author or printer. Francois Perussel has been established as the author of the first two publications but heading titles of 'London – Elise reformee' suggest each was an official stranger church document.

104 *Le nouveau testament* (Thomas Gaultier, 1553) USTC 5643; Francois Philippe, *Le livre des Prieres Communes, De l'administration des Sacre mens & autres Ceremonies en l'Eglise d'Angleterre*. (Thomas Gautier, 1553) USTC 12612.

105 Pettegree, *Foreign Protestant Communities*, pp. 2, 9, 23; further initiatives include the French church established at Canterbury under the protection and governance of Jan Utenhove, and the Flemish weavers in Glastonbury patronised by Somerset, via Valerand Poullain.

106 SP Foreign, pp. 119–120 – 6 June 1551: Francis Peyto to the Earl of Warwick; Pettegree, *Foreign Protestant Communities*, pp. 78–79; Pettegree estimates that 5000 foreigners were resident in London in 1547, and closer to 10,000 in 1553.

107 *Le temporiseur* USTC 679 and *Liturgia Sacra* USTC 504650 and Francois Perussell's *Summa Christianae religionis* USTC 504661; USTC 400829; 504623.

108 USTC 10463 – Thomas Berthelet is an inferred printer. Berthelet was active printer at this stage and had experience printing in French (USTC 47625; 49441; 49442).

109 Mierdman continued to print in Dutch and this accounts for the three other publications.

was unlikely to provide a vast quantity of work or commercial success; still, it was a mark of prestige and an example of the regime utilising an individual with the requisite skills to produce a high-quality product suitable for their French-speaking subjects.

Richard Jugge's revision of Tyndale's New Testament, first produced in 1552, was the final new biblical translation of the reign. In January 1551, Jugge was granted a license to produce his revision in 'both great and small volumes'.[110] Jugge made full use of this allowance, printing a richly decorated quarto in 1552 (fig. 4.1), before publishing three further editions, each printed by Stephen Mierdman: one sextodecimo (1552), one quarto and one octavo (1553). The patent terms include a justification: 'granted because printing by strangers has led to errors of translation as well as in the words and orthography, is to last eight years during which no other subject may print the New Testament in English'. This statement seemingly applied only to Jugge's revision; had it applied to the biblical printing industry as a whole, twelve individuals (including Grafton, Mierdman, Day, and Seres) would all have been guilty of infringement. However, nine of these twelve individuals produced their version of the New Testament in 1551, which predated Jugge's inaugural edition. On 10 June 1552, the Privy Council reaffirmed Jugge's license for the New Testament 'lately by hym set forth', fixing the cost at 'xxij^d the peece in quieres'.[111] Following Jugge's New Testament in 1552, no stand-alone New Testaments were printed before the end of the reign, though at least three projects printed alternative New Testaments as part of complete bibles, including Jugge's printer Stephen Mierdman.[112] Before 1551, independent New Testaments account for twenty Edwardian titles, in which fifteen individuals were listed in colophons.

Following Jugge's inaugural edition, his was the only translation used and he acted as printer or publisher for all four projects. Taken from the patent's first date of issue in January 1551, Jugge's patent initially appears to have been relentlessly violated, but he swiftly won a monopoly over the stand-alone New Testament market after the license was reissued in 1552. It is critical to remember how much shorter the New Testament is than the Old Testament: this was a significantly easier print job and could be retailed at a more accessible print

---

110   PR *Edward VI*, 3, p. 227.
111   APC, 4, p. 73.
112   USTC 504854; 504679; 504792; according to the STC, these three complete bibles each used the Great Bible translations and, therefore, the two printed by Hill for his publishers must have breached at least one official patent: Grafton and Whitchurch's for the Great Bible. The only New Testament texts were published in a quarto bible by Nicolas Hill for Abraham Veale (1552), Grafton's quarto Great Bible (1553) and a folio bible printed by Nicolas Hill for Stephen Mierdman.

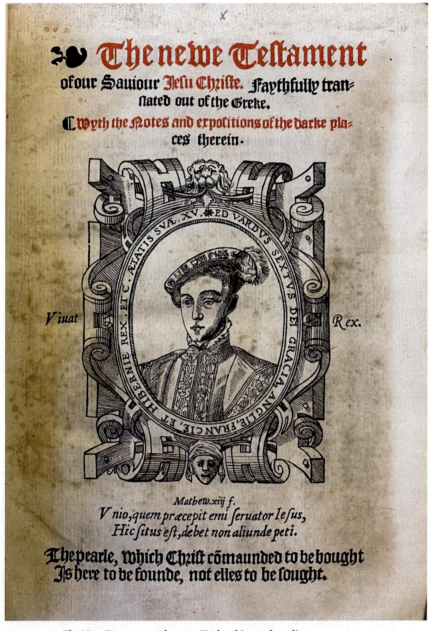

FIGURE 4.1 The New Testament title-page (Richard Jugge, [1552])
THE HUNTINGTON LIBRARY: 96524; NATIONAL LIBRARY OF SCOTLAND: HAX.45

point for readers. Jugge's ascendency continued into the reign of Mary I, galvanised by a partnership with the new Queen's Printer of Statutes, John Cawood; however, his patent was revoked as part of the catholic counter-reformation. Henry Richard Tedder and Joyce Boro have asserted that Jugge was granted a seven-year patent to print all books of common law in May 1556, though this appears to be misappropriated as this patent was held by Richard Tottell, the only Edwardian patent recipient to retain his patent following Mary I's accession.[113]

Of these limited-scope patents, Jugge's impacted broader industry practices the most. Gaultier secured a foothold upon what were naturally poorly subscribed areas of the industry due to language barriers and small markets, whilst Wolfe's patent secured only a single publication. Had the Edwardian reign progressed further than 1553, it is possible that Jugge would have emerged with a patent of significant worth, but the death of a monarch could dramatically change the state of play.

A final set of three patents, each issued only months before the young king's death, had no time to be influential to the landscape of Edwardian printing. Within this category of patents fall those issued to John Day, William Seres and Richard Tottell. Ultimately, their historical and commercial significance was not limited to Edward's reign, as each was renewed during one of the subsequent reigns of Mary I or Elizabeth I. As such, we must place these patents in their Edwardian and broader historical context to understand their significance.

The first of these patents was issued to William Seres, granting permission 'to print all manner of books of "private prayers" called Primers bothe in greate volumes and smale whiche arre and shalbe sette fourthe agreagle (sic) and accordynge to the boke of Commen prayers' for six years.[114] Seres had established himself in the industry in partnerships with Anthony Scoloker and John Day, and by 1553 stood as a prolific publisher. Following this patent, three of Seres' eight publications in 1553 are listed as independently-printed primers, but Seres was a publisher, and he also commissioned a printer for these works.[115] Four of Seres' publications during this year bear the colophon of 'Nicolas Hill for William Seres', and he may well have been the printer of choice.[116] The statesman whose hallmark is apparent upon Seres' pathway to

---

113 H.R. Tedder, 'Jugge, Richard (c.1514–1577)', ODNB, rev. Joyce Boro.
114 PR Edward VI, 5, pp. 50–51.
115 USTC 516534; 504822; 504827.
116 One of the works (*Acts in Metre for the lute*) the USTC lists as 'Nicolas Hill for William Seres' does not appear to be by Hill; sharing the same imprint as the other independently printed Seres work from 1553.

patents is William Cecil: Seres was an active servant of the Cecil household and a number of his publications were adorned with the Cecil insignia.[117]

25 March 1553 was a milestone date in the history of the Tudor printing industry: John Day was granted a patent for the works of John Ponet (bishop of Winchester), including the *ABC with brief catechism*, and the works of Thomas Becon (preacher of Canterbury cathedral).[118] This patent covered four of Day's fourteen titles produced in 1553: two titles of Becon's *Principles of Christian Religion*,[119] an *ABC*,[120] and one edition of Ponet's *Short Catechism*.[121] Day had secured influential supporters, and the duke of Northumberland wrote to champion Day's patent application.[122] This patent exemplifies the importance of high profile political support, perhaps more so than any other in the Edwardian period. Diarmaid MacCulloch and Elizabeth Evenden have discussed Archbishop Cranmer's attempts to secure this patent for Reyner Wolfe, whilst Northumberland favoured John Day.[123] The ensuing political struggle saw Wolfe compensated with the Latin *Catechismus Brevis* as his official office commanded, whilst Day received the far more commercially desirable English translation. Whilst this patent amounted to little in the short term, it bore fruit following the recreation of much of the Edwardian industry following the accession of Elizabeth I and the revival of this patent in 1558.[124] The patent promised huge commercial benefits; the inclusion of the works of Thomas Becon was a lucrative opportunity. Day was able to secure new patents during Elizabeth I's reign, including Thomas Sternhold's metrical psalter, and these became the foundations that facilitated his more ambitious projects.[125] Thomas Becon's works were printed in forty-five titles between the issue of Day's Edwardian patent and the end of the sixteenth century, forty-two of which were printed by, or in the name of, the Day family. Later in his career, patents were fundamental to Day's commercial activities, but, owing to the untimely death of Edward VI, they had little chance to affect his fortunes before Mary I's accession.

---

117 Evenden, 'The Fleeing Dutchmen?', p. 66, states that Seres 'was a clear favourite of Mildred Cecil'.
118 PR *Edward VI*, 5, p. 43.
119 USTC 504801, 504838.
120 USTC 515452.
121 USTC 504915.
122 William Cecil himself would become one of Day's lead patrons. SP 10/15, no. 3 – 7 September 1552; Evenden, *Patents, Pictures and Patronage*, p. 48.
123 MacCulloch, *Thomas Cranmer*, p. 524; Evenden, *Patents, Pictures and Patronage*, pp. 25–27.
124 Pettegree, 'Printing and the Reformation', p. 179.
125 Evenden, *Patents, Pictures and Patronage*, pp. 47–52; Andrew Pettegree, 'Day, John (1521/2–1584)', ODNB.

The patents issued to William Seres and John Day overlapped with the patents for official church documents. Peter Blayney's succinct summary disentangles the legal printers of the catechism: 'When the ABC and the Brief Catechism were printed as parts of the Book of Common Prayer they belonged to the Royal Printer, when included in a primer they belonged to Seres, and then when printed alone they belonged to John Day'. From the end of March 1553 until Edward's death, then, the text of the *ABC with Brief Catechism* could be legally printed by seven people: the four patent holders for the *Book of Common Prayer* (Grafton, Whitchurch, Oswen and Powell), the new patentees (Day and Seres), and Wolfe (in Latin). Blayney's research brings some clarity, along with some confusion, to the publication of the psalms: 'When included in an English Bible, the Book of Psalms belonged to the patentee for that particular translation, but psalms included in the Book of Common Prayer belonged to the Royal Printer. Separate psalters in prose, and any psalms included in a primer, belonged to Seres, but metrical translations of them belonged to John Day'.[126] The Psalms, then, could be printed by any one of the above six individuals or anyone printing the unpatented Tyndale, Coverdale, Taverner, or 'Matthew' translations of the bible. Considering the metrical psalms, Edward Whitchurch – rather than John Day – was the only printer to produce Sternhold's metrical psalter, generating five new titles in 1553.[127]

The final patent awarded in 1553 was granted to Richard Tottell to print books of common law. Due mainly to the type of works he produced, Tottell was the only patentee who continued to trade unobstructed by the accession of Mary I, and his patent paid dividends. Following the patents issue, Tottell produced eleven works classified by the USTC under 'jurisprudence', immediately seizing a forty-four per cent market share.[128] Tottell had previously printed only one work, *A medicine for the soule as well as for them that be sick* (1550) before leaving the trade until his patent revived his activities. Anna Greening has asserted that Tottell was already well connected with the London legal elite but that this patent marked the beginning of an exponentially improving career that would see him thrive until the latter part of Elizabeth I's tenure.[129] Such was Tottell's rise that Sir John Baker states that this was a landmark year in the history of English law printing.[130] Baker concludes that Tottell's position was a '*de facto* monopoly', claiming that other printers withdrew from the trade, but Tottell's patent ordered this monopoly. Through this patent, the

---

126 Blayney, 'William Cecil and the Stationers', pp. 22–23.
127 USTC 504880, 504887, 504916, 515449, 515454.
128 USTC eleven of twenty-five titles in total classified as 'jurisprudence' in 1553.
129 Anna Greening, 'Tottell, Richard (*b.* in or before 1528, *d.* 1593)', ODNB.
130 John Baker, ed., *The Oxford History of the Laws of England, Vol. VI, 1483–1558*, (Oxford: Oxford University Press, 2003), p. 497.

Edwardian establishment had initiated a significant reshaping of this area of the book trade.[131]

The patents awarded to members of the printing industry in 1553 had little time to alter the English printing landscape. What is clear from their legacy, however, is that these printing patents would have made a significant impact upon the trade had they had time to take root. Tottell's patent paid dividends during Mary I's reign, whilst Day and Seres had to wait until the return to evangelicalism under Elizabeth I to reap their rewards. Patents have been shown to have been critical to the business activities of premier printers under Elizabeth and, despite few publications being completed during Edward's reign under these three patents, it would not be a stretch to say that Edward's regime initiated this process.

Another patent document that merits discussion is an unsuccessful application with an inferred date of July 1550. The *Patent Rolls* record a draft patent for Nicholas Udall with the comments 'No note of delivery' and 'No warrant indicated'.[132] Udall was a man of standing within the establishment and England's book world, having worked as lead editor for the first volume of Erasmus' *Paraphrases*. Based upon what we have seen of the politically motivated distribution of Edwardian book patents, at first glance Udall and modern historians would be forgiven for questioning why this was not enough to secure the proposed patent. Primarily, the proposed patent requested the sole right to print his English translation of Peter Martyr Vermigli's *Tractio de Eucharistia* and *Disputacio de Eucharistia*.[133] The text had been printed in a high-quality Latin edition (Reyner Wolfe, 1549), but evidently Udall believed that an English translation would be commercially viable, theologically beneficial, or both.[134]

This section of the patent, had it been processed, would have secured similar terms to those issued to Gwalter Lynne in 1547. In May 1550, Martin Micronius, a leading member of the Dutch stranger church, lamented 'Peter Martyr's book on the Lord's supper could not be printed, owing to the bishops, and those too gospellers'.[135] This publication was contentious, but its eventual publication and the patent application itself suggest another reason for the failure. The Udall application also requested permission 'to print and sell the bible in English as well in the large volume for the use of churches as in any

---

131 Baydova, Anna, 'To make a career between London and Paris. Social Networks as a basis of Renaissance book production and trade', MEMS *Working Papers, Movable Types Conference Special Edition*, 5 (2014) at: [https://www.kent.ac.uk/mems/docs/n5_memswp_Baydova.pdf].
132 PR *Edward VI*, 3, p. 315.
133 USTC 504551.
134 USTC 504325.
135 OL, 2, pp. 558–562 (p. 561).

other convenient volume'. This clause, camouflaged between two sentences relating to Peter Martyr Vermigli's works, would have infringed upon the service book patents awarded to Grafton, Whitchurch, Oswen and Powell, and it is likely the reason why the warrant was not issued.[136] Printing an edition of the bible was one thing, but producing a folio edition with sufficient skill to merit provision in parish churches was another task altogether: Udall was, after all, a scholar, not a printer. Udall did not attempt to publish a bible and was listed in no publication colophons other than the requested edition. There was no attempt by any other printer to produce Udall's translations, which were ultimately published as *A discourse or traictise wherein he openly declared his whole and determinate judgemente concernynge the sacrament of the Lordes supper.*[137]

Why Whitchurch's involvement in this project was masked is uncertain – though his initials on the title-page made this a tame attempt. His employment again raises the issue of Udall attempting to encroach upon Whitchurch's service book patent.[138] If Udall's patent had been issued, it is most likely that he would have underwritten a Whitchurch edition of the Great Bible for use in the churches, saving Whitchurch the financial outlay (and risk) of an edition that Whitchurch may have expected to be superseded. What is more, it is clear from the fact that Whitchurch printed for Udall that they shared at least a commercial – if not personal – relationship, perhaps first formed during the *Paraphrases*. In an industry so close and interconnected, this proposed patent represents a tantalising snapshot of the interconnectedness and entrepreneurial character of the Edwardian book world.

The effectiveness of patents as financial inducements varied dramatically. The lucrative service book patents awarded to Grafton and Whitchurch offered a stream of projects, keeping presses occupied and income consistent. Other patents provided little more than government distinction and the right to continue their trade activities as before. The patents issued in the latter part of Edward's tenure, in hindsight, proved to be important landmarks in English printing, reshaping genres and marking the commencement of specific individuals' ascendancy within the industry. However, whilst their legacy was influential, they had little time to affect the landscape of the Edwardian industry. Patents are considered to have been the key to success for many

---

136 Blayney, 'William Cecil and the Stationers', p. 16 suggests that 'the Udall patent was intercepted at the last minute, probably at the request of an interested party with a powerful friend'.

137 USTC 504551; Alford, *Kingship and politics in the reign of Edward VI*, pp. 122–123: This edition was dedicated to the Marquis of Northampton, William Parr – further increasing the links with the Parr family from the *Paraphrases* project.

138 HEH: 45364.

individuals within the Tudor book world, but in the reign of Edward VI, Grafton and Whitchurch held the only patent of true value. Nonetheless, Edwardian printing patents are of critical historical importance: they were the forerunners of a system of patronage and patents that would define the Elizabethan book world, despite appearing for the majority of the reign to be a continuation of Henrician practices.

The regime's religious changes created a significant amount of work for England's printers. Promoting specific individuals to royal offices provided them with work and financial security. The regime was the highest patron in the land and made meaningful contributions to the development of English printing. The increase in offices created highlights a keen interest in initiating progress in the English book world. The canonical church documents generated a vast amount of work for their printers; these projects, as we have seen, were monumental. Leveraging a legally bound market of 9,000 ensured that these were the largest projects of the reign. The printers of these works had their positions secured by royal patents, which initiated further works above and beyond even these huge projects. The Edwardian reformation was inherently linked to the canonical documents; as such, their printers were crucial to the proceedings of religious change.

Charging Richard Grafton, Edward Whitchurch, John Oswen and Humphrey Powell with disseminating their new works showed a commitment to these works, and the appointment of provincial printers to expedite the process in resistant provinces reinforces the importance attributed to the printed word. The service book patent issued to these individuals was the critical patent of the reign. Whilst the patents issued to Stephen Mierdman and Gwalter Lynne promised much, each individual made their way in the world by working above and beyond the remit of their patents. The final patents and privileges of the reign, issued to Jugge, Day, Seres and Tottell, represent the germination of the patents that would come to define the careers of some of the most influential English printers of the latter half of the century. The untimely death of the young king stalled these proceedings, but the seeds were sown during his tenure.

The Edwardian protestant regime was committed to the power of print. Its members were acutely aware of the potential of print and made sure that the overwhelming majority of the reign's publications served their ends. Members of the regime invested as patrons creating a significant body of works designed and disseminated to create conformity and uniformity in religion; they sheltered and protected printers who aligned themselves with religious reform. Print was crucial to the religious policy of the reign, and religious publications continued their overwhelming dominance of printed output in England.

CHAPTER 5

A Technical and Design Examination

It is twenty years since Andrew Pettegree asserted that it was a marked failing of studies of the English publishing industry that books are seen exclusively as texts and far too little as the products of an industrial process.[1] Printing, after all, was an industrial and commercial enterprise. Much commendable research on printing as an industrial process has been completed since Pettegree's comments, and the historiography of English printing, English religious change, and early modern English society is richer for his realisation.[2]

Hitherto, however, publications considered of particular cultural, textual, or stylistic merit have drawn a level of research disproportionate to their influence upon the wider industry. The consequence of this research is that our understanding of a small number of publications and printers far outstrips that of industry convention. Analytical study of typefaces, paper quality, and illustrations, for example, has been profitably applied to the output of John Day and John Foxe.[3] Similarly, historical research upon the *Paraphrases*

---

1 Andrew Pettegree, 'Printing and the Reformation: the English exception', in *The beginnings of English Protestantism*, eds. Peter Marshall and Alec Ryrie (Cambridge: Cambridge University Press, 2002), pp. 157–180 (p. 157), Pettegree's sentiments have been echoed by Elizabeth Evenden and Thomas Freeman, *Religion and the Book in Early Modern England: the making of John Foxe's "Book of Martyrs"* (Cambridge: Cambridge University Press, 2011), p. 1; Alec Ryrie, *Being Protestant in Reformation Britain* (Oxford: Oxford University Press, 2013), p. 292.

2 For English printing, see Peter Blayney, *The Stationers' Company and the Printers of London, 1501–1557*, 2 vols (Cambridge: Cambridge University Press, 2013); John D. Fudge, *Commerce and Print in the Early Reformation* (Leiden: Brill, 2007), p. 2. For English religious change, see Catharine Davies, *Religion of the Word: The defence of the reformation in the reign of Edward VI* (Manchester: Manchester University Press, 2002); Eamon Duffy, *The Stripping of the Altars: Traditional Religion in England, c.1400–1580*, 2nd edn (New Haven, CT: Yale University Press, 2005). For English society, see Stephen Alford, *Kingship and politics in the reign of Edward VI* (Cambridge: Cambridge University Press, 2002); Peter Marshall, *Heretics and Believers: A History of the English Reformation* (New Haven, CT: Yale University Press, 2017).

3 Elizabeth Evenden, *Patents, Pictures and Patronage: John Day and the Tudor Book Trade* (Aldershot: Ashgate, 2008); John N. King, 'John Day: master printer of the English Reformation', in *The Beginnings of English Protestantism*, eds. Peter Marshall and Alec Ryrie (Cambridge: Cambridge University Press, 2002), pp. 180–208; John N. King, 'The Light of Printing: William Tyndale, John Foxe, John Day, and Early Modern Print Culture', *Renaissance Quarterly*, 54 (2001), pp. 52–85; Elizabeth Evenden, and Thomas Freeman, 'Print, Profit and Propaganda: The Elizabethan Privy Council and the 1570 Edition of Foxe's "Book of Martyrs"', *English Historical Review*, 119, 484 (2004), pp. 1288–1307; Elizabeth Evenden, 'The Michael

of Erasmus and the Great Bible is far deeper than other contemporary publications.[4] A preoccupation with the extraordinary and the noteworthy is entirely understandable, but these isolated examples at the pinnacle of the Tudor print world need to be assessed against a surer understanding of wider industrial and material conventions.

This chapter is based on a comprehensive material bibliographical study of Edwardian output, which has revealed much about industry practices and resources. Treating books as physical artefacts provides detailed information relating to format, typefaces, illustrations, initial letters and ornaments to explore what each facet reveals of the culture and economics of the Edwardian book world. These stylistic features shed light upon how individuals' respective styles evolved, how individuals' advancements prompted imitation and the development of industry-wide, and discernibly English, print conventions and practices. The basis of evidence is drawn from the USTC database, which catalogues 1,212 titles printed in England between 1547 and 1553, 967 of which have been digitised by the invaluable resource EEBO. Thereafter, the Huntington Library collections were consulted, allowing for material bibliographical analysis of 299 books printed between 1541 and 1563.[5]

Wood Mystery: William Cecil and the Lincolnshire Printing of John Day', *Sixteenth Century Journal*, 35 (2004), pp. 383–394.

4   John Craig, 'Erasmus or Calvin? The Politics of Book Purchase in the Early Modern English Parish', in *The Reception of Continental Reformation in Britain*, eds. Polly Ha and Patrick Collinson (Oxford: Oxford University Press, 2010), pp. 39–62; John Craig, 'Forming a Protestant Consciousness? Erasmus' Paraphrases in English Parishes, 1547–1666', in *Holy Scripture Speaks: The Production and Reception of Erasmus' Paraphrases on the New Testament*, eds. Hilmar M. Pabel and Mark Vessey (Toronto: University of Toronto Press, 2002), pp. 313–359; Gretchen E. Minton, 'John Bale's *Image of Both Churches* and the English Paraphrase on Revelation', in *Holy Scripture Speaks: The Production and Reception of Erasmus' Paraphrases on the New* Testament, eds. Hilmar M. Pabel and Mark Vessey (Toronto: University of Toronto Press, 2002), pp. 291–312; David Daniell, *The Bible in English: Its History and Influence* (New Haven, CT: Yale University Press, 2003).

5   Whilst not an exhaustive sample, gathering the necessary information for all Edwardian works would extend this project beyond its current remit; nonetheless, a sufficient and representative database has been created from which findings can be extrapolated with a level of caution. This sample was developed using the Huntington Library catalogue to focus upon the London industry between 1547 and 1553. Particular attention was paid to religious publications and works produced by printers or publishers with larger numbers of titles in order to develop a more comprehensive knowledge of those individuals who had the largest bearing upon the industry.

This chapter will briefly discuss industrial innovation before addressing three key areas relating to the physical output of England's presses: design conventions, technical improvements and stylistic development. Whilst often overlapping, these areas are distinct. Industrial innovation relates to new production processes in the English context, and examples are sparse. Industrial production methods, principally presswork, typecasting, typesetting, and illustration techniques, varied little from the advent of English printing.[6] Design conventions encapsulate a wider analysis of how pages were formed, incorporating an examination of formats and the sizes of pages, text blocks, columns, and margins. Production improvements tackle issues of the quality of execution by print houses: the size, frequency and intricacy of illustrations, paper quality and variations of type, for example, would all fall under this remit. Stylistic developments consider nuances and peculiarities in presentation from one print house to the next, including variations from visual convention, development of distinctive English characteristics, and the imitation of continental print traditions.

In practice, distinctive books of this period often demonstrate progress in multiple categories at once. A publication presented in a non-conventional format and a type-fount new to the English book world would be innovative in design and stylistic terms. Equally, many visually impressive volumes, in fact, offer little in terms of industrial, design or stylistic development. Erasmus' *Paraphrases* was a fine large folio, decorated with extensive and intricate illustrations, and executed with the assuredness and quality characteristic of Whitchurch's print house. This work was one of the foremost works for production quality but broke little new ground in technical terms. The specificity of these terms must be maintained, and the parameters of these terms have guided this analysis.

Between 1547 and 1553, English print output made up significant ground on many European print centres whose output fell simultaneously.[7] Given the assessments of the technical capacity of English printers at the commencement of Edward's reign and this unexpected productivity, the question of quality of output is crucial. In terms of productivity, London climbed disproportionately, but without an improvement in quality, it could not yet be seen as a printing centre of international repute. This chapter explores whether this

---

6 Lotte Hellinga, 'Printing', in *The Cambridge History of the Book in Britain, Vol III: 1400–1557*, eds. Lotte Hellinga and J.B. Trapp (Cambridge: Cambridge University Press, 1999), pp. 65–108 (pp. 82, 108).

7 Alec Ryrie, *The Age of Reformation: The Tudor and Stewart Realms, 1485–1603* (Abingdon: Routledge, 2009), p. 140.

period of astonishing growth prompted, or was prompted by, technical and stylistic innovation or whether this increased output came at the expense of quality. Moreover, it will examine how far England's printers assimilated to European conventions, how far they advanced from early Henrician styles, and how far a distinctively English style developed in this short period of 1547–1553.

The answer to these questions, of course, can vary dramatically from project to project and from print house to print house. As with any industry, the fortunes of established companies rose and fell; new enterprises could enter the fray and achieve great success or could flounder against the surrounding competition. One of the defining paradoxes of English printing under Edward VI is that few works, if any, surpassed the quality and investment of the Great Bible, but the overall quality of industry-wide output improved. This process was encouraged by investment in new materials, the growing dissemination of second-hand illustrative materials, and more print houses offering high-quality products in line with the leading examples of English print to date. In general terms, English print culture evolved little from its Henrician roots; the majority of print houses produced few genuinely innovative products. The English market seemingly resisted originality; when printers put forth dramatic changes in the presentation, these products often failed to gain a substantial foothold. The leading printers of the reign invested more readily in new materials – indicating their commitment to investing in their careers and commercial success – and pulled the overall standards of English print culture forward. This investment, and the advancing careers of successful new entrants to the trade, introduced new materials and allowed more products from England's presses to be of a higher calibre, attaching an unprecedented number of individuals to the production of prestigious works.

1   The Henrician State of Affairs

When pre-Edwardian English printing has been considered as an industrial process, it has been found trailing behind its continental counterparts. English printers were content to purchase paper and type from continental print centres and follow continental practices in production, illustration and bookbinding.[8] Such is the perception of England's subordinate print world that

---

8   Lucien Febvre and Henri-Jean Martin, *The Coming of the Book. The Impact of Printing 1450–1800*, eds. Geoffrey Nowell-Smith and David Wootton, trans. David Gerard (London: NLB, 1976), pp. 41–43; Geoffrey Dowding, *An introduction to the History of Printing Types* (London: Wace, 1961), p. 63; Robert J.D. Harding, 'Authorial and editorial influence on luxury

Andrew Pettegree assigned the English vernacular market a place amongst the peripheral European markets of Portuguese, Polish and Czech, and labelled London's industry a satellite of the Scheldt entrepôt.[9]

The English print world remained in the shadow cast by prestigious and productive European print centres. In the decade prior to Edward's accession, Parisian print houses produced six times the number of titles of London; Lyon and Venice each produced treble, and Antwerp, Basel, Nuremberg, Strasbourg and Wittenberg each out produced the English capital. The leading typefounders, illustrators and master printers all dwelled in major continental centres. Sixteenth-century master printers such as Johann Froben in Basel (fl. 1491–1527), Robert Estienne in Paris (fl. 1555–1571) and Plantin in Antwerp (fl. 1559–1588) all had international reputations, and their products influenced their contemporaries both at home and abroad.

Seeking equivalents to these prestigious master printers in English print culture brings historians to the isles' earliest printer, William Caxton who was naturally innovative in the English context. Caxton's heirs included Wynkyn de Worde and the earliest printers for the king: William Faques, Richard Pynson, and Thomas Berthelet, before Richard Grafton's graduation to King's printer of statutes under Edward. Grafton's position among the premier printers of the English book world was secured in the Henrician years by the visually unparalleled Great Bible projects of the early 1540s, but it is critical to explore his Edwardian publications not only against this preceding standard but also against other Edwardian publications. Only through this can we see which of his Edwardian contemporaries showed signs of extraordinary skillsets, improved existing practices, and brought innovative approaches to the book world. Thereafter, scholarship follows John Day's rise to prominence, beginning in the Edwardian period and reaching its zenith in the Elizabethan years. Indisputably one of the premier printers of the Tudor age, John Day's legacy is secured primarily by his Elizabethan publications, most notably John Foxe's

---

bookbinding styles in sixteenth-century England', in *Tudor Books and Readers: Materiality and the Construction of Meaning*, ed. John N. King (Cambridge: Cambridge University Press, 2010), pp. 116–137 (p. 120).

9 Bruce Gordon, 'The Authority of Antiquity: England and the Protestant Latin Bible', in *The Reception of Continental Reformation in Britain*, eds. Polly Ha and Patrick Collinson (Oxford: Oxford University Press, 2010), pp. 1–22 (pp. 4, 22); Pettegree, 'Printing and the Reformation', p. 162, this assessment of the trade is due to England's small number of native speakers, low rates of urbanisation and implied undistinguished levels of literacy; these comments on literacy are supported by Adam Fox and Daniel Woolf, eds., *The Spoken Word: Oral Culture in Britain, 1500–1850* (Manchester, 2002), p. 7; and Richard Suggett and Eryn White, 'Language, literacy and aspects of identity in early modern Wales' in *The Spoken Word: Oral Culture in Britain, 1500–1850*, eds. Adam Fox and Daniel Woolf (Manchester: Manchester University Press, 2002), p. 66; Evenden, *Patents, Pictures and Patronage*, p. 35.

Actes and Monuments, which has a rich historiography. Day's ability to improve his technical skills over time is one of the foundation stones for his reputation, but his technical development within the Edwardian years must be compared to his contemporaries, not against his Elizabethan achievements.[10]

The importation of many technical and stylistic innovations preceded Edward's accession to the throne. The rotunda fount was introduced to English printing by Richard Pynson in 1509 (in either Pietro Griffo, *Oratio* or Savonarola, *Sermo*),[11] the italic fount in 1528 by Wynkyn de Worde's (in either Lucian's *Complures Dialogi* or Robert Wakefield's *Oratio de laudibus trium linguarum*).[12] The tertiary types used in the English book world, too, had each been employed prior to Edward's accession: schwabacher and bastarda had been used since the earliest days of English print, and Siberch's Cambridge press introduced movable greek type to the English printing industry. The typographical landscape of Edwardian print, then, was steeped in Henrician influence and made few innovations.

The introduction of metal engraving illustrations, even, is a Henrician innovation. Thomas Geminus brought copper engravings to the English market first, with his 1545 edition of *Compendiosa totitus anatomiae delineatio*, attributed to John Herford.[13] These engravings imitated the work of Jan Stephan van Calcar who had been commissioned to illustrate an edition printed by the esteemed Johannes Oporinus of Basel in 1543. It has been asserted that 'A master of ornamental design' produced the work displayed in Geminus' 1545 edition. Later, these engraving plates were deployed in Nicholas Udall's English translation of the same work, printed in 1553 by Nicolas Hill. Geminus continued to use copper engravings into the Edwardian years, including in *Morysse and damashin renewed and encreased* in 1548, and *Compendios a totius*

---

10   Ian Green, *Print and Protestantism* (Oxford: Oxford University Press, 2000), pp. 22–23; Pettegree, 'Printing and the Reformation', p. 175; For Day's technical ability improved under Elizabeth I, see Foxe's *Actes and Monuments* (USTC 506141, 506152, 509575) and Cunningham's *Cosmographical Glasse* (USTC 505579). Evenden, *Patents, Pictures and Patronage*, pp. 2, 183; Elizabeth Evenden and Thomas Freeman, *Religion and the Book in Early Modern England*, p. 112.

11   USTC 501068; 501066; Hellinga, 'Printing', p. 76.

12   David Scott Kastan, 'Print, literary culture and the book trade', in *The Cambridge History of Early Modern English Literature*, eds. David Loewenstein and Janel Mueller (Cambridge: Cambridge University Press, 2002), pp. 81–116 (p. 88); (USTC 502123); Hellinga, 'Printing', p. 78.

13   Arthur Mayger Hind, *Engraving in England in the sixteenth and seventeenth centuries. Part I: The Tudor Period* (Cambridge: Cambridge University Press, 1952), plates 17–24; USTC 503674; Hellinga, 'Printing', pp. 106–107 states that the first English edition with engravings was USTC 503194 (Thomas Raynald, 1540) though there are no engravings available on EEBO.

anatomie delineati, printed in 1553 but after Mary I's accession, by Nicolas Hill.[14] Whilst Geminus' work continued into the Edwardian period, it was not a widespread Edwardian phenomenon.[15] Metal engraving illustrations made very little progress during Edward's reign as printers showed little appetite to adopt this technical innovation.

During the reign of Henry VIII, the process of gradually importing and incorporating continental developments ensured a dependency upon the speed of progress across the Channel. Innovations within the English context were numerous, but English printers imitated rather than innovated in the context of the European book world. Whilst production figures between the Henrician and Edwardian periods are dramatically different, the material conventions of the industry are closer than we might expect. Stylistically, the late Henrician print world was already making ground on the traditional centres of European printing. Edward's reign continued this progress, but the rapidity with which the industry grew in these years belies some of the core and foundational factors that defined the appearance of English books during the Henrician 1530s–40s and the Edwardian years.

2   Design Conventions

This exploration of design conventions investigates the physical construction of books. This includes how paper was folded into quires, bound and the display of text upon the pages. This chapter will first establish the industry-wide conventions before delving more specifically into particular printers who showed signs of breaking from early English print culture customs. This section will explore design features – format, page size, text block size, lines of type per page, and the use of printed commentaries and marginalia – to construct a firmer understanding of industry-wide conventions and those printers and publications deviating from these customs. These areas highlight that Edwardian printed materials broke little ground in terms of industry-wide conventions. There were pioneering publications, but they appear both innovative and extraordinary largely because the conventions surrounding them continued.

---

14   USTC 516464; Hind, *Engraving in England*, 1, plates 25–27; USTC 504930.
15   Hind, *Engraving in England*, 1, pp. 9–10: Hind casts doubt upon whether Geminus was the true engraver of the 1545 illustrations following a decreasing level of skill being used in later publications.

A TECHNICAL AND DESIGN EXAMINATION

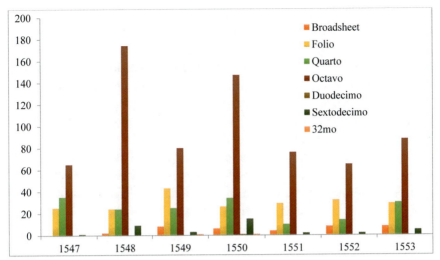

GRAPH 5.1 Format usage in English titles, 1547–1553
Note: There are eighty-seven publications in the USTC database between 1547 and 1553 not assigned a format. Fragments are often classified as 'broadsheets' so some caution must be applied to these figures.

The construction of book quires through folding sheets provided opportunities to produce books of various sizes.[16] Folding sheets in half once provided a folio, twice a quarto, three times an octavo. Octavos dominated the Edwardian print world. The two most voluminous years of title output (1548 and 1550) mirror the two years in which the octavo was most prominent and the only two years in which the market share of any format exceeded sixty per cent. In 1548, the year of most pronounced growth, the octavo format accounted for seventy per cent (174 titles) of the total output (245 titles) and almost the entirety of market growth as folio and quarto production declined. Not only did the octavo format dominate the market, but it also decided its success.

Format alone, however, can establish only a basic framework for further investigation. Oftentimes, format data has prompted broad-stroke analysis of printed output – and therefore of the character of that output – without sufficient consideration of variety within each format. Previous studies have linked format selection to readership and target audience, but this element of

---

16   For a detailed explanation and breakdown of format construction, forms and how to identify format, see Philip Gaskell, *A New Introduction to Bibliography* (Oxford: Clarendon Press, 1972), pp. 78–109, particularly figs. 46–60.

book construction can, at times, be misleading.[17] Tessa Watt's *Cheap Print and Popular Piety* champions the consideration of the amount of paper required for a publication rather than the format as a more accurate gauge, an approach that validates 'the un-literary, almost philistine, activity of mechanically counting pages to establish the likely price and audience of a book'.[18] This information provides not only an indication of the target audience but also critical information relating to the potential size of print jobs and the time and amount of work required to produce a publication.

This process, however, is hindered by two factors. First, and most significant, is the matter of print run sizes, for which evidence is endemically sparse. Historians postulate that print runs for the period averaged between 800 and 1500, potentially as high as 2000 depending on the publication in question. Larger books (bibles, chronicles, works of serious scholarship) and books for widespread use (catechisms and prayer books) were expected to have exceeded industry convention, whilst smaller works tended toward the lower end of the estimated spectrum.[19] In the case of books requiring more total sheets, of course, the amount of work added for an additional 100 books is proportionally greater than for one with fewer sheets, and inequalities in print-run sizes make Watt's practice effective only as a basic understanding. Secondly, the format and number of pages alone cannot decipher the amount of paper used. This simple multiplication of leaves/pages used against the necessary information gathered from the format provides the number of sheets used in each publication. However, printers' sheets, and therefore individual book's pages, could vary significantly in size.

Page size variation can dramatically influence the amount of paper required for any publication. The largest folio page size found within this study's Huntington Library sample was a 314 × 200mm edition of *The Workes of Chaucer* (Nicolas Hill, 1550), the smallest a 245 × 170mm edition of the *Book of*

---

17 King, 'John Day: master printer of the English Reformation', p. 185; Peter J. Thuesen, *In Discordance with the Scriptures: American Protestant Battles over Translating the Bible* (Oxford: Oxford University Press, 1999), p. 26; Pettegree, 'Printing and the Reformation', p. 160. In reaction, Joseph A. Dane and Alexandra Gillespie, 'The myth of the cheap quarto', in *Tudor Books and Readers: Materiality and the Construction of Meaning*, ed. John N. King (Cambridge: Cambridge University Press, 2013), pp. 25–45 attempts to break down scholars' assumptions of cost, size and readership drawn simply from the format.

18 Tessa Watt, *Cheap Print and Popular Piety 1550–1640* (Cambridge: Cambridge University Press, 1991), p. 262.

19 Pettegree, 'Printing and the Reformation', p. 159; Daniell, *The Bible in English*, p. 120; Elizabeth Evenden, *Patents, Pictures and Patronage*, p. 35; Fox and Woolf, *The Spoken Word: Oral Culture in Britain, 1500–1850*, p. 22; Ryrie, *Being Protestant*, p. 283.

Common Prayer (Edward Whitchurch, 1549).[20] These page area figures, in each instance, must be doubled as each page from a folio uses half a sheet of paper, allowing for two leaves (or four pages) on a single sheet. These figures, then, provide sheet areas of 125,600mm^2 and 83,300mm^2, respectively: the Chaucer sheets are fifty per cent larger than those of the *Book of Common Prayer*.[21] Even the Chaucer edition pales in comparison to the 385 × 265mm pages of the Great Bible printed for the use of parish churches in 1541.[22] The comparison of the 1541 Great Bible 770 × 530mm sheets and the 1549 *Book of Common Prayer* sheets show that the same amount of paper that produced a sheet of the 1541 Great Bible could produce 2.45 sheets of the 1549 *Book of Common Prayer*. In its simplest terms, had the *Book of Common Prayer* been printed on sheets the same size as the Great Bible, it could have been folded into quarto.

Further issues of page size variance can be seen when comparing variant formats. This 1549 *Book of Common Prayer* is only 32mm taller and 15mm wider than the largest English quarto: a 213 × 155mm English and Latin New Testament (William Powell, 1548).[23] This pattern recurs in other formats; within this sample, the largest octavo (170 × 110mm) was larger than the smallest quarto (140 × 92mm). Despite these outliers, it is important to establish some form of material convention within the industry. Ian Green has established a full-size folio as 350 × 230mm and a smaller folio at 260/280 × 170/190mm.[24] Online databases list formats but do not list sizes and, as such, the prevalence of the large folio vs smaller folio must be established. From the sample of works consulted at the Huntington, folio publications show a mean average of 281 × 188mm, quartos at 189 × 136mm, and octavos at 135 × 87mm. The median averages closely mirror the means, with 278 × 190 for folios, 192 × 136mm for quartos and 137 × 85mm for octavos. These figures suggest that sheet sizes were at least relatively stable: each format's average width would be roughly enough to incorporate the length of the smaller format, a fundamental factor in the construction of each format by equivalent folds.

---

20 One challenge for this analysis is the reliance upon extant copies. Many have been rebound and may have been trimmed. This does not affect text-block sizes but may influence margins and total page sizes. Contemporary bindings allow for greater clarification on these matters and have been sought where possible from the Huntington collection. USTC 504221.

21 (62800mm^2) × 2 and (41650mm^2) × 2.

22 (102025mm^2) × 2 = 204050mm^2.

23 The same BCP is also 15mm taller but 12mm narrower than the largest quarto examined at the Huntington, a 213 × 155mm Coverdale Bible printed between Christopher Froschauer in Zurich and Stephen Mierdman in 1550. HEH: 40533; ESTC: S122319.

24 Green, *Print and Protestantism*, p. 67.

Measurements of the text block from the highest printed point of the page (often a running header) to the lowest (often catchwords or signatures) and across the longest width (including commentaries and references) show that between sixty-eight (folio and quarto) and seventy per cent (octavo) of the page was filled with the text block. Removing the headers, commentaries and signatures from the measurements shows that between fifty-five per cent (quarto) and fifty-eight per cent (folio) of the page was assigned to the body of the core text. These figures show a strong sense of design convention within the period. The largest discrepancy by format is between the percentages of the text block made up by the body of the text, which falls from eighty-six per cent in folio down to eighty-one per cent in octavo. Whilst we might expect more comprehensive commentaries and printed marginalia in larger folios, this figure simply reflects that running headers and catchwords/signatures have a larger proportional impact upon a page with fewer lines of text.

The conventions of lines of text per page against publication format are also strong within the Huntington sample. Whilst perhaps appearing self-evident, this assumption can be problematic. The premise here, of course, rests upon the principle that each format corresponds to an 'appropriate' size of type fount, a matter which will be addressed further in the subsequent section on stylistic innovation. Nonetheless, from the sample examined, fairly stable design conventions emerge. Of the seventy-one consulted works with fewer than twenty-five lines of text in the body of the page, ninety-seven per cent were octavos (sixty-nine in total). Similarly, of the seventy works with between twenty-five and twenty-nine body of text lines, over sixty were octavos.

At the other end of the scale, the twenty publications that exhibited fifty or more body of text lines, ninety per cent were folios (eighteen in total), and the other two were quartos of international origin.[25] Moreover, in publications of over forty body of text lines, fifteen of the nineteen publications were printed in folio and the remaining four in quarto. Only within the ranges of thirty to thirty-nine lines of text is a full range of formats exhibited. Within this span, it is most informative to split the group into two categories, thirty to thirty-four and thirty-five to thirty-nine lines of text per page. Within these smaller categories, the sample shows that for publications with between thirty and thirty-four lines per page, a majority thirty-three (sixty-seven per cent) used the quarto format, and the remaining twenty-two (thirty-three per cent) used the octavo. In the range of thirty-five to thirty-nine lines per page, the folio format emerges with four of twenty titles; the quarto uses another four, whilst the octavo accounts for a further twelve.

---

25   Ibid.; USTC 206225.

The Edwardian book world was built around these relatively stable design conventions. The majority of the books produced in this period are, in design terms, what we have come to expect of a sixteenth-century book: both the number of lines per page and page sizes correspond coherently with the physical processes of book construction. There were, however, some challenges to these established protocols.

One of the more striking challenges to established design conventions was the emergence of small-format New Testaments. The process by which these formats were created ensures a significantly different material product. By folding sheets in different ways, printers produced smaller page sizes with more leaves in each gathering.

To create these format sizes, the same sheets involved for printing a larger octavo were folded again, to create a sextodecimo with thirty-two pages per sheet of paper. The duodecimo format, meanwhile, deploys a different folding technique from the onset, first folding the sheet into three in length and width, by which the final cutting of the sheet creates twenty-four pages. The lone duodecimo New Testament of this reign, along with three of the four sextodecimo New Testaments, originated from the printing house of Stephen Mierdman. In one respect, this is a matter of design evolution; in another, it is stylistic development. Prior to Edward's accession, sixty-four sextodecimo publications were produced in England, and a further thirty-six were printed during his reign. The duodecimo format, too, had appeared eighteen times from English presses during the Henrician years.

Constructing books in this manner was not a design revolution, but it certainly broke from conventional design to present scripture in this manner and therefore represents innovation within this genre. Both sextodecimo and duodecimo editions of the New Testament were new to the English book world. The first to be employed was the sextodecimo, appearing in 1548 from the print houses of Stephen Mierdman and John Herford, and later followed up by two further Mierdman editions, commissioned by publisher Richard Jugge.[26] With these four editions, the pocket-sized sextodecimo carved out a small niche in the market, a factor supported by the perception of Edward's reign as one of increased lay scripture reading and religiosity.[27]

---

26   USTC (Stephen Mierdman for Richard Jugge) 504120; 515430; ('Mierdman for John Day', actually Christopher Froschauer with preliminary leaves by Mierdman) 516499; (John Herford) 516461.
27   Ryrie, *Being Protestant*, pp. 271–275; Daniell, *The Bible in English*, pp. 245–246; 269.

The more innovative introduction was Mierdman's edition of William Tyndale's New Testament (1550), the first biblical work printed in England in duodecimo.[28] This was the only publication of Edward's reign to utilise this format and the first religious duodecimo in ten years. This work, in design terms, was a shrewd choice underpinned by solid economic considerations. Comprised of 648 pages, the duodecimo required the use of only twenty-seven sheets. This marked a significant reduction from the quarto format, which required an average of eighty-four sheets per New Testament, while Mierdman's complete octavo New Testament, from 1553, required 51.5 sheets. Mierdman also printed three of the four New Testaments published in the sextodecimo format during the period, which also averaged twenty-seven sheets of paper.[29] The duodecimo's elongated pages incorporated forty-five lines of text per page, whilst both the octavo and sextodecimo constructions include only thirty-five. Paper costs in the period were one of the largest outlays for sixteenth-century printers. Mierdman's small-format accomplishments would have reduced the price of both production and transportation and likely represent an attempt to reach a wider lay audience.[30] This innovative publication provided a valid prototype for the duodecimo as a medium for scripture, and yet the format was not used for a biblical work again until 1581 (a psalter) and was not used for a New Testament again in England during the sixteenth century.

Such limited divergence from the established design protocols of book construction during these years certainly owes something to a lack of daring and a paucity of trailblazers within the English print world. We must not, however, pin this lack of change on a collection of uninventive printers. Episodes such as this duodecimo New Testament, which failed to inspire competition or imitation, suggest that English readers were actively resistant to change. Mierdman created an alternative product with favourable financial conditions for printers (and therefore presumably readers), but the market appears to have opposed these efforts. English readers were developing a distinct taste and, with this in mind, we cannot criticise businessmen for accommodating their patrons.

Mierdman's exploits with smaller formats were innovative and unusual within the English book world. The established design conventions remained largely stable, and we must keep this in mind whilst assessing anomalies.

---

28   USTC 504521.
29   This information is gathered from the USTC and considers all small format bibles of the reign.
30   The use of the sextodecimo was a route to conserving costs: minimising illustrations and using smaller type reduced the amount of paper required; Evenden, *Patents, Pictures and Patronage*, p. 15.

Whether by printers' stubbornness or, far more likely, readers' demands, the market remained faithful to the design conventions of late-Henrician print. The Edwardian print world retained a distinctive Englishness in its products but, in design terms, this was a distinctively English character rather than a uniquely Edwardian one.

3 Technical Improvements

Many of the industrial innovations that led to improved technical assurance in English printed works occurred before Edward's accession. The 1541 Great Bible and its successors were completed to a standard with which few woodcut artists or printers in England could compete. Here, a step away from the English industry is also important. Elite print houses in internationally renowned print centres, particularly Basel, Paris, Antwerp and Venice, were showcasing products more visually impressive than any available in the English setting. Higher proficiencies and investment were yielding better material products from typesetting, formatting, fount variation, presswork, paper quality, and illustration perspectives. All in England lagged behind the European master printers. Improvements, however, could be made at different tiers in the print world and an industry-wide improvement in the quality of products did not require a ground-breaking, trade redefining product. London's print houses and their products remained imperfect; as such, this section does not seek to rebrand England on an international scale but to evaluate the Edwardian print trade in the English context.

No single publication during Edward's tenure would surpass the heights of the 1540s woodcut illustration, but through continued investment in (and the redistribution of) technical equipment, the industry at large began to close the gap between the most spectacular English publications and the routine. More so than in any preceding period, smaller printing houses began to use woodcut initials, ornaments and illustrations. One of the key measures for historians of the quality of printed material is the detail and frequency of woodcut illustrations and initials found throughout the work. In this area, continued investment from high-calibre printing houses, increasing investment from smaller enterprises, and the redistribution of illustrative equipment brought industry-wide standards to a new high.

This section will explore technical improvements both as an individual and industry-wide phenomenon. In terms of industry-wide progress, there are two critical factors we must clarify. Firstly, once a woodcut was created, it became part of the stock of one of England's printers. Whether this was a first- or second-generation owner, it was absorbed into a collective mine of resources. Secondly, if the collective resources were more widely dispersed than in previous decades, then any specific woodcut did not have to surpass the quality of all of those woodcuts preceding it to advance industry-wide standards. Comparative technical improvements in lower echelons could aid the overall industry-wide standards without necessarily challenging those in the upper reaches.

Whilst standards improved across the industry, they continued to vary dramatically from one printing house to another. Large and detailed woodcuts remained, for the most part, the preserve of the established and esteemed printing houses, which continued to invest in such marks of prestige and quality. Many of the printers of esteemed works within the Edwardian industry had roots in similar printing within the Henrician book world: Thomas Berthelet, the former King's Printer of statutes, Reyner Wolfe, and the two printers of the Great Bible, Richard Grafton and Edward Whitchurch continued their high-quality output during the Edwardian years. There was also a small number of newcomers or printers who had been involved in the Henrician industry in a more limited capacity, who sought to break into this elite and employed richly illustrated texts to make up ground. Folio and quarto bibles, as they always had in the English context, provided some of the most richly adorned and beautiful books. Editions of large-format works by rising stars such as Stephen Mierdman, Nicolas Hill and John Day drove forward technical standards, with each printer investing heavily to continue their respective rises through the ranks. These illustrations distinguished their products from their competitors, yet none of the illustrations found within the Mierdman, Hill or Day bibles could surpass the technical skill shown in the Great Bible.[31] Nonetheless, these works increased the number of individuals in the clique at the head of the English book world and thus, England could boast more accomplished printers flourishing in the capital.

It is an important realisation that woodcut quality was indicative of investment and capital rather than necessarily of skill on behalf of the printing house. Original woodcuts were commissioned from woodcut artists or purchased from existing stock within the book world, though some may have been produced 'in-house'.[32] Printing from a woodcut illustration, whether beautiful or basic, involved the same process at the press. The fact that a printing house

---

31 Hellinga, 'Printing', pp. 105–106.
32 Elizabeth Evenden, 'The Fleeing Dutchmen? The influence of Dutch immigrants upon the Print Shop of John Day', in *John Foxe at Home and Abroad*, ed. David Loades (Aldershot: Ashgate, 2004), pp. 63–77 (p. 66), states that Giles Godet was a Netherlandish emigre working in London as a 'wood engraver'.

The Gospell.

saye, he hath the deuyll. The sonne of man came eatyng and drinckyng, and they saye, beholde a glotton and drincker of wyne, and a frend vnto Publicans & synners. And f° wyse: dome is iustified of hir chyldren.

Luke.x.a Then began he to vpbrayde the cities, in whiche most of his myracles were done, because they repented not. Wo be to thee Chorasin. Wo be to thee Bethsaida: for if ye miracles which were shewed in you, had ben done in Tyre & Sydon, they had repented longe agone in sackcloth and asshes. Neuertheles I saye to you: it shalbe easier for Tyre and Sydon at the daye of iudgement, then for you. And thou Capernaum, which arte lyft vp vnto heauen, shalt be broughte downe to hell. For if the miracles which haue ben done in D thee, had ben shewed in Sodom: they had remained to this daye. Neuertheles I saye vnto you: that it shalbe easier for the land of Sodome in the day of iudgement, then for thee.

✠The Gospel on S. Mathias daye.
The wyse knew not.
Luke.x.b

At that tyme Iesus aunswered and sayed: I prayse thee O father Lorde of heauen and earth, because thou hast hid these thinges from the wise and prudente, and hast opened them vnto babes: verelye father, euen so it was thy good pleasure before thee. All thinges are geuen vnto me of my father. And no man knoweth the sonne but the g* father: neither knoweth anye man the father, saue the sonne, and he

FIGURE 5.1   Inverted woodcut: The New Testament (Richard Jugge, [1552])
NATIONAL LIBRARY OF SCOTLAND: HAX. 45

produced the most detailed and visually impressive woodcut illustrations, then, often speaks more to its capital investment than to technical proficiency. An example of this phenomenon is exposed in a 1552 New Testament where a printer's gaffe saw a woodcut printed upside down in the gospel of St Matthew.

The story of English woodcuts has largely been presented as a matter of those at the head of the industry making technical strides and pulling the industry forward. The Edwardian period, however, was quite different. Despite continuing to invest and produce high-quality illustrations, the speed of technical development in the uppermost echelons of the print world slowed. The middling individuals within the print world's hierarchy, however, were able to make up ground via continued investment in original woodcuts and an increasingly prominent trade in second-hand illustrative materials. The highest and lowliest members of the trade held their places under Edward VI, but it was those ambitious middle-tier individuals who drove forward industry-wide development and provided English readers with more high-quality print houses than ever before.

High profile publications seeking special recognition or prestige led the way in this sphere, as highly-capitalised print shops commissioned new woodcuts to secure their standing within the English printing elite. Fresh woodcuts and engravings were often exhibited first in folios or large quartos, typically bibles and New Testaments, official documents of the Edwardian church and state, histories and chronicles, and works completed in collaboration with wealthy patrons.

One of the premier examples can be found in the catalogue of works printed by Richard Grafton. Working for the most esteemed patron of them all, the King's Printer of statutes produced works for both the king and the church. Grafton and his patent-sharing business partner Edward Whitchurch were the dominant purveyors of high-quality illustrated material. Beyond the canonical church works, Grafton and Whitchurch also embarked upon several other substantial printed projects that pushed the boundaries of print quality.

Perhaps Grafton's most striking publications of the reign were his editions of Edward Hall's *The Union of the Two Noble and Illustre Families of Lancastre and Yorke*. One of the finest editions of the period, it bore all the hallmarks of a publication seeking royal approval. Following Hall's death in 1547, Grafton acted as the editor of the work, and he strove to complete the project to the best of his abilities and resources. The folio pages measure 260 × 185mm, larger than all but a handful of English books in the period.[33] Indeed, Grafton's 1548

---

33   Larger works in the Huntington sample included complete folio bibles, an edition of Thucydides' *The history of the warre, whiche was betwene the Peloponesians and*

A TECHNICAL AND DESIGN EXAMINATION   133

Edward VI (70 x 70mm)   Richard III (60 x 60mm)

FIGURE 5.2   Woodcut initials: Edward Hall, *The Union* (Richard Grafton, 1550) (USTC 504475)

Union was the largest English edition since the Great Bible in the Huntington sample. *The Union* was printed clearly and accurately in a single column of forty-five lines, in 95 textura, with a single line title header and signature on each page. Edward Hall had provided a dedication to the king, and his text lamented the 'Tragical doynges of Kynge Richard III' before showing his unwavering support for the 'governaunce politique of Kyng Henry VII' and the 'Triumphaunt reigne of Kynge Henry VIII'.

The woodcut initials used during this volume range from simple 18 × 18mm initials to magnificent heraldic dedication initials of 70 × 70mm. Many of the initials used within *The Union* came from Grafton's existing stock, but he commissioned others afresh. Each earlier monarch's reign is introduced by a slightly smaller 60 × 60mm initial, another bow to the reigning monarch. Richard III's is one of few reigns not to be introduced with a heraldic initial, speaking directly to the narrative of the Tudor claim overpowering that of the later Plantagenet monarchs, and conferring legitimacy during the king's minority.

The central woodcut title-page border of Grafton's collection depicts the young king at Court in the top compartment, shown below, and the printer's mark upon a shield held by two cherubs at the foot of the page.

---

the *Athenyans* (William Tylle, 1550), USTC 504507; Erasmus', *Paraphrases* (Edward Whitchurch, 1551), USTC 517915; Geoffrey Chaucer, *The Workes* (Nicolas Hill for William Richard Kele, Thomas Petyt, and Abraham Veale, 1551), USTC 504408, 504409, 504415, 504436; and *Concordance* (Richard Grafton, 1550), USTC 504506.

FIGURE 5.3 Head compartment of Grafton's title-page border: *A concordance* (Richard Grafton, 1550)
NATIONAL LIBRARY OF SCOTLAND: RB.M.115

The image of Edward upon the throne takes a dominant position at the centre directly above the title – a reflection of how Grafton and Whitchurch had presented Henry VIII in their 1541 edition of the Great Bible.[34] Edward is shown at the heart of a group of twenty individuals with members of the church at his right and nobles at his left, again, mirroring the Great Bible title-page imagery. Grafton used this title-page header throughout the period in editions including the *The Union* (1548), *Statutes* (1548), the *Book of Common Prayer* (1549) and the *Concordance* (1550), highlighting that printers of the period would recycle their woodcuts, particularly those which associated their products with powerful patrons.[35] Grafton held on to this woodcut, despite commissioning a new and more elaborate woodcut border for the subsequent 1550 edition of *The Union*, which was designed specifically for the purpose and portrayed the topic of the work itself.

The new edition of *The Union* also includes a full-page engraving of Edward's father at court on the verso facing the colophon and printer's mark.[36] The engraving, signed 'IF' for Jacque le Fevre, measures 205 × 135mm, and sits above the words 'God save the Kyng'.[37] This was an astute move by the printer, as it furthered his association with the late king – and therefore successive

---

34 Border matching HEH: 61300; image taken from the NLS copy of *The Concordance* (Richard Grafton, 1550) (NLS: RB.m.115); *P&PD* 110.
35 USTC 504506, (HEH: 20891); 516510 (62285); 504006 (61078).
36 HEH: 47767, This image is taken from the NLS copy.
37 Hind, *Engraving in England*, 1, plate 8; Ruth Samson Luborsky Elizabeth Morley Ingram, eds., *A Guide to English Illustrated Book 1536–1603*, 2 vols (Temple, AZ: Arizona Centre for Medieval and Renaissance Studies, 1998), 1, p. 422.

A TECHNICAL AND DESIGN EXAMINATION 135

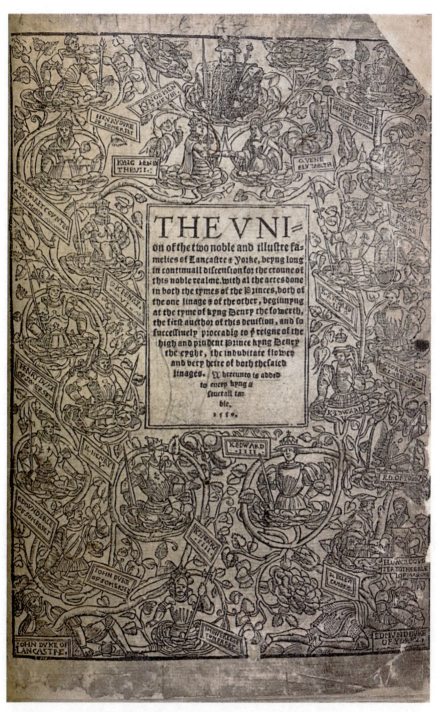

FIGURE 5.4 Edward Hall, *The Union* (Richard Grafton, 1550)
NATIONAL LIBRARY OF SCOTLAND: C.7.B8; MCKERROW & FERGUSON 75

FIGURE 5.5
Illustration of 'John Wycliffe'
THE HUNTINGTON LIBRARY:
30710, USTC 504508, FOL. 2

Tudor monarchs – which conveyed a unique prestige to his works. Grafton employed this tactic repeatedly during the period.[38]

Grafton's high-quality new woodcuts did not end with *The Union*. He continued to invest heavily in this area, ensuring that his output was visually striking and completed with a technical assurance rivalled by few in England. There is evidence to suggest, however, that he was also acquiring woodcuts from established printers. Grafton printed a portrait of the newly adopted martyr John Wycliffe in the preface to his edition of Purvey's *True Copye of a Prolog* by Wycliffe, which he printed on behalf of, and in the name of, Robert Crowley.[39]

This woodcut was first employed in 1530 in the Antwerp printing house of J. Hoochstraten, in *A compe[n]dious old treatyse, shewing, howe that we ought to haue the scripture in Englysshe*, before passing to Derek van der Straten, who also produced English-language works for clandestine export.[40] Van der

---

38 Along with the small printer's device at the foot of the title-page, Grafton also printed a 145 × 105mm woodcut on the final recto of the edition. This woodcut was employed in other Grafton editions before 1553. A second printer's device was used in smaller works including USTC 504671 (HEH: 69748), 504702 (59433) 504619 (35272).

39 USTC 504508 (HEH: 30710).

40 USTC 410237.

Straten employed this woodcut in the prefatory matter to John Bale's *Illustrium Maioris Britanniae scriptorum* ([Wesel, 1549]).[41] The woodcuts purchased from the Continent were not all commissioned new: the second-hand trade was also international.

The second-hand trade in illustrative materials allowed a broader spectrum of printers to improve their products. Purchasing second-hand material would undoubtedly reduce the cost of procuring woodcuts, allowing the industry-wide standard of English printing to improve. This trickle-down of resources disseminated them across a wider number of printing houses than those who were actively commissioning new initials, illustrations or title-page borders. The fact that these resources were being acquired by second, third, and fourth printers by legal means is suggested in no small part by the size of the English industry. Whilst imitations and pirate copies of illustrations can be seen in the engravings of Thomas Geminus and many continental editions of the period, this was chiefly a concern for the international book world, where the ability to regulate (or interest in regulation) spanned different jurisdictions and fell to each respective legislative body. The English print world remained small and largely inward facing. In the same way that the English authorities would have been able swiftly to recognise the typefaces, illustrations and ornaments within any illicit materials, the printers themselves would have known that any level of theft or unauthorised use of another printer's patented material could be swiftly identified.[42]

Until a successful method of visual recognition software is added to the principal databases of digital copies of publications, the second-hand trade in woodcuts is most effectively explored by tracing a series of woodcuts first found in prominent publications or through title-page borders. This method allows historians to rest upon two invaluable resources: Luborsky and Ingram's *A Guide to English Illustrated Books 1536–1603* and McKerrow and Ferguson's *Title-Page Borders Used in England & Scotland 1485–1640*.[43] These databases have explored illustrations of the period with sufficient scrutiny to allow for conclusions to be drawn with relative conviction.[44] Personal associations within the industry, too, often highlight paths by which these woodcuts were

---

41   USTC 665137, 665413; van der Straten printed twenty-three titles between 1543 and 1554 from his Wesel press: nine (all before 1548) were in English; he printed seven Latin and five Dutch works between 1547 and 1554.
42   Pettegree, 'Printing and the Reformation', p. 167.
43   Luborsky and Ingram, *A Guide to English Illustrated Books*; M&F.
44   Due to the number of texts to examine, precision beyond these databases falls outside of the current remit of this study.

transferred from one printer to the next. These personal associations, alongside the ease with which the English print world could be controlled, suggests that a physical displacement of resources rather than underhand imitation was occurring.

The Tyndale bible published by Matthias Crom at Antwerp for Richard Grafton and Edward Whitchurch in 1537 employed ninety-one woodcuts, and yet its illustration legacy is limited.[45] Crom passed at least four of these illustrations to Stephen Mierdman when the latter, having married Crom's daughter, assumed control of his business after Crom's retirement.[46] Mierdman used them in two publications in 1549 and 1552.[47] Thereafter, a decade passes before R. Harrison employed two of those same four and another of Crom's woodcuts. The next known use was not for another decade when Richard Jugge employed the same four that had passed to Mierdman between 1572 and 1574. Finally, the assigns of Christopher Barker used these same four illustrations in 1578. The pattern of usage for these woodcuts suggests that the most likely passage of ownership is a simple transaction from each printer to the next. In contrast, the illustrations of the Great Bible, printed first by François Regnault at Paris for Grafton and Whitchurch in 1539, passed into their publishers' hands. It is known that Grafton and Whitchurch moved the operation to London before its completion, and the woodcuts were part of this repatriation.[48] Either Grafton or Whitchurch continued to utilise these woodcuts until at least 1549, and they largely stayed with these owners.

The 1535 Coverdale bible, meanwhile, has a remarkable illustration legacy.[49] The publication's sixty-four woodcut illustrations were sold, inherited or otherwise acquired by many printers and remained in use for twenty-five years. The illustrations appear to have been acquired first by James Nicolson, who utilised all but one between 1535 and 1538 and loaned one to Thomas Gibson in 1537.[50] Thereafter, upon Nicolson's withdrawal from the industry, John Mayler employed at least twenty-nine of them, including at least one of these

---

45   USTC 410342.
46   Willem Heijting, 'Mierdman, Steven [*pseud.* Niclaes van Oldenborch] (*c.*1510x12–1559)', ODNB.
47   USTC 504300, 504760.
48   Daniell, *The Bible in English*, pp. 200–203.
49   Luborsky and Ingram, *Guide to English Illustrated Books*, pp. 85–92.
50   Nicolson: USTC 518577, 502736, 502912, 516385, 516386, 516387. This woodcut was more likely loaned than sold to Gibson, it was one used by Mierdman in 1549 and had acquired woodcuts from Mayler, and potentially more which Nicolson had not sold to Mayler.

A TECHNICAL AND DESIGN EXAMINATION 139

FIGURE 5.6
Illustration of St John:
Miles Coverdale (ed.),
The Bible (Cologne:
[Eucharius Cervicornus
and Johann Soter], 1535)
(USTC 502736;
also 504165)
NATIONAL LIBRARY OF
SCOTLAND: CWN.45

twenty-nine illustrations across nine of his editions between 1542 and 1546.[51] During the Edwardian period, Richard Grafton used four of the Coverdale bible illustrations (plates 57, 59, 60, 62, depicting the four evangelists) in four editions between 1548 and 1549.[52]

---

51   There are two 'Nicolson' editions from 1540 (both Thomas Becon) and the Coverdale Psalms in 1549, but Nicolson printed nothing in the four-year interim between each of these works and his 1539 editions. Mayler: USTC 503300, 503293, 503392, 503388, 503395, 503435, 503385, 503698; Mayler also acquired a 77 textura, a 54 textura from Nicolson. Peter Blayney has also traced a path of woodcuts from Nicolson to Mayler and later to Scoloker USTC 503980, 503904, 503831; Blayney, *The Stationers' Company*, pp. 646–647.
52   USTC 504031, 504032, 504267, 517964.

It is possible that Grafton acquired these illustrations from Nicolson directly, as no Mayler publication ever utilised them and, thus, there is no evidence he ever owned them.[53] After Grafton, these four images passed to Stephen Mierdman – who had since, or in this same transaction, acquired twenty-five of the original woodcut illustrations from the Coverdale bible, thirteen of which had been used by Mayler. Mierdman made use of these twenty-five woodcuts in his 1549 'Matthew' bible. Again, as neither Mayler nor Grafton used sixteen of the Coverdale woodcuts used by Mierdman, the exact circumstances of his acquisition of these particular woodcuts remain ambiguous. Mierdman used the images of the four evangelists in a joint project with Whitchurch and Nicolas Hill for an edition of the Great Bible in 1553 and in a New Testament printed for Richard Jugge, before Jugge took ownership and used them (along with John Cawood) in four editions of Elizabethan acts of parliament in 1559.[54]

Meanwhile, in 1549, John Day and William Seres employed an illustration of the 'Death of Absalom' from the same 1535 Coverdale bible in two titles of John Cheke's *The hurt of Sedition*.[55] No use of this woodcut is known since Nicolson's 1537 Coverdale bible. How this woodcut came to pass to the Day/Seres partnership is, again, uncertain.[56] In the Elizabethan period, Day employed two further 1535 Coverdale bible illustrations in Morwen's translation of the *History of the latter tymes of the Jewes* and the *Workes* of Thomas Becon.[57] Stephen Mierdman had previously obtained these two woodcuts, having used them in the 'Matthew' bible of 1549. The passage of these woodcuts to Day could have been through direct transfer (he and Mierdman collaborated during Edward's reign) or may have taken the route of plates 57–60, via Richard Jugge and John Cawood during the Marian period.[58]

---

53   We also know from that Grafton and Whitchurch acquired some typefounts previously used by the Nicolson within this period some of which were employed by Mayler (54 textura), but others that were not (95 and 78 texturas) lending credence to the idea that materials could have been sold in separate transactions. See stylistic development section below for information on the second-hand type trade.
54   STC: 2091, 9458, 9459, 9459.3, 9459.5; HEH: 96524, 59951.
55   STC: 5109 & 5109.5.
56   It is, however, known that Day printed a work published by T. Gibson in 1548, and it may be through some association thereof; I. Gadd, 'Gibson, Thomas', ODNB.
57   STC: 14795 & 1710.
58   It is likely that Mierdman passed on the woodcuts to Jugge, who in turn passed them on to Cawood. Mierdman printed two editions of Jugge's Tyndale Bible with these woodcuts. STC: 2873.7. Jugge also acquired some biblical woodcuts from Mierdman that had been used by Matthias Crom in 1537.

This fascinating legacy of the Coverdale bible illustrations reveals many of the frustrations of the study of early modern printing. The scarcity of tangible evidence makes definitive conclusions difficult to form. Nonetheless, this lack of clarity tells us much about English print culture. It highlights that printers cared little for consistency or retaining a set of woodcuts to use together. Coverdale woodcuts 57 (Matthew), 59 (Mark), 60 (Luke) and 62 (John) were the only collection that provided continuity in appearance for their owners (Nicolson, Grafton, Mierdman, Jugge and Cawood), whom each employed them as a set. In total, this set of four images of the evangelists was utilised together on fourteen separate titles within the sixteenth century, with three of the four deployed on three further occasions.

Whilst design features highlighted that English readers were attached and committed to conventions within the industry, the use of illustrative material was a distinct phenomenon. The printer's stock was a resource to be mined whenever possible, and these illustrative devices could be used in any number of scenarios.[59] The deeper we delve into the distribution and use of illustrations in this period, the more apparent this becomes. The following sections will further explore the realities of woodcuts as multi-purpose illustrative objects that printers used whenever they could be accommodated.

4 Woodcut Title Borders and Initials

Freshly commissioned woodcuts, particularly elaborate borders, were an expensive outlay. Printers in the lower echelons of the English print world tended towards not only more straightforward designs – which woodcut artists of lesser ability could produce at a smaller fee – but also woodcut borders of less specificity. The title-page commissioned by Grafton for the second edition of the *Union* provided little opportunity for recycled use: its theme was inextricably linked to that single publication. For the majority of publications (and the majority of printing houses), this was not a sustainable model. For publications of lesser grandeur and lesser political importance, printers favoured generic borders, which could be reused for various purposes. This is a particularly valuable realisation when it comes to the second-hand trade. Generic borders of myriad sizes and levels of detail were passed through legacies, loans and sales between the tradesmen, and this trickle-down process stimulated the general standard of English products. Thus, woodcut title-page borders

---

59 Joseph A. Dane, *What is a book? The study of Early Printed Books* (Notre Dame, IN: University of Notre Dame Press, 2012), p. 128.

had 'careers' of their own. Many of the woodcut title-page borders found in Edwardian works changed hands, moving from print-house to print-house before, during and beyond Edward's reign. There are clear instances of title borders changing hands permanently, but others where they were loaned and returned.

Historians of the English print world are indebted to R.B. McKerrow and F.S. Ferguson, whose *Title-Page Borders Used in England & Scotland 1485–1640* is foundational to any research into stylistic and technical development. For Edward VI's reign, fifty-one unique woodcut title-page borders are highlighted across 233 publications, being used between them by twenty-eight printing houses. McKerrow and Ferguson's analysis and attribution of texts to specific print houses have been much amended by subsequent research involved in compiling the STC, ESTC and USTC. Thirty-one from McKerrow and Ferguson's total fifty-one woodcut title-page borders utilised within Edward's reign were first employed during the Henrician period. This majority immediately implies a substantial inheritance of style and design from preceding decades. The industry was, however, developing and maturing in this area and patterns of woodcut usage and distribution across the industry-at-large emphasise that this was an area of significant development from Henrician production.

In the year of Edward's accession, three new woodcut title-page borders were printed for the first time in England, procured and utilised by Richard Grafton (*M&F* 63), John Day (*M&F* 65), and one other print house (*M&F* 55).[60] Each of these woodcuts was sufficiently generic to be used in multiple publications during the Edwardian years. This was no doubt an active choice by each printer.

Grafton, one of the most affluent of Edwardian printers, maintained ownership of *M&F* 63 throughout these years, using it in 1547, 1549 and 1553. In contrast, John Day later shared the use of his freshly-commissioned woodcut with William Tylle in 1549 and Richard Jugge in 1550. Day had links to both Tylle and Jugge in his wider activities in the industry, and it seems he only loaned this border, as he had recovered it by at latest 1553 when he deployed it again. *M&F* 55, in contrast, has an uncertain origin. The three publications for which it was used in 1547 emerged from three different printing houses, William Myddleton, William Powell and a collaborative project by Thomas Raynald and William Hill. From 1548 onwards, this woodcut was in the ownership of William Powell, and it is possible that he commissioned the border. It is most likely, however, that William Myddleton – the successor to Robert Redman's law printing

---

60   *M&F* 55 was used in 1547 by three different print houses: William Myddleton, William Powell and William Hill.

business, who used three different woodcut borders within this year – commissioned this woodcut. Myddleton died in 1547, and two of his other woodcuts (*M&F* 7; *M&F* 8) moved from Myddleton's stock to William Powell.[61] The transition of materials from Myddleton to Powell occurred as Powell married the widowed Elizabeth Myddleton and assumed control of the business. It, therefore, seems most logical that William Hill borrowed the cut from Powell, as it was returned to him before he made use of it in twelve further publications between 1549 and 1553. This woodcut border was the most frequently appearing border of the Edwardian period, noted in twenty-two extant publications.

Like the printed output for the year, 1548 was a bumper year for woodcut artists. English printers deployed seven new title-page borders in 1548. Individuals at the pinnacle of the industry were the major investors in new woodcuts in this year: Grafton (*M&F* 61 and 67), Whitchurch (*M&F* 68), Reyner Wolfe (*M&F* 66) and Nicolas Hill/Gwalter Lynne (*M&F* 71). When examining the works in which these woodcuts were printed, it is clear that some of these projects were considered to be particularly worthy of investment. Nicolas Hill printed an English translation of the *Catechism* of the archbishop of Cologne, Hermann von Wied (which was attributed to Archbishop Cranmer as he authored the preface to the work) for his publisher Gwalter Lynne.[62] This edition also included a woodcut following the title-page of Edward VI presenting the bible to bishops and nobles, attributed to the 'School of Holbein'.[63] Edward Whitchurch was commencing the first volume of Erasmus' *Paraphrases* (one of the canonical works of the Edwardian reformation); Richard Grafton produced the inaugural edition of Hall's *The Union*; and both Grafton and Reyner Wolfe produced editions of Lord Protector Somerset's *An espistle or exhortacion to unitie and peace*: Grafton's in English, and Wolfe's in Latin. These titles each represented an opportunity for the printers to earn prestige whilst proving their alignment with the new establishment. The only two freshly-commissioned woodcuts from this year not to fit this mould were those commissioned by John Day and William Seres (*M&F* 64 and 69). Still relative newcomers to the trade, Day and Seres were building their enterprise and favoured more generic styles instead; it was not until 1550 that Day commissioned a woodcut of the calibre that we now expect in hindsight. Nonetheless, their investment in these two woodcuts proved enduring: they were used in nineteen and seven titles respectively

---

61 *M&F* 7 was used in 1547 by Myddleton, then in 1552 by Powell; *M&F* 8 by Myddleton in 1547 before Powell in 1548.
62 The theological alignment of the edition soon proved compromising for England's prelate, who rapidly sought to distance himself from the project, see Diarmaid MacCulloch, *Thomas Cranmer: A Life* (New Haven, CT: Yale University Press, 1996), pp. 386–390.
63 Hind, *Engraving in England*, 1, plate 10a.

between 1547 and 1553, either during their partnership or subsequently in Day's solo products. It is noteworthy that as the octavo showed a new level of dominance over the English market in 1548, four of the seven woodcut borders commissioned in this year were employed first in octavos (M&F 61, 64, 69, 71). Whilst landmark publications were considered to be more deserving of freshly-commissioned borders, and printers were often content to use their existing stock for octavos, two of these four were the first Day/Seres borders, and Hill's was also a first octavo commission; with the octavo so dominant in the market, it made sense for these printers to have a readily-available octavo border.

Between 1549 and 1553, the flow of original woodcut title-page borders slowed. Only six new borders emerged between these years: three first used by Reyner Wolfe (M&F 72, 73 and 77), one by Tylle (M&F 74), one by Grafton (M&F 75) and another by Day (M&F 76). Wolfe commissioned two relatively basic octavo borders but his third, designed for Cranmer's *A Defence*, was striking. Richard Grafton's commission in 1550 was the richly detailed border for the second edition of *The Union*. John Day's rise to prominence is cemented in 1551 with his 251 × 143mm title border, which incorporated the iconic phrase 'Arise for it is Day' in the foot piece of a folio edition of the bible.[64] Three of these borders fit the conventional mould for freshly-commissioned woodcuts perfectly: they were specifically designed for prestige editions, designed to catch the eye and signify the importance of the work to the reader.

Given the financial implications of commissioning a new woodcut, it is perhaps surprising that a printer whose name appears in only two colophons shown by the USTC should have deployed the largest woodcut title border of the period. According to the USTC, William Tylle printed only a quarto Tyndale New Testament in 1549 and Thucydides' *History of the Peloponesian War* in 1550, though Peter Blayney has since linked Tylle to a second New Testament, in octavo.[65] For his first publication, Tylle utilised a woodcut title border that had been commissioned by John Day in 1547 for his edition of Anthony Cope's *A Godly Meditacion upon the xx select psalmes of David*, and also used in an edition of *The comparison betwene the antipus and antigraphe* in 1548, before being passed to Tylle in 1549. Identified as both a witness and an overseer to Tylle's will, proved in July 1551, John Day clearly held more than a simple commercial relationship with Tylle. Day recovered this woodcut border – despite it having passed through the print house of Richard Jugge either en route to or following a return from Day – so it is reasonable to assume this was loaned to Tylle rather

---

64   USTC 504663.
65   USTC 516384; Blayney, *The Stationers' Company*, pp. 631, suggests this is misattributed by the STC.

A TECHNICAL AND DESIGN EXAMINATION

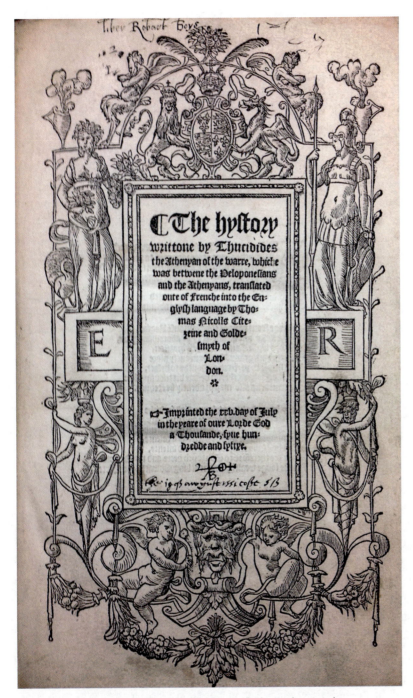

FIGURE 5.7 Thucydides, *the hystory of the warre, whiche was betwene the Peloponesians and the Athenyans* ([William Tylle], 1550)
USTC 504547; NATIONAL LIBRARY OF SCOTLAND: K.15.B

than sold. For his second publication, however, Tylle showcased a woodcut new to the English print world: a 298 × 160mm enclosing 133 × 69mm border, which is the largest deployed by any Edwardian printer.[66] Indeed, this border was too large for the pages of the vast majority of Edwardian publications.[67]

McKerrow and Ferguson's assignment of this border's first use to Tylle, however, is questionable due to the prominence of the initials 'E.R.' that frame the border in its side columns. The English book world up to this point shows no trace of an appropriate printer by the initials 'E.R.' to which this woodcut could be attributed. As we have seen from Grafton's acquisition of the Wycliffe woodcut, the market for illustrative devices could be international, and it is most likely that Tylle acquired the woodcut border from abroad. Peter Blayney's research into Tylle has suggested that he was a man of some means. These findings account both for Tylle's fleeting involvement within the trade working only on prestigious projects and, perhaps, for the capital invested in commissioning the largest woodcut of the period for a work that could hardly be expected to have been widely popular or fast-moving stock.

Freshly-commissioned woodcuts indicate a printer's preparedness to invest in materials for upcoming work or works. These twenty woodcut borders, however, tell only part of the story. A further thirty-one woodcuts had roots in the Henrician industry, and other methods existed for creating borders that would not warrant inclusion in McKerrow and Ferguson's study, including patchworks of ornaments to frame the title-page text. These existing woodcut borders created a thriving second-hand market already in place before Edward's reign, but the frequency with which borders changed hands increased, which allowed a greater number of printers to employ such devices, and a great number of publications to bear them.

One of the most widely used woodcut title-page borders during the Edwardian period was a 104 × 64mm encompassing 67.5 × 36mm border for octavos (*M&F* 33).[68] Originally employed by Thomas Gybson and John Nicholson in the 1530s, this border was subsequently used by John Mayler and Henry Smyth in the late Henrician years, before being acquired by the Netherlandish émigré Nicolas Hill. Having first used the woodcut in 1546, Hill deployed it again in 1548, 1550, 1552 and 1553, establishing that, at this stage, he was the principal owner. During Edward's reign, Hill's woodcut was also used by five other printing houses or publishers: Whitchurch (1547 and [1550]); William Powell (1548),

---

66   *M&F* measures this border: 295 × 162.
67   The Huntington Sample includes only nine books with pages large enough for this border.
68   *M&F* 33; USTC (Whitchurch) 516450; (Whitchurch for J. Turke) 504498; (Powell) 504142; (Thomas Raynald for John Wyght) 504236; (Copland for Walley) 516485; (Seres) 504645.

A TECHNICAL AND DESIGN EXAMINATION

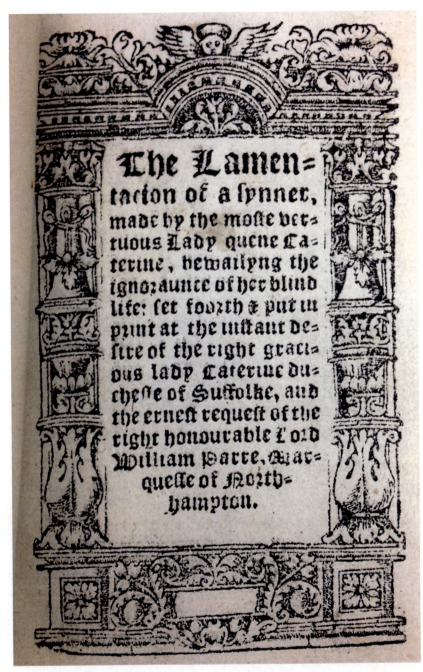

FIGURE 5.8 Octavo border, used 1530–1553: Katherine Parr, *The Lamentacion of a Synner* (Edward Whitchurch, 1548)
THE HUNTINGTON LIBRARY: 349595; MCKERROW AND FERGUSON 33

[Thomas Raynald for] John Wyght ([1549]), William Copland (1550), and John Kingston and Henry Sutton ([1553]).[69]

Hill is sure to have received some form of remuneration from printers borrowing his woodcut, and it likely served as a useful (albeit minor) source of income whilst the woodcut would otherwise have been gathering dust in the corner of his print house. This woodcut border was used for seventeen publications in the Edwardian period alone and fifty-five titles in total. As the border is appropriately sized for an octavo volume, we can conservatively estimate that print-run sizes for publications would be at the smaller end of our estimated spectrum, which would help prolong the life of the woodcut.

The process of printers both adding to their stock and simultaneously reusing existing equipment can be seen in a curious case of Nicolas Hill's edition of *The Workes* of Chaucer in 1550. Hill acquired this border via either John Byddell or John Wayland, whom both deployed it during 1539, after acquiring it from James Nicolson.[70] Hill first exhibited the border in 1547 in a quarto edition of the *Salesbury Bible*, printed for John Walley, and next in a 1549 quarto of Bernardino Ochino's *A Tragoedie or Dialoge* printed for Gwalter Lynne. In each of these instances, this 176 × 120mm border filled most of the page.[71]

Two years later, however, Hill employed the same title border upon a folio edition of Geoffrey Chaucer's *Works*, printed for a syndicate of publishers including Thomas Petyt, William Bonham and Richard Kele, which is further explored below in chapter seven.

Instead of framing the page, the border is employed at the centre of a 315 × 200 mm page, creating an initial impression that the work might have been cobbled together from existing parts.[72] To an extent, this is true. A syndicate of publishers funded the publication, and it may well be the case that the collective of publishers behind the project would not fund a freshly-commissioned woodcut, and Hill was unwilling to invest heavily with his commercial margins already cut. Moreover, this border consisted of four composite pieces; for example, the side columns are used to frame a freshly commissioned illustration to accompany the 'knyghtes tale'. With movable parts, extending the columns with additional pieces would have been a relatively small expense to fill more of the title-page. Nonetheless, this substantial folio volume of over

---

69 John Kingston and Henry Sutton may have acquired the border in the Marian period.
70 *M&F* 38; Byddell likely used the woodcut first as Hill's 1548 publication was printed for publisher Wayland. William Salesbury, *A dictionary in Englyshe and Welshe* (N. Hill for J. Wayland, 1547) USTC 515066.
71 Bernardino Ochino, *A Tragoedie or Dialoge* (Nicolas Hill for Gwalter Lynne, 1549) HEH: 30116; USTC 504308.
72 USTC 504408, 504409, 504415, 504436; *M&F* 38.

A TECHNICAL AND DESIGN EXAMINATION 149

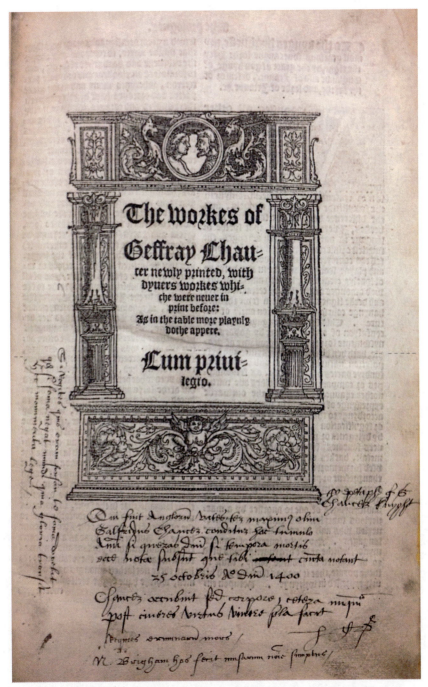

FIGURE 5.9 Quarto border on folio: Geoffrey Chaucer, *The Works* (Nicolas Hill [for the Paul's Cross publishing syndicate], 1550)
USTC 504408, 504409, 504415, 504436

350 leaves boasts high-quality illustrations, initials, and frames throughout and certainly exceeds expectations following the underwhelming title border.

The Workes of Chaucer surpasses its humble title-page border, but this principle was also displayed in reverse. The quality and assurance displayed by woodcut title-page borders did not necessarily indicate the level of illustrations or the financial outlay for each work in question. Often, a title border would be the sole illustration used, presumably in a bid to catch the eye of patrons or purchasers. In any instance where that printer was not using the title-page border for the first time, the illustration had already simply become part of their stock, and the only potential cost of re-use was that the woodcut would be worn away more rapidly.

Whilst woodcut title borders and illustrations have been shown to move through the capital and the provinces' print houses, nowhere is this phenomenon more visible than with illustrative initials. Here, without consulting each page of each publication from the period, a comprehensive analysis of any initial's exact 'career' is difficult to trace. Woodcut initials were not used in uniform sets; only rarely would a single woodcut initial size be standardised within any publication. Initials of multiple sizes often appear in one text, and there are many examples of over five and up to ten different sizes of woodcut initials being employed within a single edition.[73] Richard Grafton deployed three different initial 'W's within two leaves – two woodcuts and one type – in his 1549 edition of *The Ordinal*.[74] Grafton is likely to have only owned one of each initial, so once set for a page, it could not be set again for the same sheet, but seemingly it was adjudged to be more important to show off more initials than to maintain a matching style. The aesthetic continuity that we now expect of printed material was not cemented in the sixteenth-century print world.

The scale of stock that premier printing houses held allowed this variety, which distinguished their products from others on the market, and aided the process of constructing page layout, as initials could be exchanged to account for the space required to be filled. Despite these benefits, England's premier printing houses were rarely territorial regarding their smaller woodcuts. Naturally, landmark and exceptionally detailed woodcuts were retained more frequently than those smaller styles, which required smaller outlays. As a result, some of the most striking woodcut initials of the period are used in very few publications. Some of the largest and most outstanding within the Huntington collection have already been shown from Grafton's publication

---

[73] USTC 504155, 504300, 504776, 504803, 516510, 516510 for six printers using five or more variants in one publication.

[74] USTC 518597, leaves g4v. and h1r.

A TECHNICAL AND DESIGN EXAMINATION 151

FIGURE 5.10
Initials from *Book of Common Prayer*
(Richard Grafton, 1552)

of *The Union*, and he also included an array of finely executed initials in the *Concordance* (1550) and his *Books of Common Prayer* (1549 and 1552) with Edward Whitchurch. Though visually impressive, these initials were not breaking new ground for either printer.[75] Each had played a pivotal role in the Great Bible projects of the Henrician 1540s, which too had boasted some magnificent title-pages, illustrations and initials.

Whitchurch's publications during the Edwardian years maintained a comparable standard of woodcut initials to those shown in the Great Bible, and many of them maintained a similar style and character. He continued to use many of the same styles, commissioned woodcut initials afresh, and shared some of the Great Bible initials with other printers either by loan or resale. One of Whitchurch's more noteworthy publications in this regard highlights how some woodcut initials were guarded in this period.

In 1550, Whitchurch deployed the shown woodcut initial alphabet edition of Vigo's *The most excelent worckes of chirurgery* (Figure 5.11). Although significantly less detailed than many of his others, this set was distinct in style and the reverse of the convention. Rather than the typically paper-coloured letter within a printed background, this alphabet maintained the letter as the inked and impressed section of the initial. Despite not being the grandest or most beautiful initials, these pieces initials were found nowhere else within the Huntington sample. Whether Whitchurch was personally more territorial regarding his woodcuts is unclear; he alone used two of his woodcut title borders, including the border he commissioned for the *Paraphrases*. Whitchurch may have been more reluctant to engage with this portion of the trade than many of his contemporaries; only once did he loan a woodcut title-page border to another printer without reclaiming it later in the reign.

For smaller and less unique woodcut initials, however, a far greater level of mobility is shown. Richard Grafton's 1549 editions of the *Ordinal* and the *Book of Common Prayer* include many woodcut initials, both great and small. Some are directly traceable through other leading printing houses, including those run by John Day and William Seres, William Powell and Stephen Mierdman. If indeed Whitchurch was more territorial with his illustrative materials, then it is possible that his co-patent holder was the conduit through which these illustrations were passed to London's wider printing community.

---

75   Woodcuts from this range are also used in USTC 516510, leaf A1r; USTC 504506, Leaf a2r.

FIGURE 5.11
Giovanni da Vigo, *The most excelent worckes of chirurgery* (Edward Whitchurch, 1550)
THE HUNTINGTON LIBRARY: 60096

FIGURE 5.12   23 × 23mm 'I'
NATIONAL LIBRARY OF SCOTLAND: C7.B8

This 23 × 23mm 'I' initial was one of the most mobile of Edwardian woodcuts.[76] Following its use in Grafton's *Ordinal*, it was used by Stephen Mierdman in 1549, before passing to William Powell during 1549 and 1550, before being moved again to John Day, who used it in at least four different titles during 1550. Grafton appears to have reclaimed the initial in 1550; he deployed it in his edition of Hall's *The Union*. Following its use in 1550 by John Day, this initial was not found in any other publications produced between 1550 and 1551 within the Huntington sample. By at latest 1552, however, it had been returned to the printing house of William Powell, who used it in Boorde's *The Breviary of Healthe*. Grafton, it seems, did not forget the initial and he too utilised it in 1552 in editions of Caius' *Boke against the sweating sickness* and Thomas Wilson's *The rule of reason*. The exact passage of this initial through these print houses remains unclear. The fact that this small and simple woodcut changed hands a minimum of four times within four years highlights the mobility of these illustrative materials in the Edwardian book world.

---

76   Image from the NLS copy of ESTC: S120059; HEH: (Grafton) 61102, 79924, 59433; (Mierdman) 62185; (W. Powell) 96531, 486008, 12855; (Day) 447795, 230049, 69482.

A TECHNICAL AND DESIGN EXAMINATION 155

FIGURE 5.13   23 × 23mm 'T'
NATIONAL LIBRARY OF SCOTLAND: C7.B8

Despite being only 23 × 23mm, this initial 'T' appeared in many prestigious texts, including Grafton's *Books of Common Prayer* and Whitchurch's second volume of Erasmus' *Paraphrases*, but this is no reflection upon the initial itself.[77] This small woodcut initial appeared earliest chronologically in the Huntington sample in *A Short Treatise upon the Turkes Chronicles*, printed by Edward Whitchurch in 1546. Thereafter, it takes the well-trodden route between Grafton and Whitchurch's enterprises between 1547 and 1549, before moving to John Day and William Seres in 1550. There is one example of the initial being used by Richard Grafton in the 1552 *Book of Common Prayer*, but it may not have been returned to him. Cyndia Susan Clegg's research upon the first Elizabethan Prayer Book of 1558/9 has explained a system of draft copy production and holding stock in warehouses and the construction of

---

77   Image from the NLS copy of ESTC: S093758; HEH: (Grafton) 61102, 62284, (Whitchurch) 62279, 62282, 60448; (Day) 61600, 447795, 51631; (Mierdman) 66534.

these editions from remaining and additionally printed sheets.[78] This critical analysis has offered a solution to the mystery of the various *Book of Common Prayer* imprints (and therefore titles) of the Edwardian years but also provided a glimpse into the unique stockpiling of assets that Grafton and Whitchurch's service book patent permitted. An extension of this same notion suggests that they may well have stockpiled assets from the 1548 *Book of Common Prayer* and reused them in 1552.

In some cases, such as the Coverdale bible illustrations, woodcuts were sold or loaned with a specific purpose in mind. The passage of small woodcut initials shows that printers also requested additional generic materials. In short, a 23 × 23mm woodcut initial 'I' or 'T' is not important or eye-catching enough to request specifically. It is far more likely, however, that a printer who currently owned a relatively small number of initials would request a range of additional materials to ensure that their upcoming publications could be richly adorned.

This chapter has explored the passage of woodcuts throughout the industry and the thriving loan and purchase pathways of these illustrative materials in the Edwardian book world. This system allowed for the industry-wide improvement of the products of English presses whilst ensuring that capital investment as an industry-wide total was decreased. Whilst the level of financial remuneration for the borrowing or second-hand purchase of these woodcuts cannot be found, any level thereof would be beneficial for the original purchaser of the woodcuts that in certain instances would simply be idle stock. The principal investors in original woodcut illustrations were those print houses at the height of the industry, whilst those ascending towards the pinnacle employed both second-hand woodcuts and an increasing number of original cuts. Whilst there was little new ground broken by the technical improvements within this period, the realms of highly skilled printers increased, and the number of high-quality printed works increased substantially. In isolation, the Henrician industry saw the production of the best quality pre-Elizabethan publication but as an industry-wide entity, the Edwardian printing industry produced works of a stronger overall standard. In European terms, many limitations of pre-Edwardian print culture remained but a collaborative approach to illustrative materials was allowing general quality improvements to occur even whilst the landmark publications of the reign stagnated. England was still not a print world to investigate for the highest-quality illustrations or publications of the period but quality was improving despite coinciding with new levels of printed output.

---

78   Cyndia Susan Clegg, 'The 1559 Books of Common Prayer and the Elizabethan Reformation', *Journal of Ecclesiastical History*, 67 (2016), pp. 94–121.

5 Stylistic Conventions and Development

The final area under consideration is the stylistic conventions and development in English printing during the Edwardian years. The factors by which stylistic development can be gauged are often easily discerned when one opens any early modern printed book, but the least easily defined by catalogue entries or database building. For this section, it is a scholarly necessity that we rely more heavily upon interpretation and contextualisation for detailed analysis.[79] There are, nonetheless, some basic conventions that can be drawn from figures and databases that clarify the stylistic conventions of the period. This chapter will explore variations in the style and use of different typefounts between printers at all levels in the industry before exploring those printers who represented a significant break from the stylistic conventions of the period.

The style and display of English printed works were distinctively English, particularly in the vernacular market. Few printers of the Edwardian period clung to the print culture of the earliest English printers, and the influence and standards of contemporary continental printers were aspired to more so than in previous generations. The assimilation towards continental styles had always been part of the English print world, but as ever, the selective adoption of these stylistic characteristics from European printing centres created a specific English character of print.

Type is one of the central factors in addressing stylistic variation. Both stylistically and commercially, England was reliant upon the Continent in this sphere. Before, during and after the Edwardian period, English printers relied upon importing these materials. Typefounders, typically in France and the Netherlands but also further afield, were a key component in the European book world being a continental trade.[80] An exploration of sixteenth-century English typography, therefore, is essentially a story of exploring which types were acquired and how they were distributed rather than who was behind the typefounding.

As in the case of woodcut borders and the database drawn up by McKerrow and Ferguson, historians are indebted to Frank Isaac's monumental study of English typefaces to 1558.[81] Filtering Isaac's survey to the fifty-five individuals

---

79   Quantifying the proportional use of any given typefount within a single printed work, for example, would be extraordinarily laborious and reap little beyond what can be readily discerned by sight.
80   Hellinga, 'Printing', pp. 72–73.
81   Isaac's study continues to be approved by a number of historians, including Dane, *What is a book?*, p. 113; though the individual treatment of printers has been challenged by Blayney, *The Stationers' Company*, pp. 624, 637–638.

found in English colophons within the Edwardian period highlights 560 combinations of printers using different typefaces. This is not to say that there were 560 typefaces used: each instance of any given printer using any given typeface counts as one entry. If five different printers used a single typeface, this would count as five different combinations; if one printer used five different typefaces, each would account for a different combination. For example, Richard Grafton and Edward Whitchurch shared many of their typefaces, and their two print houses alone account for fifty-one of these 560 combinations, forty-one of which were employed in the Edwardian period.

Nonetheless, many of the stylistic conventions for type use can be gleaned from Isaac's database. Of these fifty-five printers, every single one employed the use of at least one textura fount, and seven individuals used ten or more different textura founts during their careers. There were 331 combinations of printers and textura founts, which establishes the textura as the dominant fount within the English book world. The two secondary typefount styles were rotunda and italic, employed by forty-one and thirty-eight of our fifty-five printers. Only eight of the fifty-five printers whose names were found in Edwardian colophons used neither a rotunda nor italic fount at some point in their career, though a further fifteen employed either rotunda or italic, but not the other. Printers understood the significance of contrasting types within publications. They often used different fount styles to emphasise commentaries, references, or highlight different languages within the text. The tertiary founts of the English print world, however, were utilised by significantly fewer printers. Edwardian printers used four further classifications of typefount: greek (nine individuals), fraktura (six), bastarda (five), and schwabacher (three).

For four printers, one of these tertiary typefounts replaced one of the secondary. In the majority of instances, however, these tertiary typefounts were the preserve of those printers who displayed a wide variety and range of typefounts within their publications.[82] Of the nine individuals who employed a greek typefount, we find the top five printers in terms of variety of typefaces used and four more individuals who utilised at least ten variant typefaces during their careers. The rotunda style, too, was the preserve of those printers who favoured variety. Six printers who used rotundas all used at least twelve different faces, and three of them (Thomas Berthelet, William Powell and William Myddleton) also used multiple sizes of rotunda. The bastarda

---

82   Hugh Singleton used Schwabacher and not italic; Robert Crowley used bastarda fount and not rotunda fount; two generations of the Wyer family press used rotunda and bastarda founts and not italic.

typeface was less common within the industry's upper echelon; the top eight proponents of typeface variety veered away from that typefount, likely due to its associations with early printing in the vernacular.

The leading proponents of type variety across their careers who printed at least one Edwardian publication were John Day (twenty-seven), Richard Grafton (twenty-five), Edward Whitchurch (twenty-six), Thomas Berthelet (twenty-five) and Reyner Wolfe (twenty-two). In the specific years under consideration, however, this line-up changes: Day and Grafton share first place (twenty-two) and Whitchurch (nineteen) retains the third spot, but Thomas Gaultier (seventeen) and Nicolas Hill (fifteen) come next. Berthelet was a Henrician printer; he published less frequently during the Edwardian period, once his official post had been passed on to Richard Grafton. Wolfe's career began in the 1530s, and he had already deployed ten typefaces before Edward's accession. Moreover, his career continued during the Elizabethan period, and he acquired two more types in these years. On the other hand, Hill and Gaultier had shorter periods of productivity and prominence in England, and the variety of types they used was almost entirely exhibited within their Edwardian output.[83] Gaultier appears on Isaac's list almost by default and, according to Peter Blayney, by mistake. Hill's reputation as a printer-for-hire is significant, and Blayney highlights works attributed to Gaultier that were printed, in fact, by Hill. Isaac's identification of Gaultier as the printer and not the publisher of these works significantly contributes to his inclusion on this list.[84]

The printers on this list were at the top of the English print world. There were strides made in the Edwardian industry for printers to acquire and employ a variety of types in their publications. This was not simply a case of finding a type that worked for a particular size of page or publication. Employing various types in a single publication created a more stimulating page for readers and afforded the printers extra flexibility for sizing, emphasis and notes. A wide range of founts was a significant investment, acquired over time, but reinvestment of profits into new type suggests commercial success or printers investing in materials in a bid to improve.

---

83   Only one of Hill's types was used in the Henrician period and not in the Edwardian.
84   Blayney, *The Stationers' Company*, p. 628, shows that the initials used came from five different alphabets, all owned by Nicolas Hill. The title-page border (*M&F* 38) was also Hill's at this date, and all of the types match ones owned by Hill, so there can be little doubt that the books were printed for Gaultier by Hill.

From the sample considered, clear correlations link the format of a publication and the size of the fount used. Of those twenty-three publications consulted that used a fount of 60mm or smaller, twenty-one are listed as octavos, one is listed as a broadsheet (owing to the fact that it is only a fragment of a far smaller publication), and one is listed as folio: Grafton's *Concordance* of 1550. In the next range, from 60–70mm founts, the balance again is heavily towards the octavo, with twenty of twenty-one publications listed in this size. Within the ranges of 70–79mm and 80–89mm, a span of all three major publication formats (folio, quarto and octavo) can be seen, though the octavo continues to dominate as a reflection of the industry conventions rather than proportionally. Once we reach the upper reaches of type size (90–99mm and 100mm+), the octavo's prominence begins to fade. Within the 90–99mm range, where we find 104 total titles, the octavo accounts for sixty-four titles, the quarto rises to twenty-five and folios to fourteen.

Only eight printers utilised a fount of over 100mm for the body of the main text during the years 1547 to 1553 in the Huntington sample. This list includes prominent printers of the period: Grafton, Whitchurch, Wolfe, William Powell, William Copland and John Cawood and the partnerships of Nicolas Hill and Gaultier, and Day and Seres. They deployed these founts most frequently in folios, many of which would have been considered of particular cultural, religious or political importance. Works commissioned by royal order for the English church or French churches in England were among this list, alongside Copland's *A prayer sayd in the kings chappell in the tyme of hys graces sicknes*, Cranmer's *Response* to conservatives Stephen Gardiner and Richard Smith (1551), and John Cawood's edition of Northumberland's discourse from the scaffold following the accession of Mary I (1553).[85] The use of this size of fount for the body of text in a publication, then, was primarily restricted to the upper tiers English print, but also to publications considered politically or socially important. Quite simply, this is an economic consideration and one of practicality. This size of fount could be helpful for publications where group or public reading was anticipated. For printers, unless this specific mode of reading were expected, it would not make economic sense to print in such a manner: larger type meant more paper, and more paper meant greater costs.

---

85   'John Dudley', *The saying of John late Duke of Northumberlande uppon the scaffolde* (John Cawood, 1553) USTC 504918.

FIGURE 5.14 *A prayer sayd in the kings chappell in the tyme of hys graces sicknes*
(William Copland, [1553])
THE HUNTINGTON LIBRARY: 18291

Within the 80–89mm range, we see the prominence of two particular printers producing octavos. Of the twenty-four octavo publications employing an 80–90mm fount for the body of the text, either Robert Wyer or Anthony Scoloker completed twelve. By convention, most printers within the period printed their octavos in a smaller fount than this range, but the Wyer press and that of Anthony Scoloker inclined towards printing octavos in their respective 86 bastarda and 81 textura. The Scoloker 81 textura is a text on the edge of this category and is extremely close to the equivalent 78 and 80 texturas employed by many of the printers within the industry at this time. The products of his press, therefore, have a categorical difference from many of his contemporaries but look similar. In comparison, the material output of the Wyer press is visually distinct from many of their competitors despite falling into many of the same categories. Herein lies one of the difficulties of conducting such research by database building and the collection of figures: pre-defined categories can be misleading, particularly relating to characteristics of printing style. In the following section, therefore, a series of publications are explored in finer detail by visible rather than quantifiable variations.

Texturas continued to be the dominant fount for vernacular works, thereby making them the most prominent fount used at England's presses. There are examples, however, of the continued use of other styles of type or new adaptations. In each instance, these typographical variants appeal to an element of style and presentation or a particular printed material genre. Whilst the typographical practices of the English print world were, throughout Edward's reign, reasonably stable, these printers sought to distinguish their products from the competition around them in one manner or another.

Few of the elite printers in the English book world exhibited the bastarda fount.[86] Robert Wyer's press maintained a distinctive style during the Edwardian period that may be perceived as outdated and lagging behind the industry's current standing. A reluctance to shirk the bastarda type and the style of images and initials that he employed created an easy to distinguish house style. Robert Wyer and Richard Wyer (believed to be brothers) are each named in the colophons of multiple Edwardian publications and printed in this style.

Robert Wyer's style was closely connected to the earliest English printed editions and painted an antiquated picture of English printing. His adherence to more traditional styles that had since been superseded means that his publications look more akin to those of previous decades than his Edwardian contemporaries. In typographical terms, not only did Wyer employ a bastarda type,

---

86   The bastarda fount was used in Edward's reign by Richard Jugge, William Copland, Robert Crowley and the Wyer press.

but he also never employed any italics even as many of his forward-thinking contemporaries were beginning to incorporate them. Moreover, Wyer's octavos used an 86 bastarda which was not only a stylistic variance from the industry standard but was noticeably larger than those of his contemporaries, who instead were typically utilising texturas between 60 and 80mm.

In a period where increasing numbers of printers were employing elaborate and illustrative printers' devices, Wyer opted either for initials alongside an existing illustration or for a simple statement of his name in a bold woodcut. Wyer's illustrations and initials, too, appear antiquated in the light of his competitors. N.F. Blake has noted that a set of small woodcuts used by Robert Wyer was created in imitation of those employed by Antoine Verard of Paris, and the initials he employed were linked to the house of Wynkyn de Worde.[87]

FIGURE 5.15
The Wyer press illustration style: John Coke, *The debate betwene the heraldes of Englande and Fraunce* ([London, Robert Wyer for Richard Wyer, 1550])
THE HUNTINGTON LIBRARY: 60045

---

87 N.F. Blake, 'Wyer, Robert (*fl.* 1524–1556)', ODNB.

Figure 5.15 highlights the Wyer family press illustration style, the inspiration for which can be traced back to European standards showcased by printers such as Antoine Verard in his 1501 edition of Doolin de Mayence's *La fleur des Batailles*. Henrician printing took much from the Continent in terms of stylistic traits, and these Wyer illustrations exemplify this practice. Verard, like many other French printers and publishers before and after him, had a significant stylistic impact upon the printers of England, and it is in Robert Wyer's publications that this is most noticeable in the Edwardian years. The pace of printing change in England, however, is much slower. The European printing style to which the Wyer press connected is almost fifty years old. While the European print centres had adopted rotunda and italic founts, producing finely printed comparatively modern works, the Wyer press continued to forge its output in this antiquated style.

Robert Wyer's illustrations and initials have a direct heritage from Wynkyn de Worde. *The Kalender of Shepeherdes*, produced by de Worde in 1528, shows bold initials that Wyer later used in place of a printer's device in a 1552 publication *The compost of Ptholomeus*, which was a reprint of an edition Wyer had produced periodically since 1530.[88] Wyer employed an alphabet of similar woodcut initials throughout his Henrician and Edwardian publications, and it was through this significant continuity with the bygone era of England and Europe's earliest printers that his stylistic variation from his Edwardian contemporary conventions is secured. Wyer's work appears outmoded against his contemporaries, demonstrating that significant stylistic development had occurred since the advent of print. The imagery involved in the broader output of Edwardian printed woodcut illustrations, initials and printers' devices had evolved into more modern conventions.

Wyer's 86 bastarda also provided continuity with early print culture.[89] From the Huntington sample, *The Antidotharius* (1548), *The Compost of Ptolemeus* (1552), and *The cronycle of all the kynges* (1552) each utilised this 86 bastarda.[90] For this very reason, Wyer's publications are immediately set apart from his textura-using counterparts. Wyer, too, employed textura typefount for some of his publications, but his commitment to his bastarda fount for the body of many publications represents a significant stylistic deviation. Prior studies' assertions that Wyer employed the bastarda 'perhaps more by chance than design' are unnecessarily dismissive of his, albeit antiquated, character and

---

88 ESTC: S110521.
89 HEH: 18279; John Lydgate, *The Cronycle of all the kynges: that haue reigned in Englande: sythe the Conquest of Wyllyam Conqueroure* (Robert Wyer, 1552).
90 HEH: 59179; 59438.

FIGURE 5.16   John Lydgate, *The Cronycle of all the kynges* (Robert Wyer, 1552)
THE HUNTINGTON LIBRARY: 18279

style of printing. This stylistic variation of type was compounded by illustrations that presented publications with an inherited style from the Henrician period. Classifications of type are helpful in so far as they suggest patterns and characteristic styles, but for a product to be truly distinctive in stylistic terms, it takes a combination of type, illustration and initials. Wyer's output showcased them all. This antiquated style highlights that whilst areas of the trade were developing towards contemporary continental styles, the English print world did not move as one. The industry-at-large was a fluid collection of individuals: as one persevered, another progressed. The Wyer press became distinctive for its lack of advancement, by which the stylistic links with England's earliest printers can be shown to be dissipating.

In contrast, one printer who exhibited a transitional style during the Edwardian period was the King's Typographer and Bookseller for the ancient languages: Reyner Wolfe. The government instituted this official office to encourage English printing towards conventions of contemporary continental printing centres and improve the reputation of English printing. In terms of Isaac's database, Wolfe utilised twenty-two typefaces throughout his career: eight texturas, six rotundas, five italics, and one each of greek, fraktura and schwabacher. He was the joint leading proponent of variety, using italic scripts across the Henrician and Edwardian periods.[91] Within the Edwardian period, however, these figures fall to three texturas and italics, two rotundas and one schwabacher.

Lotte Hellinga credits Wolfe as the producer of a work that 'heralds a change in the presentation of printed books' in the English book world. The publication in question, however, was printed in the Marian period: Robert Record's *The Castle of Knowledge*. Hellinga's assessment of this volume speaks of 'an excellent balance of a combination of contrasting types', 'good illustrative material' and 'judicious use of italic'.[92]

Wolfe also employed these features during the Edwardian period, though not in an English-language publication. The requisite skills for *The Castle of Knowledge* were honed and developed under the protection and assurance provided by his official appointment to the king. This section will cast light upon when Wolfe employed this continental style and how its direct contrast with vernacular equivalents – both of competitors' creation and his own – shows that there were clearly defined parameters and stylistic expectations for specific categories of books. The vernacular and Latin markets in the English book world operated to contrasting stylistic conventions.

---

91   Wolfe used five italic types in the period covered by Isaac, equal to Day and Grafton.
92   Hellinga, 'Printing', p. 77.

FIGURE 5.17   Wolfe's rotunda and italic fount: Peter Martyr Vermigli, *Tractatio de Sacramento Eucharistæ* (Reyner Wolfe, 1549)
THE HUNTINGTON LIBRARY: 631121

A comparison that highlights these conventions can be seen in the publications of Peter Martyr Vermigli. The Italian reformer, installed as Regius Professor of Divinity at Oxford University, produced his Latin treatise on the sacrament (Reyner Wolfe, 1549), and his work was soon translated into English by Nicholas Udall and printed under the false imprint of Edward Stoughton [= Whitchurch] for Nicholas Udall, 1550.[93] These two quarto editions highlight that products of English presses, even those from highly esteemed printing houses, could vary dramatically in style.

Wolfe's 1549 edition begins with a simple text-only title-page using rotunda and italic typefaces, mirroring a contemporary continental printing style. The Latin market in England, particularly during these reformation years, was small; Wolfe's remit under his official office was to serve this readership and bolster English production in this market area. To do so, Wolfe adopted a continental style. Fine, elaborate illustrated woodcuts, varying in four sizes from

---

93   Peter Martyr Vermigli, *Tractatio de Sacramento Eucharistae* – (Latin: Wolfe USTC 631121) (English: 'Stoughton' 54364).

45 × 44mm to 28 × 28mm, adorned this edition, and his 93 rotunda and 121 italic typefaces reflect continental designs distinct from the texturas to which readers of English-vernacular works were accustomed.[94] English readers who engaged with academic texts did so in continental imported books, and he thus accommodated their expectations of style.

The 'Stoughton for Udall' English edition of Vermigli's *Discourse or traictise*, figure 5.18, employed what had long been the conventional style for English-printed works. The woodcut title border bearing Whitchurch's initials and his symbol of the sun is followed by two ornamental woodcut initials (Sigs. *2r; A1r) to open the preface and body of the text before giving way to a body of the text in a 95 textura, employing italic and rotunda typefaces only sparingly throughout.[95]

Even within Wolfe's catalogue of printed works, we see this inclination toward more modern continental-style typefaces for Latin works whilst maintaining the conventional textura for English-language works. Wolfe printed editions of Archbishop Cranmer's *Defence of a true catholike doctrine of the sacrament* in English (1550) and in Latin (1553).[96] The English quarto edition, figure 5.19, employed a 95 textura with an elaborate full-page and freshly commissioned title-page border.[97]

In comparison, the later Latin edition, figure 5.20, bore a plain-text title-page and was printed in an 88 italic typeface with a rotunda preface. Whilst both were adorned with a combination of illustrated and ornamental woodcuts, these two editions varied greatly in style. Although this style was adopted by only a small number of academic tracts in Latin, this is a significant step for the English industry and one rarely acknowledged by historians. England is known to have been a subordinate market for scholarly printing, but Wolfe's financial investment in type and development as a printer gave England its first scholarly printer to challenge this status quo.

---

94   For comparison, see Peter Martyr Vermigli, *In selectissimam s. Pauli priorem ad Corinthios epistolam* (Zurich, Christopher Froschauer, 1551); USTC 666475.
95   Italic was used only for emphasis within the body of the text, and rotunda for margin notes.
96   Thomas Cranmer, *Defence of a true catholike doctrine of the sacrament* – (Latin: Wolfe, USTC 56568) (English: Wolfe, 333197).
97   170 × 113mm encompassing 78 × 56mm.

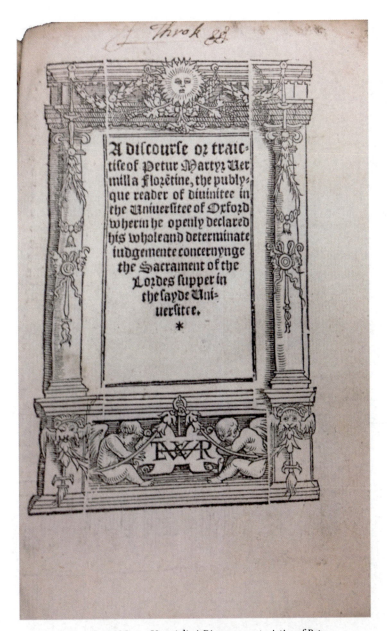

FIGURE 5.18   Peter Martyr Vermigli, *A Discourse or traictise of Peter Martyr Vermilla* ([Robert Stoughton [=Edward Whitchurch] for Nicholas Udall, 1550])
THE HUNTINGTON LIBRARY: 45364

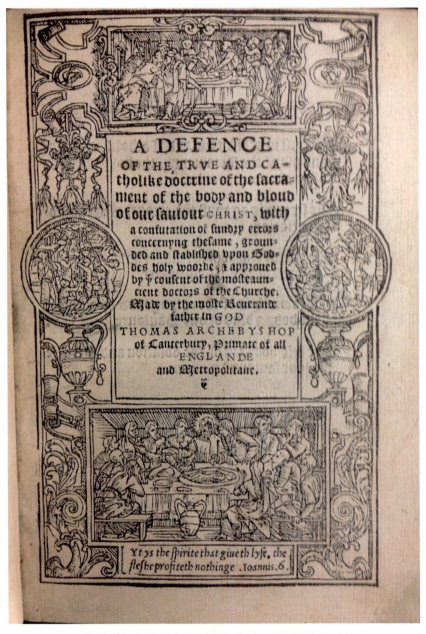

FIGURE 5.19   Thomas Cranmer, *A Defence of the True and Catholike Doctrine* (Reyner Wolfe, [1550])
THE HUNTINGTON LIBRARY: 333197

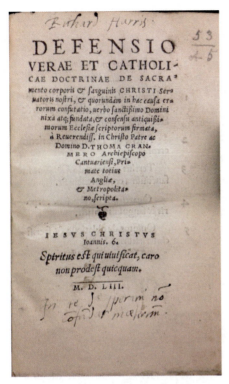 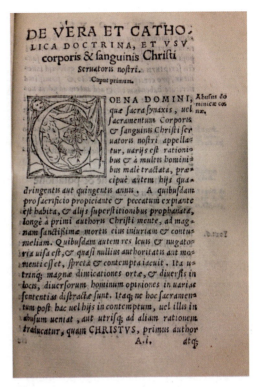

FIGURE 5.20   Thomas Cranmer, *Defensio* (Reyner Wolfe, 1553)
THE HUNTINGTON LIBRARY: 56568

A second possibility for this stylistic variation is that English printers were, for the first time, setting their sights upon audiences beyond the confines of their domestic market. Both Peter Martyr Vermigli and Thomas Cranmer were esteemed figures in the evangelical world, and their publications may have been expected to gain traction abroad. Many of the territories in which scholarly printing occurred were in the midst of conservative clampdowns. Edwardian England became 'the best hope for the continued progress of the reformation in Europe', 'one of the international capitals for Protestant thought' and the reign was the period when English evangelicalism 'was most integrated into the mainstream of the continental Reformation'.[98]

---

98   Diarmaid MacCulloch, 'Sixteenth-century English Protestantism and the Continent', in *Sister Reformations: The Reformation in Germany and in England*, ed. Dorothea Wendebourg (Tübingen: Mohr Siebeck, 2010), pp. 1–14 (p. 7); N. Scott Amos, 'Strangers in a Strange Land: The English Correspondence of Martin Bucer and Peter Martyr Vermigli', in *Peter Martyr Vermigli and the European Reformations: Semper Reformanda*,

The story of the interaction between England and the continental reformations during these years has primarily been depicted as one of English evangelicals attempting to further the English reformation with influences from abroad.[99] This adherence to continental styling may suggest a new degree of reciprocity and an outward focus of English evangelicals and printers, which has hitherto been assumed not to have occurred. This evolution of England's reformation and its printing industry to becoming outward-facing is crucial in understanding the Edwardian reformation's position in its contemporaneous political and religious climate. Neither of these works fell under Reyner Wolfe's role as the King's Typographer and Bookseller for the ancient languages – he would only have printed them if he, or his patrons, believed they could sell. The ambition shown by Wolfe here highlights that at the very least, England had a readership sufficiently engaged with the ancient languages to prefer tracts in Latin to English or, more excitingly, that a London printer was hoping to target academic audiences abroad.

There are precedents for such international outreach of English scholarship from the Henrician period. Bishop John Fisher – who would later face martyrdom in 1535 for his objection to the Henrician reforms – developed a continental reputation, which saw his works printed and disseminated widely across Europe.[100] In the Edwardian period, Richard Smith (an outspoken conservative theologian in exile) and Stephen Gardiner (the deposed bishop of Winchester) each had Latin tracts printed in conservative cities on the Continent. These works, considered by contemporaries and historians to have been created for clandestine import into England, would also have had an international appeal. There is little doubt that some copies of these works circulated around catholic Europe rather than simply being boxed up and shipped wholesale to England.[101] These conservative authors were printed in conservatively governed cities, with a mind to targeting conservative audiences. English printers had never printed for continental audiences; political opportunity and skills had always rested simultaneously in better-equipped continental printing centres. The Edwardian period, however, saw evangelical ascendancy in England

---

ed. Frank A. James III (Leiden: Brill, 2004), pp. 26–46 (p. 28); Andrew Pettegree, *Marian Protestantism: Six Studies* (Aldershot: Scolar Press, 1996), p. vii.

99   Cranmer and Somerset were key to drawing theologians to England, and the attempt to persuade Melanchthon to England is one of the 'what might have beens' in the English reformation, see MacCulloch, *Tudor Church Militant*, p. 170.

100 Andrew Pettegree, *The Book in the Renaissance* (New Haven, CT, Yale University Press, 2010), p. 107.

101 Susan Brigden, *London and the Reformation* (Oxford: Clarendon Press, 1989), p. 454.

whilst pressures mounted upon the evangelicals in Europe. Robert Barnes' literary career had shown that Latin works by English scholars could win a European readership, and it is possible that Wolfe's publications represented the next step in this integration with international evangelical scholarship.[102] English readers, theologians and scholars had been provided with an English edition of Cranmer's *Defensio* three years previously, and this publication suggests (on behalf of either Cranmer as an author or Wolfe as a printer) an attempt to gain prominence with the international evangelical community.

The fact that the English book world was part of an international trade of books can often be understated in relation to the Edwardian industry. English printing indeed moved towards self-sufficiency and, under the banner of the reformation, to a new focus upon vernacular works that would be of little value elsewhere in the European book world. England remained a subordinate market, but that is not to say that it had no export potential.

In a change as much cultural as stylistic, Edward's reign saw, for the first time, significant non-English vernacular printing in England. Between 1550 and 1553, thirty titles were printed in Dutch (seventeen), French (twelve) and Italian (one). This market sphere was monopolised by three individuals: Stephen Mierdman, Nicolas Hill and Thomas Gaultier. Primarily, these works were printed for Edward's French-speaking subjects in the Channel Islands and the stranger churches of London.[103] Whilst the French provinces held by the English monarch had depleted significantly, the Channel Islands and Calais remained important territories, particularly as the English reformation brought greater instability to a continent with deep religious divisions.

It is worth noting that French vernacular biblical readerships had been poorly served during the 1540s. Geneva was only slowly emerging as a centre for evangelical printing, and French printing centres were under the increasingly repressive regime of Henri II. French biblical production in Paris had declined rapidly. When Gaultier completed his octavo *Nouveau Testament* in 1551, Genevan and Parisian presses had not produced a French New Testament, or a complete bible, for five years. Moreover, presses at Louvain, Antwerp and Lyon had combined for only six New Testaments and eight complete bibles

---

102   Carl R. Trueman, 'Barnes, Robert, (c.1495–1540)', ODNB.
103   Blayney, *The Stationers' Company*, p. 628–24 August 1552 Jan a Lasco wrote to William Cecil. The letter asked Cecil to procure a royal grant to print English church books in French for his majesty's islands (STC 16430); Andrew Pettegree, *Foreign Protestant Communities in Sixteenth-Century London* (Oxford: Clarendon Press, 1986), p. 95 states 'The French liturgies, the Geneva catechism, and two editions of the Bible in French were all printed by Gualtier for their use'.

between 1546 and 1550. Furthermore, the stylistic convention for these bibles and New Testaments favoured the sextodecimo or folio formats; in these same five years, only Bartholomeus van Grave (Louvain, 1549) produced a French octavo New Testament.[104]

Having only recently reached a period in which evangelical books could be openly sold and purchased, the English book world was well acquainted with the international clandestine print trade. Some of the Gaultier New Testaments may have been exported to France to be sold at least at Calais or smuggled further afield. The paths from the English book world to areas of evangelicalism that were under increasing pressures from their respective monarchies were well-trodden. Jan a Lasco's letter to William Cecil requesting a patent for Gaultier to print French service books for the Channel Islands underpins our understanding of this publication – but does not necessarily mean that Gaultier printed these works for this purpose alone.[105] Nicolas Hill and Stephen Mierdman may also have set their sights upon international markets alongside the London stranger populations with their seventeen Dutch-language publications.[106] Gaultier's New Testaments can now only be found in modern French libraries, including Bibliothèque de la ville de Caen (ESTC: S469842)[107] and the Société de l'histoire du protestantisme francais (ESTC: S92029,[108] S91028),[109] whilst Dutch-language publications from Edwardian London can be found in Amsterdam University Library (ESTC: S93428,[110] S94178,[111] S91080,[112] S90838)[113] and Leiden University Library (ESTC: S94178).[114] Whether this disproportionately large concentration of known copies being held in European libraries reflects contemporary circulation or modern acquisition strategies is unclear, but it encourages the idea of an international outreach of English printers during these years.

---

104 Francis Higman, *Piety and the People: Religious Printing in French, 1511–1551* (Aldershot: Routledge, 1996), appendices; USTC 5615, FB: 5391, NB: 4611.
105 Blayney, *The Stationers' Company*, p. 628.
106 Evenden, 'The Fleeing Dutchmen?', p. 69; Heijting, 'Mierdman, Steven'.
107 Only listed copy on ESTC.
108 *Ibid.*
109 One of three copies, also held by the British Library and the Zion Research Library, MA, USA.
110 Only listed copy on ESTC.
111 Two known copies, both in the Netherlands.
112 Only listed copy on ESTC.
113 *Ibid.*
114 Two known copies, both in the Netherlands.

This exploration of the stylistic conventions and developments within the Edwardian printing industry has shown that there were specific and defined fields of the English book world. Printers accommodated readers' expectations in their presentation of specific works. The world of Latin scholarship and theological discourse moved more quickly than the English vernacular in this regard, partly to accommodate English readers' stylistic expectations but also to reach a continental audience. Printing in the vernacular for the stranger churches has hitherto been seen as an inward-facing process for subjects living within Edward's realms, but there was potential for outreach to other European populations. Without specific figures of print runs, this is a difficult prospect to consider and one that historians have marginalised.

Returning to Hellinga's comments about Wolfe's Marian edition of *The Castle of Knowledge*, it is true that Wolfe did not make the transition to printing English vernacular works consistently in the Latin typefount within the Edwardian period, but there is little surprise that this jump was made soon after Mary I's accession considering the progress Wolfe had already made under Edward VI. The English book world unquestionably took much inspiration from the European book world but as a whole the pace of developments was much slower. Industry-wide stylistic conventions during this period were fairly stable: English readers knew what to expect from their printing houses, and printing houses knew what English readers expected from their books. The balance of different typefounts saw a clearly defined three-tier system where texturas dominated English books, followed by second-tier types of rotunda and italic, thereafter the same tertiary types that endured from the Henrician period. Type to page ratios offered some variation by printers, in large part due to their stock and the option to be flexible and employ different type for different formats.

This chapter has highlighted that the material products of the Edwardian print world had a deeply rooted connection with late-Henrician print culture. Design conventions that developed in early English printing endured, and readers developed distinct preferences to which printers largely adhered. There were specific standards of appearance for how each format was expected to look, which works would be printed in which format and how words should be presented on a page. English readers, as we have seen, were committed – through conviction or stubbornness – to these design conventions and resisted those publications attempting to present works in new or innovative manners.

The Edwardian industry broke little fresh ground in terms of industrial or technical improvements. There were few industrial advances as the Edwardian industry maintained its pattern of gradually importing skills and techniques from continental centres of print. Moreover, English printers continued to exhibit typefaces and paper imported from Europe. The Edwardian period saw the successful completion of several landmark publications, accomplished with a technical acumen shown by few English printers up until this point. These years saw advancement in the technical capacity of the industry at large, as the lower and middle reaches of the printing industry were brought into closer parity with the uppermost. Grafton and Whitchurch, upon the commencement of Edward's reign, had few, if any, rivals to their position as the premier English printers. Whilst their material products continued to be in this uppermost tier of English products, they began to be caught up. Increasing numbers of print houses were able to print with this level of confidence and sureness: John Day, Stephen Mierdman, Reyner Wolfe and Nicolas Hill each exhibited work of the quality of some of the finest of the Grafton or Whitchurch publications. It was through the number of high-quality printed works available, from a larger number of print houses, rather than through a particular landmark publication, that Edwardian print was technically superior to Henrician print.

Stylistically, Edwardian printed works show the embryonic stages of reaching greater parity with their continental contemporaries. Reyner Wolfe's adherence to existing styles of continental academic printing was a step forward for English print culture. Latin was an international language of scholarship and, thus, the printers of such works served an international audience.[115] Such was the reliance of English readers upon continental printing centres up to this point that little attempt had been made in the English sphere to produce scholarly texts. Wolfe's appointment to King's Typographer and Bookseller for the ancient languages changed this. In the English context, Wolfe was a pioneer, albeit maintaining a style to which both readers at home and abroad were accustomed.

The stylistic conventions of the core of the late-Henrician and Edwardian trade were, however, as removed from the antiquated products of the Wyer press as they were from its most progressive proponent Reyner Wolfe. Continuities from late-Henrician conventions highlight that the Edwardian industry was not one of design, technical or stylistic revolution. The evolution of individual styles and technical improvement as an industry-wide process was not enough to generate demand for the level of production that we saw in this period. The output of the presses doubling between 1546 and 1548, and London

---

115   Andrew Pettegree and Malcolm Walsby, eds., *Netherlandish Books: Books Published in the Low Countries and Dutch Books Printed Abroad before 1601* (Leiden: Brill, 2011), p. i.

rising from the ninth most productive European city between 1540 and 1546 to the third most productive between 1547 and 1553 cannot be attributed to design, technical or stylistic developments. The technical capacity of the English printing industry within this period improved because the products of individual printers improved. England's printers were becoming both more productive and proficient, but one did not come as a result of the other. An increased number of high-quality products emerged from English presses as a greater number of printers became highly skilled, not because any level of industrial, design, technical or stylistic innovation made doing so easier.

CHAPTER 6

Commercial Networks

This chapter explores the English book world's professional networks and interpersonal relationships between 1547 and 1553. This under-explored area is critical to understanding the Edwardian printing trade as a commercial and industrial enterprise. The English book world was made up of three key components: an industrial process resulting in material products, an economy to sustain it and, critical to this examination, people.

The sixteenth-century English book world was small relative to some of its continental counterparts. A small population with low literacy levels ensured that English readers could be provided for by a heavily centralised trade comprehensively weighted towards vernacular production. Principally, the Edwardian printing trade is the story of the seventy-seven individuals named in the colophons of one or more of the 1,212 titles produced between 1547 and 1553.[1] Thirty-five active printers operated at some stage during the Edwardian years, whilst those other colophon-listed individuals played roles of funding publishers and printing collaborators. These figures belie the breadth of individuals making their living in the English book world. They obscure the employees of these individuals and the plethora of associated tradespeople who contributed to the smooth running of this industry. Crucial contributions were made by craftsmen, artisans, skilled and unskilled labourers, men of commerce and men of learning without whom the smooth running of the industry would be undermined.

Navigating these personal and commercial relationships was fundamental to maintaining a successful position within the English print world. No printing house was a fiefdom of its own. The proximity and competition within the trade could easily have caused instances of conflict and contention, but it fostered a spirit of cooperation and collaboration. The interconnectedness of each occupation within the trade was fundamental to the trade's rapid growth. This chapter will first outline the underpinnings of the printing industry itself and the driving forces of the printing houses: master printers. Thereafter, it will

---

1 The number of individuals in Edwardian colophons is debated: Patricia Took claiming '80 or so', Elizabeth Evenden stating 72, Peter Blayney 80, and the USTC highlighting 77. Peter Blayney, *The Stationers' Company and the Printers of London, 1501–1557*, 2 vols (Cambridge: Cambridge University Press, 2013), p. 605; Elizabeth Evenden, *Patents, Pictures and Patronage: John Day and the Tudor Book Trade* (Aldershot: Ashgate, 2006), p. 40.

explore three different types of workers in the English printing world: industrial, craft and commercial. The second focus of this chapter will be an exploration of the interpersonal relationships found within the printing industry.

This analysis will demonstrate that the book world displayed more dynamic commercial relationships under Edward VI than ever before. The Henrician years demonstrated that the print world could be navigated through individual projects and business acumen. However, a characteristic of the Edwardian print world was an unprecedented level of collaboration between individuals and enterprises whose connections have not been fully appreciated. Rather than a disparate collection of competitors, the Edwardian print landscape became a more unified 'world' for the first time, as webs of collaboration created a spike in the number of individuals involved in the trade and spurred forward output.

1 The Composite Parts of the English Book World

The web of individuals involved in the book world extended far beyond authors and owners of print houses. The industrial process involved many individuals working together towards a single end. Workers housed within the print house were, of course, critical, but their efforts were supplemented and supported by tradesmen, artisans and merchants who also played roles in the creation and dissemination of publications. This chapter will explore a series of positions within the English book world, the foremost of which were the printers and publishers. Printers were the individuals who occupied premises where publications were produced. Their enterprises owned the presses and type and employed the necessary staff to create their works. Publishers, meanwhile, were not necessarily responsible for the act of printing but commissioned the creation of works by a printer. This boundary was, as we shall see, fluid and many individuals bridged both professions.

Of the thirty-five printers who operated under Edward, the active number at its zenith surpassed any number of concurrently active printers under Henry VIII and was significantly higher than following the contraction of the trade after the accession of Mary I.[2] It is not until the recovery and reconstruction of the Edwardian industry under Elizabeth I that the number of active printers

---

2   Blayney's research shows that there was a maximum of twenty-one printers working simultaneously in 1548, and thirty-four in total over the course of the reign. The USTC lists thirty-five, though this includes 1553 where reigns are uncertain, Blayney compares this with the twenty-seven who worked under Mary I. Blayney, *The Stationers' Company*, p. 605.

surpassed the Edwardian years. As our period preceded the 1557 charter of the Stationers' Company, printers belonged to merchant companies including Grocers, Drapers, Haberdashers, Stringers and Salters, and the Stationers.[3] These companies were the lifeblood of England's mercantile economy; personal associations from these companies were found within the English book world, but new wider networks also developed.

Non-printing publishers, too, came to the fore. At least six individuals listed in the colophons of five or more publications between 1547 and 1553 did not operate a printing press in England before, during, or after the reign.[4] A further thirty individuals contributed to fewer than five publications purely as publishers. Elizabeth Evenden's estimate that only thirty-nine of the ninety-one traders in books active between 1547 and 1558 were master printers highlights that the book world was significant and extensive beyond printers alone.[5] Like our aforementioned printers, the publishers of London were associated with larger merchant guilds.[6]

Printers and publishers are the best-evidenced individuals in the history of the trade. Colophons are a central tool in establishing works created and their passage through the press. Beyond these names in the colophon, the English book world relied upon many others employed by these named parties and a far wider network of individuals whose living was made in a mutually dependent trade or supplemented by the print trade. When considering the array of individuals within the English book world, a critical factor must be kept in mind: the English book world, and the printing industry, in particular, was a small economy centred overwhelmingly within one city. Those involved were often mutually dependent, and economic decisions were made with the activities of one another in mind.

This chapter will explore three occupation classifications in the book world: industrial workers, craftsmen and commercial businessmen. Within the first category fall those individuals working within the printing house. These were

---

3   Grocers (Richard Grafton, Anthony Scoloker), Drapers (Thomas Raynald), Haberdashers (Edward Whitchurch), Stringers (John Day) and Salters (Robert Wyer) and Stationers (William Hill, William Powell and Humphrey Powell); Blayney, *The Stationers' Company*, pp. 635–636, 646, Peter Blayney, *The Stationers' Company before the charter, 1403–1557* (London: Worshipful Company of Stationers and Newspaper Makers, 2003), pp. 39, 47.

4   William Bonham, Richard Kele, Gwalter Lynne, Robert Toy, Henry Sutton and John Walley.

5   Evenden also states that seventy-two residents of England were named in imprints or colophons as printers, publishers or distributors of books during the Edwardian years. Evenden, *Patents, Pictures and Patronage*, p. 40.

6   For example, among the Drapers were Abraham Vele, John Wyght, Thomas Petyt; Peter W.M. Blayney, *The Bookshops in Paul's Cross Churchyard* (London: Bibliographical Society, 1990), pp. 29, 50–51, 57.

the workers whose combined labours turned raw materials into a finished material product and included pressmen, compositors and proofreaders. Secondly, we consider those individuals who work in the pre- or post-printing associated crafts. Those workers who prepared the raw materials (papermakers, typefounders and woodcut artists) combined with individuals who later dealt with the finished product from the presses (bookbinders) to make up the body of craftsmen who served England's print houses. Finally, commercial businessmen were the 'front of house' of the English book world; booksellers ranging from pedlars of small numbers of tracts and editions to rural communities to the publishing booksellers of Paul's Cross were critical to the English book world. These categories create a more comprehensive understanding of the extended English book world. This section will highlight the number of individuals required for the smooth running of the print trade. The Edwardian years caused more people to be employed before, during and after the printing of a book. A host of underappreciated individuals made their living in the English book world, contributing to products so central to our understanding of the period.

Due to the scarcity of archival evidence, the employees of England's printing houses have been marginalised in favour of the study of master printers and their respective catalogues of output. Nonetheless, the proficiency of this cast of pressmen, typesetters and proofreaders ensured the effective execution of any given publication. The endeavours of these individuals were the basic machinery upon which the printing industry was built. Only through effective delegation and management could master printers thrive. The eponymous naming of printing houses in the period ensures that sixteenth-century books are listed as the products of one individual; instead, the delegation skills of these listed individuals rather than their technical proficiency ensured the quality of their wares.

The evidence that we can glean from archival material relating to these individuals primarily comes from the subsidy records of the master-printers with whom they are associated. Aided, in part, by Ernest James Worman's *Alien members of the book-trade during the Tudor period*, both Andrew Pettegree and Elizabeth Evenden have procured evidence on the personnel and activities involved in this sphere of the trade, though both instances deal with the Dutch stranger communities of London, or specifically those in the employ of John Day.[7] The Dutch and French communities were crucial in this area and

---

7   Ernest James Worman, ed., *Alien members of the book-trade during the Tudor period: Being an index to those whose names occur in the returns of aliens, letters of denization, and other documents published by the Huguenot Society* (London: Bibliographical Society, 1906);

elsewhere within the English book world. Many of the most esteemed printing houses of the Edwardian years employed Netherlandish workers, including those of Grafton, Whitchurch, John Day and Dutch émigrés Nicolas Hill and Stephen Mierdman.[8] Alongside the over seventy émigrés working within the trade, there was also a multitude of English individuals who practised these occupations. The running of a single press would require two pressmen, one compositor and one corrector. When operating two presses, only the number of proofreaders could be proportionally reduced, as one proofreader could handle the output of multiple presses. Thirty-five printers were active during the Edwardian years, and as many as twenty-one printing houses operated simultaneously. With these figures to guide us, it can be estimated that at least twenty-five presses, and potentially as many as forty presses, were running at any point during the reign.[9] To man this number of presses at least fifty, but often closer to 100, individuals must have been employed in this capacity alone at any point.

Elizabeth Evenden and Thomas Freeman's evidence suggests that a 'reasonably successful' printing house in the sixteenth century consisted of three presses and a staff of six pressmen, three compositors and a corrector.[10] Three presses was a level of production and activity that few printers in the Edwardian period were likely to have employed. Grafton, Whitchurch, Day, Hill and Mierdman are all likely to have been operating at this capacity, or more, along with William Powell and Thomas Berthelet.[11] Printing operations rivalling this production run by William Copland, William Myddleton (in 1547 only), and Reyner Wolfe may have been operating two or more presses.

Andrew Pettegree, *Foreign Protestant Communities in Sixteenth-Century London* (Oxford: Clarendon Press, 1986), pp. 82–84; Elizabeth Evenden, 'The Fleeing Dutchmen? The Influence of Dutch Immigrants upon the Print Shop of John Day', in *John Foxe at Home and Abroad*, ed. David Loades (Aldershot: Ashgate, 2004), pp. 63–78 (p. 64).

8   Andrew Pettegree, *Marian Protestantism: Six Studies* (Aldershot: Scolar Press, 1996), pp. vii, 128; Susan Brigden, *London and the Reformation* (Oxford: Clarendon Press, 1989), p. 430; Pettegree, *Foreign Protestant Communities*, pp. 85–86; David Loades, 'Books and the English Reformation prior to 1558', in *The Reformation and the Book*, ed. Jean-Francois Gilmont, trans. Karin Maag (Aldershot: Ashgate, 1998), pp. 264–291 (p. 273).

9   Blayney, *The Stationers' Company*, pp. 605–606.

10 Elizabeth Evenden and Thomas Freeman, *Religion and the Book in Early Modern England: the making of John Foxe's "Book of Martyrs"* (Cambridge: Cambridge University Press, 2011), pp. 12–13; Evenden and Freeman's work explores the history of Foxe's *Actes and Monuments*, the 1570 edition of which was printed in house by Day over three simultaneously running presses – which casts some light on the inflated sense of reasonable success. Pettegree, 'Day [Daye], John (1521/2–1584)', ODNB.

11 John Day is known to have operated four presses in 1583, Evenden and Freeman, *Religion and the Book in Early Modern England*, pp. 8–9.

Willem Heijting states that Stephen Mierdman employed at least three men, though, with a printing house of such productivity, Mierdman's employ was likely far larger.[12] Nicolas Hill, too, is listed as having employed three apprentices, though they would have supplemented more experienced and educated staff members, which likely amounted to at least five (though probably more) employees.[13]

For these printing houses, staffing was a significant outlay and crucial component of their business. The laborious work of a pressman was physically demanding, with the expectation of 2,500–3,000 impressions per ten-hour day, six days per week.[14] They are believed to have been working seventy-two-hour weeks, paid by the impression. Alongside these hardy pressmen, compositors' work required precision and judgement to ensure neat page alignment and correct spelling. Compositors were paid comparatively well and by the rate at which they set lines.[15] Finally, correctors perused copy sheets for mistakes, studiously correcting and amending issues. For works of serious scholarship and theology, this was of critical importance, and the endeavours of compositors and correctors alike could make or break a publication. The importance of these individuals in the world of continental Christian Hebraism has been noted by Stephen G. Burnett, though the principle extends to Latin and Greek scholarship, particularly in the English context.[16] Correctors' wages no doubt depended greatly upon their level of expertise. An individual of significant learning had to be hired to cross-examine works of theological scholarship or translations into, or from, the ancient languages. This was an entirely different task from correcting pamphlet literature in the vernacular. The workforce wage alone of running a single press could easily have been 28s. per week, and a printing house of two presses at least 48s. per week.[17] The engine room of the English printing house, then, was operated by a deceptively large number of individuals compared to the thirty-five named printers active within Edward's reign.

12 Willem Heijting, 'Stephen Mierdman', ODNB.
13 Andrew Pettegree, 'Hill, Nicolas [Nikolaos van den Berghe] (d. 1555)', ODNB.
14 Evenden and Freeman, *Religion and the Book in Early Modern England*, p. 19.
15 Elizabeth Evenden, 'Patents and Patronage: The life and career of John Day, Tudor Printer' (unpublished doctoral thesis, York University, 2002), p. 20; Evenden and Freeman, *Religion and the Book in Early Modern England*, p. 20.
16 Stephen G. Burnett, *Christian Hebraism in the Reformation Era 1500–1660: Authors, Books and the Transmission of Jewish Learning* (Leiden: Brill, 2012), pp. 202–206, 302.
17 Celyn Richards, 'Printing for the Reformation: The Canonical Documents of the Edwardian Church of England, 1547–1553' in *Print and Power in Early Modern Europe (1500–1800)*, eds. Nina Lamal, Jamie Cumby and Helmer J. Helmers (Leiden: Brill, 2021), pp. 111–133 (pp. 120–122).

Correspondence of the period betrays authors' and readers' criticism of the diligence shown in corrections and composition. Peter Martyr Vermigli's correspondence offers some insight from an author's perspective on the importance of proofreaders and correctors. He wrote to both Heinrich Bullinger and Rudolph Gwalther about their role in shepherding his publications through the Zurich presses.[18]

> I much wish you would salute all your fellow-ministers individually in my name, especially my friend Gualter, who has employed himself so laboriously in the revision of my book.
>
> to HEINRICH BULLINGER, 6 August 1551[19]

> Though I have before offered you my thanks for the pains you have taken that my book might be accurately printed ... I would not, however, have you in future bring so heavy a charge against your young men, as though it were through their fault that so many errors have crept into my book. They were indeed of great assistance to me in copying, and I am very much indebted to their kindness, and am grieved that the favour they have conferred upon me should be met by such a requital.
>
> to HEINRICH BULLINGER, 26 October 1551[20]

> Were I not to thank you, most learned sir, for the pains you have taken in the revision and correction of my book when it was in printing ... I plainly perceive that you have bestowed no small labour upon this matter; for in copying out the book I send you, there was not such care taken as there ought to have been. But I will endeavour that greater accuracy shall be observed, when I next forward anything to you to be printed.
>
> to RUDOLPH GWALTHER, 6 March 1552[21]

Bullinger and Gwalther were preeminent theologians and the successive heirs to Huldrych Zwingli as the head of the Zurich reformation. It is likely that they were primarily concerned with revisions to the translation and text rather than the process of shepherding the book through the printing house. The comment relating to Bullinger's 'young men', however, indicates the concerns and

---

18 Either: *Disputatio de eucharistae sacramento* (Zurich, Andreas Gessner and Rudolph Wissenbach, 1552) (USTC 683622, 683623) or more likely *In selectissimam s. Pauli priorem ad Corinthios epistolam* (Zurich, Christopher Froschauer, 1551) (USTC 666475, 666476).
19 OL, 2, pp. 496–498 (p. 498).
20 OL, 2, pp. 498–501 (pp. 498–499).
21 OL, 2, pp. 501–503 (p. 501).

pitfalls of having the text run through a second or third pair of hands before the end product. Whether this episode speaks more to Martyr's humility or Bullinger's perception of Martyr (that the mistakes would not have been present in his work) is unclear, but in either case, it is clear that authors and readers were concerned that editors, typesetters and proofreaders could introduce additional errors.

On occasion, the fear of poor execution prompted printers and authors to work in direct coalition. Ensuring that the end product arrived with readers as the author intended was vital for both authors' and printers' reputations. One example, identified by David Daniell, places the repatriated Henrician émigré John Rogers in the printing house of Edward Whitchurch during the spring of 1548, working as a translator.[22] As the editor of the 1537 'Matthew' bible, Rogers was a star on the rise, securing positions as the vicar of St Sepulchre (May 1550) and the prebend of St Pancras in St Paul's Cathedral (Aug 1551). John Rogers' association with Whitchurch certainly stemmed from the Henrician years, when Grafton and Whitchurch published Mathias Crom's printing of the 'Matthew' Bible. They developed a strong relationship; both printers signed as securities for the first fruits for Rogers in 1550 and 1551.[23] Securing a highly educated man such as Rogers to translate the works of Philipp Melanchthon was undoubtedly a coup for Whitchurch. Melanchthon himself described Rogers in glowing terms when proposing his instalment as pastor and superintendent of Meldorf.[24] Whitchurch's output in these years included works of significant standing. During 1548 and 1549, the Whitchurch press produced editions of Erasmus' *Paraphrases* (volumes one and two), the *Book of Common Prayer* and a quarto bible – each a work of political and religious importance. Rogers' 'Mathew' translation had proven his credentials; Whitchurch knew he had a skilled translator on board. It is only given the critical importance of Whitchurch and Grafton's official publications to the regime's dissemination of religious change, that someone of Roger's standing could have been involved in the process.

A second example, initially put forward by A.B. Emden, suggested that Robert Crowley, a former fellow of Magdalen College Oxford, had worked as a proofreader in the printing house of John Day.[25] Peter Blayney has since

---

22   David Daniell, *The Bible in English: Its History and Influence* (New Haven, CT: Yale University Press, 2003), p. 192.
23   David Daniell, 'Rogers, John (c.1500–1555)', ODNB.
24   J.F. Mozley, *Coverdale and his bibles* (London, 1953), pp. 122–123 cited in Daniell, 'Rogers, John (c.1500–1555)', ODNB.
25   John N. King, *English Reformation Literature: The Tudor Origins of the Protestant Tradition* (Princeton, NJ, Princeton University Press, 1982), pp. 96–97.

attacked this notion as lacking archival foundations; further emphasising that Crowley would have been 'distinctly overqualified for the job'.[26] The implication here for the cast of individuals working as proofreaders and correctors within the printing house would be that those of a university education would be beyond the power (and financial clout) of printing houses. The process of proofreading and correcting sheets was an exercise in diligence and accuracy, rather than a scholarly pursuit. The suggestion that Crowley was working as a proofreader has endured, but the reality of any association with Day and Seres more likely stems from the author playing an active role in his first three publications (all printed by Day and Seres) rather than from Crowley working as a day-to-day component of Day's printing team.

Another association between printer and scholar within the period was that between Anthony Scoloker and Richard Argentine. Following Scoloker's move to Ipswich in 1548, he embarked upon an evangelical printing campaign. This reform-minded town was stationed upon the river Orwell with links to England's eastern seaboard and positioned under the eye of Archbishop Cranmer and privy councillor Thomas First Baron Wentworth.[27] John N. King has stated that Scoloker and Argentine were under the direct patronage of Baron Wentworth and Edward Grimstone.[28] Scoloker's edition of Martin Luther's *A ryght notable sermon, of absolution and the true use of the keyes full of great comforte*, translated by Richard Argentine, has a prefatory dedication from the translator to Lord Wentworth.[29] Argentine also translated editions of Bernardino Ochino and Huldrych Zwingli for printing at Scoloker's press, with the Zwingli work bearing a prefatory dedication to Grimstone.[30] Argentine, who proved supple in his religious convictions in the coming years, was undoubtedly a skilled translator. Along with his work for Scoloker, he was commissioned to produce an English translation for the Ipswich Borough Charter in 1552, for which he was paid 40s.[31] Whether he dirtied his fingers at the compositor's tray or proofing recently inked sheets remains uncertain, but it is possible considering the amount of collaboration between the pair in quick succession in 1548. What is certain, however, is that collaboration between scholars and printers enabled original translations, even in the provincial market.

---

26   Blayney, *The Stationers' Company*, pp. 637–638.
27   P.R.N. Carter, 'Wentworth, Thomas, first Baron Wentworth (1501–1551)', ODNB; Diarmaid MacCulloch, *Tudor Church Militant: Edward VI and the Protestant Reformation* (London: Allen Lane, 1999), p. 97.
28   King, *English Reformation Literature*, p. 104.
29   USTC 504065.
30   USTC 504162.
31   J.M. Blatchly, 'Argentine, Richard (1510/11–1568)', ODNB.

Those individuals who began as editors, translators, or proofreaders, and graduated to producing publications, show another collaborative dynamic within the English print world. A first example is highlighted by the employment of William Baldwin in the printing house of Edward Whitchurch, an example put forward, again, by John N. King. Baldwin is believed to have occupied the role of corrector from 1547 onward.[32] Baldwin's influence is listed in the colophon of four USTC listings for Whitchurch titles in 1550: three editions of Jean Calvin's *An epistle both of Godly consolacion* (translated by Lord Protector Somerset), and one original text, *A treatise of morall phylosophye*.[33] There are thirty-two works authored by Baldwin in the USTC, the first seven of which appeared in the Edwardian years, and five of which came from Whitchurch's printing house.[34] Baldwin also had works printed by William Powell and Thomas Gaultier in 1552.[35] Of the five from Whitchurch's house, only one colophon reads 'William Baldwin in the shop of Edward Whitchurch'; the remaining three each list 'imprinted at London by Edward Whitchurch', with credit inferred to Baldwin by the USTC. Baldwin's standing in the print trade remained small, and all of his credits as a printer came from associations with other printers. He rose to prominence, however, as a translator and author after Whitchurch printed his early works. Following Mary I's accession, Baldwin wrote a number of anti-catholic polemics, and many of his works appeared or reappeared during the reign of Elizabeth I.

The second example, which bridged the Henrician and Edwardian years, is Robert Copland's working in the printing house of Wynkn de Worde. Mary C. Erler places Copland as a translator of French works for de Worde for almost a decade, from 1505 until his first printing in 1514.[36] Following Edward's accession, Copland is credited by the USTC for the printing of two titles: Andrew Boorde's *The pryncyples of astronomye*, and an anonymous *A boke of the propertyes of herbes*, both in 1547.[37] Robert's son William assumed control of the family business in 1548, though he had already begun printing independently by 1545. Robert developed a commercial relationship with publisher Richard Kele, producing three titles authored by John Skelton in 1545 and another of his authorship, and his son continued this relationship.[38] William Copland became an influential printer-for-hire and is considered in more detail below. The graduation of Robert Copland from translator to active

---

32 John N. King, 'William Baldwin (d. in or before 1563)', ODNB.
33 USTC (Jean Calvin) 504428, 504432, 504439; (Baldwin) 504384.
34 USTC (Whitchurch) 503814, 504384, 504684, 504800, 504183.
35 USTC (William Powell) 515432; (Thomas Gaultier) 504777.
36 Mary C. Erler, 'Copland, Robert (*fl.* 1505–1547)', ODNB; USTC 501267.
37 USTC 515357, 503871.
38 USTC 503666, 503667, 503668.

printer highlights that, at least in some instances, the academic pursuit of translation was not entirely removed from the printing house itself. Copland proved skilled enough to translate and edit, but also willing and able to pursue a career in book production.

Employing educated and diligent translators, proofreaders and correctors, then, was of critical importance. Whether scholars or educated men of particular esteem could be coaxed into employment likely hinged upon the importance of the works they were printing, and the financial means of the printing house. Elizabeth Lane Furdell has postulated that some printing houses 'enlisted wives and daughters to compare the original texts with proofs' and this may well have been the reality for small outfits.[39] What we have seen in the Edwardian period, however, is that printers and authors alike attempted to enlist the aid of educated individuals wherever possible. Eminent theologians, authors, and university graduates were all involved in shepherding printed works from ideas and drafts to printed end products.

Throughout this period, with such an influx in printed material being created and an influx in individuals becoming involved in the trade, the number of pressmen, compositors and correctors must have increased significantly. Between 1547 and 1553, it is within the realms of possibility that upwards of 100 individuals might have been working in these industrial roles at any time. This supporting cast of workers was of great importance. Printers' reputations and the authors' credibility depended upon these marginalised pressmen and much-maligned compositors and correctors, the sum of whose efforts turned raw materials and concepts into material products.

English print culture relied upon and fed into existing and related crafts. The effective running of the trade required skilled typefounders, illustrators, papermakers and bookbinders. For many of these artisans and craftsmen, England relied upon mainland Europe and represented only a subordinate part of an international industry. Master printers were required to develop effective trade links with national and international merchants and artisans in order to facilitate the gathering of equipment. It is important to remember, when we discuss these artisan crafts, that the book world did not begin with the advent of print. The scribal and manuscript culture that predated print required both paper and bindings. These were established trades, which were boosted significantly by the introduction and increasing prosperity of print, but already had foundations.

---

39   Elizabeth Lane Furdell, *Publishing and Medicine in Early Modern England* (New York: University of Rochester Press, 2002), p. 122.

During the Edwardian years, there were no paper mills operating in England.[40] Previous attempts to produce paper in England had quickly ceded to international competition.[41] It was not until the seventeenth century that domestic production could provide the necessary paper supply for the trade to be self-sufficient. In the meantime, paper continued to flow from the Continent, particularly France, handled largely through English merchants rather than any international reach of printing houses.[42]

Paper is known to have been one of the most expensive components of book construction in the period, expected to sell wholesale in 1540s Paris for between ten sols and thirty sols per ream, depending on quality.[43] Assessments of the quality of paper remain throughout the historiography an inexact science. In the Edwardian period, paper quality was judged by weight per ream, replication of which is impossible. An extensive trade-wide study of watermarks could shed light upon which mills supplied English printers but falls outside of the confines of this study. Indicative research by Elizabeth Evenden and Thomas Freeman suggests that the majority of paper used in early English printing originated in France, particularly Normandy.[44] Research into official church publications in Edwardian England have validated Jean François Gilmont's estimate of paper accounting for around forty per cent of the cost of a book.[45] Peter Blayney's discovery of Humphrey Powell being successfully sued by Thomas Stanbridge in 1549 for £13 6s and 8d for 100 reams of 'good quality and saleable paper' also supports these guideline figures for paper pricing.[46] 100 reams of paper equates to 50,000 sheets (one ream = 500 sheets) and could have been used to produce around over two thousand copies of Powell's largest

---

40 Evenden, 'Patents and Patronage', p. 13.
41 Stephen W. May and Heather Wolfe, 'Manuscripts in Tudor England', in *A Companion to Tudor Literature*, ed. Kent Cartwright (Chichester: Wiley Blackwell, 2010), pp. 125–139 (pp. 125–126); Evenden and Freeman, *Religion and the Book in Early Modern England*, pp. 10, 28–29.
42 Blayney, *The Stationers' Company*, p. 17.
43 Lucien Febvre and Henri-Jean Martin, *The Coming of the Book. The Impact of Printing 1450–1800*, eds. Geoffrey Nowell-Smith and David Wootton, trans. David Gerard (London: NLB, 1976), p. 112.
44 May and Wolfe, 'Manuscripts in Tudor England', p. 126; Evenden, 'Patents and Patronage', p. 13; Evenden and Freeman, *Religion and the Book in Early Modern England*, p. 28.
45 Jean Francois Gilmont, *Bibliographie des éditions de Jean Crespin, 1550–1572*, 1, p. 54 cited in Evenden and Freeman, *Religion and the Book in Early Modern England*, p. 10; Celyn Richards, 'Printing for the Reformation: The Canonical Doucments of the Edwardian Church of England 1547–1553' in *Print and Power in Early Modern Europe (1500–1800)*, eds. Nina Lamal, Jamie Cumby and Helmer J. Helmers (Leiden: Brill, 2021), pp. 111–133 (pp. 120–121).
46 Blayney, *The Stationers' Company*, p. 614.

extant publication (a 340-page quarto psalter printed for Whitchurch in 1549), though the real print run size is unlikely to have used more than half of the contested paper.[47] This same contested paper would have been enough for 330 copies of the first volume of Erasmus' *Paraphrases* printed by Whitchurch in 1549.

Lucien Febvre and Henri-Jean Martin estimated that each press could use three reams of paper in a single day. Annie Parent's estimates, based on a print house running four or five presses, that each press could use as many as six reams per press per day are overly ambitious for a printer of this period.[48] Few Edwardian printers operated this number of presses. Using the guide range of 1,250–1,500 sheets per day highlights a more reasonable expectation of output. Powell and Stanbridge's contested 100 reams could have been sufficient to last Powell from 33 to 40 days if Powell was running a single press, or as few as 16–20 days if running two. This level of outlay, for what is a relatively small portion of the working year, highlights that the most productive English printers could easily have been spending well over £100 per annum on paper alone.[49] Effective links to international papermakers, therefore, were critical to business. Printers could not afford simply to buy the required paper years in advance due to its high cost. Examples of paper quality varying within a single publication highlight this reality, and further emphasise the importance of these commercial networks providing efficient opportunities to purchase the raw materials.

England also lacked the necessary typecasters to be self-sufficient. This, again, necessitated reliance upon the continental book world.[50] This was detrimental to English printing only in so far as it increased costs incurred by importing such materials, which naturally had to be passed on incrementally to readers. The international trade in type appears to have flowed relatively freely, as we have seen a wide variety of typefaces acquired and deployed. Elizabeth Lane Furdell has claimed that for the uppermost echelons of the Tudor book trade, it was 'normal practice' for typefounding to have occurred

---

47   USTC 504230.
48   Febvre and Martin, *The Coming of the* Book, p. 40; Evenden and Freeman, *Religion and the Book in Early Modern England*, p. 10, states 'Annie Parent estimated that 25–30 reams would be used per day to supply four or five presses'.
49   If we estimate Whitchurch to have used 100 reams on 666 copies of the *Paraphrases*, even a conservative estimate total number of copies at 5000 given their provision in every parish church and nothing else printed in that year amounts to over £105.
50   Evenden and Freeman, *Religion and the Book in Early Modern England*, p. 27; Pettegree, *Foreign Protestant Communities*, pp. 85–86.

in-house.[51] Whilst England's industry was on the rise, even with the new influx of foreign émigrés, it is unlikely that this was the case. Elizabeth Evenden has noted that there is no evidence that John Day cast his own type and, as we have seen, he employed the widest variety of type in these years and a greater variety of type in his career than any Edwardian printer. If Day was purchasing type from external craftsmen, it is unlikely that other print houses were creating their own; type production remained a distinct craft rather than an in-house pursuit.[52] Mentions of these unaffiliated skilled artisans are found infrequently in archival material. There are rare identifications of these workers in London, but it appears that reliance upon imports was the convention.[53] The patent awarded to Grafton and Whitchurch in December 1547 permitted the printers to hire an increased number of 'such and as many prynters compositors and founders' suggests the presence of at least some domestic typefounders.[54] Hubert D'Anvillier (or Dauville), who arrived in England in 1553, is one of few who have been identified, and it appears that he and other typefounders in England only partly fulfilled the needs of the trade.[55] Those typefounders operating on English soil were most likely, like D'Anvillier, religious émigrés escaping persecution in the Netherlands or France who brought with them skills that the English industry lacked.

More prominent than domestic production, however, was the import of type from the Continent.[56] This heritage of importing type, particularly specialist types, is evident throughout the Henrician and Edwardian years: Reyner Wolfe purchased his Greek type in Basel, Richard Pynson imported type from Parisian typefounders, and John Day bought his musical type from Robert Granjon.[57] For the wider industry, too, we see that types made their way over

---

51 Furdell, *Publishing and Medicine*, p. 122.
52 Andrew Pettegree, 'Printing and the Reformation: the English Exception', in *The Beginnings of English Protestantism*, eds. Peter Marshall and Alec Ryrie (Cambridge: Cambridge University Press, 2002), pp. 157–180 (p. 175).
53 Joad Raymond, *Pamphlets and Pamphleteering in Early Modern Britain* (Cambridge: Cambridge University Press, 2003), p. 74.
54 Blayney, *The Stationers' Company*, p. 723.
55 E.G. Duff, *A Century of the English Book Trade* (London: Bibliographical Society, 1948), pp. 36–37; Pettegree, *Foreign Protestant Communities*, p. 84; Evenden, 'The Fleeing Dutchmen?', p. 66.
56 Lotte Hellinga, 'Printing', in *The Cambridge History of the Book in Britain, Vol. III: 1400–1557*, eds. Lotte Hellinga and J.B. Trapp (Cambridge: Cambridge University Press, 1999), pp. 65–108 (pp. 72–73); Evenden and Freeman, *Religion and the Book in Early Modern England*, p. 27; Pettegree, 'Printing and the Reformation', p. 175; Pettegree, *Foreign Protestant Communities*, pp. 85–86.
57 Pamela Robinson, 'Materials: Paper and Type', in *A companion to the Early Printed Book in Britain, 1476–1558*, eds. Vincent Gillespie and Susan Powell (Cambridge: Brewer,

from Europe. For some printers, of course, this import of materials occurred when they themselves relocated. Grafton and Whitchurch repatriated the English bible projects from France in the early 1540s, where a transfer of materials is evident. For Stephen Mierdman, the import of European types was simply a case of following their owner in his relocation. As an extension of this largely imported craftsmanship, European typefounders led many of the stylistic conventions of English print culture, though the balance and use of various printing types created a discernible English pattern of usage.

Historiographical convention has long stipulated that bookbinding and printing were mutually-dependant but autonomous trades.[58] Bookbinding predated the advent of print, and both native Englishmen and resettled Europeans prospered in the craft. After 1534, legislative measures defended English bookbinders by prohibiting the importation of pre-bound books.[59] It has been argued that English bookbinders of the previous decade continued to lack the quality of their continental counterparts, and this initiative was designed both to protect the interests of the English craftsmen and galvanise improvements in quality.[60] In binding, as in many other areas of the book world, the English industry responded to and imitated European conventions.

For the most part, only bindings of particular material quality or stylistic relevance have received scholarly attention. Mirjam Foot's exploration of gold leaf tooling on Henrician bindings, for example, has highlighted the increasing influence of Italian and French design and style.[61] It is clear, though, that English-based bookbinders were active and flourishing. Alexandra Gillespie

---

2014), pp. 61–74 (p. 71); A.F. Johnson, cited in 'Printing in England from William Caxton to Christopher Barker, An Exhibition: November 1976–April 1977', *Virtual Exhibitions of Special Collections material*, at http://special.lib.gla.ac.uk/exhibns/printing/; Evenden, 'Patents and Patronage', p. 129.

58 Febvre and Martin, *The coming of the book*, p. 105; Alexandra Gillespie, 'Bookbinding and Early Printing in England', in *A Companion to the Early Printed Book in Britain, 1476–1558*, eds. Vincent Gillespie and Susan Powell (Cambridge: Brewer, 2014), pp. 75–94 (pp. 84–85); Mirjam Foot, 'Bookbinding 1400–1557', in *Cambridge History of the Book in Britain, Vol. III: 1400–1557*, eds. Lotte Hellinga and J.B. Trapp (Cambridge: Cambridge University Press, 1999), pp. 109–127 (p. 120).

59 25 Henry VIII, c.15; Alan Coates, 'The Latin Trade in England and Abroad', in *A Companion to the Early Printed Book in Britain, 1476–1558*, eds. Vincent Gillespie and Susan Powell (Cambridge: Brewer, 2014), pp. 45–60 (pp. 55–56); Cyndia Susan Clegg, *Press Censorship in Elizabethan England* (Cambridge: Cambridge University Press, 1997), p. 6.

60 Robert J.D. Harding, 'Authorial and editorial influence on luxury bookbinding styles in sixteenth-century England', in *Tudor Books and Readers: Materiality and the Construction of Meaning*, ed. John N. King (Cambridge: Cambridge University Press, 2010), pp. 116–137 (p. 120).

61 Foot, 'Bookbinding', p. 117.

lamented the lack of attention paid to bindings by book historians in 2014, duly noting that the bookbinder's craft was 'integral to the manufacture, importation and sale of books in England'.[62] Whilst Gillespie's concern is entirely justified, there are several challenges facing any prospective industry-wide study of bookbinding. Previous research on binding between 1400 and 1555 has detailed that bindings can seldom be attributed to a particular workshop.[63] Individual tooling and detailing of bindings and the issue of discovering whether printer, publisher or patron bore the responsibility for any given binding shroud bookbinders in mystery. Moreover, a comprehensive study of bindings would require the examination of an extraordinarily large number of historical artefacts currently scattered across the world. For any number of reasons books initially bound in the same manner and style might have since been rebound. The study of bindings, as a result, is largely confined to the discussion of general conventions or the in-depth bibliographical analysis of single objects or collections. Furthermore, many books not bound by their contemporaries have since become noteworthy historical artefacts in the modern world and have been bound according to a modern perception of their importance and in a bid to preserve them. The *British Library Database of Bookbindings* (BLDB) currently catalogues 340 sixteenth-century English bindings from its collections. Some forty-two individual binders are identified among this collection by initial or house rather than by name.

Gillespie has also challenged the historiographical accord that books of the period were sold unbound, noting that books could be bound at various points during their passage to the open market: via the printer, publisher, bookseller or reader.[64] The participation of printers and publishers within this artisanal craft not only extends their influence beyond the production of finished leaves but also reinforces the level of interconnectedness of the English book world. The case for further involvement by author, printer or publisher within the binding process is supported by the role that bindings could play in any given book's reception. Gérard Genette and Robert J. Milevski have highlighted that once accompanying a text, the binding becomes part of a single material object playing a paratextual and peritextual role and a vital component of

---

62   Alexandra Gillespie, 'Bookbinding and Early Printing in England', in *A Companion to the Early Printed Book in Britain, 1476–1558*, eds. Vincent Gillespie and Susan Powell (Cambridge: Brewer, 2014), pp. 75–94 (p. 93).
63   Foot, 'Bookbinding', p. 120; Robert J. Milevski 'A Primer on Signed Bindings', in *Suave Mechanicals. Essays on the History of Bookbinding Volume 1*, ed. Julia Miller (Ann Arbor, MI: Legacy Press, 2013), pp. 165–179 (p. 179).
64   Gillespie, 'Bookbinding and Early Printing in England', pp. 84–85.

the book.[65] With these factors in mind, it is hardly surprising that authors, printers, publishers and booksellers might have wished to have an input in the binding process.

Robert J.D. Harding's research upon luxury bookbinding has highlighted the proficiency with which Tudor publications could be bound at the pinnacle of this craft.[66] These bindings, typically examples gifted to prominent individuals or housed in prominent libraries, are disproportionately likely to have survived. The study of these presentation copy bindings has informed the clearest understanding we have of specific English binderies. Nowell Havy, who was nicknamed 'The Edward and Mary binder' (fl.1545–1558), the 'Medallion binder' (fl.1544–1559) and the 'Greenwich Binder' (fl.1520s–1530s) have each been noted for their distinctive use of luxury leathers including goatskin, buckskin and kidskin.[67] However, these luxury binders represent only a small portion of the bookbinding craft and, thus, a smaller-still part of the output of England's printers. Very few published works received such investment, and those fine bindings remain uncommonly luxurious and expensive.

What we do know of industry-wide practice is that quality and standards of bookbinding were standardising. Calf leather was the most prominent material for substantial full bindings, whilst sheep, goatskin and textile bindings were reserved for works of particular esteem.[68] Ephemeral works were less likely to be bound at all but could be bound quickly and inexpensively in a heavy parchment called forel.[69] One indication that bindings were standardising is the Henrician proclamation of 1541, which allowed for a two-shilling increase in price between copies of the Great Bible sold loose and those sold bound.[70] This proclamation suggests that individuals or parishes had the option to purchase pre-bound copies in more standardised calf leather or unbound copies which they could bind to their specification. Other official proclamations, too, speak of particular binding materials, with unbound, forel (+8d.), sheepskin (+1s. 1d.) and calf leather (+1s. 10d.) outlined in the proclamation for the pricing of the 1549 *Book of Common Prayer*.[71]

---

65   Milevski, 'A Primer on Signed Bindings', p. 165.
66   Harding, 'Authorial and editorial influence on luxury bookbinding styles'.
67   Foot, 'Bookbinding', p. 113; Gillespie, 'Bookbinding and Early Printing in England', pp. 84–85.
68   Foot, 'Bookbinding', p. 113.
69   Parchment bindings are mentioned in the 1534 Act against the importation of unbound books, 25 Henry VIII, *c*.15.
70   *H&L*, 1, pp. 296–298 – 6 May 1541 – Whilst this proclamation had now expired following the king's death in 1547, it provides some insight into the anticipated selling price of the Great Bible.
71   *H&L*, 1, p. 464 – 3 June 1549.

With book production highly centralised, the highest concentration of active binderies could be found in the capital. The literary and manuscript worlds that had supported binders before the upsurge in printed documents were centralised in London and near universities and the cathedrals; as print developed, it is a natural commercial development that new binders appeared where printing occurred. The vast majority of bindings required in London would have been low-quality, low-cost protective coverings to protect works during transit both pre- and post-purchase. For works of particular importance, a higher quality binding might have been sought, but the majority of the output of print houses would not have justified substantial investment in high-quality bindings.

Isolated examples of high-quality bookbinding skills and investment can be found. The famous 'King Edward and Mary binder' has seven listings on the BLDB, including English, Parisian and Venetian publications ranging from 1546 to 1555, including a translation of Thomas Cranmer's *Defence de la vraie et catholique du sacrement* printed by Thomas Gaultier in 1552. The *British Library* has also digitised three works credited to the 'Medallion Binder', two of which place the binder close to the circles of Edwardian power: firstly, a Basel-printed Greek bible of 1545 owned by Edward VI, and secondly, *The Decameron of Boccaccio*, produced in France in the fifteenth century and believed to have been owned by Lord Protector Somerset. According to the USTC, this work was not printed in France until the 1520s.[72] Such illustrious company among the Medallion binder's commissions is a testament that this bindery was among the most proficient and high quality in England.

It has been argued that English binders dominated this adjunct trade of the book world by 1534.[73] Whilst the skillset boasted a more national outlook than type production, it remained an area of the trade where foreigners had a significant stake. The French party of bookbinders, in particular, has been noted as significant and Dutch émigrés also played a role.[74] French influence did not arrive with the stranger churches, with a number of binders having been denizened during Henry VIII's reign, including Jaques Coiplett and John Pennys.[75] Isaac de Bruges and Thomas Hacket, too, have been identified as among this

---

72 BL Shelfmarks: Davis86, Add Ms 35323; Foot, 'Bookbinding', p. 126, states that 'a number of folios from Edward VI's library were bound here' including *Le livre Cameron* (Paris, veuve Michel Le Noir, 1521), USTC 8377.
73 Clegg, *Press Censorship*, p. 6.
74 Evenden, 'The Fleeing Dutchmen?', p. 65; Pettegree, *Foreign Protestant Communities*, pp. 85–86, 94.
75 1 July 1554, Westm. Deniz. Roll, 36 Hen. 8. cited in William Page, ed., *Letters of Denization and Acts of Naturalization for Aliens in England, 1509–1603* (Lymington: Huguenot Society

group operating in the Edwardian years, whilst James Sheres, who had family links to the Cambridge stationer Peter Sheres, was a contemporary bookbinder among the Netherlandish community in London.[76]

Elizabeth Evenden has stated that a bookbinder could be employed directly by the printer and paid by the item bound.[77] This would allow for the closest interaction between specific binders and printers, whose commercial relationships would have suited both parties. Evenden's assertion that the printing and binding trades were more interconnected than autonomous is supported by Robert J.D. Harding's examination of a presentation binding of Martin Bucer's *De regno Christi* gifted to Edward VI in 1550. Harding has noted that panels in the binding were printed with Robert Estienne's Hebrew and Greek founts rather than hand tooled.[78] Whilst an international example, this book represents that there was trade collaboration between printers and binders. Moreover, it exemplifies that, in certain circumstances and for works of importance, even the centralised London printing industry still lacked the finesse of its continental counterparts.

Whether as a full-time occupation or falling under a wider remit for booksellers and stationers, bookbinders would have been active in larger commercial and scholarly centres.[79] They were present certainly in the university towns of Oxford and Cambridge and probably within the provincial print centres of Ipswich and Worcester.[80] For provincial printers to benefit from being closer to their customers, local binders must have operated. Without nearby binders, sheets would need to be transported to the capital to be bound, nullifying any benefits from printing the work outside of London. Furthermore, it is possible that provincial population centres, where scribal culture surrounding cathedrals and monasteries (before their dissolution) would have required their skills, also had binderies or stationers capable of binding books.

---

of London, 1893), pp. 49, 189; E.G. Duff, *A Century of the English Book Trade* (London: Bibliographical Society, 1948), p. 118.

76 Pettegree, *Foreign Protestant Communities*, pp. 85–86, 94; David McKitterick, *A History of the Cambridge University Press, Vol I: Printing and the Book Trade in Cambridge, 1534–1698* (Cambridge: Cambridge University Press, 1992), p. 47.

77 Evenden, 'Patents and Patronage', p. 21.

78 Harding, 'Authorial and editorial influence on luxury bookbinding styles', pp. 130–133.

79 Peter Moreux is noted as a bookbinder in York in the late fifteenth century, for example, in Duff, *A Century of the English Book Trade*, p. 107.

80 Reginald Oliver is a known Henrician stationer in Ipswich mentioned in the colophon of a 1534 publication from Antwerp (USTC 437710), though it is not known whether these books were shipped bound or unbound.

McKitterick has spoken of a close-knit but 'rather more extensive than might at first be expected' community of stationers and bookbinders in Cambridge.[81] Among the Cambridge binders found in the *BLDB*, we find four listings for Garrett Godfrey (fl.1502–1539) and ten for Nicholas Spierinck (d.1546), whom both plied their craft at Cambridge in the early sixteenth century.[82] Godfrey's business was handed over to the Dutchman Nicholas Pilgrim, who also died before Edward's accession. To fill the void left by these stationers and binders, another émigré, Peter Sheres (d.1569), became attached to the University and flourished.[83] The Oxford contingent is known to have included Giles, who bound for Magdalen College in the early sixteenth century, Philipe Cuttier, who appears to have arrived in England in the early 1550s, and Christopher Cavye who was binding books at least from the mid-1550s.[84] The universities were a natural focal point for English scholarship, which allowed stationers and binders to thrive upon local demand.

Examples have been found of printers accepting a necessary waiting period for a book to be returned bound to their exacting specifications and standards. Thomas Wotton, who was appointed the commissioner of heresies in Kent 1552 and the son of an Edwardian privy councillor, is believed to have had his books bound by a Parisian bookbinder.[85] This bindery has twenty-three listings in the *BLDB*, some of which were bound for Wotton and some which remained on the Continent. Exporting completed publications to Paris to be bound and returned to England on a large scale would have contravened Henrician legislation (not to mention would have been incredibly expensive) but preventing this occurring on a limited scale for individual owners would hardly have been a priority for the authorities.

These artisans and craftsmen who fulfilled the typographical and binding needs of printers and readers were critical to the book world, and yet continue to be shrouded in mystery. The number of individuals employed in these specific trades remains incredibly difficult to establish. In 1548, English printing output escalated beyond any reasonable expectation. The production of 243 titles in this year, and 1,212 titles across the reign, must have demanded an influx of type production and created a significant opportunity for bookbinders.

---

81 McKitterick, *A History of the Cambridge University Press*, p. 53.
82 John S. Lee, *Cambridge and its Economic Region, 1450–1560* (Hatfield: University of Hertfordshire, 2005), p. 80; Kathryn McKee, 'Judging a Book by its cover?', *Special Collections Spotlight* (2014), at https://www.joh.cam.ac.uk/judging-book-its-cover.
83 McKitterick, *A History of the Cambridge University Press*, pp. 46–47.
84 Duff, *A Century of the English Book Trade*, pp. 23, 36, 55.
85 Foot, 'Bookbinding', p. 124; S.T. Bindoff, *The History of Parliament: The House of Commons 1509–1558*, vol 2 (London: Secker & Warburg, 1982), p. 659.

The international, and smaller national, trade in type provided essential material for England's printers. In this design and technical analysis, it has been shown that English printers sought to use a wider variety of types than ever before, prompting ongoing commissions for new founts. This was an investment in the trade and the number of people involved in the wider English book world must have expanded, even if their involvement was short lived. The sheer productivity of Edwardian printers and the magnitude of the projects initiated by the regime created enormous opportunities for England's binders. As the print world expanded, the associated crafts had to keep pace.

Members of the mercantile economy were also critical to the commercial success of publications. Within this group were those merchants who imported print houses' raw materials and books, and more prominently England's booksellers. These booksellers ranged from those prominent individuals housed at London's Paul's Cross churchyard to those occupying marginal distribution networks that facilitated the effective dissemination of books to England's rural readers.[86]

England's economy was centralised around its capital, which was by far the largest population centre in the realm. Greater London's 60,000–75,000-strong population at the commencement of the Edwardian period was swiftly becoming one of the largest in Europe. The national population was also rising and had reached three million by 1551.[87] Robert Tittler's division of English urban areas into London, regional capitals (around seven in total), major provincial centres (around thirty), lesser provincial centres, and smaller market towns highlight the variant degrees of influence that urban centres held, and their likely outreach beyond their immediate population.[88] Whilst mercantile ports were active – particularly surrounding the wool trade – the English economy, on the whole, was inward facing.[89] Jan de Vries' research has shown that of the 173 European cities with over ten thousand inhabitants in 1550, only five were in England; furthermore, only 2.4 per cent of the English population dwelt in these cities.[90] Whilst England's mercantile economy was overwhelmingly

---

86   For Paul's Cross booksellers, see Peter W.M. Blayney, *The Bookshops in Paul's Cross Churchyard* (London: Bibliography Society, 1990).
87   E.A. Wrigley and R.S. Schofield, *The population history of England 1541–1871: A reconstruction* (Cambridge, MA: Harvard University Press, 1981), p. 528; supported by Loach, *Edward VI*, p. 58.
88   Robert Tittler, *Townspeople and Nation: English Urban Experiences 1540–1640* (Stanford, CA: Stanford University Press, 2001), pp. 19–22, 30.
89   G.R. Elton, *England under the Tudors*, 3rd edn (London: Routledge, 1997), p. 235.
90   Jan de Vries, *European Urbanisation, 1500–1800* (Cambridge, MA: Harvard University Press, 1984), p. 39 cited in Andrew Pettegree, *Europe in the Sixteenth Century* (Oxford: Blackwell, 2002), pp. 72–73.

centralised in London and the major urban centres, the population evidently was not. With this in mind, it is clear that unless print served only a tiny portion of the population, far-reaching commercial networks must have existed. The recommencement of printing at Worcester and Ipswich, two of Tittler's major provincial centres, but not provincial capitals, shows that these centres could operate as regional hubs for the printing trade, or at least that the printers' sponsors believed they could. Bishop John Hooper's 1551 diocese visitations in Worcester recorded a rate of twenty per cent of clergymen as university graduates, which D.G. Newcombe's research has shown was representative for the period.[91] This reinforces the fact that while the education and literacy divide in sixteenth-century England was significant, the realm outside of the capital was not devoid of educated individuals and cannot have been devoid of readers.

Two critical transitions dominate our understanding of mid-Tudor economics. The reformation prompted significant economic restructuring. Following the dissolution of various church lands, an estimated half-million pounds' worth of land was distributed: largely to crown ministers and chief servants, but the reassignment and resale of these lands involved men of means above and beyond the commercial classes.[92] The second fundamental transition, with a more immediate impact on the print world, was the Tudor price rise. The debilitating financial repercussions of foreign warfare under Henry VIII and Lord Protector Somerset's regency prompted successive debasements of both gold and silver coins between 1526 and 1551, the ramifications of which continued to be felt in the latter half of Edward's reign: debasements reduced the buying power of English merchants abroad and created an unstable and unsustainable increase in exports for the wool trade.[93] The export trade of wool had been

---

91 Newcombe, D.G., 'John Hooper's visitation and examination of the clergy in the diocese of Gloucester, 1551', in *Reformations Old and New: Essays on the Socio-Economic Impact of Religious Change c.1470–1630*, ed. Beat A. Kümin (Aldershot: Scolar Press, 1996), pp. 57–70 (p. 62).

92 Jennifer Loach, *Edward VI*, ed. George Bernard and Penry Williams (New Haven, CT: Yale University Press, 1999), p. 182.

93 Nuno Palma 'Reconstruction of annual money supply over the long run: The case of England, 1279–1870', *European Historical Economics Society Working Papers in Economic History*, 94, (2016), pp. 10–11; Li Ling-Fan, 'Bullion, bills and arbitrage: exchange markets in fourteenth- to seventeenth-century Europe' (unpublished doctoral thesis, London School of Economics, 2012), pp. 75, 88. For the decreased buying power of English currency and the wool trade, see Elton, *England under the Tudors*, pp. 242–243; Loach, *Edward VI*, p. 58, Loach has contested that the 1540s was a period of prosperity for many and that inflation did not reach the 'staggering proportions sometimes suggested', and rents lagged behind prices', though does accept the 'disastrous economic circumstances of the early 1550s', p. 46.

gradually declining since the turn of the century, but the 1550s saw a spike in exports.[94] Manufactured cloth exports, in a period of ascent for both London and the national export levels, also spiked dramatically in the 1540s, followed by a crash in 1552.[95] With the printing industry so reliant upon international imports for illustrations, type and paper, price hikes for imported goods must have impacted merchants and have been passed on to their print house clients, and thus to readers.

John N. King has postulated that the Edwardian period saw booksellers gaining ascendency over printers. James Raven, too, has claimed that 'Booksellers benefitted from the state sponsorship of official publications and from a lucrative multitude of Protestant catechisms and evangelical literature'.[96] These discussions of 'booksellers' in the Edwardian years include publishing houses, not simply the permanently housed and itinerant booksellers under discussion here. Nonetheless, even making allowance for Raven and King's comments by including the bookseller/publishers who were indeed in the ascendancy, their ideas remain speculative. This exploration of booksellers will deal not with the publishing booksellers of the capital but will consider those individuals who played a retail role in the industry.

The economics underpinning both London's and provincial booksellers mirrored those of the printing industry. Some booksellers purchased collections of texts wholesale from printers, thereby assuming the risk for any given collection's success or failure. With this in mind, booksellers (both metropolitan and rural) are far more likely to have maintained their businesses on the fast-moving staples of the industry such as almanacs and ephemeral works rather than focusing solely upon specialist works.[97]

In the same manner as English binders, the fraternity of London booksellers attempted to restrict foreign émigrés' impinging upon their trade. In 1538, Miles Coverdale and Richard Grafton had to petition Thomas Cromwell for permission for François Regnault, who was soon to be integral in the early Great Bible

---

94   Elton, *London under the Tudors*, pp. 242–243.
95   Martin Rorke, 'English and Scottish Overseas Trade, 1300–1600', *Economic History Review*, 59 (2006), pp. 265–288 (pp. 269–274, 280).
96   King, *English Reformation Literature*, p. 95n.; James Raven, *The Business of Books: Booksellers and the English Book Trade, 1450–1850* (New Haven, CT: Yale University Press, 2007), p. 47.
97   E.S. Leedham Green, 'Booksellers and libraries in sixteenth-century Cambridge', in *Libraries and the Book Trade: The Formation of Collections from the Sixteenth to the Twentieth Century*, eds. Robin Myers, Michael Harris and Giles Mandelbrote (New Castle, DE: Oak Knoll Press, 2000), pp. 1–14 (pp. 1–3); Raven, *The Business of Books*, p. 51.

projects, to sell his wares in the capital.[98] Non-wholesale booksellers had been required to become naturalised Englishmen following an act in 1534. Tudor governments also kept their eyes on the capital's booksellers. The Henrician 1540s saw substantial pressures placed upon London's evangelical booksellers, with two imprisoned in 1543 and at least twenty-five brought before the council in a period of reactionary conservative policies.[99] Moreover, following the Marian accession, the new catholic authorities arrested some sixty individuals involved in the evangelical book trade.[100] For the Edwardian period, the booksellers were, as we have seen, under less immediate threat.

At the top end of the industry, the centre of English bookselling was St Paul's churchyard. These booksellers invested in leases for premier retail space and established themselves at the summit of the industry. Peter Blayney's research into the collection of stationers and booksellers operating in this area is critical to current historical understanding.[101] Throughout this period, publishers and stationers occupied premises here, and it is indicative of the location's importance that Reyner Wolfe, John Cawood, Richard Jugge, Thomas Petyt and Abraham Veale were among the illustrious occupants. This was the shopfront of the English book world and a hive of activity and commerce. This area also hosted a wide range of stationers, non-printing publishers and non-publishing booksellers.[102] Churchyards likely played a similar role in other regional centres. It is known, for example, that the south side of York Minster became known as 'booksellers alley' by the early seventeenth century, and stationers and binders are known to have occupied the area much earlier.[103] These provincial centres of bookselling were likely the areas where stationers and non-publishing booksellers remained the central actors in their local book worlds; meanwhile, in London, the publishing bookseller rose to prominence.

Booksellers who did not act as printers or publishers are often hidden below the surface of the book world. From an economic standpoint, though, there

---

98 James Gairdner, ed., *Letters and Papers, Foreign and Domestic, Henry VIII, Volume 13 Part 2, August–December 1538* (London, H.M. Stationery Office, 1893), p. 129; Clegg, *Press Censorship*, p. 14.
99 Alec Ryrie, 'The Strange Death of Lutheran England', *Journal of Ecclesiastical History*, 53 (2002), pp. 64–92 (p. 87).
100 Andrew Pettegree, *Marian Protestantism: Six Studies* (Aldershot: Scolar Press, 1996), p. 164.
101 Blayney, *The Bookshops in Paul's Cross Churchyard*; Peter W.M. Blayney, *The Stationers' Company before the Charter, 1403–1557* (London: Worshipful Company of Stationers and Newspaper Makers, 2003); Blayney, *The Stationers' Company*.
102 Blayney, *The Bookshops in Paul's Cross Churchyard*, p. 57.
103 Rosamund Oates, *Moderate Radical: Tobie Matthew and the English Reformation* (Oxford: Oxford University Press, 2018), p. 166; Duff, *A Century of the English Book Trade*, throughout, including pp. 107, 109.

is little doubt that businesses spanned regional trade networks and wider national networks with wholesalers and retailers. Only the booksellers of the capital could have worked exclusively within one location, and their enterprises could only have carved out a smaller niche due to the prominence of the printing/publishing booksellers who dominated the marketplace. Alan Coates' exploration of the Latin book world in Oxford and Cambridge has highlighted that some booksellers imported from the Continent alongside dealing with the centralised London industry.[104] These markets had a discernible academic and literary character, with a pronounced emphasis upon Latin scholarship, which necessitated reliance upon continental printing centres including Antwerp, Paris, and Basel.[105] Examples of bookselling stationers in Oxford included the Dutch émigré Garbrand Harkes (who supplied books to Magdalen College following the dissolution of the monasteries) and the stationers John Gore and Pole, who were based side-by-side in St. Mary Parish after 1551.[106] Cambridge's known contemporaries include Richard Noak and Seger Nicholson.[107] These university towns required large numbers of books and were a natural hotbed for booksellers to set up independent businesses as satellites of the London and continental book markets.

For those regional markets with less scholarly focus, the importance of the international market will have been less significant, and the reliance upon the London market more evident and easier to navigate. From a commercial standpoint, the city of Worcester was a crucial trading post for the West Midlands and Wales, a fact Oswen built upon by building a second bookshop in Shrewsbury, immediately on the Welsh border.[108] Worcester also presented the opportunity to use established trade routes to larger population centres of Bristol, Exeter and Coventry, and potentially Salisbury (via Bristol). Worcester, then, provided a central trading post in the West of England. For other regional centres in England, equivalent trade networks would have been exploited, including Norwich, York and Canterbury.

Minor peddlers of books in this period are notoriously difficult to trace. Catherine Armstrong's dour caricature of itinerant book peddlers 'often on the margins of society, prosecuted for vagrancy and suffering extreme financial

---

104   Coates, 'The Latin Trade in England and Abroad', p. 56.
105   Coates, 'The Latin Trade in England and Abroad' in particular, explores custom rolls. For evangelical works left in Cambridge wills, see Andrew Pettegree, 'The Reception of Calvinism in Britain', in *Calvinus Sincerioris Religionis Vindex: Calvin as Protector of the Purer Religion*, eds. Wilhelm H. Neuser and Brian G. Armstrong (Kirksville, MO: Sixteenth Century Journal Publishers, 1997), pp. 267–290.
106   Duff, *A century of the English Book Trade*, pp. 58, 66.
107   Duff, *A century of the English Book Trade*, pp. 111–112.
108   MacCulloch, *Tudor Church Militant*, p. 82.

hardship' suggests that the furthest reaches of England's book networks were built upon under-funded, unregulated trade practice.[109] Whilst there was likely an element of this involved, effectively running distribution networks out from the capital existed and had been improving as the export economy had become more centralised and booksellers could utilise these same networks.[110] Satellites of the London market in towns and at fairs, however, suggest that independent and associated booksellers and peddlers played a significant role in disseminating works further afield, hardly consistent with Armstrong's depiction.[111] Moreover, English print culture was built around the trade in vernacular literature, with a non-academic audience in mind: this was not the lofty and esteemed academic centre of Basel. An effective infrastructure for reaching popular audiences must have been in place for the English printing trade to survive and thrive. It is far more likely, like in other trades, that the capital was the fulcrum of broader distribution networks, reaching larger population and trade centres such as Norwich, York and Bristol, before smaller-still distribution networks in less centralised areas of the rural population.[112] Moreover, like the continental book trade, the national trade had a calendar of book fairs, including those at Stourbridge (to serve Cambridge) and St Frideswide's (Oxford), where booksellers and possibly printing houses and publishers held a presence – whether directly, or through agents.[113] These fairs and smaller equivalents would have presented opportunities for outreach to the lesser-served readerships outside the capital and wholesale booksellers.

During the Edwardian years, printing remained heavily centralised in London. Whilst the capital was the largest population centre in England, printers needed to access wider audiences. This was particularly true with the return of provincial printing at Ipswich, Worcester and Canterbury. From peddlers to the illustrious booksellers at Paul's Cross, booksellers played a critical

---

109 Catherine Armstrong, 'The Bookseller and the Peddler: the spread of knowledge of the New World in Early Modern England, 1580–1640', in *Printing Places: Locations of Book Production and Distribution Since 1500*, eds. John Hinks and Catherine Armstrong (London: British Library, 2005), pp. 15–30 (p. 23).
110 R.H. Britnell, 'The English Economy and the Government, 1450–1550', in *The End of the Middle Ages? England in the Fifteenth and Sixteenth Centuries*, ed. John L. Watts (Stroud: Sutton Publishing, 1998), pp. 89–116 (pp. 94–95).
111 Raven, *The Business of Books*, p. 51.
112 Tittler, *Townspeople and Nation*, pp. 19–22, Tittler's regional capitals were: Norwich, York, Bristol, Newcastle, Exeter, and perhaps Coventry, Colchester, and Salisbury.
113 John Feather, *A History of British Publishing*, 2nd edn (London: Routledge, 2005), pp. 10–11; Eleanor Chance, Christina Colvin, Janet Cooper, C.J. Day, T.G. Hassall, Mary Jessup, and Nesta Selwyn, 'Markets and Fairs', in *A History of the County of Oxford: Volume 4, the City of Oxford*, eds. Alan Crossley and C.R. Elrington (London: Victoria County History, 1979), pp. 305–312.

role in bridging the printing houses and their readerships. The rapid increase in production under Edward VI and the need quickly to gather profits to reinvest in the next project demanded a smooth-running system of distribution, and often little-known traders in wider goods and specific booksellers provided this link.

2   Commercial Relationships between Printers and Publishers

This section explores the commercial relationships between variant combinations of printers and publishers who worked together to share risk and resources and rise through the industry's ranks. Many of these relationships result in an enduring and immediately visible association. The rising importance of the non-printing publisher and the phenomenon of 'printers-for hire' create colophons by which these associations are instantly identifiable. This exploration of commercial associations, however, will delve deeper into links between printers and the extent to which these associations affected publications. This section will also address those commercial relationships greater than the sum of their parts. This leads directly to chapter seven, where I will argue that a collaborative network which I describe as the St Paul's publishing consortium, operated between c.1546 and 1554 on a scale that scholars have not previously acknowledged, chiefly because many of its members were not involved in the handful of landmark publications that have dominated the historiography.[114] This group produced a landmark bible, but its wider activities exemplify the interconnectedness of the print world and highlights how personal and commercial relationships were foundational in the industry.

Few printers maintained their presence in the market without occasionally reaching out to other trade members to collaborate. As we have seen, even those printers who printed and published independently within the period did not exist as islands. Whilst the industry was moving towards increasing collaboration, some printers continued effectively to combine the printing and publishing trades. For some of these self-publishing printers, as we shall see, their presence in table 6.1 is simply a reflection of failing to share credit in colophons; for others, it reflects the support of powerful patrons who underwrote a presence in the industry; finally, for others it was a business practice that was rooted in the Henrician industry, that came to look increasingly antiquated as the Edwardian reign progressed.

---

114   Abraham Veale, for example, has no *ODNB* profile, despite publishing eleven titles in the Edwardian years, and many more under Elizabeth.

TABLE 6.1   Independent printers, 1547–1553

	Total projects	Solo projects[a]	Percentage
Richard Grafton	210	186	86
John Day	155	73	47
William Powell	69	67	97
Edward Whitchurch	87	62	71
Thomas Berthelet	61	61	100
Robert Wyer	47	44	94
Reyner Wolfe	36	35	97
John Oswen	31	31	100
William Myddleton	25	25	100
Richard Tottell	17	16	94
John Cawood	16	16	100

a   During this section the phrases 'solo projects' and 'collaborative projects' will be used to identify those titles in which only a single individual, or multiple individuals, are recognised by the USTC to have contributed as a printer or publisher to any title.

Despite almost three-quarters of the books printed in the Edwardian years bearing only one name in their colophon, there were surprisingly few prominent printers who almost exclusively acted independently.[115] Scouring the USTC highlights that many of the most prominent names in the industry collaborated on projects even if it was not their usual practice. This measure of single name colophons can, however, be misleading. For this reason, simply counting titles to establish printers who worked independently most frequently will not suffice. According to single-name colophons alone, the top two of our list are simply the most active printers: Richard Grafton and John Day. However, as we know, many of Richard Grafton's works were commissioned by the Crown (which acted as the funding publisher) and he also worked together with Edward Whitchurch without sharing colophons. Day, as we shall see, was wide-reaching in his collaborative circles. Thereafter, the printers who produced the most titles with only their name in the colophon were William Powell, Edward Whitchurch and Thomas Berthelet.

115   The figure for Robert Wyer includes three titles by 'R. Wyer', which could mean Richard rather than Robert Wyer, though with Robert leading the printing house, caution suggests Robert is the more likely party. This figure also considers a Robert and Richard Wyer's collaboration to have been the fruits of one printing house, and therefore independent.

For those same reasons ascribed to Grafton, Reyner Wolfe's thirty-five of thirty-six titles being printed without a publisher comes with the caveat that he was, at least in part, supported by the Crown too. Thomas Berthelet and John Oswen also garnered some support from the regime, though to a lesser extent than Wolfe. Thomas Berthelet, who had been the official printer to Henry VIII's regime, produced sixty-one titles independently, though it appears he retained a stipend from the Crown. Richard Grafton's appointment promised an additional annuity following Berthelet's death, but he lived and his shop printed throughout Edward's reign, so it is reasonable to expect he retained the annuity.[116] Berthelet's sixty-one titles included yearbooks, statutes and acts of parliament from Henry VIII's reign, psalms and homilies from John Fisher, Erasmus and the church fathers, and two vast folios of the Latin-English *Bibliotheca Eliotae*, printed over almost 1200 dual column pages.[117] Whilst E. Gordon Duff and K.F. Pantzer suggest Berthelet became 'much less active' following Edward's accession (indicating that he left much of the work to his nephew), Berthelet continued to print official and pseudo-official works and seemingly retained a position of esteem and wealth within the print world. The Berthelet house may not have maintained its outstanding prominence between 1547 and 1553, but even with a downturn in prestige and production, his print house made a considerable and independent contribution to the trade.[118]

Ipswich-based John Oswen began his career printing independently without official support. He produced twelve titles in his first active year in 1548, though four of these are editions of Jean Calvin's *What a faithful man*.[119] Oswen printed short, small-format evangelical tracts in this first year. Following his accrual of official support, Oswen's press began to take on more significant printing projects, culminating with his two folio *Books of Common Prayer* in 1549 and 1552. The fact that Oswen increasingly adopted the quarto and folio formats (and embarked upon larger projects) lends itself to the assertion that royal support had emboldened him in his business and that this fledgling provincial press was flourishing. Due purely to its reappearance, provincial printing is considered to have flourished during Edward's reign, but the Oswen press provides an indicator that provincial printing could prosper if political and economic conditions aligned.

Of the printing houses without official offices that show the greatest penchant for working independently, those headed by William Myddleton, William Powell, and Robert Wyer were the most prominent. William Myddleton was

---

116 K.F. Pantzer, 'Berthelet [Berthelot], Thomas (*d.* 1555)', ODNB.
117 USTC 504035, 515948.
118 Duff, *A Century of the English Book Trade*, pp. 11–12; Pantzer, 'Berthelet, Thomas (*d.* 1555)'.
119 USTC 503961, 503962, 503983, 503994.

a remnant of the Henrician book world. Before his death in 1547, he produced a further twenty-five independent publications. The vast majority of Myddleton's output was, like Berthelet's, either official or pseudo-official, including works for the courts and yearbooks. Myddleton's progress into the world of legal printing occurred through the inheritance of the printing house of Robert Redman in the early 1540s, and following Myddleton's death, the house changed hands again. In 1547, William Powell married Myddleton's widow Elizabeth, and the business model endured.[120] The press of William Powell continued in the vein of his predecessors, surviving on a diet of staple yearbooks and almanacs, though he did attempt more substantial projects, including a diglot New Testaments designed to fulfil the need for clergy to own copies of the text. In many respects, the Myddleton-Powell press diverged very little from the practices and processes upon which it had been built. Whilst one might imagine this lack of innovation and development failed to keep up with those new ascending printers surrounding it, this press fulfilled an enduring need in the market that transcended the reigns.

Robert Wyer ran another printing house that followed the self-publishing printer model without patronage. As we saw in chapter five, Wyer operated in an increasingly antiquated style, and his output suggests a slightly beleaguered living rather than evident prosperity.[121] The Wyer press printed on behalf of John Day in 1548, John Goodale in 1550 and Richard Kele in 1552, though the family seemingly preferred to print in isolation. They printed a sporadic combination of works across various genres, including evangelical polemic, primers, prognostications and classical authors, which suggests that they assessed the commercial viability of projects and attempted to fill holes in the market. The Wyer press printing style, both in imagery and type, represents a more medieval approach, though the press' operation throughout and beyond the Edwardian tenure makes clear that they were making a sufficient living to create a consistent output.

In the final years of the reign, two English printers played a role in re-establishing previous production patterns. Richard Tottell and John Cawood both printed briefly in 1550 before vanishing from the trade and then reappearing to produce sixteen titles each in 1553. They each produced their publications as independent printer/publishers, though both flourished under official support: Tottell under patent and Cawood with an official office under Mary I. Working as an independent printing publisher without the support of

---

120   R.E. Graves, revised Anita McConnell, 'Middleton [Myddylton], William (d.1547)', ODNB.
121   Tamara Atkin A.S.G. Edwards, 'Printers, Publishers and Promoters to 1558', in *A Companion to the Early Printed Book in Britain, 1476–1558*, eds. Vincent Gillespie and Susan Powell (Cambridge: Brewer, 2014), pp. 27–44 (p. 42).

a powerful patron in these years was challenging. It is clear from these examples, however, that whilst the dominance of the English market by independent publishing printers was waning, it remained a feasible business model.

Despite these examples highlighting the persistence of individualism, collaboration was increasingly prevalent within the Edwardian printing world. From the uppermost echelon of the printing hierarchy down to the lowest, printers, publishers and funders relied upon one another to ensure their wares could reach readers. Some printers or publishers built their entire business presence around these commercial relationships. Peter Blayney's research has shown that output in books printed on behalf of others in England was a developing trend: under five per cent of all works between 1521 and 1534, to seventeen per cent from 1535 until Edward's accession. The Edwardian period saw a significant increase to accommodate over one-quarter of all publications.[122]

The colophons of Edwardian works begin to demonstrate the networks and connections within the trade: 328 of the total 1,212 titles listed in the USTC between 1547 and 1553 credit more than one individual with some part in the printing, publishing or retailing spheres of book production. These publications typically bear the imprints 'and', 'for', 'in the house of', 'at the cost of' or 'sold by' to acknowledge or itemise the input of respective partners. With these variations in the formula, there was no standard practice of listing which party was the lead printer or whether a non-printing publisher or patron was involved. Members of the Edwardian book world were adaptable and collaborative in output.

The leading collaborative forces in the Edwardian industry were not necessarily of one profession or another. Publishers, who by necessity had to collaborate with printers, were matched by the printers they hired to complete their works. The range and number of publishers who commissioned works infrequently, or fewer than three times, was high, whilst the printers-for-hire proved willing to accommodate them, thus increasing their visible collaboration networks. Of the seventy-seven names listed in the colophon of at least one publication between 1547 and 1553, thirty-three were names that only appear alongside another name in the imprint or colophon.[123] Many of these individuals (thirty-one) were present in the trade only fleetingly, with three

---

[122] Blayney, *The Stationers' Company*, p. 653.
[123] These individuals were Pierre Angelin, William Awen, William Baldwin, John Bale, William Bonham, Edmund Campion, Roger Car, John Case, Richard Field, Richard Foster, Christopher Froschauer, Thomas Geminus, Thomas Gibson, John Goodale, John Gybkyn, John Harrington, Andrew Hester, George Joye, Richard Kele, Anthony Kingston, John Kingston, Gwalter Lynne, Cutbere Mathew, John Mayler, Thomas Purfoot, William Rastell, William Salisbury, John Sheffield, Anthony Smith, Edward Sutton, Henry Tab, Nicholas Udall and Egidius van der Erve.

or fewer titles bearing their names, and the most feasible route for them to produce a book was to commission an established printer and act as a funding publisher.[124]

The following table highlights the reign's most productive collaborators, the individuals with the highest propensity for collaboration, and those who collaborated most widely and forms the basis of our exploration of the trade's interpersonal commercial networks. The idiosyncratic manner in which publishers and printers shared credit masks some collaborations from view, but this section will cast light upon both the immediately observable and hidden collaborations in the book world.

The leading producer of collaborative works in the period was publisher William Seres, the bulk of whose works were created by his partnerships with printers John Day and Anthony Scoloker.[125] Due to his role as publisher, these ninety-four collaboration projects account for ninety-five per cent of Seres' business. After Seres follow the prolific printers John Day, Nicolas Hill and Stephen Mierdman for whom the percentage of their business completed in collaboration falls, but their sheer productivity places them second, third and fourth places on our list. This phenomenon is best displayed by comparing seventh and eighth places on our list: Richard Grafton and Gwalter Lynne. Whilst Grafton rarely shared credit in colophons (and made little effort to collaborate

TABLE 6.2   Printers' collaboration, 1547–1553

	Occupation	Total projects	Total collaborations	Percentage of collaborations	Number of collaborators
William Seres	Publisher	99	94	95	7
John Day	Printer	155	81	52	10
Nicolas Hill	Printer	89	63	70	18
Stephen Mierdman	Printer	81	58	72	21
Richard Kele	Publisher	28	28	100	8
William Copland	Printer	56	27	48	9
Richard Grafton	Printer	210	24	11	11
Gwalter Lynne	Publisher	22	22	100	4
John Walley	Publisher	26	21	81	8
Richard Jugge	Publisher/printer	28	18	64	6

124 Removing only Richard Kele and Gwalter Lynne from the above list.
125 Partnerships years active: Day and Seres (fl.1546–1550) and one title (USTC 517974) inferred for 1551 Scoloker and Seres: (fl.1548) and one title (USTC 504404) inferred for 1550.

beyond his connection with Edward Whitchurch), his extraordinary output means that with only twelve per cent of his output qualifying, he out-produced one of the more influential and esteemed publishers of the Edwardian years. These figures only tell part of the story of collaboration in the English book world, but they serve as critical markers for those who played a significant role in the increasingly collaborative outlook of the industry.

3   Partnerships

A fundamental story of Edwardian printing at large was of thriving partnerships. These partnerships came in an array of different dynamics. Printers collaborated to share the production of single editions or multiple editions of the same work; printers also collaborated with publishers and booksellers. The importance and influence of specific partnerships within the English book world have long been acknowledged in the period's historiography, often to the detriment of whoever is considered the minor party. This section will further explore these partnerships to redress this imbalance, treating each individual's career as an entity meriting examination rather than as a supplement to bolstering our knowledge of another in the trade. Naturally, business collaborations varied dramatically in their endurance and their productivity. Furthermore, it will shed light on influential partnerships whose combined efforts made a meaningful contribution to printed output and drove forward English print through collaboration.

The average number of publications per collaborative partnership was low, but these combinations can be separated into two categories: those who produced nine titles or more and those who produced fewer. The premier colophon-sharing partnership of the reign is the printer/publisher partnership of John Day and William Seres, with seventy titles amassed, which ultimately made up seventy-one per cent of Seres' market presence. There are typically two classes of these nine titles or more collaborative partnerships: those enduring connections resulting in a steady flow of production over three or more years and those flash-in-the-pan associations that resulted in a flurry of activity before dissipating.

Richard Grafton and Edward Whitchurch formed the premier printing partnership of the age. Having begun their working relationship as co-publishers of the 1537 Coverdale bible, they embarked upon their printing career. They shared credit on nine titles during the Henrician years, though this convention soon ceased. Curiously for our method of establishing partnerships and collaborations within this period, Grafton and Whitchurch shared no Edwardian colophons.

TABLE 6.3 Prominent partnerships

	Collaboration titles	Years active	Total titles A	Total titles B	Percentage of titles A	Percentage of titles B
A – John Day and B – William Seres	69	1547–1551	169	99	41	70
A – Anthony Scoloker and B – William Seres	14	1548–1550	31	99	45	14
A – Gwalter Lynne and B – Stephen Mierdman	12	1548–1550	23	83	52	14
A – Gwalter Lynne and B – Nicolas Hill	9	1548–1550	23	89	39	10
A – Thomas Raynald and B – William Hill	9	1548–1549	41	31	22	29

Nonetheless, it is evident that they were close partners – they shared materials, worked cooperatively on projects and covered for one another when the other was completing a major assignment. It appears they also stockpiled assets, including printed sheets and may well have held warehouse premises together to this end.[126] The Grafton and Whitchurch partnership is more difficult to quantify than many others within the English print world. The combined seventy publications that Grafton and Whitchurch produced for the English church can feasibly be quantified as a result of this partnership. They were peers and partners in the official service book patent acquired in 1547; this patent required enormous exertion on behalf of both men, and it prompted a corpus of printed material rivalled by few if any of their contemporaries. Grafton and Whitchurch held the closest active association in English printing upon the Edwardian accession, and this association endured atop the hierarchy of printers throughout the reign.

Whitchurch and Grafton worked incredibly closely, but whilst sharing a patent and projects, Whitchurch retained some commercial independence. He was one of the premier printers of the period in his own right, successfully completing some of the reign's most demanding projects and finest editions. The *Paraphrases* project represents the pinnacle of this success. During this

---

126 Cyndia Susan Clegg, 'The 1559 Books of Common Prayer and the Elizabethan Reformation', *Journal of Ecclesiastical History*, 67 (2016), pp. 94–121 (pp. 110–112).

two-part project, Whitchurch worked with some of the reign's premier patrons and produced a canonical volume for the Edwardian church and the second *Paraphrases* volume for private sale.

Despite their enduring and prolific partnership, these printers also looked for collaboration beyond one another to advance their respective businesses. Grafton completed twenty-five further collaborative projects, in which he shared credit with eleven individuals.[127] Chief among these collaborative partners was Robert Crowley, for whom Grafton printed thirteen titles between 1549 and 1551.[128] Whitchurch, too, branched out to collaborate with other individuals, from as early as 1542 when he produced works with John Judson and Richard Bankes.[129] This continued in the Edwardian years, when Whitchurch collaborated with nine other individuals, resulting in fifteen further titles.[130] Whilst their businesses were not angled towards outside collaboration, Grafton was the seventh most active collaborator between 1547 and 1553, whilst Whitchurch was the eleventh. The English printing world was rich in collaboration, and even printers we associate with thriving independent businesses or steadfast partnerships sought to develop and nurture broader commercial networks within the trade.

The Grafton/Whitchurch partnership was not the only printer/printer partnership in the English print world. In stark contrast, in almost every way, was another printing partnership shared by Thomas Raynald and William Hill. The men embarked upon a two-year collaboration between 1548 and 1549 that created nine titles. Both printers emerged in the second year of Edward's reign

---

127   Grafton shared colophons with: John Day, Robert Crowley, Richard Kele, Kingston, Stephen Mierdman, John Mychell, William Salisbury, William Seres, Robert Stoughton and John Walley.

128   USTC 504213, 504215, 504216, 504422, 504223, 504492, 504495, 504505, 504508, 504530, 504533, 504579, 518523, three of these titles are variant titles of William Langland's, *The Vision of Pierce Plowman* (1550) and two are Crowley's *The voyce of the laste trumpet* (1549).

129   USTC (with Judson) 503312; (with Bankes) 503369, Bankes had been particularly collaborative in his approach to printing and publishing during the Henrician 1530s and 1540s, with twenty-five of his fifty titles having been produced with another individual listed in the colophon. Judson is only ever listed in one colophon. Judson is listed as a bookseller by Charles Henry Timperley, *The Dictionary of Printer and Printing, with the Progress of Literature, Ancient and Modern* (London: H. Johnson, 1839), p. 411. Duff, *A Century of the English Book Trade*, pp. 81–82, claims Judson was a printer, a senior member of the Stationers' Company on its incorporation and later thrice Warden of the Company and once Master in the Elizabethan period.

130   Individuals who collaborated with Whitchurch include William Baldwin, John Day, Thomas Gaultier, Nicolas Hill, Stephen Mierdman, Humphrey Powell, William Seres, John Turke and Nicholas Udall.

and contributed to the sudden flood of publications coming from England's presses in 1548, adding a combined forty titles and collaborating directly on six.[131]

William Hill's career was brief but productive, spanning only two years (1548 and 1549) and resulting in a flurry of thirty-one titles. William Hill's projects included fourteen total collaborations, with the additional five collaborations being printed for publishers William Seres and Hugh Singleton. Thomas Raynald's career, meanwhile, continued. He is associated with forty-one titles, though his productivity declined to only three titles in each of his final two printing years in 1551 and 1552. Raynald's output between 1548 and 1552 included fourteen collaboration projects. Beyond his independent printing and partnership with William Hill, Raynald also printed for John Wyght, Humphey Toy, John Harrington, William Seres and Richard Kele.

Hill's thirty-one-strong catalogue shows a specialisation in the small-format polemical tracts that formed the basis of the rapid growth in England's printing industry in 1548.[132] With his engagement with the world of printing spanning only two years, 1548 (the year of maximum Edwardian output) and 1549, historians have too readily overlooked this interesting albeit short career.[133] Thomas Raynald, the former apprentice and printing successor to Thomas Petyt, appears to have printed on a broader religious spectrum, including works by prominent reformers, but also one by conservative Richard Smith and four by the radical polemicist John Mardeley.[134] Raynald, it seems, suffered no repercussions or sanctions from the production of these works and continued to print until 1552.

Unlike Grafton and Whitchurch, Raynald and William Hill shared credit in their colophons, using 'Thomas Raynald and William Hill' (eight) or the reverse (one). Raynald was the more prolific printer and the fact that his name is listed first in the majority of the shared colophons may imply that he led these projects, but this can only be conjecture. This partnership has been discussed in chapter four in terms of its evangelical alignment and attempt to print some of the official works of the Edwardian church. Peter Blayney's assessment that these printers' careers 'collapsed when zeal proved no match for economics'

---

131   Twenty-five for William Hill and fifteen for Raynald, six collaborations together: USTC 503995, 504012, 504048, 504144, 504159, 504073.
132   Edmund Gest, William Punt, William Turner, Robert Barnes and continental theologians Heinrich Bullinger and John Calvin were all among his published authors.
133   William Hill, for example, has no ODNB biography.
134   Blayney, *The Stationers' Company before the Charter*, p. 47. Raynald's evangelical authors included William Tyndale, George Joye, John Hooper and Thomas Becon.

TABLE 6.4   William Hill and Thomas Raynald's collaborations

	Projects	Total collaborations	Percentage of business	Titles printed for publishers	Percentage of business	Number of collaborators	Number of publishers
William Hill	31	14	45	5	16	3	2
Thomas Raynald	41	14	34	5	12	5	4

may indeed reflect careers fuelled by evangelical fervour. Equally, Raynald and Hill may simply have been overly ambitious.[135] Among their collaborations was the grandest project that either individual undertook: a 1,576-page folio 'Mathew' bible, printed upon huge 301 × 200mm pages, in 54-line dual columns in a 95 textura, with large illustration borders to herald each testament.[136] The title-page bore the second largest woodcut used in an Edwardian publication; this border would later pass to Nicolas Hill who used it for the Paul's Cross Syndicate's folio Bible of 1551 (see figure 7.1).

To make commercial matters more difficult, this huge undertaking was produced in the same year as John Day and Stephen Mierdman – two heavyweights of the English book world – combined to produce their folio of the same translation.[137] In a period when Great Bible editions were competing with several Coverdale, 'Mathew', Taverner and Becke translations, and a full range of formats were now available to purchase, this bold move from Hill and Raynald put them in a precarious position, and sharing the risk may have been the most feasible route to publication.

The printer/printer partnerships shown in the combined and individual catalogues of work by Grafton and Whitchurch and Raynald and William Hill are only one of many partnership dynamics found in the English book world. The most prominent form of partnership was the combination of a printer and publisher.

The most famous partnership between printer and publisher during this period is that of John Day and William Seres. This partnership accounts for sixty-nine titles printed within the Edwardian years, which immediately

---

135   Blayney, *The Stationers' Company*, p. 629.
136   USTC 504299.
137   USTC 504300.

establishes them as the two leading collaborators found in Edwardian colophons. The partnership appears to have been led by Day, as their respective catalogues show Day to have been more proactive and prolific outside of their collaboration. The Day/Seres partnership lasted only until 1551, for which sixty-nine titles represent a substantial commercial enterprise.

Day and Seres' partnership worked towards popular audiences, with sixty-eight of sixty-nine titles being small-format publications: the lone folio was *A lamentation of the death of the moost victorious Prynce Henry the eyght* co-produced for John Tucke in 1547.[138] The partners focused heavily upon the market for religious publications, which has naturally led to assertions of their protestant zeal.[139] They played a meaningful role in creating the wave of evangelical pamphlet literature that characterises 1548. Only eleven of their sixty-nine titles are not primarily classified by the USTC as either religious or biblical; even among these, we find Robert Crowley's confutation of Miles Huggarde, Thomas Becon's *Fortress of the faithful agaynst ye assautes of povertie and honger*, and two accounts of the news of the Devonshire and Cornish rebels in 1549.[140] The English reformation fuelled their presses, and their presses fuelled the reformation in turn by disseminating works of leading theologians, controversialists and producing scripture between 1548 and 1551.[141]

Such is Day's prominence in the historiography that it will suffice to frame his lesser-known Edwardian accomplishments within the context of the wider industry. Day produced 155 titles during the Edwardian years, including his thirteen publications in 1553, some of which were anti-Marian publications following her accession.[142] Of these 155 titles, seventy-three were independently printed and published, whilst eighty-two were handled in collaboration with at least one other partner. Day's output, then, was scattered with the influence of other individuals, be it funding partners (primarily via publishers such as Robert Toy and Abraham Veale) or where Day acted as a publisher, outsourcing the printing, as in the eleven instances of works printed 'by Stephen Mierdman

---

138   USTC 503838.
139   Peter Blayney, 'William Cecil and the Stationers', in *The Stationers' Company and the Book Trade 1550–1990*, eds. Robin Myers and Michael Harris (Winchester: St Paul's Bibliographies, 1997), pp. 11–34 (p. 21); Brigden, *London and the Reformation*, p. 438; Evenden and Freeman, *Religion and the Book in Early Modern England*, p. 64.
140   USTC 504020; 504365, 504383; 504285, 518565.
141   USTC 517974, 504121, 504289, 504307, 504528, 504552.
142   Within these titles are publications under the pseudonym 'Michael Wood', now known to have been Day's alias whilst printing in Lincolnshire, and his publications of Bale's edited editions of Stephen Gardiner's *De vera obediencia* USTC 517667, 517668.

for', either Day or Day and Seres together.[143] The fact that Day's work aligned with, and at times outstripped the pace of, the evangelical trajectory of the authorities has been well documented in previous scholarship, and his ascendancy in terms of technical capacity has been explored earlier in this study and particularly in the work of John N. King and Elizabeth Evenden.[144]

Seres' role in this partnership – and thus his historiography at large – has been marginalised due to John Day's remarkable Elizabethan exploits. William Seres, in fact, is listed in a startling number of colophons between 1547 and 1553 (ninety-nine titles in total), more than printers Stephen Mierdman and Edward Whitchurch and more than any other publisher. While most of Seres' output was made up of publications he worked on with John Day, he also commissioned works from other printers (thirty titles).[145] Reaffirming these figures is critical in establishing Seres as a formidable publisher in his own right. Of the ninety-nine titles that he published, he also collaborated with Anthony Scoloker (fourteen titles), Stephen Mierdman (four), Nicolas Hill (four), William Hill (three), Edward Whitchurch (three), Thomas Raynald (two), and Richard Grafton, Richard Kele and Thomas Gaultier once each.[146] These were the premier printers of the period, and Seres fostered commercial networks that catapulted him to the pinnacle of print production. Many of these collaborations included Seres and Day's overriding partnership as Whitchurch, Mierdman and Grafton printed for the partnership rather than exclusively for Seres. Beyond his partnership with Day, Seres continued to target a popular audience and his entire catalogue of works independent of John Day was printed solely in the octavo format, aside from one sextodecimo primer in 1553, by which time he had procured an official patent for its production.[147]

Seres, then, also worked in another partnership with Anthony Scoloker, following Scoloker's return to the capital, resulting in a flurry of fourteen titles spanning 1548 (twelve titles), 1549 (one) and 1550 (one). As with Seres' partnership with Day, most Scoloker/Seres publications supported the reformation,

143   Day also commissioned works by Grafton (two), Whitchurch (two), and Robert Wyer (one).
144   John N. King, 'The Light of Printing: William Tyndale, John Foxe, John Day, and Early Modern Print Culture', *Renaissance Quarterly*, 54 (2001), pp. 52–85; Evenden and Freeman, *Religion and the Book in Early Modern England*; Evenden, *Patents, Pictures and Patronage*.
145   This figure includes five titles currently attributed to Seres alone, where no printer is inferred; though it is possible that Day printed them.
146   This amounts to thirty-three collaborators, three of the projects overlapped: Whitchurch Grafton and Mierdman each collaborated with John Day and William Seres on their projects.
147   USTC 504822; PR *Edward VI*, 5, pp. 50–51.

including editions by Tyndale, John Frith, Huldrych Zwingli, and the archbishop of Cologne, Hermann von Wied.[148] The partnership adopted the pseudonym 'Michael Boys' of Geneva in 1548 to repatriate the printing of recently deceased social and religious polemicist Henry Brinklow's *Complaint of Roderyck Mors*.[149] Brinklow's rhetoric remained controversial even in the Edwardian years, and it was likely a fear of censorship and prosecution that prompted the use of the pseudonym.[150] This partnership, as with Seres' independent output in these years, followed a similar outwardly popular evangelical direction. The Scoloker/Seres publications, visually, were characteristic of Scoloker's previous output, but it is clear that Seres was not simply being drawn into publications by printers. Seres was deliberately publishing works of a particular genre and style. His impressively large catalogue of publications was also matched by the influential company he kept. As will be discussed below, Seres' ties to the man who would become the premier statesman of Elizabethan England – William Cecil – aided his integration with the regime and contributed to his rise to prominence.[151] Seres ultimately secured letters patent for primers and psalters in March 1553, which indicates the proficiency he had displayed, and the administration's willingness to put their faith in him. Seres produced three titles in 1553 which fall under this patent, discussed in chapter four, for which Seres was given sole credit, though it seems he commissioned to be printed under his name alone.

It has suited Day's legacy as Tudor England's premier printer to marginalise Seres' influence in these years, but a partnership with a formidable publisher, particularly in close association with the circles of power, undoubtedly facilitated Day in a broader sense than the sharing of financial risk. The Day/Seres partnership was the mainstay of Seres' output and influence within the industry, but his output was significant beyond his role with Day. Excluding all Day/Seres publications, Seres still ranks as at least the second most prolific publisher of the period.[152]

---

148   USTC (Tyndale) 504329, 504138; (Frith) 504051; (Zwingli, Veron transl.) 504544; (von Wied) 516470.
149   Alec Ryrie, 'Brinklow, Henry (*d.* 1545/6)', ODNB.
150   USTC 514977, 541978.
151   Evenden and Freeman, *Religion and the Book in Early Modern England*, pp. 66–67; Evenden, 'The Fleeing Dutchmen?', p. 66; Stephen Alford, *Kingship and Politics in the reign of Edward VI* (Cambridge: Cambridge University Press, 2002), p. 133.
152   The qualifier of this statement is that the five sole-credit publications were only published by Seres rather than printed by him, and not printed by John Day.

4   Printers for Hire

The English print world became more cooperative and collaborative. The increasing interconnectedness of individuals within the trade and the number of individuals seeking collaboration ensured that non-printers could produce publications and that trusted print houses were seldom inactive. The increased presence of the publisher in this period is demonstrable but owes much to the corresponding, and prerequisite, escalation in printing for hire.

Within the 327 publications bearing the name of one or more individuals between 1547 and 1553, 206 are listed with the clearly stated 'for' colophons or imprints, which itemise a printer and publisher relationship.[153] Four more are highlighted by colophons reading 'cost of'.[154] From these publications, it can be reasonably suggested that at least fifty-nine individuals acted as a publisher on one or more titles during these years.[155] The number of active printing houses serving these publishers, however, was comparatively small. In total, thirty individuals or print houses were commissioned to produce one or more publications on behalf of a publisher. Still, the surge to prominence of those printing houses that produced more than twenty-five publications on behalf of others began to reshape the commercial and interpersonal dynamics of the industry. Each major printer-for-hire was operating multiple presses and inviting business from private sources, which fuelled their remarkable productivity. Their success marks a significant evolution in the English context. Peter Blayney has suggested that a printer working for a publisher would make 'less than half the profit margin he could make by publishing it himself'.[156] Even this margin, when completed at the scale of output of the reign's major printers-for-hire, was enough to be a sustainable approach to business whilst exposing the printers-for-hire to far less risk.

The most expansive visible collaboration networks stem from the most prominent printers-for-hire: Nicolas Hill and Stephen Mierdman. One or other of these two individuals is listed in 121 of the 327 Edwardian publications that recorded more than one individual in its colophon. As contract printers, these Netherlandish émigrés played a central role in the dramatic increase of

---

153   Blayney's figures for the Edwardian years highlight 298 items printed for others, though some variation may be accounted for with 1553 publications printed during Mary I's reign, Blayney, *The Stationers' Company*, p. 653.
154   USTC 504066, 516489, 516490, 518679.
155   There is significant overlap as between printers and publishers in this context. Printers who outsourced the printing of a project would be considered to have published that work.
156   Blayney, *The Stationers' Company*, p. 652.

TABLE 6.5   Major printers-for-hire

	Total projects	Collaboration projects	Percentage of business	Number of collaborators
Stephen Mierdman	81	58	72%	21
Nicolas Hill	85	63	74%	18

individuals credited in colophons. Ten individuals who are otherwise absent from the print world during these years contracted one of these two printers.[157] Alongside a single collaboration together, Hill's name shares a colophon with eighteen different individuals between 1547 and 1553, and Mierdman shares credit with twenty-one individuals. As nine parties acted as publishers for both Mierdman and Hill, twenty-eight people employed either Mierdman, Hill, or both during Edward's reign.

Stephen Mierdman and Nicolas Hill were atypical members of the book world due to this high percentage of output being produced on behalf of, or in collaboration with, others. Functioning as printers-for-hire dominated their respective businesses, accounting for around three-quarters of each printer's respective Edwardian output. Hill is credited with fifty-five titles during Henry VIII's tenure, forty-four of which were produced in collaborations. This pattern continued during the Edwardian period, amounting to sixty-three of his eighty-five projects. Mierdman, meanwhile, had printed for an English readership from his Antwerp press, but it was not until 1548 that he relocated to Billingsgate, London. Over the next five years, he produced eighty-one titles, fifty-eight of which were multi-party publications.

The expansive networks shown by these printers may reflect an 'open door' policy held by the printers in terms of being open for commissions. In this small economy, it would have been readily known which printers operated in this contract printing mould. For both Mierdman and Hill, few of these publisher-funded publications can be seen as forming part of a coherent and enduring partnership rather than one-off projects. Of the 121 total titles printed by one of these two printers by commission, only four began collaborative relationships that resulted in more than ten titles, whilst eleven of these collaborative relationships lasted only one title.

---

157   Mierdman shared colophons with William Awen, John Bale, Richard Foster, John Gybkyn, Andrew Hester, George Joye and Edward Sutton; Nicolas Hill shared colophons with Thomas Geminus, Thomas Purfoot, and John Sheffield.

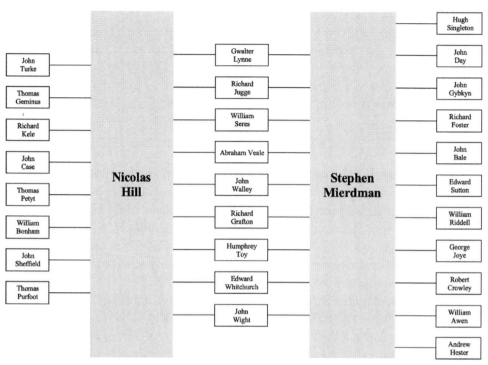

FIGURE 6.1 The commercial networks of Nicolas Hill and Stephen Mierdman

There was a significant crossover between the publishers and booksellers who collaborated with Nicolas Hill and Mierdman, including some of the leading active publishers. The most impactful relationships between these two printers-for-hire and non-printing publishers were with Gwalter Lynne (nineteen in total) and Richard Jugge (fourteen). For Gwalter Lynne, who never printed his works, reliance upon printers-for-hire was vital. It also made sense for Lynne to lean upon his compatriots among the Dutch population in London. Richard Jugge was, at this time, a substantial publisher within the industry, and turning to the premier printers-for-hire was a natural process for a man developing his industrial presence. Later in Edward's reign and during the subsequent reigns, Jugge rose to prominence as a printer, following his receipt of a privilege to print his newly revised version of the Tyndale Bible. The works for which Jugge relied upon a printer-for-hire in these years included quarto, octavo and sextodecimo New Testaments, two almanacs and a polemic discourse by John Fryth, all handled by Stephen Mierdman, and a polyglot dictionary and two Hooper translations by Nicolas Hill.[158]

---

158   USTC (Mierdman) 504071, 504078, 504110, 504120, 504920, 504921, 515375, 516491; (Hill) 504463, 504534, 504708, 515441, 516000.

We see a wide range of materials within both printers' catalogues of collaborative works. Among Mierdman's fifty-eight collaborative publications, outputs ranged from seemingly insubstantial projects, such as the thirty-two-page octavo edition of Robert Crowley's *The way to wealth* in 1550, to the magnificent 'Mathew' bible printed for John Day and William Seres in 1549, or the 436-page folio *Abcedarium anglico latinum* for William Riddell in 1552.[159] Nicolas Hill, too, produced quality works for others, including a striking 1,418-page folio edition of *The Workes* of Chaucer printed for The Paul's Cross publishing syndicate in 1550.[160] Quicker job lot jobs, too, played a role, including a sextodecimo *Of the preparation to the crosse*, for John Walley in 1550.[161] Mierdman appears to have been the go-to printer-for-hire for one-time and small-scale publishers of works. Of the eleven publishers who employed only Mierdman and not Nicolas Hill, nine collaborated with only Mierdman and collaborated on only one or two publications.

In these two premier printers-for-hire, we do not find individuals who shaped the nature of texts produced during these years, yet we find two printers who were paramount to the material output of the industry. This development had broad implications for the trade, potential patrons and society. By facilitating individuals who had the capital but not the capacity to print works, printers-for-hire opened a route for texts to become printed books. The decision to produce a book could now be made with a different economic model in mind: a wealthy patron or non-printing publisher could be motivated to fund an edition via a printer-for-hire for any number of reasons rather than the primary motivation of profits. Hill and Mierdman were emblematic of this growing opportunity, and the rapidity with which non-printers came to publish works through them suggests that people within and without the print world were keen to engage.

There were other printers occupying the same business territory as Mierdman and Hill but on a smaller scale. Four more of London's printers produced substantial bodies of work for other individuals: William Copland, Thomas Gaultier, William Hill and Thomas Raynald. Among their list of clients, we see familiar London booksellers: each printed at least one work for Robert Toy and Richard Kele, whilst two of the three also printed for Richard Jugge, John Walley and William Seres.[162]

---

159   Bible – USTC 504300; *Abcedarium anglico latinum* – USTC 504780.
160   In this instance, the syndicate included: Kele, Petyt, Bonham and Toy (see chapter seven).
161   USTC 515493.
162   Richard Jugge published works printed by Copland and Gaultier; Walley commissioned works by Copland and Gaultier; Seres published works printed by Gaultier and Hill (also Thomas Raynald, who was William Hill's partner).

TABLE 6.6 Minor printers-for-hire

	Total projects	Total collaborations	% of business	Titles for publishers	% of business	Total number of collaborators	Number of publisher collaborators
William Copland	56	27	48	27	48	9	9
Thomas Gaultier	16	10	63	9	63	9	8
William Hill	31	14	45	5	16	3	2
Thomas Raynald	41	14	34	5	12	5	4

These minor printers-for-hire were contracted for works by a range of individuals, including premier printers and publishers, established booksellers, and relative unknowns of the book world. As we can see, these printers occupied comparatively less of their time at the presses printing things for other individuals.

Chief among these minor printers-for-hire, we find the Copland family press. William, believed to be the son of Wyken de Worde's printing heir Robert Copland, produced fifty-six titles during the Edwardian years, twenty-seven of which were printed on behalf of others. These publications include some known associates of Robert Copland, including John Walley and Henry Tab, for whom Robert's name is attached to projects in 1548. Robert's date of death is uncertain, and this may have been William using his deceased father's name to bestow legitimacy upon his early publications. The Copland press printed nine titles for a syndicate of booksellers based at Paul's Cross, thereby adding Richard Kele, John Wyght and Richard Jugge to its clients. It printed further works for publishers amongst the syndicate's ranks that do not qualify as syndicate publications as they were two-party projects rather than being collectively funded.[163] The Copland family press and its clients highlight how small the English printing and publishing world was, and London publishers could rely upon the Coplands at the sign of the Rose Garland on Fleet Street. William Copland produced mainly small works for his publishers; however, they did increase in size to include an octavo New Testament for John Walley in 1550 and an impressive edition of *The four sons of Aimon* for the Paul's Cross

---

163 Copland printed for Richard Kele in 1547, 1549 and 1550; and Abraham Veale in 1552.

publishers in 1554.[164] Despite this high level of collaboration shown, over fifty per cent of the Copland press' Edwardian work was produced independently, including a 368-page folio edition of *The recuile of the histories of Troie* completed in 1553.[165]

Thomas Gaultier had the highest rate of collaboration, in part, because he printed an edition of Thomas Paynell's *The piththy and moost notable sayinges of al scripture* for the Paul's Cross publishing syndicate in 1550, which accounts for three titles. Gaultier worked as a printer in England between 1550 and 1553, quickly establishing himself with both English and French texts. His catalogue of works culminated with a New Testament in English for John Cawood in 1550 and his independently printed French New Testaments in 1551 and 1553, the second of which followed his receipt of royal support. Gaultier worked in collaboration on ten projects, each seemingly only fleeting associations as nine individuals are listed among these ten texts.

As discussed above, William Hill and Thomas Raynald's respective catalogues of works were stories of independent and printer-printer partnerships rather than printing for hire: the majority (sixty-four per cent) of their collaborations were together. They, too, both worked for William Seres, though otherwise did not step on each other's toes; William Hill worked for Seres and Hugh Singleton, whilst Raynald picked up projects for Robert Toy, John Harrington, and Richard Kele.

For these middling printers-for-hire, job printing was often a secondary concern and a means to ensure their presses did not stand idle. In order to pay wages and overheads, it was paramount that presses were active and making money. In instances where they printed for others, printers must have accepted a smaller portion of returns from sales, but they also assumed a more negligible, if any, risk.[166] These printers-for-hire induced individuals to become involved in the trade, and these contracts helped buoy the printers' businesses in a perilous commercial environment.

---

164   USTC 504985, 515473, 515474.
165   USTC 504906.
166   Blayney, *The Stationers' Company*, p. 652, has argued that printers who printed on behalf of others rather than publishing their own could expect to make less than half the profit.

5   Publishers

Hand-in-hand with the rise of printers-for-hire during this period is the ascent of non-printing publishers. These co-dependent roles in the industry owed a great deal to one another, but there are instances where they were mutually exclusive. While Hill and Mierdman carried much of the burden of publishers' commissions, there remain 206 of the 327 titles bearing the name of multiple parties in their colophons still to be accounted for. William Seres' role as a publisher has been discussed, but other individuals played the same role.

Chief among England's publishers were Richard Kele (twenty-eight titles), Gwalter Lynne (twenty-two titles), and John Walley (twenty-one titles). Kele and Walley's businesses included many collaborative projects, but even these colophon listings mask the true level of interconnectivity between trade members. Opportunities presented themselves for many individuals to publish works without investing heavily or immersing themselves in the trade. This portion of our examination will cover those publishers ranging from the lowest level of involvement to those leading the rise of non-printing publishers.

The Edwardian period saw a disproportionately large number of one-off publishers who dipped their toes into the waters of print. On some occasions, these individuals can be seen to have funded works of particular esteem, perhaps attempting to garner prestige and standing from their involvement; others invested in what appear to be bewilderingly mundane volumes. Single-publication publishers account for twenty-one of the collaborative partnerships in the reign, whilst raising the limit to five titles increases their ranks to thirty. Small-scale publishers were, therefore, whilst not individually noteworthy, an important part of the landscape of Edwardian print collaboration. These thirty individuals whose doors remained open for this steady flow in outsourced titles allowed for the development of the printers-for-hire trade. The exact circumstances discouraging each of these one-time or short-term publishers from investing in publications again are, of course, unique to each investor and each project. In many instances, these individuals may have only ever intended to publish a single work of specific importance to them; in others, they may have proven to be economic misadventures.

Beyond those individuals exploring print as one-time or short-term ventures, six publishers produced at least ten publications or more during the reign, three of whom could be classed as 'middling' publishers.

These three publishers form the second tier of Edwardian publishing and exemplify the willingness of English publishers to work somewhat indiscriminately with a variety of printers. Toy worked with a wide network of printers, seven in total, Singleton worked with six and Veale with four. It is difficult to ascertain whether publishers actively shopped around for lower prices or simply scheduled their commissions when printers had inactive presses, but in a volatile market where commercial acumen governed success or failure, the reality was likely a combination of both. The existence of multiple printers-for-hire in London invited more publishers into the trade, but also will have allowed publishers to seek the best deal.

Both Robert Toy and Abraham Veale are elevated to this tier of middling publishers, in part, due to their investments in the Paul's Cross publishing syndicate. Their participation in this syndicate will be explored in chapter seven, but it is noteworthy that their involvements overlapped on only two occasions: a folio bible of 1551, and Erasmus Sarcerius' *Common Places*, 1553, both printed by Nicolas Hill.[167] In total, they invested in eight syndicate publications between 1547 and 1553. Outside their participation with the publishing

TABLE 6.7   Middling publishers

	Total projects	Collaborative projects[a]	Number of printers	Printers of choice
Hugh Singleton	16	11	6	Humphrey Powell; John Herford; John Mychell; William Hill; Thomas Raynald; Thomas Gaultier
Robert Toy	16	15	7	John Day; John Herford; Thomas Gaultier; Nicolas Hill; William Copland; Stephen Mierdman; Thomas Raynald
Abraham Veale	11	11	5	Stephen Mierdman, Nicolas Hill, John Day, William Copland, John Wyer

a   'Collaborative projects', here, are defined as USTC listings that have more than one individual listed in the colophon, either on the original document or inferred by USTC.

167   USTC 504679, 504644; 504884, 504888, 504902.

syndicate, they also co-commissioned an edition of Tyndale's translation of Erasmus' *Enchiridion militis christiani*, printed by John Day in 1552.[168]

Stationer Robert Toy, whose son Humphrey would secure setting-up costs and a patent for the printing of the *Book of Common Prayer* in Ireland in 1550, operated at the sign of the Bell in Paul's Cross churchyard and seems to have achieved a steady living as a bookseller and publisher. His son was able to matriculate at Queen's College Cambridge in 1551 – albeit receiving financial assistance from the college – and Robert bequeathed property interests in Paternoster Row and St Paul's churchyard to his wife.[169] Peter Blayney's research suggests Toy's career began with a 1541/2 primer, co-funded by William Bonham and printed by John Herford, although the USTC records two primers published the same year for Toy, by Richard Grafton and Nicholas Bourman.[170] Toy's Edwardian publications were geared towards religious literature, including works by John Foxe and John Clerk and translations of Erasmus. Robert Toy also funded one of two Edwardian trigesimo-secundos (thirty-twomos): a primer by Thomas Gaultier in 1550.[171] The extent of Toy's outreach to printers highlights him as having one of the widest spanning commercial networks. Toy's daughter, Rose, married the stationer Arthur Pepwell and his widow Elizabeth worked closely with John Walley in the reign of Mary I.[172] Robert Toy's commercial networks provide us with another indication of the interconnectedness of English printing and publishing.

Abraham Veale, based at the sign of the Lamb in St Paul's churchyard, is noted by E. Gordon Duff to have begun printing in 1548.[173] In fact, Veale was a publishing bookseller who published alone and with the Paul's Cross syndicate. There is only one Edwardian edition to which only Abraham Veale's name is attached in the USTC, which Peter Blayney has since inferred to have been the work of John Wyer.[174] Whilst belonging to the network of publishers and booksellers at Paul's Cross, Veale's publication record shows a surprisingly small network of trusted printers. Veale collaborated primarily with Nicolas Hill (six titles), who produced the majority of, and the most impressive of, Veale's publications although he also commissioned works from Stephen

---

168   USTC 504734, 504735.
169   I. Gadd, 'Toy, Humphrey (*b.* in or before 1537, *d.* 1577)', ODNB; Blayney, *The Stationers' Company*, p. 468.
170   Blayney, *The Stationers' Company*, p. 438; USTC 503367, 503346, 503289.
171   USTC 504411.
172   Gadd, 'Toy, Humphrey'.
173   Duff, *A Century of the English Book Trade*, pp. 161–162.
174   Blayney, *The Stationers' Company*, p. 635.

Mierdman (two), John Day (one), William Copland (one) and John Wyer (one). Veale's investments were religious in genre, including folio and quarto bibles printed by Hill, Thomas More's *Utopia* and Heinrich Bullinger's *Christen state of matrymonye*.[175] Veale's book world associations often only emerge through his chosen printer's commissions. His network, however, was significantly more extensive than the four individuals with whom he shared colophons.

Hugh Singleton's life mirrors the religious tumult of the period; he is believed to have grown up in Wesel, returned to England in 1547, and later fled to Wesel during Mary I's reign.[176] Based at the signs of St. Augustine (1548–1550) and the double hood (1551 onwards), Singleton was involved in sixteen projects between 1547 and 1553, to which can be added a further two titles printed in Wesel at the press of Joos Lambrecht.[177] These two titles, Stephen Gardiner's *De vera obedientia* and John Bale's *The vacacyon of Johan Bale to the bishiprick of Ossorie in Irelande*, were doubtless designed to undermine the new Marian religious policies and sit alongside Singleton's efforts to promote evangelicalism when he published works by continental reformers Urbanus Rhegius, Martin Luther, Johannes Oecolampadius and Hermann von Wied. Singleton also published works by the martyred Robert Barnes (printed by John Herford) and two texts by evangelical poet William Samuel (both printed by Humphrey Powell).[178] Singleton represents perhaps one of the surest notions of the religious conviction of an Englishman within the Edwardian printing world. Singleton's overwhelming focus upon evangelical works and his subsequent exile and return to the fold under the reformed government of Elizabeth I denote his religious inclinations. Singleton's role as the publisher also meant that he had more freedom in commissioning works he believed to be profitable economically and socially.

This middling tier of publishers significantly contributed to the book world. Their forty-one titles make up only three per cent of the publications of the reign, but they characterise the phenomenon of a growing spirit of cooperation and collaboration, where non-printing publishers could make their mark on a trade that had been traditionally led by printers alone.

The publishing career of Gwalter Lynne, who received a catch-all patent in 1547 for any new works 'consonant to godliness' published at his expense,

---

175 USTC 518466, 504679, 504664, 504715.
176 Natalie Mears, 'Singleton, Hugh (*d.* in or before 1593)', ODNB; Mears' exploration of Singleton's life focuses on his Elizabethan exploits, following his publishing career from 1553, and his printing from (at earliest) 1555.
177 Blayney, *The Stationers' Company*, p. 662; USTC 504811, 504859.
178 Brian Cummings, 'Samuel, William (*fl.* 1551–1569)', ODNB.

resulted in works being commissioned from four printers, most notably and consistently his Netherlandish compatriots Stephen Mierdman and Nicolas Hill. Lynne's publishing career resulted in the publication of twenty-two titles between 1548 and his withdrawal from the trade in 1550. Of these publications, all but three were outsourced to either Mierdman (twelve) or Hill (seven), with John Herford (two) and William Powell (one) picking up the final projects. Lynne's preference to collaborate with these two Netherlandish printers speaks to the quality of products that each printer delivered, a state of affairs supported not only by the books themselves but also the number of publishers who turned to them.

Having developed a close working relationship with Nicolas Hill and Mierdman, Lynne had little need to explore the option of employing other printers. It is possible that his first project picked up by John Herford, the patented publication of 1548, simply preceded any working relationship with Mierdman and Hill. The reasons for turning to William Powell in 1549 to print a translation of one of Heinrich Bullinger's sermons before returning to Herford again in 1550 for a Nicholas Lesse translation of Augustine's *A worke of the predestination of saints*, at least on the surface, remains curious. Attempting to rationalise why Lynne decided to revisit commissioning works to Herford and introducing business to Powell can only be conjecture. The Bullinger sermon was only a 68-page octavo, a project that could have been completed quickly by any efficient printer. The timing might have denied Stephen Mierdman from the commission, as he printed an edition of the complete bible for John Day in 1549, but this explanation would hinge upon exceptionally poor timing and is far from watertight. With Nicolas Hill producing fewer titles in 1549 than in any other year of the reign and printing another project for Lynne in the same year, it is difficult to see why (from a purely business standpoint) Hill's press could not have assumed the project even if Mierdman was unable to complete it. Similarly, the return to using Herford as the printer of a 388-page octavo edition of St. Augustin's *A worke of the predestination of saints* in 1550 could correspond with Mierdman working with Richard Grafton on the folio edition of *The Union of the two noble and illustre famelies of Lancastre and Yorke*, and Nicolas Hill completing *The Workes* of Chaucer for the Paul's Cross publishing syndicate. There are, of course, any number of social, health, travel or economic factors that could have prevented either of the printers from taking on any of these projects, so we must not assume that it was the result of any commercial grievance.

Gwalter Lynne presents an intriguing case for the Edwardian print world. In many respects, he exemplifies a definitively Edwardian approach to the industry. He provided work for others and built up meaningful collaborative relationships. But for his withdrawal from the trade in 1550, in favour of the trading of wine (which shows nothing more than that Lynne was above all a businessman), Lynne might well have been considerably more prolific and prosperous as a publisher.

Richard Kele produced the second most extensive catalogue of works by a non-printing publisher (twenty-eight titles). His catalogue spanned many genres, including religious works (sermons, polemic and scripture), calendars and almanacs, and jurisprudential works. Active between 1540 and 1552 before withdrawing from the trade, Kele represents part of the distinctively Edwardian boom of publishing.[179] Whilst five of Kele's fourteen titles printed in the Henrician period bear only his name in the colophon, there is little evidence to suggest he ever owned or ran a printing house. He was, instead, a publishing bookseller, dwelling at the sign of the eagle on Lombard Street, one of the central districts for Tudor London's merchants.[180]

Kele's commercial network included not only the eight individuals who printed his commissions but also the booksellers based in Paul's Cross churchyard. Kele commissioned eight different printers in the Edwardian years.[181] His publication catalogue favours two printers: Nicolas Hill (ten titles) and William Copland (eight titles). Kele's association with the Copland printing house spanned two generations, having commissioned three octavos from Robert Copland in 1545, and son William to print octavo editions following his assumption of control of the business. On the other hand, Nicolas Hill was the printer of choice for Kele's more extensive works, including folio almanacs in 1547 and 1552, the *Workes* of Geoffrey Chaucer in 1550 and a complete bible in 1551. The latter two of these works were completed in conjunction with a wider syndicate. Kele's association with Nicolas Hill extended beyond the Paul's Cross syndicate. He was the only publisher to collaborate with Hill on more than ten occasions during the Edwardian years, building on their two Henrician

---

179 Kele's first colophon listing was printed by Richard Bankes in 1540, USTC 515313. This was followed by titles in 1542 and 1543, before Kele's association with the Copland and Hill printing houses began in 1545.
180 Peter Brimacombe, *Tudor England* (Norwich: Jarrold Publishing, 2004), p. 71.
181 Kele hired Robert Copland (1545, four titles); William Copland (1547–1552, eight titles); Nicolas Hill (1550–1552, ten titles); Robert Wyer (1552, one title); Richard Grafton (1550, one title); Thomas Raynald (1550, one title); Thomas Gaultier (1550–1551, three titles); John Herford (1547–1548, three titles).

collaborations.[182] As we have seen, Nicolas Hill's presence in the industry was driven by his propensity for collaboration and this same opportunity allowed Kele to develop a significant standing within the industry from the publisher's vantage point.

John Walley's name first appears in an English colophon in 1543, where he is credited for the publication of Gaspar Laet's almanac.[183] Thereafter, his career turns more clearly to that of a publisher, with only six of his twenty-six Edwardian titles giving him sole credit.[184] Walley's career extended beyond the Edwardian period; he was listed in the Stationers' Company charter of 1557 and remained in business until his three final publications in 1585.[185] Walley's publications where sole credit is offered can often be linked to variants with differing title-pages, and there is little evidence that he ran a press. Walley published works in eleven genres specified by the USTC, though his output centred around his seven religious works and four further biblical texts. The most surprising publication listed in the USTC as having been printed by John Walley is a 1551 folio bible. Catalogues of the period have yet to credit the work's printer, Nicolas Hill, for his contribution, instead naming Walley as the printer rather than crediting him as just one of seven investors.

The majority of his works in the Edwardian period were collaborative. Nicolas Hill, William Copland, Robert Copland, Richard Grafton, Thomas Gaultier, John Herford, and Stephen Mierdman all 'printed for' Walley. He also shared colophons with Cuthbert Matthew and Henry Tab. The collaboration with Matthew claimed to have been 'printed for' Walley, though it has been unearthed that this was also printed by Nicolas Hill, and Henry Tab was a co-publisher of an edition of *the Treasure of pore men* printed by Robert Copland in 1548.[186] The fact that Walley employed such a wide range of printers during the Edwardian period may reflect that he was shopping for the best deals available. Spreading his twenty-one collaborative projects among seven printers may well have been Walley's vehicle to success that allowed him to endure in an industry where many others did not.

These three individuals who formed the uppermost tier of Edwardian English publishing created a significant number of publications. Whether these publications were publisher-led or printer-led remains a cause for some uncertainty, but it seems likely that, given the variety of publications in their

---

182   USTC (Henrician) 503702, 503742; (Edwardian) 503883, 504408, 504512, 504706, 504737, 504740, 504746, 504748, 516516, 518679.
183   USTC 516420.
184   USTC 504181, 515409, 515045, 515363, 515996, 518065.
185   Blayney, *The Stationers' Company*, p. 512; USTC 510289, 510157, 510190.
186   Blayney, *The Stationers' Company*, p. 1032; USTC 516467.

catalogues, and their propensity to use multiple printing houses to complete their works, they were more likely to have been publisher-led. The seeming lack of loyalty shown by publishers to their chosen printers muddies the waters of which printer was responsible for certain projects but exposes the true interconnectedness and complexity of the commercial networks upon which the industry was coming to rely.

The Edwardian reign developed a series of characteristic commercial dynamics quite unlike any created within the industry under Henry VIII. The day-to-day activities of the print trade's industrial workers, artisans and commercial workers changed little but developed to accommodate Edwardian presses' increased output. Meanwhile, there were distinct shifts in the balance of the trade among printers and publishers. Edwardian print culture saw a disproportionate growth in two or more party publications and was built upon a wide range of commercial and personal connections. Fuelled by a new spirit of collaboration, the industry was spurred to new levels of production. Publishers, seeing that the quality of English printed output was improving, invested more readily and more widely. One-off and small-scale publishers injected capital into the printing houses, ensuring that a continuous flood of works, both large and small, made their way to readers. Printers-for-hire accommodated not only the small-scale publishers whose collective commissions made a meaningful contribution to the printed output of the reign but also worked extensively with larger publishers who, between them, developed a higher proportion of collaborative projects than the print world had ever experienced. This proportional rise in publishers providing commissions to printers-for-hire, and printers-for-hire affording the opportunity to produce works brought the English industry forward, increasing production levels and the output quality of the industry at large.

CHAPTER 7

The Growth of the Wider English Book World

This final core chapter casts light upon the expansion of England's book world to new scales under Edward VI. The previous chapter demonstrated an increasing appetite for collaboration within the print trade, whilst this chapter seeks to emphasise the new extent to which collaborative relationships acted within and without the trade. The first consideration is a fluid collective of booksellers and printers who emerged in 1546 and thrived during Edward's reign. This web of individuals exemplifies the budding collaborative spirit in the English print trade; with the trade so heavily centralised in the capital and the collective so heavily centralised around Paul's Cross, we see a number of publications emanating from this dynamic hub of England's booksellers. England's book world also showcases a growing influence of patrons from beyond the print trade who contributed by funding authors, printers and publishers throughout the reign. Literary or printing patronage is traced in this chapter through dedications and enduring partnerships where collaborative partnerships worked together as printers capitalised on prominent patrons' appetite for prestige and religious reform.

1 'Certayne Honest Menne of the Occupacyon Whose Names Be upon Their Bokes': The Paul's Cross Publishing Syndicate

This section explores a collection of individuals who published and sold books from Paul's Cross and the surrounding areas.[1] This interconnected association of individuals has only been briefly examined in connection with their collective underwriting of an edition of the 'Matthew' bible, printed by Nicolas Hill in 1551.[2] Further exploration of the catalogues of published works of those who funded Hill's bible has revealed that these individuals had overlapped on numerous other projects between 1546 and 1555. The first of these three-or-more party collaborations occurred in 1546. This publishing method via syndicate grew to involve at least eleven publishers who invested to varying

---

[1] Christopher Anderson, *The Annals of the English Bible*, vol 2 (London: William Pickering, 1845), p. 242.
[2] Ibid., Peter Blayney, *The Stationers' Company and the Printers of London, 1501–1557*, 2 vols (Cambridge: Cambridge University Press, 2013), p. 675.

degrees in at least twenty-two publications. The collection of individuals I call the Paul's Cross publishing syndicate did not have a firm membership and did not have a process of obligatory investment. This collaborative network was fluid, with individuals cherry-picking investments and projects. The parameters for considering any project as a product of this syndicate is an extant copy surviving into the USTC bearing the name of at least two or more publishing booksellers in London and a printer known to have completed the project on their behalf.[3] In order to establish which of these publications linked which individuals, the publishing catalogues of those involved were compared and compiled to reveal matching publications. Much of this process could be completed in reverse stemming from the reign's two largest and most subscribed syndicate-funded publications: Nicolas Hill's 1550 edition of the *Workes of Chaucer* and his 1551 folio bible. The publications that fall under this remit range from the very small to the very large. This is one compelling factor to suggest that publishers may have led this process rather than printers-for-hire canvassing for investors. Moreover, the collection of publishers used multiple printers as their route to production and publication. The legacy of these collaborations in short title catalogues and physical artefacts may be the product of close personal relationships or the pooling of limited resources; however, when seen as a catalogue of publications, it represents a significant contribution to the book trade.

The process of this syndicate was to print editions with personalised title-pages or colophons, presumably used to itemise respective financial input and allow each investor to sell their portion with clear accreditation. Due to the manner in which these publications were printed, they have a disproportionate impact on the output statistics of their chosen printer and the commercial balance of the industry. For the twenty-two editions published via this syndicate, the result is over sixty titles listed in the USTC database due to single print runs using multiple variant title-pages or colophons.[4] Removing those publications which spanned into other reigns, the Paul's Cross publishing syndicate is responsible for more titles during the Edwardian years (forty-one) than all but the largest printing houses or publishing enterprises. Andrew Pettegree has highlighted the regularity of publication via consortium in the sixteenth-century Parisian book world, but its prominence in England was far

---

3 Shared investment in this manner meant that fewer copies with each colophon were produced. If the total print run was 1500 copies and was split into five equal parts, fewer copies would need to be lost or destroyed for one title not to have survived.
4 The process of this syndicate was to print single editions with personalised title-pages or colophons. Due to these variations, each is listed as a separate title by the major catalogues of the sixteenth century.

TABLE 7.1 The Paul's Cross syndicate publications[a]

Author	Title	Printer	Date	Named editions	Titles	Format	Pages
Giles Duwes	*Introductorie ... to French*	Nicolas Hill	1546	Walley, Smyth	2	quarto	364
Law forms	*Parvus Libellus*	Nicolas Hill	1546	Hill, Kele, Toy, Walley, Smyth	5	octavo	88
Courts	*Manner of kepynge*	Nicolas Hill	1546	Hill, Kele, Toy, Walley, Smyth	5	octavo	72
Courts	*Modus tenendi*	Nicolas Hill	1546	Hill (2), Kele, Toy, Walley	5	octavo	28
Anthony Fitzherbert	*The boke for a justice*	Nicolas Hill	1546	Hill, Kele, Toy, Walley	4	octavo	328
Presidentes	*The boke of presidents*	Nicolas Hill	1546	Walley, Smyth	2	octavo	310
Exchquer	*Ordinance ...*	Nicolas Hill	1546	Hill, Kele, Toy, Walley, Smyth	5	octavo	16
Juliana Berners	*Boke of Hawkynge*	W. Copland	1547	Tab, Walley	3	quarto	86
Geoffrey Chaucer	*Works*	Nicolas Hill	1550	Bonham, Kele, Petyt, Toy	4	folio	660
Thomas Paynell	*The Piththy*	Thomas Gaultier	1550	Bonham, Kele, Toy	3	octavo	310
Customs	*The rates of the custom house*	Nicolas Hill	1550	Petyt, Toy	2	octavo	16+
Biblia	*Bible (folio)*	Nicolas Hill	1551	Bonham, Kele, Patyt, Toy, Veale, Walley, Wyght	7	folio	1,460
Heinrich Bullinger	*Christian state of matrimonye*	Nicolas Hill	1552	Hill (2), Kele, Toy, Veale,	5	octavo	190

a Toy and Veale also commissioned John Day to produce an edition of Erasmus', *Enchiridion militis christiani* (1552) which has not been considered part of the syndicate's catalogue due to having multiple named publishers upon the title-page and is thus seen as a three-party project between Toy, Veale and Day. USTC 504734, 504735.

TABLE 7.1   The Paul's Cross syndicate publications (*cont.*)

Author	Title	Printer	Date	Named editions	Titles	Format	Pages
Coverdale / Bale	*A Christe exhortation*	Nicolas Hill	1552	Kele, Veale, Wyght	3	octavo	72
Anthony Fitzherbert	*The boke of husbandry*	Nicolas Hill	1552	Kele, Jugge, Walley	3	octavo	126
Herbs / Copland	*Properties of herbes*	W. Copland	1552	Kele, Tab, Walley, Wyght	4	octavo	160
Thomas Paynell	*The Piththy*	W. Copland	1552	Jugge, Walley, Wyght	3	octavo	384
Erasmus Sarcerius	*Common places*	Nicolas Hill	1553	Toy, Veale (x2), Walley	4	octavo	352
Dionysius	*Disticha mordlia*	Nicolas Hill	1553	Toy, Walley	2	octavo	136
John Skelton	*a iittle booke, whiche hathe to name …*	W. Copland	1554	Toy, Wyght	2	octavo	62
Aymon	*Four sons of Aymon*	W. Copland	1554	Petyt, Toy, Walley	3	folio	358
Stephen Hawes	*Amoure and la bel Pucelle*	W. Copland	1555	Walley, Tottell	2	quarto	226

smaller, and this Paul's Cross collective is the first clearly demonstrable and enduring publishing consortium.[5]

Peter Blayney provided a thorough analysis of the booksellers of Paul's Cross in 1990 since built upon in his 2013 study of England's sixteenth-century printers before the Stationers' Charter.[6] These works highlight the number of publishing booksellers who were operating in and around Paul's Cross churchyard in the mid-Tudor years. Among them were William Bonham (The King's Arms,

---

5   Andrew Pettegree, *The Book in the Renaissance* (New Haven, CT, Yale University Press, 2010), p. 72.
6   Peter W.M. Blayney, *The Bookshops in Paul's Cross Churchyard* (London: Bibliography Society, 1990); Peter W.M. Blayney, *The Stationers' Company before the Charter, 1403–1557* (London: Worshipful Company of Stationers and Newspaper Makers, 2003); Blayney, *The Stationers' Company*.

later the Red Lion), Richard Jugge (The Bible), Thomas Petyt (The Maiden's Head), Henry Tab (The Judith), Robert Toy (The Bell), Abraham Veale (The Lamb) and John Wyght (The Rose), whom each had bookshops nearby, whilst Richard Kele (The Eagle, Lombard Street) Henry Smyth (The Trinity, without Temple Bar) and John Walley (Hart's Horn, Foster Lane) dwelt outside the churchyard but still collaborated.[7] These individuals all collaborated through a printer-for-hire with at least one other individual on the same list. Whilst many of the publishers did not collaborate with one another directly, often they were removed by only one degree of separation. The concentration of individuals publishing in and around Paul's Cross fostered and encouraged cooperation, but the links between these individuals were often far deeper than simple proximity.

The foremost participants within the syndicate were Richard Kele, Robert Toy, and John Walley – whom each contributed to the publication of at least twelve titles. The second tier of participants includes Abraham Veale, William Bonham, John Wyght, Henry Smyth and Thomas Petyt, who contributed to three or more publications. Finally, Henry Tab, Richard Jugge and Richard Tottell contributed to two or fewer titles.

TABLE 7.2 The Paul's Cross syndicate publishers, 1546–1555

Participating publishers	Number of contributions	Years active
John Walley	15	1546–1555
Robert Toy	14	1546–1554
Richard Kele	12	1546–1552
John Wyght	6	1551–1554
Abraham Veale	5	1551–1553
Henry Smyth	4	1546
Thomas Petyt	4	1550–1554
William Bonham	3	1550–1551
Richard Jugge	2	1552
Henry Tab	1	1547
Richard Tottell	1	1555

7 H.R. Tedder, 'Jugge, Richard (c.1514–1577)', ODNB, rev. Joyce Boro; I. Gadd, 'Toy, Humphrey (b. in or before 1537, d. 1577)', ODNB; Alexandra Gillespie, 'Petyt [Petit], Thomas (d. 1565/6)', ODNB; E.G. Duff, *A Century of the English Book Trade* (London: Bibliographical Society, 1948); Blayney, *The Bookshops in Paul's Cross Churchyard*.

Thomas Petyt appears to have been a central character in this syndicate. Whilst he invested in only four of the twenty-three editions, the three-time warden of the Drapers' company had many personal connections in the book world.[8] Petyt personally invested in Hill-printed editions of Chaucer's *Works* (1550), *The rates of the custom house* (1550) and the folio bible (1551), but his involvement also brought further members. John Wyght and Abraham Veale, two of Petyt's former apprentices, both invested in publications.[9] Petyt and these two former apprentices enjoyed more than a simple employer/employee relationship. Petyt bequeathed items to both Veale and Wyght (and Wyght's son, Thomas), and his influence may well have opened doors for his apprentices or, at the least, his role with the syndicate encouraged his apprentices to follow suit. Abraham Veale first entered the syndicate for the folio bible of 1551. He developed thereafter a significant commercial relationship with Nicolas Hill, who printed at least five works funded, either entirely or in part, by Veale.[10] The year following Veale's introduction, John Wyght invested by part-funding an edition of Heinrich Bullinger's *Christian State of Matrimony*.[11] Petyt and another participant in the syndicate, Robert Toy, also had a deeper relationship than proximity. The will of Peter Turner (landlord to both Petyt and Toy) lists the printer/booksellers as the co-executors responsible for the paying of Turner's legacy to his son William.[12]

The syndicate utilised numerous printers between 1546 and 1554. The syndicate was founded when four publishers of London commissioned seven works to be printed by Nicolas Hill in 1546. These publishers (Kele, Walley, Smyth and Toy) began their collaboration by commissioning works exclusively in octavo format, the largest of which was 364 pages. These works were well within Hill's skillset and represented a successful if unadventurous start to the enterprise. Hill's involvement with these publishers then gave way to other projects until his skills were enlisted again between 1550 and 1553. The commissions grew more ambitious, and following the small projects came two large folios, one edition of the *Workes of Chaucer* (contributed to by four publishers) and one

---

8   Gillespie, 'Petyt [Petit], Thomas'; Petyt's first publication: (inferred date) Henry VIII, *The copye of the kynges gracyous letters patentes* ([London, Thomas Petyt, 1538]) USTC 515290 or Girolamo Savonarola, *A goodly exposycyon, after the maner of a contemplacion, upon the .li. Pslame called Miserere mei deus* (London, Thomas Petyt, 1540).
9   Blayney, *The Stationers' Company*, p. 661.
10 USTC 504679, 504715, 504751, 504885, 504888, 518466.
11 Heinrich Bullinger, *Christian State of Matrimony* (Nicolas Hill for Richard Kele, Robert Toy, Abraham Veale and John Wyght, 1552) (USTC 504685, 504706, 504711, 504715, 516034, 516035).
12 Blayney, *The Stationers' Company*, p. 528.

complete bible (seven publishers). The fact that Nicolas Hill produced the two most substantial and impressive publications of the syndicate's history suggests that he was their printer of choice; despite this, the publishers were not above selecting other printers-for-hire depending on surrounding circumstances. Thomas Gaultier received a commission in 1550, and William Copland served the syndicate in 1552 before becoming their printer of choice following Nicolas Hill's flight into exile at Emden following the Marian accession.[13]

During Hill's absence, it was to William Copland that the publishers first turned in 1547. Only one of the 1546 syndicate engaged with this publication, John Walley, who was supported this time by Henry Tab. Copland would go on to be the printer of two further syndicated projects in 1552, when he picked up another project by Walley and Tab, joined this time by John Wyght and Richard Kele, and a second project with Walley, Wyght and Jugge. The labyrinthine connections between these booksellers highlight how interrelated the syndicate was and emphasises that projects were picked up on an ad-hoc basis at the publishers' discretion.

The final printer to whom the syndicate turned was Thomas Gaultier, who printed the previously mentioned 310-page edition of *The piththy and moost notable sayinges of al scripture* for William Bonham, Thomas Petyt, Richard Kele and Robert Toy in 1550. It is possible that Hill was engaged with printing the *Works of Chaucer* simultaneously and was therefore unable to produce the work. The Chaucer project involved, among others, all four of *The piththy and moost notable sayinges of al scripture* publishers, and it is possible that they were using this smaller project with Gaultier to raise funds in preparation or to make ends meet with some faster-moving stock – both through the press and off the shelves.

The consortium was far more active in some years than others. 1546 was the most significant year in these terms, as members of the syndicate invested in seven different publications – resulting in twenty-eight titles. Following a single publication in 1547 (two titles), publishing by syndicate disappeared until 1550, when three publications (nine titles) were produced. The next major year of activity was 1552, in which five publications (seventeen titles) were produced.

The Paul's Cross syndicate collaborated on and commissioned a wide variety of publications. The USTC categorisations for the works include 'educational books' (one); 'jurisprudence' (five), 'ordinances' (one), 'agriculture' (one), 'economics' (one), 'religious' (four), 'bibles including parts' (one), 'science' (one),

---

13   Andrew Pettegree, 'Hill, Nicolas', ODNB.

THE GROWTH OF THE WIDER ENGLISH BOOK WORLD

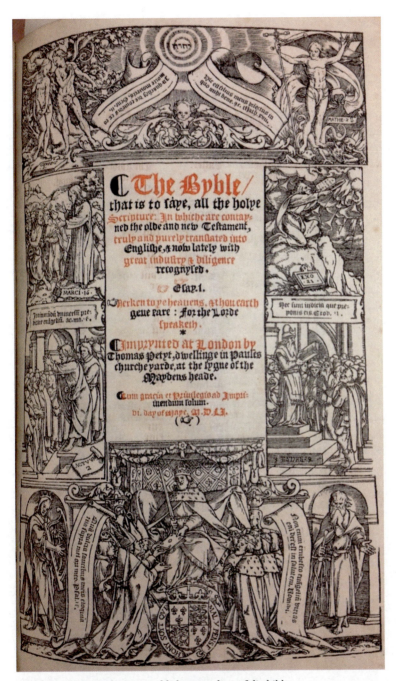

FIGURE 7.1   The Paul's Cross publishing syndicate folio bible
(Nicolas Hill for Thomas Petyt, 1551)
USTC 504570

'classical authors' (one), 'poetry' (one) and 'literature' (five).[14] Indeed, the products the syndicate commissioned were as varied as their themes, ranging from small octavos of eight leaves to the substantial 609-leaf folio *Workes* of Chaucer (1550) or complete bible (1551).[15] These smaller projects lend credence again to the notion that this process was syndicate-led rather than printer-led. There would be little need for the printer actively to seek out multiple investors for a 28-page octavo law book (*Modus tenendi unum hundredum sive curiam de recordo*) or a 16-page octavo ordinance, each of which was ultimately published as five separate titles.[16]

The landmark publication of this consortium, and therefore the best studied, is the folio bible printed in 1551 by Nicolas Hill. There are seven known variants, bearing imprints of 'Nicolas Hill for': William Bonham, Thomas Petyt and Abraham Veale, 'Nicolas Hill at the cost of' Richard Kele; and three variants in which Hill is not credited, instead attributing the publication to John Wyght; Robert Toy; and John Walley independently.[17] Thus, this folio bible accounts for seven titles despite having been completed from a single print run, and at the hands of one print house.

This folio edition of richly adorned 300 × 190mm pages was printed in dual columns, in a 55 textura, with initials ranging from 20 × 20mm to the 40 × 40mm initials that begin each book. The four-compartment woodcut making the title-page, reused for the beginning of the New Testament, is an elaborate depiction of biblical passages and royal heraldic imagery – though not discernibly of Edward VI. Whilst the title-page bears the statement '*Cum gracia et privilegio ad imprimendum solum*', this almost ubiquitous statement of legality is not indicative of privilege or a patent granted to Hill or the Paul's Cross syndicate, but of compliance with pre-licensing processes required of Edwardian printers.[18]

---

14 1546 publications: five 'jurisprudence' (twenty-one titles), one 'educational' (two titles), one 'ordinance' (five titles); 1554 publication: one 'religious' (three titles); one 'literature' (three titles); one poetry (two titles); 1555: one literature (two titles).

15 Chaucer: USTC 504408, 504409, 504415, 504436; Complete Bible: USTC 'Hill for …' 504570, 504679, 504792, 518466, 518678, 518679; 515045 ('Waley'), 504643 ('Wyght'), 504644 ('Toy').

16 *Modus tenendi unum hundredum sive curiam de recordo*, printed by Nicolas Hill (x2), also for Kele, Toy, Walley; *Ordinance* by Nicolas Hill, also for Kele, Toy, Walley, Smyth.

17 USTC 504570; 504643; 504644; 515045; 518466; 518678; 518679.

18 Pre-publication licensing had been expanded by official proclamation on 28 April 1551 – a mere eight days before the completion date of 6 May 1551 listed on the edition's title-page. This proclamation, however, simply furthered existing licensing procedures re-instituted in 1549 whereby Thomas Smith, William Petre and William Cecil were appointed to vet every publication coming off English presses (see chapter three).

The sheer scale of this bible ensures that this is the type of work that lends itself to a broader funding effort – the financial outlay would have been large, and the opportunity to recoup investment tied to a naturally slow-moving stock. Bibles in this period could be lucrative, the maximum selling price set by Henrician proclamation of 6 May 1541 (though now expired) was 10s loose and 12s bound, but that remained tied to the fact that they would, indeed, sell.[19] Having successfully and commendably produced the *Works* of Chaucer the previous year, this project was one that the syndicate bought into en masse. It had the highest number of contributing partners of any project in which they took part. Alongside the scale of this work came an opportunity for prestige building. For any single publisher of the group, this project might well have proved beyond their means but, as a collection of the sum of its parts, the syndicate produced something far beyond their individual means.

The Paul's Cross syndicate was an anomaly among the English printing landscape.[20] While publishers were on the rise, their associations, for the most part, involved publisher and printer connections. This syndicate bound eleven publishers together in a unique business model that allowed each publisher to retain their independence and financial autonomy. Having the option to invest in these projects provides us with an insight into some of the most attractive business and cultural opportunities of the period. The syndicate provides a disproportionately large influence upon short title catalogue statistics due to the number of titles coming from a single print run with alternate title-pages, but the Paul's Cross syndicate also provides a disproportionately large amount of insight into the English book world. The syndicate collaborated to produce over sixty titles, creating an impressive catalogue of works that included some of the more visually impressive and substantial publications of the reign.

2 'Private' Patronage

The Edwardian polity, controlled as it was by a 'Protestant clique', allowed for a range of individuals to act within both official and unofficial capacities.[21] As such, private patronage in the Edwardian book world is difficult to disentangle from the role of the ruling government and official influence. The forms of

---

19 *H&L*, 1, pp. 296–298 – 6 May 1541. This proclamation was now expired but suggests a retail price for the Great Bible, there is little chance that the syndicate could have marketed this bible beyond this price.

20 USTC 504570, HEH: 45910.

21 Alec Ryrie, *Protestants: The Faith that Made the Modern World* (New York: Viking, 2017), p. 46.

official inducements discussed in chapters three and four are examples where patrons were operating as officers of the Edwardian state, whilst those considered in this chapter present examples of patrons acting as private citizens. Patronage, in these two variant forms, can be identified by whether the agent in question was acting within or outside their official capacity. Private patronage within the English book world typically took one of two forms: the patronage of authors (facilitating and subsidising their living costs) and of printers (either through one-off, or the on-going underwriting of costs).

Edwardian England boasted a significant number of scholarly theologians, statesmen and nobility who together formed a community of scholarship and religious discourse. The nobility patronised key authors whose message struck a chord with developing religious reform. Previous explorations of the world of literary and printing patronage have identified a number of key patrons. Lord Protector Somerset and Archbishop Cranmer have been identified as chief patrons of the English reformation, whilst the duchesses of Richmond and Suffolk, and the Queen Dowager Katherine Parr have been identified as influential literary patrons.[22]

The reformations under the Tudors were not popularly driven. Mass-produced ephemeral propaganda did not fuel the Edwardian reformation. Certain texts were promoted and produced at particular moments to incite religious change. As we shall see, promoting religious change was not the only reason for private patronage. There are many reasons why an individual may choose to promote a particular publication or particular printer or publisher.

---

22 For Somerset and Cranmer, see Catharine Davies, *A Religion of the Word: The defence of the reformation in the reign of Edward VI* (Manchester: Manchester University Press, 2002), p. x; John N. King, *English Reformation Literature: The Tudor Origins of the Protestant Tradition* (Princeton, NJ, Princeton University Press, 1982), pp. 106–107; Cyndia Susan Clegg, *Press Censorship in Elizabethan England* (Cambridge: Cambridge University Press, 1997), p. 24; Bruce Gordon, 'The Authority of Antiquity: England and the Protestant Latin Bible', in *The Reception of Continental Reformation in Britain*, eds. Polly Ha and Patrick Collinson (Oxford: Oxford University Press, 2010), pp. 1–22 (p. 2); John Norman King, 'Protector Somerset, Patron of the English Renaissance', *The Papers of the Bibliographical Society of America*, 70 (1976), pp. 307–331. For the duchesses of Richmond and Suffolk and Katherine Parr, see Gretchen E. Minton, 'John Bale's *Image of Both Churches* and the English Paraphrase on Revelation', in *Holy Scripture Speaks: The Production and Reception of Erasmus' Paraphrases on the New Testament*, eds. Hilmar M. Pabel and Mark Vessey (Toronto: University of Toronto Press, 2002), pp. 291–312 (p. 299); Stephen Alford, *Kingship and Politics in the reign of Edward VI* (Cambridge: Cambridge University Press, 2002), pp. 122–123; King, *English Reformation Literature*, pp. 104–106; John N. King, 'John Day: master printer of the English Reformation', in *The Beginnings of English Protestantism*, eds. Peter Marshall and Alec Ryrie (Cambridge: Cambridge University Press, 2002), pp. 180–208 (p. 186).

In this spirit, private patronage was not freely given to, or exclusively funnelled into, either heavyweight academic texts to occupy the minds of the elites, or the ephemeral texts to fuel the conversion of public opinion. The hallmarks of private patronage are found in a full range of genres and qualities of publications.

This section will explore hallmarks of patronage and support found in Edwardian books – dedications and the major patrons of the arts – before turning to more collaborative and enduring patronage partnerships that contributed to the budding collaborative mentality of printing and publishing. In some instances, these patronage partnerships afforded the patronised party enduring support and political protection, whilst others encouraged publications and commissions by enabling authors within their courts and houses. Patronage can be indicated through illustrations, coats of arms, written dedications and many other methods, though these indicators are not necessarily a receipt or acknowledgement of financial aid or incentive.

The prefaces of Edwardian books are littered with the names of evangelical reformers, statesmen and nobility. Those names include Edward's successive regents, key privy councillors, and wider governmental players, the Archbishop, churchmen and independent theologians. Dedications within the book world could serve many purposes. As John N. King and Catharine Davies have argued, the presence of a preface dedication is by no means a guaranteed indicator of patronage.[23] Dedications could reflect any number of possible scenarios including pleas for support and patronage, mockery and satire, attempts to feign or bolster legitimacy, simple nods of recognition or, indeed, to reflect political or financial support from the named party.[24] Prefatory dedications too could reflect the will of the author, the printer or the publisher, or any combination thereof. Indeed, Elizabeth Evenden and Thomas Freeman have noted that John Foxe, who translated editions of continental theologians Martin Luther, Johannes Oecolampadius and Urbanus Rhegius dedicated his works seemingly without acknowledgement of patronage, nor seeking employment, nor to men of particular esteem, wealth or status.[25]

---

23   King, *English Reformation Literature*, p. 103. Davies, *Religion of the Word*, p. 171, n.80, has noted that attempts to attract patronage via dedications were very rare in Edwardian England and suggested that dedications 'can only be used to indicate the dedicatee's religious commitment rather than anything more substantial'.

24   Jennifer Loach, *Edward VI*, ed. George Bernard and Penry Williams (New Haven, CT: Yale University Press, 1999), p. 45; King, *English Reformation Literature*, p. 103.

25   Elizabeth Evenden and Thomas Freeman, *Religion and the Book in Early Modern England: the making of John Foxe's "Book of Martyrs"* (Cambridge: Cambridge University Press, 2011), pp. 36–37.

Recent contemplations of Tudor book dedications have poured cold water on their ability to determine patronage. Archival evidence, however, shows that the political importance of book dedications was high, even if their motives cannot be discerned. The Henrician exile John Hooper dedicated *A declaration of Christe and of his offyce* (Zurich, Augustin Fries, 1547), to Lord Protector Somerset, which paved the way for his return to the English evangelical fold.[26] Later, the post-script of Hooper's letter of 5 February 1550 encouraged Heinrich Bullinger:

> you will remind masters Gualter, Bibliander and my other Zurich friends, that if they are about to print any religious work, they should dedicate it either to our king, a most excellent and learned youth, or to some one or other of the nobility. I charge and enjoin you, my most learned gossip, and every way most esteemed master, to send me something of yours in print for our king. I will take care that the work shall come to his hands, and that the offering shall not want a commendation from myself.[27]

This plea for dedications to, and presentation copies to be bestowed upon, both the young king and his evangelical advisors show that even when the act of dedications came without additional attachments, it was nonetheless significant. The Swiss reformers answered Hooper's call. Bullinger wrote prefatory dedications to Edward VI in volumes two and three of his seminal work, the *Decades* (1550), and a subsequent part to Lady Jane Grey's father, Henry Grey.[28] Bullinger's dedication to Edward VI included the rousing words:

> Proceed, therefore, proceed most holy king, to imitate the most godly princes, and the infallible rule of the holy scripture: proceed, I say, without waiting for man's authority, by the most true and absolute instrument of truth – the book of God's most holy word – to reform the church of Christ in your most happy England.[29]

---

26   USTC 632072; Andrew Pettegree, *Foreign Protestant Communities in Sixteenth-Century London* (Oxford: Clarendon Press, 1986), pp. 29–30.
27   *OL*, 1, pp. 74–78 (p. 78).
28   Peter Opitz, 'Bullinger's Decades: Instruction in Faith and Conduct' in *Architect of Reformation: An introduction to Heinrich Bullinger, 1504–1575*, eds. Bruce Gordon and Emidio Campi (Grand Rapids, MI: Baker Academic, 2004), pp. 101–116 (p. 105); Carrie Euler, *Couriers of the Gospel: England and Zurich, 1531–1558* (Zurich: Theologischer Verlag Zürich, 2006), pp. 90–91.
29   Thomas Harding, ed., *The Decades of Henry Bullinger, (1504–1575), Minister of the church of Zurich* (Cambridge: Cambridge University Press, 1849–1852), p. xxvii.

In April 1550, Hooper presented a copy of the *Decades* to Edward VI.[30] Even amidst the tumult of the Swiss reformers attempting to forge the *Consensus Tigurinus*, a process inspiring collaboration but also division, it was not only the Zurichers who directed dedications to the English monarch. Basel scholar and fastidious translator Sebastian Castellio dedicated his 1551 Latin bible to Edward VI.[31] Jean Calvin, whose astronomic rise was beginning in French-speaking Geneva, penned a dedication to Lord Protector Somerset in his commentaries on Timothy in 1548.[32] He also dedicated an edition of his commentaries on Isaiah to the king (written by Nicholas des Gallares based on Calvin's lectures), ultimately published in 1551 from the Genevan print house of Jean Crespin.[33] Later, Crespin reprinted the work and Calvin sent a copy of this Isaiah commentary, with a new dedication, to a freshly crowned Queen Elizabeth I in 1559.[34] The international world of book dedications was one of political game-playing. England's importance and integration in the continental reformations reached its zenith in the Edwardian period, with great minds and powerful politicians looking to England as a leading evangelical force. Dedications were used to inspire, flatter and create stronger links with the continent's evangelicals.

The central recipients of dedications within the English context were the king and Lord Protector Somerset.[35] John N. King has calculated that 123 printed dedications were made to Edwardian royalty, courtiers and peers, fifty-three to the king himself and a further thirty-five to members of the Seymour family.[36] Jennifer Loach counts a total of forty-nine dedications to the king.[37] The Huntington sample underpinning this monograph includes eighty-three prefatory dedications by authors, printers or editors. Within the sample,

---

30 Euler, *Couriers of the Gospel*, pp. 92–93.
31 Gordon, 'The Authority of Antiquity: England and the Protestant Latin Bible', p. 20; Diarmaid MacCulloch, *Tudor Church Militant: Edward VI and the Protestant Reformation* (London: Allen Lane, 1999), p. 174, MacCulloch also notes that this dedication was largely reproduced in his 1554 publication against the persecution of Heretics, published amid the Severetus affair.
32 Emidio Campi, *Shifting Patterns of Reformed Tradition* (Göttingen: Vandenhoeck & Ruprecht, 2014), p. 163.
33 USTC 450035; Wulfert Greef, *The Writings of John Calvin: An Introductory Guide* (Louisville, KY: Westminster John Knox Press, 2008), pp. 84–85.
34 Andrew Pettegree, 'The Reception of Calvinism in Britain', in *Calvinus Sincerioris Religionis Vindex: Calvin as Protector of the Purer Religion*, eds. Wilhelm H. Neuser and Brian G. Armstrong (Kirksville, MO: Sixteenth Century Journal Publishers, 1997), p. 272; USTC 450085.
35 Loach claims twenty-four, King claims twenty-five for Somerset in total. Loach, *Edward VI*, pp. 43–44; King, *English Reformation Literature*, p. 107.
36 King, *English Reformation Literature*, p. 107.
37 Loach, *Edward VI*, pp. 43–44.

as in the wider Edwardian book world, the chief recipient of book dedications was Edward VI. Twenty dedications to the young king are found, including three from John Bale, two from John Hooper and one each from fifteen others.[38] These dedications came predominantly from the primary authors of publications (seventeen) but also editors (John Bale and Miles Coverdale) and publishers (Gwalter Lynne).[39]

Lord Protector Somerset's reputation as a central patron for evangelicalism is supported by book dedications addressed to him. Among those to dedicate works to Somerset were émigré continental theologians Martin Bucer, Peter Martyr Vermigli and Bernardino Ochino, a still-in-exile John Hooper, James Harrison, Henry 1st Baron Stafford, and chronicler Thomas Cooper.[40] Each of these individuals had gained something or had something to gain from the new evangelical regime. Bucer and Peter Martyr had secured positions as Regius chairs of theology at Cambridge and Oxford, respectively, and Stafford had been restored to his barony under the protectorate.[41] Harrison, whose preface wished for the 'graunte to the kynges Maiestie of England his righteous monarchie of Britayn, to thadvanucement of Gods glory', is now remembered as an ambitious opportunist who sought to achieve favour by aiding the English expeditions into Scotland.[42] The Huntington sample dedications to Somerset were penned by Harrison, Stafford and Cooper, and John Hooper and highlight a different element in the politics of book dedications of the period. While the historiography has noted Somerset as a patron of the arts, these three dedications highlight that political motives also stood behind engaging with the country's elites. Dedications to Somerset's immediate family members are found in the Huntington sample, including two dedications from Gwalter Lynne and one from William Samuel to Somerset's wife, Anne.[43]

---

38   USTC (John Bale) 504304, 504373, 504564; (John Hooper) 504772, 504450; (Nicholas Bodrugan) 503973; (Thomas Cooper) 504035; (Miles Coverdale) 518639; (Thomas Cranmer) 504011; (Edward Hall) 504075; (Arthur Kelton) 516459; (Thomas Lancaster) 504498; (Gwalter Lynne) 504410; (John Marbecke) 504506; (Bernardino Ochino) 504308; (Thomas Sternhold) 504280; (Robert Recorde) 504669; (Thomas Wilson) 504781; (Phillippe Gerrard) absent from USTC, HEH: 59967, ESTC: S103091.

39   Dedications from authors include Arthur Kelton, Bernardino Ochino, Archbishop Cranmer, Edward Hall, John Hooper, John Marbeck, Nicholas Bodrugan, Robert Recorde, Thomas Cooper, Thomas Lancaster, Thomas Sternhold, Thomas Wilson.

40   King, *English Reformation Literature*, pp. 106–107; USTC (James Harrison) 503893; (Lord Stafford) 504016; (Thomas Cooper) 504301; (John Hooper at Zurich, Augustin Fries) 632072.

41   C.S.L. Davies, 'Stafford, Henry, tenth Baron Stafford (1501–1563)', ODNB.

42   King, 'Protector Somerset, Patron of the English Renaissance', pp. 313–314; USTC 503893.

43   King, *English Reformation Literature*, pp. 106–107 adds the wider Seymour family as the recipient of twelve dedications: USTC (Lynne to Anne) 504433, 515417; (William Samuel to Anne) 504665.

Within the Huntington sample, the usual who's who of Tudor statesmen and theologians are found as dedicatees. After the king and Somerset, several influential nobles and statesmen were named, including John Dudley, William Cecil, and William Paget.[44] More minor influencers among the political elite are also found, with the earls of Pembroke and Hertford each receiving a dedication. The presence of a dedication is not a definitive hallmark of association and less so of patronage; still, the presence of these prefatory texts and the individuals they address remains significant. Whether reciprocated or not, the English book world was reaching out beyond its borders to the wider world; its authors, translators, publishers and printers were engaging with the reign's important religious and political powers.

3   Patronage Partnerships

This section will explore commercial and personal associations which allowed individuals within the printing industry to further their careers and produce works with the support of influential patrons. Personal relationships which helped printers and publishers secure patents have been discussed in chapter four, but other patronage partnerships could also offer political shelter and financial support. The involvement of wealthy and powerful patrons brought political influence and capital to the book trade and ensured that more titles and more firmly protestant literature could be produced.

The first partnership considered is the relationship between Gwalter Lynne and Anne Seymour, duchess of Somerset and the wife of the Lord Protector. Seymour is presented as a 'learned and pious lady, a strong follower of the Protestant faith' by Mirjam Foot, who has examined an edition of William Roye's catechism dedicated to her by Lynne and bound for presentation to Edward VI, which has yet to be digitised by the British Library.[45] This publication, *The true beliefe in Christ and his sacramentes*, represents one of two editions in the Huntington sample printed by Stephen Mierdman in 1550, commissioned by

---

44   Loach, *Edward VI*, pp. 44–45 counts fourteen for Warwick, whilst King, *English Reformation Literature*, p. 107 counts only seven in total: Christopher Burlinson, 'Hurlestone, Randall', ODNB. USTC 504926 (Thomas Wilson to John Dudley), 504664 (Ralph Robinson to William Cecil), 504112 (William Patten to William Paget).
45   Mirjam Foot, 'Bookbinding 1400–1557', in *Cambridge History of the Book in Britain, Vol. III: 1400–1557*, eds. Lotte Hellinga and J.B. Trapp (Cambridge: Cambridge University Press, 1999), pp. 109–127 (pp. 122–123).

publisher Gwalter Lynne.[46] Outside our sample, another edition commissioned by Lynne, *A worke of the predestination of saints*, bears a prefatory dedication by Nicholas Lesse to Anne Seymour.[47] Retha Warnicke credits Lynne with the production of another work dedicated to Seymour by Lesse, but in fact, this came from a collaboration between John Day and William Seres.[48]

Anne was the dedicatee for several further publications throughout the reign; one other is found in the Huntington sample, authored by William Samuel in his *The abridgemente of goddes statutes in myter*, printed in 1551 by Richard Grafton for Robert Stoughton.[49] Outside of the sample, Anne's patronage for the second volume of the *Paraphrases* of Erasmus, which will be discussed shortly, is acknowledged with another prefatory dedication, this time by John Olde. Anne Seymour is established and known as an influential patron of the period. Seymour's visible connection with Lynne lasted only one year, and the extent to which this was a genuine relationship of commercial patronage remains unclear. Lord Protector Somerset, whose recent fall had been confirmed by parliament in this same year, had his translations of Jean Calvin printed by 'William Baldwin in the shop of Edward Whitchurch' rather than by Lynne, which further suggests that the link was direct to Anne.[50] Whilst Lynne secured his printing patent during the Somerset protectorate, Lynne's dedication to 'the most worthy patrones' and 'most worthy example of al noble women', from her 'humble and bounded dayly draytor' suggests that he was in her service.[51]

John Day's links with Catherine Brandon, dowager duchess of Suffolk, have been established and solidified by John King, Elizabeth Evenden and Stephen Alford. Described by John King as 'the great Protestant patroness' and by Susan Wabuda as a patron whose 'inexhaustible purse helped to shape a new protestant culture', Brandon's reputation as a powerful patron is secure in the historiography.[52] Evenden has contested King's assertions of a local connection linking these individuals, based on Day having grown up in Suffolk. She instead postulates that they connected through the émigré stranger churches

---

46 USTC 504433; The second is Heinrich Bullinger, *A briefe and compendiouse table, in a maner of a concordaunce* USTC 515417.
47 USTC 518039; Retha M. Warnicke, 'Seymour [née Stanhope] Anne, Duchess of Somerset (c.1510–1587)', ODNB. Warnicke also includes another Nicholas Lesse translation to Lynne, though the USTC credits Day and Seres for its production.
48 USTC 504062; Warnicke, 'Seymour [née Stanhope] Anne, Duchess of Somerset'.
49 USTC 504665.
50 USTC 504428, 504432, 504439.
51 USTC 504433.
52 King, *English Reformation Literature*, p. 105; Susan Wabuda, 'Bertie [née Willoughby; *other married name* Brandon], Katherine, duchess of Suffolk', ODNB.

of London and that William Cecil may have been an intermediary between the two parties, owing to connections shown by Stephen Alford.[53] John N. King's research has attributed a significant role to Brandon's financial involvement; he suggests that she underwrote Day and William Seres' activities, which facilitated their astronomical rise through the industry, whilst Evenden refers to them as clients of the duchess.[54]

The Huntington sample bears witness to the strength of the connection between Brandon and the literary and print worlds. Evangelical theologian Thomas Solme penned a dedicatory preface to Brandon to accompany Hugh Latimer's sermons produced by John Day and William Seres in 1549, which also bore a full-page 119 × 80mm Brandon coat of arms.[55] Whether Solme, who describes himself as Catherine's 'humble and faythful Oratour', represents a direct connection to Brandon is uncertain, though this has been claimed in the historiography.[56] In a publication missing from the USTC (HEH: 350574), Nicholas Lesse dedicated his translation of Aepinus, Johann, *A very fruitful & godly exposition vpo[n] the. xv. Psalme of Dauid* to Lady Katerin Dowches of Suffoke, which, too, was printed by Day.[57]

Outside the sample, Day and Seres are known to have produced at least four editions between 1548 and 1549 that bear the Brandon coat of arms.[58] These printings of the Brandon coat of arms may indicate that Day and Seres were under the patronage or protection of the dowager duchess in 1548. However, this woodcut may indicate no more than the fact that Day and Seres were a well-connected rising force who secured a commission from a prominent individual; Brandon may have commissioned the woodcut to announce her alignment with these evangelical texts publicly.

John N. King has postulated that Thomas, first Baron Wentworth was a central patron of the evangelical regime under Edward VI. Wentworth is given the illustrious tag of having 'converted Bale and served as a patron to both Bale and Thomas Becon'. King has also asserted that this patronage was turned to Anthony Scoloker and Richard Argentine, who acted under the protection

---

53 Elizabeth Evenden, *Patents, Pictures and Patronage: John Day and the Tudor Book Trade* (Aldershot: Ashgate, 2006), pp. 4–5, 17–18; Alford, *Kingship and Politics in the reign of Edward VI*, pp. 118–122.
54 King, *English Reformation Literature*, p. 105; Evenden, *Patents, Pictures and Patronage*, p. 18.
55 USTC 504302.
56 Whitney R.D. Jones, 'Solme [Some], Thomas (b.1509–1510, d.in or after 1553)', ODNB.
57 HEH: 350574; ESTC: S101644; STC: 166.5: Aepinus, Johann, *A very fruitful & godly exposition vpo[n] the. xv. Psalme of David* (John Day, [1548]).
58 King, 'John Day: master printer', pp. 186, 189.

of Wentworth and Edward Grimstone.[59] Argentine dedicated his edition of Luther's *A ryght notable sermon, of the true use of the keyes* (Ipswich, Anthony Scoloker, 1548) to Wentworth but literary, rather than printing, patronage is the more likely scenario here.[60] Scoloker had links to Argentine, made clear in their three successive collaborations and printings.[61] The only Scoloker work among the thirteen in the Huntington sample to bear a dedication is this edition of Luther's sermon. Wentworth's standing as a patron was acknowledged by translator Rychard Schityre [Richard Sherry], who produced an edition of Johannes Brenz's *A verye fruitful exposicion upon the syxte chapter of Saynte John* (John Day and William Seres, 1550). This title would have likely made its way to the press of Scoloker (by this time, relocated to London) had he been the patronised party. There is no indication then that Scoloker was under the direct protection or patronage of Thomas Wentworth.

Private patronage links, as we can see, are intertwined and difficult to verify. At least, these temporary alliances between prominent individuals and book-producing enterprises caused projects to be commissioned and thus generated work for printers and publishers, which ought not to be underappreciated. It is evident that these projects were on a smaller scale and offered a significantly lower opportunity for the printers than officially-granted patents. It was, however, possible for printers to experience the best of both worlds.

State and private patronage in the Edwardian period often overlapped. In 1547, the first volume of the *Paraphrases* of Erasmus was added to the list of canonical documents of the English church. Archbishop Cranmer and Lord Protector Somerset supported the publication in an official capacity by providing a 9,000-strong, legally obligated market. There was, however, another force behind this same publication acting as a private individual: the queen dowager, Katherine Parr.[62]

Parr maintained an extensive correspondence network. Janel Mueller's edited volume of her letters and complete works casts light upon the connections she held with England's elite.[63] Parr's patronage networks, too, were

---

59   King, *English Reformation Literature*, p. 104.
60   USTC 504065.
61   USTC 504102, 504150, 504162.
62   Minton, 'John Bale's *Image of Both Churches*', p. 299; John Craig, 'Forming a Protestant Consciousness? Erasmus' Paraphrases in English Parishes, 1547–1666', in *Holy Scripture Speaks: The Production and Reception of Erasmus' Paraphrases on the New Testament*, eds. Hilmar M. Pabel and Mark Vessey (Toronto: University of Toronto Press, 2002), pp. 313–359 (pp. 315–317).
63   Janel Mueller, ed., *Katherine Parr: Complete Works and Correspondence* (Chicago, IL: University of Chicago Press, 2011).

extensive and included leading musicians, artists, portraitists, engravers, and jewellers.[64] The queen dowager, who survived Henry VIII until September 1548, also provided literary patronage and facilitated the return of Miles Coverdale (appointed her almoner in 1547).[65] Whilst Parr's association with the print world was considerable, she acted as a private, albeit influential, individual. Following the inaugural edition of the *Prayers or Meditations* (Thomas Berthelet, 1545), which would prove hugely popular, Katherine Parr's voice began to be heard, though her influence within the book world was still being bridled.[66] It was not until after Edward's accession that her influence would genuinely come to the fore. Parr had harboured and patronised the project to translate Erasmus' *Paraphrases* into English since its inception in the late Henrician years. Following the absorption of the *Paraphrases* into the canonical church documents in July 1547, it was clear that Katherine's evangelical inclinations were welcome in Edwardian England. The stoicism that had forestalled the publication of her second tract, *The Lamentacion of a Synner*, dissipated, and the printer of the *Paraphrases* (and a favourite of the regime) Edward Whitchurch released it only months later in November 1547. This was soon followed by a second edition in 1548, after a request by William Cecil, who penned an introduction to the text.[67]

Katherine had already installed Nicholas Udall as lead editor of the *Paraphrases* project before Henry VIII's death, but the work remained unfinished. The Udall and Parr family connection carried further than the *Paraphrases* project. Udall added a prefatory dedication to his officially patented translation of Peter Martyr Vermigli's *A discourse ... concernynge the sacrament of the Lordes supper* ([Edward Whitchurch], 1550), addressed to William Parr.[68] This connection to the evangelical establishment saw Udall pen a dedication to the king in 1553 in his translation of *Compendios a totius anatomie delineation* – printed by Nicolas Hill for Thomas Geminus in two titles in 1553.[69] Parr's influence was instrumental in ensuring this first volume of the

---

64   Susan E. James, 'Katherine [Katherine Parr] (1512–1548)', ODNB.
65   Within the Huntington sample, Katherine Parr received a dedication from Spanish Humanist Juan Luis Vives USTC 503909.
66   USTC 503601; 503622; 503863; 516429; 517788.
67   USTC 503860, 503984; Evenden, *Patents, Pictures and Patronage*, p. 18, Janel Mueller, 'Literature and the Church', in *The Cambridge History of Early Modern English Literature*, eds. David Loewenstein and Janel Mueller (Cambridge: Cambridge University Press, 2003), pp. 257–310 (p. 289); Alford, *Kingship and Politics in the reign of Edward VI*, p. 124.
68   Alford, *Kingship and Politics in the reign of Edward VI*, pp. 122–123; USTC 504551; Matthew Steggle, 'Udall, Nicholas (1504–1556)', ODNB.
69   USTC 504930, 516525; Steggle, 'Udall, Nicholas (1504–1556)'.

Paraphrases was completed, and it subsequently secured official approval.[70] With the economic support of the establishment and the cultural and literary support of Parr, the project proved a significant success and a milestone publication. The resulting book grants credit to Parr's influence, bearing the Parr coat of arms on its title-page and a dedication to Katherine in the preface.[71] The first volume of the *Paraphrases*, as we have seen in chapter four, was ultimately printed as seven titles, six in 1548 and one in 1550, and represented a large part of the printed output of one of the regime's favourite patented printers.

The common strand running between the two volumes of this project, however, is their editor, Miles Coverdale. The former exile was appointed Katherine Parr's Almoner in 1548, thus granting legitimacy and power to his publications. This appointment coincided with a dramatic increase in his publication output, which proceeded from three titles in 1547 to eleven in 1548 and nine in 1549. A royal endorsement highlighted to the printers of England that Coverdale's evangelicalism had been approved: nine individuals were listed in the colophons of Coverdale-authored or Coverdale-edited publications in 1548, and seven more are seen in 1549.[72] Coverdale's reintegration exemplifies self-censorship and the importance of patronage, both state and private.

In many respects, the second volume of the *Paraphrases*, also printed in 1549 by Edward Whitchurch, was an entirely different literary project. Miles Coverdale headed a new editorial team who completed the work under the guiding hand of another familiar and esteemed patron, Anne Seymour; the second volume is widely accepted as more radical in character.[73] Gretchen Minton has argued that the popularity of the first volume of the *Paraphrases* was sufficient to incite the production of the second volume.[74] The reality, though, is that the royal command for the presence of the first volume enforced a market, thus ensuring popularity. Sales and public acclaim, nonetheless, likely expedited the project's expansion to create the second volume, though the same canonical status was not granted. The spirited patronage of Anne Seymour was fundamental in securing the efforts of its translators and editors to complete the mammoth task at hand, but without canonical church document status,

---

70   Minton, 'John Bale's *Image of Both Churches*', p. 299.
71   Alford, *Kingship and Politics in the Reign of Edward VI*, pp. 122–123.
72   1548 included John Herford, John Day (four), William Seres (two), Roger Car, Anthony SmithThomas Raynald, William Hill (two); 1549 added: John Mychell, Edward Whitchurch (two), James Nicolson, Humphrey Powell, John White, Cutbere Matthew, John Walley, Reyner Wolfe and John Oswen.
73   Minton, 'John Bale's *Image of Both Churches*', p. 300; Craig, 'Forming a Protestant Consciousness', p. 318.
74   Minton, 'John Bale's *Image of Both Churches*', p. 300.

regular financial restraints remained in place. Print runs are likely to have been far smaller for the second volume than the first, and the total number of copies much lower. This second volume remains one of the larger and more visually impressive Edwardian printing projects, but it highlights that independent private patronage could not rival the official support given to the first volume.

John N. King stated that a circle of aristocratic women (including the duchess dowager of Suffolk and the duchesses of Somerset and Richmond) that surrounded Katherine Parr in the late Henrician years moved away from their leader before her death and that she had 'relatively little direct impact' during Edward's tenure.[75] The first volume of the *Paraphrases* began as a Henrician project, it is true, but few (if any) Edwardian publications prompted more work to be generated. Without Katherine Parr's patronage, the project may never have been completed, and without the supporting official legislation, any print run may have remained at the conventional size. As such, despite having only lived until September 1548, Parr's impact upon the top tier of English printing was significant, as was her role as a patron for the Edwardian reformation. The first volume of the *Paraphrases* represents the perfect storm of private and state patronage, whilst the second represents the extent of private patronage in the Edwardian book world.

The book world under Edward VI fostered a new spirit of cooperation and collaboration with striking results. Nowhere is this reality more evident than in the myriad connections between the publishers encircling Paul's Cross churchyard, who published via syndicate between 1546 and 1555. The combination of these factors displayed increasing entrepreneurialism and commercial dynamism hitherto lacking in the English context. The world of patronage, too, contributed to the advancement of particular individuals within the trade. Patronage offered shelter and funding to printers aligning themselves with the rapidly progressing protestant cause. While the Crown remained the biggest patron of the book trade, these patronage links drove forward production and gave opportunities, large and small, for more work to be printed. These new and distinctive characteristics made a significant contribution to the print trade's growth between 1547 and 1553; the interconnectedness of individuals before, during and after a book's production saw the consolidation of a more extensive book world than England had ever seen.

---

75   King, *English Reformation Literature*, pp. 104–105.

CHAPTER 8

Conclusion

The Edwardian period was tumultuous as newly-empowered evangelicals hurriedly enacted their reformation. With this shift in religious alignment came the need for new evangelical church documents, increased access to scripture, and persuasive rhetoric to encourage their burgeoning reform movement. The print world expanded with this religious change. Buoyed by the cultivation of a climate of reformist freedom and official engagement with the trade, the Edwardian print world grew rapidly and disproportionately compared to its predecessors. New entrepreneurial printers and publishers bolstered the ranks of the English book world. These individuals sparked change in the construction of the trade; a new cooperative spirit developed alongside the increasing separation of printing and publishing. Printers-for-hire allowed more individuals to participate in the trade, whether fleetingly or to build their careers. Personal relationships were fundamental to the trade, and connections formed by commercial, personal or political links governed English print culture.

The English Print Trade in the Reign of Edward VI, 1547–1553 has highlighted that Edward's reformed protestant government was an essential driving force behind the development of the print world. The regime did not dissolve censorship and simply allow events to unfold; instead, it built upon Henrician precedents, appointing more official printers and enshrining more compulsory texts for churches than ever before. The sponsorship of these individuals and texts prompted the most substantial printing projects of the reign. It is difficult to overstate the importance of this support for the regime's chosen printers. The premier printers of the period were all favourites of the government. The regime drove the English print world forward with huge projects underpinned by legally obligated markets, namely the canonical church documents. They also protected selected printers by offering patents for popular and specialist works, creating commercial opportunities and securing solid market foundations. Whilst many of the patents issued later in the reign had little time to pay dividends, the reconstruction of the Edwardian industry under Elizabeth I, particularly John Day's patent-fuelled ascent, suggests that these were significant inducements scuppered only by the young king's death. The Crown remained the principal benefactor and patron of English printing in this period of growth and development.

Outside their clique of selected favourites, the Edwardian programme of reform stimulated the wider industry. Previously attributed to a simple change in legislation, this stimulus can now be more accurately attributed to the creation of a climate of protestant enablement that emboldened printers. A tacit understanding of the religious trajectory of the Crown and Church of England allowed printers to outstrip the pace of official religious change in 1548, prompting an outpouring from English presses double the size of any preceding year. The late Henrician industry had been characterised by restriction and control; under Edward VI, the industry can be characterised by facilitation and encouragement.

The analysis of design and technical features in Edwardian printed material that underpinned chapter five has highlighted previously underappreciated continuities from the Henrician years. The stability observed in this sphere allows us to sharpen our focus upon which areas in this multifaceted industry developed during Edward's reign. The book trade did not see a changing of the guard or a stylistic revolution; it evolved from its Henrician precursors and more quickly in some areas than in others. This chapter has also clarified that the English market developed its own print culture distinct from many of its continental counterparts. The pace of innovation and stylistic development in England was slower than in the major centres of European print, but Edward's reign saw London become the fourth highest title-producing city in Europe whilst preserving this same print culture.

The Edwardian years were not characterised by stylistic or technical innovation, and yet the quantity and general quality of output from presses improved discernibly. Whilst no printers produced works that exceeded the Henrician Great Bible in terms of illustrations or stature, the ranks of high-quality printers and the number of high-quality publications swelled. John Day, Stephen Mierdman and Nicolas Hill joined Richard Grafton, Edward Whitchurch and Thomas Berthelet at the pinnacle of the industry and newcomers, including Richard Jugge, made an impact. These printers pushed their technical development after rising through the ranks of the trade by securing valuable patronage or commercial backing from commissioning publishers. *The English Print Trade in the Reign of Edward VI, 1547–1553* has also highlighted that print houses cooperated. The second-hand market in woodcut illustrations contributed to the rising industry-wide quality of printed material between 1547 and 1553. This trade helped fund new investments in new illustrative materials and brought more of these materials into the hands of established printers and newcomers.

Building on earlier foundational prosopographical research on England's early modern printers, more detailed study of the types of commercial relationships within the trade has highlighted some critical underexplored areas. The rapid development of a new printer-publisher dynamic within the English context shows that early publishers, so often overshadowed in the historiography by master printers, warrant more credit and further investigation. It also places the importance of printers-for-hire at the fore as a gateway into the book world. The industrial and commercial construction of the trade demanded that an array of commercial and personal relationships be navigated shrewdly to ensure success.

From the individuals setting type and pulling the press, through national and international merchants and booksellers, up to the political classes of the regime, the heads of printing houses had to please many people. This project has highlighted a wide breadth of commercial relationships even within an industry that remained largely inward-facing and self-serving in the European context. The complexity of the commercial relationships and the interconnectedness of the trades of book printing, book publishing and bookselling are best displayed by the fluid syndicate of publishing booksellers of Paul's Cross, who make a marked impact on how we view Edwardian print, despite hiding under the surface of preliminary statistical analysis. Collaborating in this way meant that publishers could invest with confidence; they could share in the prestige and profit without saturating the market. The advantages of operating in a small and inward-facing print world became more evident as the composite parts worked together to drive the print trade forward.

These developments in printing were stunted by the early death of the young monarch. Following the accession of Mary I and the return to catholicism, the print world regressed significantly. The leading printers of Edward's reign were forced out of the industry or into the protestant underground at home or in Europe. The Marian trade became more reliant again upon Europe, and the new regime's favourites acquired assets and equipment from their displaced protestant-printing predecessors. Following the accession of Elizabeth I, the legacy of the Edwardian years begins to become more apparent. The more tempered protestantism that Elizabeth I's reign brought forth did not inspire the same outpouring from the presses that the climate of freedom of 1548 had initiated. The 243 titles produced in 1548 would remain the highest single-year output from England's presses for thirty years, only finally surpassed in 1579. The continuities between the printing worlds of these reigns remain to be adequately explored to seek out the enduring legacy of the Edwardian tenure.

It is clear, however, that 1547–1553 was a period of decisive development in English print culture. Marked by the substantial official investment, disproportionate growth in output, improvements in industry-wide quality and an increasing commercial dynamism forged by developing commercial relationships, the English print world made up ground on its continental counterparts.

Edwardian print maintained significant continuities with its Henrician forerunners in crown patronage and stylistic conventions but rolled them out on a broader scale and more sophisticated level. The English print world also matured into a more complex industry, spurred on by the religious change of the establishment. In a reign often characterised as one of destruction and iconoclasm, this religious change was fundamental to the advancement of the print world in the face of challenging economic conditions. A climate of protestant ascendancy galvanised England's printers and publishers, who made rapid progress and rejuvenated and reshaped the English book world for the length of Edward's tenure.

Bibliography

Databases

British Library English Short Title Catalogue at http://estc.bl.uk.
British Library Database of Bookbindings at https://www.bl.uk/catalogues/bookbindings/.
Consortium of European Research Libraries Thesaurus at https://data.cerl.org/thesaurus.
Early English Books Online at https://eebo.chadwyck.com/home.
The Universal Short Title Catalogue at https://www.ustc.ac.uk.
Pollard, A.W., and Redgrave, G.R., (eds.), begun by W.A. Jackson, and F.S. Ferguson, completed by Pantzer, K.F., *A Short-Title Catalogue of Books Printed in England, Scotland and Ireland, and of English Books Printed Abroad 1475–1640*. Second edition revised and enlarged (London, 1986–1991).
Pettegree, Andrew and Malcolm Walsby, eds., *French Books III and IV: Books published in France before 1601 in Latin and Languages other than French*, 2 vols (Leiden: Brill, 2011).
Pettegree, Andrew and Malcolm Walsby, eds., *Netherlandish Books (Books Published in the Low Countries and Dutch Books Printed Abroad before 1601)*, 2 vols (Leiden: Brill, 2010).
Pettegree, Andrew and Malcolm Walsby, eds., *French Books I & II: French Vernacular Books / Livres vernaculaires français*, 2 vols (Leiden: Brill, 2007).

Primary Sources

Burgess, Clive, ed., 'Churchwardens' Accounts: nos 151–180.', *The Church Records of St Andrew Hubbard, Eastcheap, c1450–c1570* (London: London Record Society, 1999).
Calendar of the Patent Rolls Preserved in the Public Record Office, Edward VI: Vol. I–IV, A.D. 1547–1553 (London: H.M. Stationery Office, 1924–1926).
Cartwright, T.J.J., James Macmullen Rigg, and Sophia Crawford Lomas, eds., *Calendar of the Manuscripts of Marquis of Bath preserved at Longleat, Wiltshire. Volume II: [Harley Papers, 1515–1772]* (London: H.M. Stationery Office, 1907).
Cox, J. Charles, ed., *Churchwardens' Accounts from the fourteenth century to the close of the seventeenth century* (London: Methuen & Co, 1913).
Crawford, Anne, ed., *Letters of the Queens of England, 1100–1547* (Stroud: Sutton Publishing, 1997).
Dasent, John Roche, ed., *Acts of the Privy Council of England*, new series, 4 vols (Burlington, Ontario, Canada: Tanner Ritchie, 2004–2005).

Gairdner, James, ed., *Letters and Papers, Foreign and Domestic, Henry VIII, Volume 7, 1534* (London: H.M. Stationery Office, 1893).

Gough Nichols, John, ed., *Narratives of the days of the Reformation, chiefly from the manuscripts of John Foxe the Martyrologist* (London: Camden Society, 1859).

Hamilton, Hans Claude, ed., *Calendar of State Papers relating to Ireland of the reigns of Henry VIII, Edward VI, Mary and Elizabeth 1509-1573* (London: Longman, Green, Longman & Roberts, 1860).

Heinz, R.W., *The Proclamations of the Tudor Kings* (Cambridge: Cambridge University Press, 1976).

Hughes, Paul L., and James F. Larkin, *Tudor Royal Proclamations, Vol. II The Later Tudors (1553-1587)* (New Haven, CT: Yale University Press, 1969).

Hughes, Paul L., and James F. Larkin, *Tudor Royal Proclamations, Vol. I: The Early Tudors (1485-1553)* (New Haven, CT: Yale University Press, 1964).

Hume, Martin A.S., and Tyler, Royall, eds., *Calendar of Letters, Despatches and State Papers relating to the negotiations between England and Spain preserved in the archives of Vienna, Simancas and elsewhere, Vol. 9: [Edward VI, 1547-1549]* (London: H.M. Stationery Office, 1912).

Isaac, Frank, ed., *English and Scottish Printing Types 1535-1558 * 1552-1558* (Oxford: Bibliographical Society and the Oxford University Press, 1932).

Kirk, R.E.G., and Kirk, E.F., eds., *Returns of aliens dwelling in the city and suburbs of London, from the reign of Henry VIII to that of James I*, Huguenot Society of London, 10/1 (1900).

Knighton, C.S., ed., *Calendar of State Papers: Domestic Series of the reign of Edward VI 1547-1553* (London: H.M. Stationery Office, 1992).

Littlehales, Henry, ed., 'Churchwardens' accounts: 1547-8.', *The Medieval Records of A London City Church St Mary At Hill, 1420-1559* (London: Trübner, 1905).

Mears, Natalie, Alasdair Raffe, Stephen Taylor, and Philip Williamson, (with Lucy Bates), eds., *National Prayers: Special Worship since the Reformation. Volume 1: Special Prayers, Fasts and Thanksgivings in the British Isles, 1533-1688* (Woodbridge: Boydell Press, 2013).

Page, William, ed., *Letters of Denization and Acts of Naturalization for Aliens in England, 1509-1603*, (Lymington: Huguenot Society of London, 1893).

Pollard, A.W., and G.R. Redgrave, eds., *A Short-Title Catalogue of Books Printed in England, Scotland and Ireland, and of English Books Printed Abroad 1475-1640*, begun by W.A. Jackson, and F.S. Ferguson, completed by K.F. Pantzer, 2nd edn revised and enlarged (London, 1986-1991).

Luborsky, Ruth Samson and Elizabeth Morley Ingram, eds., *A Guide to English Illustrated Books 1536-1603* (Temple, AZ: Arizona Centre for Medieval and Renaissance Studies, 1998).

Lunders, A., T.E. Tomlins, J. France, W.E. Taunton, and J. Raithby, *Statutes of the realm, from original records and authentic manuscripts, 1101–1713*, 12 vols (London: Dawsons of Pall Mall, 1810–1828).

McKerrow, Ronald B., *Printers' & Publishers' Devices in England & Scotland, 1485–1640* (London: Bibliographical Society, 1949).

McKerrow, R.B., and F.S. Ferguson, *Title-Page Borders Used in England & Scotland 1485–1640* (Oxford: Bibliographical Society at the Oxford University Press, 1932).

Mueller, Janel, ed., *Katherine Parr: Complete Works and Correspondence* (Chicago, IL: University of Chicago Press, 2011).

Robinson, Hastings, ed., *Original Letters Relative to the English Reformation: Written during the Reigns of King Henry VIII., King Edward VI., and Queen Mary: Chiefly from the Archives of Zurich*, vols 1–2 (Cambridge: Cambridge University Press, 1846–7).

Selwyn, D.G., ed., *A Catechism set forth by Thomas Cranmer From the Nuremberg Catechism translated into Latin by Justus Jonas* (Appleford: Sutton Courtney Press, 1978).

Strype, John, ed., *Memorials of the most reverend father in God, Thomas Cranmer, sometime lord archbishop of Canterbury*, 2 vols (Oxford: Oxford University Press, 1840).

Strype, John, ed., *Ecclesiastical Memorials, relating chiefly to Religion, and the reformation of it, and the emergencies of the Church of England, under King Henry VIII, King Edward VI and Queen Mary I, with large appendixes, containing original papers, records, &c.*, 7 vols (Oxford: Clarendon Press, 1822).

Tanner, Joseph Robson, *Tudor Constitutional Documents A.D. 1485–1603: with an historical commentary* (Cambridge: Cambridge University Press, 1930).

Turnbull, William B., ed., *Calendar of State Papers: Foreign Series of the Reign of Edward VI 1547–1553* (Burlington, Ontario, Canada: Tanner Ritchie, 2005).

Worman, Ernest James, ed., *Alien members of the book-trade during the Tudor period: Being an index to those whose names occur in the returns of aliens, letters of denization, and other documents published by the Huguenot Society* (London: Bibliographical Society, 1906).

Secondary Literature

Alford, Stephen, *Kingship and politics in the reign of Edward VI* (Cambridge: Cambridge University Press, 2002).

Ames, Joseph, *Typographical antiquities: an historical account of printing in England, Scotland and Ireland*, 4 vols, ed. Thomas Frognall Dibdin (London: William Miller, 1810).

Amos, N. Scott, 'Strangers in a Strange Land: The English Correspondence of Martin Bucer and Peter Martyr Vermigli', in *Peter Martyr Vermigli and the European Reformations: Semper Reformanda*, ed. Frank A. James III (Leiden: Brill, 2004), pp. 26–46.

Amos, N. Scott, 'Protestant Exiles in England. Martin Bucer, the Measured Approach to Reform, and the Elizabethan Settlement – "Eine gute, leidliche Reformation"', in *Sister Reformations: The Reformation in Germany and in England*, ed. Dorothea Wendebourg (Tübingen: Mohr Siebeck, 2010), pp. 151–174.

Anderson, Christopher, *The Annals of the English Bible*, vol 2 (London: William Pickering, 1845).

Armstrong, Catherine, 'The Bookseller and the Peddler: the spread of knowledge of the New World in Early Modern England, 1580–1640', in *Printing Places: Locations of Book Production and Distribution Since 1500*, eds. John Hinks and Catherine Armstrong (London: British Library, 2005), pp. 15–30.

Atkin, Tamara, and A.S.G. Edwards, 'Printers, Publishers and Promoters to 1558', in *A Companion to the Early Printed Book in Britain, 1476–1558*, eds. Vincent Gillespie and Susan Powell (Cambridge: Brewer, 2014), pp. 27–44.

Auchter, Dorothy, *Dictionary of Literary and Dramatic Censorship in Tudor and Stuart England* (Westport, CT: Greenwood Press, 2001).

Austin, Kenneth, *From Judaism to Calvinism: The Life and Writings of Immanuel Tremellius (c.1510–1580)* (Aldershot: Ashgate, 2007).

Baker, J. Wayne, 'Church, State and Dissent, The Crisis of the Swiss Reformation, 1531–1536', *Church History*, 57 (1988), pp. 135–152.

Baker, J. Wayne, 'Christian Discipline, Church and State, and Toleration: Bullinger, Calvin and Basle 1530–1555', *Zwingliana*, 19, 1 (1992), pp. 35–48.

Baker, John, ed., *The Oxford History of the Laws of England, Vol. VI, 1483–1558* (Oxford: Oxford University Press, 2003).

Barnett, Richard C., *Place, Profit, and Power: A Study of the servants of William Cecil, Elizabethan Statesman* (Chapel Hill, NC: The University of North Carolina Press, 1969).

Baydova, Anna, 'To make a career between London and Paris. Social Networks as a basis of Renaissance book production and trade', MEMS *Working Papers, Movable Types Conference Special Edition*, 5 (2014) at [https://www.kent.ac.uk/mems/docs/n5_memswp_Baydova.pdf].

Beer, Barrett L., 'Episcopacy and Reform in Mid-Tudor England', *Albion: A Quarterly Journal Concerned with British* Studies, 23 (1991), pp. 231–252.

Beer, Barrett L., 'A Critique of the Protectorate: An Unpublished Letter of Sir William Paget to the Duke of Somerset', *Huntington Library Quarterly*, 34 (1971), pp. 277–283.

Bevan Zlatar, Antoinina, *Reformation Fictions: Polemical Protestant Dialogues in Elizabethan England* (Oxford: Oxford University Press, 2011).

Bindoff, S.T., ed., *The History of Parliament: The House of Commons 1509–1558* (London: Secker and Warburg, 1982).

Blayney, Peter W.M., T*he Stationers' Company and the Printers of London 1501–1557*, 2 vols (Cambridge: Cambridge University Press, 2013).

Blayney, Peter W.M., *The Stationers' Company before the Charter, 1403–1557* (London: Worshipful Company of Stationers and Newspaper Makers, 2003).

Blayney, Peter, 'William Cecil and the Stationers', in *The Stationers' Company and the Book Trade 1550–1990*, eds. Robin Myers and Michael Harris (Winchester: St Paul's Bibliographies, 1997), pp. 11–34.

Blayney, Peter W.M., *The Bookshops in Paul's Cross Churchyard* (London: Bibliography Society, 1990).

Borot, Luc, 'The Bible and Protestant Inculturation in the Homilies of the Church of Engand', in *The Bible in the Renaissance: Essays on Biblical Commentary and Translation in the Fifteenth and Sixteenth Centuries*, ed. Richard Griffiths (Aldershot: Ashgate, 2001), pp. 150–175.

Boulton, Jeremy, 'London 1540–1700', in *The Cambridge Urban History of Britain, Vol. 2: 1540–1840*, ed. Peter Clarke (Cambridge: Cambridge University Press, 2000), pp. 323–336.

Bracco, Donald Carl, 'The Influence of King Edward VI (1547–1553) on English Ecclesiastical History' (unpublished doctoral thesis, Wisconsin State University, LaCrosse, 1968).

Brigden, Susan, *London and the Reformation*, (Oxford: Clarendon Press, 1989).

Brimacombe, Peter, *Tudor England* (Norwich: Jarrold Publishing, 2004).

Britnell, R.H., 'The English Economy and the Government, 1450–1550', in *The End of the Middle Ages? England in the Fifteenth and Sixteenth Centuries*, ed. John L. Watts (Stroud: Sutton Publishing, 1998), pp. 89–116.

Brooks, Douglas A., *From Playhouse to Printing House: Drama and authorship in Early Modern England* (Cambridge: Cambridge University Press, 2000).

Bryson, Alan, 'Order and Disorder: John Proctor's History of Wyatt's Rebellion (1554)', in *The Oxford Handbook of Tudor Literature: 1485–1603*, eds. Michael Pincombe and Cathy Shrank (Oxford: Oxford University Press, 2009), pp. 323–336.

Burnett, Stephen G., *Christian Hebraism in the Reformation Era (1500–1660): Authors, Books, and the Transmission of Jewish Learning* (Leiden: Brill, 2012).

Campi, Emidio, *Shifting Patterns of Reformed Tradition* (Gottingen: Vandenhoeck & Ruprecht, 2014).

Cavanagh, Harrison Dwight, ed., *Colonial Chesapeake Families: British Origins and Descendants*, vol 1, 2nd edn (Bloomington, IN: Xlibris, 2017).

Chance, Eleanor, Christina Colvin, Janet Cooper, C.J. Day, T.G. Hassall, Mary Jessup, and Nesta Selwyn, 'Markets and Fairs', in *A History of the County of Oxford: Volume 4, the City of Oxford*, eds. Alan Crossley and C.R. Elrington (London: Victoria County History, 1979), pp. 305–312.

Clark, Peter, *The Cambridge Urban History of Britain* (Cambridge: Cambridge University Press, 2000).

Clegg, Cyndia Susan, 'The 1559 Books of Common Prayer and the Elizabethan Reformation', *Journal of Ecclesiastical History*, 67 (2016), pp. 94–121.

Clegg, Cyndia Susan, 'The authority and subversiveness of print', in *The Cambridge Companion to the History of the Book in Britain*, ed. Leslie Howsam (Cambridge: Cambridge University Press, 2015), pp. 125–142.

Clegg, Cyndia Susan, *Press Censorship in Elizabethan England* (Cambridge: Cambridge University Press, 1997).

Coates, Alan, 'The Latin Trade in England and Abroad', in *A Companion to the Early Printed Book in Britain, 1476–1558*, eds. Vincent Gillespie and Susan Powell (Cambridge: Brewer, 2014), pp. 45–60.

Collinson, Patrick, *From Cranmer to Sancroft* (London: Hambledon Continuum, 2006).

Collinson, Patrick, 'Night schools, conventicles and churches', in *The Beginnings of English Protestantism*, eds. Peter Marshall and Alec Ryrie (Cambridge: Cambridge University Press, 2002), pp. 209–235.

Craig, John, 'Erasmus or Calvin? The Politics of Book Purchase in the Early Modern English Parish', in *The Reception of Continental Reformation in Britain*, eds. Polly Ha and Patrick Collinson (Oxford: Oxford University Press, 2010), pp. 39–62.

Craig, John, 'Forming a Protestant Consciousness? Erasmus' Paraphrases in English Parishes, 1547–1666', in *Holy Scripture Speaks: The Production and Reception of Erasmus' Paraphrases on the New Testament*, eds. Hilmar M. Pabel and Mark Vessey (Toronto: University of Toronto Press, 2002), pp. 313–359.

Dane, Joseph A., and Alexandra Gillespie, 'The myth of the cheap quarto', in *Tudor Books and Readers: Materiality and the Construction of Meaning*, ed. John N. King (Cambridge: Cambridge University Press, 2013), pp. 25–45.

Dane, Joseph A., *What is a book? The study of Early Printed Books* (Notre Dame, IN: University of Notre Dame Press, 2012).

Daniell, David, *The Bible in English: Its History and Influence* (New Haven, CT: Yale University Press, 2003).

Davies, Catharine, *Religion of the Word: The defence of the reformation in the reign of Edward VI* (Manchester: Manchester University Press, 2002).

Davis, David J., *Seeing Faith, Printing Pictures: Religious Identities during the English Reformation* (Leiden: Brill, 2013).

Davis, J.F., 'Joan of Kent, Lollardy and the English Reformation', *Journal of Ecclesiastical History*, 32 (1982), pp. 225–233.

Diethelm, Roland, 'Bullinger and Worship: "Thereby Does One Plant, and Sow the True Faith"', in *Architect of Reformation: An introduction to Heinrich Bullinger, 1504–1575*, eds. Bruce Gordon and Emidio Campi (Grand Rapids, MI: Baker Academic, 2004), pp. 135–158.

Dlabčová, Anna, *Literatuur en observantie: De Spieghel der volcomenheit van Hendrik Herp en de dynamiek van laatmiddeleeuwse tekstverspreiding* (Hilversum, Netherlands: Uitgeverij Verloren, 2014).

de Vries, Jan, *European Urbanisation, 1500–1800* (Cambridge, MA: Harvard University Press, 1984).

Dowding, Geoffrey, *An introduction to the History of Printing Types* (London: Wace, 1961).

Duff, E. Gordon, *A Century of the English Book Trade: Short Notices of all printers, stationers, book-binders, and others connected with it from the issue of the first dated book in 1457 to the incorporation of the company of stationers in 1557* (London: Bibliographical Society, 1948).

Duffy, Eamon, *Fires of Faith: Catholic England under Mary Tudor* (New Haven, CT: Yale University Press, 2009).

Duffy, Eamon, and David Loades, eds., *The Church of Mary Tudor* (Aldershot: Ashgate, 2006).

Duffy, Eamon, *The Stripping of the Altars: Traditional Religion in England, c.1400–1580*, 2nd edn (New Haven, CT: Yale University Press, 2005).

Durkan, John, 'Some Scottish Bookmen', *The Innes Review*, 57, 2 (2006), pp. 216–218.

Eisenstein, Elizabeth L., *The Printing Press as an Agent of Change* (Cambridge: Cambridge University Press, 1980).

Elton, G.R., *England under the Tudors*, 3rd edn (London: Routledge, 1997).

Euler, Carrie, *Couriers of the Gospel: England and Zurich, 1531–1558* (Zurich: Theologischer Verlag Zürich, 2006).

Evenden, Elizabeth, and Thomas Freeman, *Religion and the Book in Early Modern England: the making of John Foxe's "Book of Martyrs"* (Cambridge: Cambridge University Press, 2011).

Evenden, Elizabeth, *Patents, Pictures and Patronage: John Day and the Tudor Book Trade* (Aldershot: Ashgate, 2008).

Evenden, Elizabeth, 'The Fleeing Dutchmen? The influence of Dutch immigrants upon the Print Shop of John Day', in *John Foxe at Home and Abroad*, ed. David Loades (Aldershot: Ashgate, 2004), pp. 63–77.

Evenden, Elizabeth, and Thomas Freeman, 'Print, Profit and Propaganda: The Elizabethan Privy Council and the 1570 Edition of Foxe's "Book of Martyrs"', *English Historical Review*, 119 (2004) pp. 1288–1307.

Evenden, Elizabeth, 'The Michael Wood Mystery: William Cecil and the Lincolnshire Printing of John Day', *Sixteenth Century Journal*, 35 (2004), pp. 383–394.

Evenden, Elizabeth, 'Patents and Patronage: The life and career of John Day, Tudor Printer' (unpublished doctoral thesis, York University, 2002).

Feather, John, *A History of British Publishing*, 2nd edn (London: Routledge, 2005).

Febvre, Lucien, and Henri-Jean Martin, *The Coming of the Book. The Impact of Printing 1450–1800*, eds. Geoffrey Nowell-Smith and David Wootton, trans. David Gerard (London: NLB, 1976).

Fincham, Kenneth, and Nicholas Tyacke. *Altars Restored: The Changing Face of English Religious Worship, 1547–c.1700* (Oxford: Oxford University Press, 2007).

Foot, Mirjam, 'Bookbinding 1400–1557', in *Cambridge History of the Book in Britain, Vol. III: 1400–1557*, eds. J.B. Trapp and Lotte Hellinga (Cambridge: Cambridge University Press, 1999), pp. 109–127.

Fox, Adam, and Daniel Woolf, eds., *The Spoken Word: Oral Culture in Britain, 1500–1850* (Manchester: Manchester University Press, 2002).

Freeman, Thomas, 'Dissenters from a dissenting church: the challenge of the Freewillers, 1550–1558', in *The Beginnings of English Protestantism*, eds. Peter Marshall and Alec Ryrie (Cambridge: Cambridge University Press, 2002), pp. 129–156.

Fudge, John D., *Commerce and Print in the Early Reformation* (Leiden: Brill, 2007).

Furdell, Elizabeth Lane, *Publishing and Medicine in Early Modern England* (New York: University of Rochester Press, 2002).

Gardiner, James, *Lollardy and the Reformation in England: An Historical Survey* (Cambridge: Cambridge University Press, 2010).

Gaskell, Philip, *A New Introduction to Bibliography* (Oxford: Clarendon Press, 1972).

Gillespie, Alexandra, 'Bookbinding and Early Printing in England', in *A Companion to the Early Printed Book in Britain, 1476–1558*, eds. Vincent Gillespie and Susan Powell (Cambridge: Brewer, 2014), pp. 75–94.

Gillespie, Vincent, and Susan Powell, eds., *A Companion to the Early Printed Book in Britain 1476–1558* (Cambridge: Brewer, 2014).

Gilmont, Jean Francois, 'Printers by the Rules', *The Library* 6th series, 2 (1980), pp. 129–155.

Gilmont, Jean Francois, *The Reformation and the Book*, trans. Karin Maag (Aldershot: Ashgate, 1998).

Gordon, Bruce, 'The Authority of Antiquity: England and the Protestant Latin Bible', in *The Reception of Continental Reformation in Britain*, eds. Polly Ha and Patrick Collinson (Oxford: Oxford University Press, 2010), pp. 1–22.

Gordon, Bruce, *Calvin* (New Haven, CT: Yale University Press, 2009).

Gordon, Bruce, and Emidio Campi, eds., *Architect of Reformation: An Introduction to Heinrich Bullinger, 1504–1575* (Grand Rapids, MI: Baker Academic, 2004).

Gordon, Bruce, *The Swiss Reformation* (Manchester: Manchester University Press, 2002).

Greef, Wulfert, *The Writings of John Calvin: An Introductory Guide* (Louisville, KY: Westminster John Knox Press, 2008).

Green, Ian, *Print and Protestantism in Early Modern England* (Oxford: Oxford University Press, 2000).

Greengrass, Mark, 'The theology and liturgy of Reformed Christianity', in *Cambridge History of Christianity, Vol 6: Reform and Expansion 1500–1660*, ed. R. Po-chia Hsia (Cambridge: Cambridge University Press, 2006), pp. 104–124.

Gunter, Karl, *Reformation Unbound: Protestant Visions of Reform in England, 1525–1590* (Cambridge: Cambridge University Press, 2014).

Harding, Robert, J.D., 'Authorial and editorial influence on luxury bookbinding styles in sixteenth-century England', in *Tudor Books and Readers: Materiality and the Construction of Meaning*, ed. John N. King (Cambridge: Cambridge University Press, 2010), pp. 116–137.

Heal, Felicity, 'The Bishops and the Printers, from Henry VII to Elizabeth I', in *The Prelate in England and Europe, 1300–1560*, ed. Martin Heale (York: York Medieval Press, 2014), pp. 142–170.

Heal, Felicity, *Reformation in Britain and Ireland* (Oxford: Oxford University Press, 2003).

Hellinga, Lotte, and J.B. Trapp, eds., *The Cambridge History of the Book in Britain Vol. III: 1400–1557* (Cambridge: Cambridge University Press, 1999).

Hellinga, Lotte, 'Printing', in *The Cambridge History of the Book in Britain, Vol III: 1400–1557*, eds. Lotte Hellinga and J.B. Trapp (Cambridge: Cambridge University Press, 1999), pp. 65–108.

Henrich, Rainer, 'Bullinger's Correspondence: An International News Network' in *Architect of Reformation. An Introduction to Heinrich Bullinger, 1504–1575*, eds. Bruce Gordon and Emidio Campi (Grand Rapids, MI: Baker Academic, 2004), pp. 231–241.

Higman, Francis, *Piety and the People: Religious Printing in French, 1511–1551* (Aldershot: Routledge, 1996).

Hind, Arthur Mayger, *Engraving in England in the sixteenth and seventeenth centuries. Part I: The Tudor Period* (Cambridge: Cambridge University Press, 1952).

Hunter, Michael, ed., *Printed Images in Early Modern Britain. Essays in Interpretation* (Aldershot: Ashgate, 2010).

Hutton, Ronald, 'Local Impact of the Tudor Reformations', in *The English Reformation Revised*, ed. Christopher Haigh (Cambridge: Cambridge University Press, 1987), pp. 114–138.

James, Frank A., *Peter Martyr Vermigli and the European Reformations: Semper Reformanda* (Leiden: Brill, 2004).

Jordan, W.K., *Edward VI: The Threshold of power. The Dominance of the Duke of Northumberland* (Cambridge, MA: Harvard University Press, 1970).

Jordan, W.K., *Edward VI: The Young King: The protectorship of the Duke of Somerset*, (Cambridge, MA: Harvard University Press, 1968).

Jordan, W.K., ed., *The Chronicle and political papers of Edward VI* (Ithaca, NY: Cornell University Press, 1966).

Kastan, David Scott, 'Print, literary culture and the book trade', in *The Cambridge History of Early Modern English Literature*, eds. David Loewenstein and Janel Mueller (Cambridge: Cambridge University Press, 2002), pp. 81–116.

King, John N., 'Paul's Cross and the implementation of Protestant Reforms under Edward VI', in *Paul's Cross and the culture of persuasion in England, 1520–1640*, eds. W.J. Torrance Kirby and P.G. Stanwood (Leiden: Brill, 2013), pp. 141–159.

King, John N., 'John Day: master printer of the English Reformation', in *The Beginnings of English Protestantism*, eds. Peter Marshall and Alec Ryrie (Cambridge: Cambridge University Press, 2002), pp. 180–208.

King, John N., 'The Light of Printing: William Tyndale, John Foxe, John Day, and Early Modern Print Culture', *Renaissance Quarterly*, 54 (2001), pp. 52–85.

King, John N., 'The Book Trade under Edward VI and Mary I', in *Cambridge History of the Book in Britain, vol. III: 1400–1557*, eds. Lotte Hellinga and J.B. Trapp (Cambridge: Cambridge University Press, 1999), pp. 164–178.

King, John N., *English Reformation Literature: The Tudor Origins of the Protestant Tradition* (Princeton, NJ: Princeton University Press, 1982).

King, John Norman, 'Protector Somerset, Patron of the English Renaissance', *The Papers of the Bibliographical Society of America*, 70 (1976), pp. 307–331.

Kirby, W.J. Torrance, 'Religion and Propaganda: Thomas Cromwell's Use of Antoine de Marcourt's Livre des Marchans', in *Persuasion and Conversion: Essays on Religion, Politics and the Public Sphere in Early Modern England*, ed. W.J. Torrance Kirby (Leiden: Brill, 2013), pp. 37–52.

Kirby, W.J. Torrance, Emidio Campi, and Frank A. James, *A Companion to Peter Martyr Vermigli* (Leiden: Brill, 2009).

Kirby, W.J. Torrance, *The Zurich Connection and Tudor Political Theology* (Leiden: Brill, 2007).

Kirby, W.J. Torrance, 'Wholesale or Retail? Antoine de Marcourt's *The Boke of Marchauntes* and Tudor Political Theology', *Renaissance and Reformation / Renaissance et Réforme*, 28 (2004), pp. 37–60.

Kümin, Beat A., *The European World 1500–1800*. (London: Routledge, 2009).

Lee, John S., *Cambridge and its Economic Region, 1450–1560* (Hatfield: University of Hertfordshire, 2005).

Leedham-Green, E.S., and Teresa Webber, eds., *The Cambridge History of Libraries in Britain and Ireland* (Cambridge: Cambridge University Press, 2006).

Leedham Green, E.S., 'Booksellers and libraries in sixteenth-century Cambridge', in *Libraries and the Book Trade: The Formation of Collections from the Sixteenth to the Twentieth Century*, eds. Robin Myers, Michael Harris and Giles Mandelbrote (New Castle, DE: Oak Knoll Press, 2000), pp. 1–14.

Lewis, Jack P., *The Day After Domesday: The Making of the Bishops' Bible* (Eugene, OR: Wipf & Stock 2016).

Lewycky, Nadine, and Adam David Morton, eds., *Getting Along? Religious Identities and Confessional Relations in Early Modern England* (Farnham: Routledge, 2012).

Ling-Fan, Li, 'Bullion, bills and arbitrage: exchange markets in fourteenth- to seventeenth-century Europe' (unpublished doctoral thesis, London School of Economics, 2012).

Loach, Jennifer, *Edward VI*, ed. George Bernard and Penry Williams (New Haven, CT: Yale University Press, 1999).

Loach, Jennifer, 'The Marian Establishment and the Printing Press', *The English Historical Review*, 101, 398 (1986), pp. 135–148.

Loades, David, *The Religious Culture of Marian England* (London: Pickering & Chatto, 2010).

Loades, David, *The Cecils: Privilege and Power Behind the Throne* (Kew: National Archives, 2007).

Loades, David, 'Books and the English Reformation prior to 1558', in *The Reformation and the Book*, ed. Jean Francois Gilmont, trans. Karin Maag (Aldershot: Ashgate, 1998), pp. 264–291.

Loades, David, *John Dudley, Duke of Northumberland, 1504–1553* (Oxford: Clarendon Press, 1996).

Loewenstein, David, *Treacherous Faith: The Spectre of Heresy and Religious Conflict in the English Reformation* (Oxford: Oxford University Press, 2013).

Loewenstein, David, and Janel Mueller, eds., *The Cambridge History of Early Modern English Literature* (Cambridge: Cambridge University Press, 2002).

Lowe, Ben, *Commonwealth and the English Reformation: Protestantism and the Politics of Religious Change in the Gloucester Vale, 1483–1560* (Farnham: Ashgate, 2010).

Löwe, J. Andreas, *Richard Smyth and the Language of Orthodoxy: Re-Imagining Tudor Catholic Polemicism* (Leiden: Brill, 2003).

Luborsky, Ruth Samson, and Elizabeth Morley Ingram, eds., *A Guide to English Illustrated Book 1536–1603*, 2 vols (Temple, AZ: Arizona Centre for Medieval and Renaissance Studies, 1998).

MacCulloch, Diarmaid, *Thomas Cromwell: A life* (London: Allen Lane, 2018).

MacCulloch, Diarmaid, 'Sixteenth-century English Protestantism and the Continent', in *Sister Reformations: The Reformation in Germany and in England*, ed. Dorothea Wendebourg (Tübingen: Mohr Siebeck, 2010), pp. 1–14.

MacCulloch, Diarmaid, *A History of Christianity. The First Three Thousand Years* (London: Allen Lane, 2009).

MacCulloch, Diarmaid, *Reformation: Europe's house divided, 1490–1700* (London: Penguin, 2004).

MacCulloch, Diarmaid, *Tudor Church Militant: Edward VI and the Protestant Reformation* (London: Allen Lane, 2001).

MacCulloch, Diarmaid, *The Later Reformation in England 1547–1603*, revised edn. (Basingstoke: Macmillan Education, 2000).

MacCulloch, Diarmaid, *Thomas Cranmer: A Life* (New Haven, CT: Yale University Press, 1996).

Macek, Ellen A., *The Loyal Opposition: Tudor Traditionalist Polemics, 1535–1558* (New York: Peter Lang, 1996).

Marshall, Peter, *Heretics and Believers: A History of the English Reformation* (New Haven, CT: Yale University Press, 2017).

Marshall, Peter, ed., *The Oxford Illustrated History of the Reformation* (Oxford: Oxford University Press 2015).

Marshall, Peter, *Reformation England 1480–1642*, 2nd edn (London: Bloomsbury Academic, 2012).

Marshall, Peter, Religious Identities in Henry VIII's England (Aldershot: Ashgate, 2006).

Marshall, Peter, and Alec Ryrie, eds., *The Beginnings of English Protestantism* (Cambridge: Cambridge University Press, 2002).

Martin, J.W., Religious Radicals in Tudor England (London: Hambledon Press, 1989).

Martin, J.W., 'Miles Hogarde, Artisan and aspiring Author in Sixteenth century England', *Renaissance Quarterly*, 34 (1981), pp. 359–383.

May, Stephen W., and Heather Wolfe, 'Manuscripts in Tudor England', in *A Companion to Tudor Literature*, ed. Kent Cartwright (Chichester: Wiley Blackwell, 2010), pp. 125–139.

McKee, Kathryn, 'Judging a Book by its cover?', *Special Collections Spotlight* (2014) at: https://www.joh.cam.ac.uk/judging-book-its-cover.

McKitterick, David, *A History of the Cambridge University Press, Vol I: Printing and the Book Trade in Cambridge, 1534–1698* (Cambridge: Cambridge University Press, 1992).

McLean, Matthew, 'Between Basel and Zurich: Humanist Rivalries and the works of Sebastian Münster', in *The Book Triumphant. Print in Transition in the Sixteenth and Seventeenth Centuries*, eds. Malcolm Walsby and Graeme Kemp (Leiden: Brill, 2011), pp. 270–291.

Mears, Natalie, and Alec Ryrie, eds., *Worship and the Parish Church in Early Modern Britain* (Farnham: Ashgate, 2013).

Milevski, Robert J., 'A Primer on Signed Bindings', in *Suave Mechanicals. Essays on the History of Bookbinding Volume I*, ed. Julia Miller (Ann Arbor, MI: Legacy Press, 2013), pp. 165–179.

Minton, Gretchen E., 'John Bale's *Image of Both Churches* and the English Paraphrase on Revelation', in *Holy Scripture Speaks: The Production and Reception of Erasmus' Paraphrases on the New Testament*, eds. Hilmar M. Pabel and Mark Vessey (Toronto: University of Toronto Press, 2002), pp. 291–312.

Mueller, Janel, 'Literature and the Church', in *The Cambridge History of Early Modern English Literature*, eds. David Loewenstein and Janel Mueller (Cambridge: Cambridge University Press, 2003), pp. 257–310.

Munro, John H., 'The Coinages and Monetary Policies of Henry VIII (r. 1509–1547): Contrasts between Defensive and Aggressive Debasements', *University of Toronto Working Paper*, 417 (2010).

Neville-Sington, Pamela, 'Press, politics and religion', in *The Cambridge History of the Book in Britain Vol. III: 1400–1557*, eds. Lotte Hellinga and J.B. Trapp (Cambridge: Cambridge University Press, 1999), pp. 576–607.

Newcombe, D.G., 'John Hooper's visitation and examination of the clergy in the diocese of Gloucester, 1551', in *Reformations Old and New: Essays on the Socio-Economic Impact of Religious Change c.1470–1630*, ed. Beat A. Kümin (Aldershot: Scolar Press, 1996), pp. 57–70.

Null, Ashley, 'Princely Marital Problems and the Reformers' Solutions', in *Sister Reformations: The Reformation in Germany and in England*, ed. Dorothea Wendebourg (Tübingen: Mohr Siebeck, 2010), pp. 133–149.

Oates, Rosamund, *Moderate Radical: Tobie Matthew and the English Reformation* (Oxford: Oxford University Press, 2018).

Opitz, Peter, 'Bullinger's Decades: Instruction in Faith and Conduct' in *Architect of Reformation: An introduction to Heinrich Bullinger, 1504–1575*, eds. Bruce Gordon and Emidio Campi (Grand Rapids, MI: Baker Academic, 2004), pp. 101–116.

Palma, Nuno, 'Reconstruction of annual money supply over the long run: The case of England, 1279–1870', *European Historical Economics Society Working Papers in Economic History*, 94 (2016).

Pettegree, Andrew, and Malcolm Walsby, eds., *Netherlandish Books: Books Published in the Low Countries and Dutch Books Printed Abroad before 1601*, 2 vols (Leiden: Brill, 2011).

Pettegree, Andrew, 'Afterword', in *The Reception of Continental Reformation in Britain*, eds. Polly Ha and Patrick Collinson (Oxford: Oxford University Press, 2010), pp. 229–236.

Pettegree, Andrew, *The Book in the Renaissance* (New Haven, CT: Yale University Press, 2010).

Pettegree, Andrew, *The French Book and European Book World* (Leiden: Brill, 2007).

Pettegree, Andrew, *Reformation and the Culture of Persuasion* (Cambridge: Cambridge University Press, 2005).

Pettegree, Andrew, 'Printing and the Reformation: the English exception', in *The beginnings of English Protestantism*, eds. Peter Marshall and Alec Ryrie (Cambridge: Cambridge University Press, 2002), pp. 157–180.

Pettegree, Andrew, *Europe in the Sixteenth Century* (Oxford: Blackwell, 2002).

Pettegree, Andrew, ed., *The Reformation World* (London: Routledge, 2000).

Pettegree, Andrew, 'The Reception of Calvinism in Britain', in *Calvinus Sincerioris Religionis Vindex: Calvin as Protector of the Purer Religion*, eds. Wilhelm H. Neuser and Brian G. Armstrong (Kirksville, MO: Sixteenth Century Journal Publishers, 1997).

Pettegree, Andrew, *Marian Protestantism: Six Studies* (Aldershot: Scolar Press, 1996).

Pettegree, Andrew, *Emden and the Dutch Revolt: Exile and the Development of Reformed Protestantism* (Oxford: Clarendon Press, 1992).

Pettegree, Andrew, *Foreign Protestant Communities in Sixteenth-Century London*, (Oxford: Clarendon Press, 1986).

Poleg, Eyal, *A Material History of the Bible, England 1200–1553* (Oxford: Oxford University Press for The British Academy, 2020).

Powell, Susan, 'The Secular Clergy', in *A Companion to the Early Printed Book in Britain, 1476–1558*, eds. Vincent Gillespie and Susan Powell (Cambridge: Brewer, 2014), pp. 150–175.

Raven, James, *The Business of Books: Booksellers and the English Book Trade, 1450–1850* (New Haven, CT: Yale University Press, 2007).

Raymond, Joad, *Pamphlets and Pamphleteering in Early Modern Britain* (Cambridge: Cambridge University Press, 2003).

Reeves, Ryan M., *English Evangelicals and Tudor Obedience, c.1527–1570* (Leiden: Brill, 2014).

Reimer, Jonathan, 'The Life and Writings of Thomas Becon, 1512–1567' (unpublished doctoral thesis, Cambridge University, Pembroke College, 2016).

Richards, Celyn David, 'Printing for the Reformation: The Canonical Documents of the Edwardian Church of England, 1547–1553' in *Print and Power in Early Modern Europe (1500–1800)*, eds. Nina Lamal, Jamie Cumby and Helmer J. Helmers (Leiden: Brill, 2021), pp. 111–133.

Richards, Celyn David, 'Print and Faith in the Swiss Reformation, 1517–1575' (unpublished master's thesis, University of St Andrews, 2013).

Robinson, Pamela, 'Materials: Paper and Type', in *A companion to the Early Printed Book in Britain, 1476–1558*, eds. Vincent Gillespie and Susan Powell (Cambridge: Brewer, 2014), pp. 61–74.

Rorke, Martin. 'English and Scottish Overseas Trade, 1300–1600', *Economic History Review*, 59 (2006), pp. 265–288.

Ryrie, Alec, *Protestants: The Faith that Made the Modern World* (New York: Viking, 2017).

Ryrie, Alec, *The Age of Reformation: The Tudor and Stewart Realms, 1485–1603*, 2nd edn (Abingdon: Routledge, 2017).

Ryrie, Alec, *Being Protestant in Reformation Britain* (Oxford: Oxford University Press, 2013).

Ryrie, Alec, 'The slow death of a tyrant: learning to live without Henry VIII, 1547–1563', in *Henry VIII and his afterlives: literature, politics and art*, eds. Mark Rankin, Christopher Highley and John N. King (Cambridge: Cambridge University Press, 2009), pp. 75–93.

Ryrie, Alec, 'Paths not taken in the British Reformations', *Historical Journal*, 52 (2009), pp. 1–22.

Ryrie, Alec, *The Gospel and Henry VIII: Evangelicals in the Early English Reformation* (Cambridge: Cambridge University Press, 2003).

Ryrie, Alec, 'Counting sheep, counting shepherds: the problem of allegiance in the English Reformation', in *The beginnings of English Protestantism*, eds. Peter Marshall and Alec Ryrie (Cambridge: Cambridge University Press, 2002), pp. 84–110.

Ryrie, Alec, 'The Strange Death of Lutheran England', *Journal of Ecclesiastical History*, 53 (2002), pp. 64–92.

Schofield, John, *Philip Melanchthon and the English Reformation*, (Farnham: Routledge, 2006).

Schutte, Valerie, *Mary I and the Art of Book Dedications: Royal Women, Power and Persuasion* (New York: Palgrave and Macmillan, 2015).

Shagan, Ethan H., *The Rule of Moderation: Violence, Religion and the Politics of Restraint in Early Modern England* (Cambridge: Cambridge University Press, 2011).

Shagan, Ethan, 'Confronting compromise: the schism and its legacy in mid-Tudor England' in *Catholics and the 'Protestant nation': Religious politics and identity in early modern England*, ed. Ethan Shagan (Manchester: Manchester University Press, 2005), pp. 49–68.

Shagan, Ethan H., *Popular Politics and the English Reformation* (Cambridge: Cambridge University Press, 2003).

Shamir, Avner, *English Bibles on Trial: Bible burning and the desecration of Bibles, 1640–1800* (London: Routledge, 2017).

Shuger, Debora, *Censorship and Cultural Sensibility: The Regulation of Language in Tudor-Stuart England* (Philadelphia, PA: University of Pennsylvania Press, 2006).

Smith, Malcolm, *Montaigne and Religious Freedom: The Dawn of Pluralism* (Geneva: Librairie Droz, 1991).

Spinks, Bryan D., 'German Influence on Edwardian Liturgies', in *Sister Reformations: The Reformation in Germany and in England*, ed. Dorothea Wendebourg (Tübingen: Mohr Siebeck, 2010), pp. 170–181.

Stephens, Peter, 'The Sacraments in the Confessions of 1536, 1549, and 1566 – Bullinger's Understanding in the Light of Zwingli's', *Zwingliana*, 33 (2006), pp. 51–76.

Suggett, Richard, and Eryn White, 'Language, literacy and aspects of identity in early modern Wales', in *The Spoken Word: Oral Culture in Britain, 1500–1850*, eds. Adam Fox and Daniel Woolf (Manchester: Manchester University Press, 2002), pp. 52–83.

Thuesen, Peter J., *In Discordance with the Scriptures: American Protestant Battles over Translating the Bible* (Oxford: Oxford University Press, 1999).

Timperley, Charles Henry, *The Dictionary of Printers and Printing, with the Progress of Literature, Ancient and Modern* (London: H. Johnson, 1839).

Tittler, Robert, *Townspeople and Nation: English Urban Experiences 1540–1640* (Stanford, CA: Stanford University Press, 2001).
Trueman, Carl R., 'Early English Evangelicals: Three examples', in *Sister Reformations: The Reformation in Germany and in England*, ed. Dorothea Wendebourg (Tübingen: Mohr Siebeck, 2010), pp. 15–28.
Trueman, Carl R., and Carrie Euler, 'The Reception of Martin Luther in Sixteenth- and Seventeenth-Century England', in *The Reception of Continental Reformation in Britain*, eds. Polly Ha and Patrick Collinson (Oxford: Oxford University Press, 2010), pp. 63–81.
Tyacke, Nicholas, ed., *England's Long Reformation 1500–1800* (London: UCL Press, 1998).
Wallis, Patrick, Justin Colson and David Chilosi, 'Structural change and economic growth in the British Economy before the Industrial Revolution, 1500–1800', *Journal of Economic History*, 78 (2018), pp. 862–903.
Walsby, Malcolm, and Graeme Kemp, eds., *The Book Triumphant: Print in transition in the sixteenth and seventeenth centuries* (Leiden: Brill, 2011).
Wandel, Lee Palmer, *The Eucharist in the Reformation* (Cambridge: Cambridge University Press, 2006).
Wansbrough, Henry, 'History and Impact of English Bible Translations', in *Hebrew Bible / Old Testament: The History of Its Interpretation, Vol II: From the Renaissance to the Enlightenment*, ed. Magne Sæbø (Göttingen: Vandenhoeck & Ruprecht, 2008), pp. 536–552.
Watt, Tessa, *Cheap Print and Popular Piety 1550–1640* (Cambridge: Cambridge University Press, 1991).
Watts, John L., ed., *The End of the Middle Ages? England in the Fifteenth and Sixteenth Centuries* (Stroud: Sutton Publishing, 1998).
Westbrook, Vivienne, *Long Travail and Great Paynes, A Politics of Reformation Revision* (Dordrecht: Kluwer Academic Publishers, 2001).
Whitfield White, Paul, *Theatre and Reformation: Protestantism, Patronage, and Playing in Tudor England* (Cambridge: Cambridge University Press, 1993).
Winters, Jennifer, 'The English Provincial Book Trade: Booksellers Stock-Lists, c.1520–1640' (unpublished doctoral thesis, University of St Andrews, 2012).
Wrightson, Keith, *Early Necessities: Economic Lives in Early Modern Britain, 1470–1750* (New Haven, CT: Yale University Press, 2000).
Wrigley, E.A. and R.S. Schofield, *The population history of England 1541–1871: A reconstruction* (Cambridge, MA: Harvard University Press, 1981).
Yarnell, Malcolm B., *Royal Priesthood in the English Reformation* (Oxford: Oxford University Press, 2014).

Oxford Dictionary of National Biography

Armstrong, C.D.C., 'Gardiner, Stephen, c.1495–1555'.
Baker House, Seymour 'Becon, Thomas (1512/13–1567)'.
Betteridge, Thomas, 'Harte, Henry (*d.* 1557)'.
Betteridge, Thomas, 'Champneys, John (d. in or after 1559)'.
Bradshaw, C., 'Huggarde, Miles (*fl.* 1533–1557)'.
Blake, N.F., 'Wyer, Robert (*fl.* 1524–1556)'.
Blatchly, J.M., 'Argentine, Richard (1510/11–1568)'.
Carter, P.R.N., 'Wentworth, Thomas, first Baron Wentworth (1501–1551)'.
Cummings, Brian, 'Samuel, William (*fl.* 1551–1569)'.
Daniell, David, 'Rogers, John (*c.*1500–1555)'.
Davies, C.S.L., 'Stafford, Henry, tenth Baron Stafford (1501–1563)'.
Devereaux, Janice, 'Shepherd, Luke (*fl.* 1548)'.
Erler, Mary C., 'Copland, Robert (*fl.* 1505–1547)'.
Gadd, I., 'Gibson, Thomas (d.1562)'.
Gadd, I., 'Toy, Humphrey (*b.* in or before 1537, *d.* 1577)'.
Gillespie, Alexandra, 'Petyt [Petit], Thomas (*d.* 1565/6)'.
Greening, Anna, 'Tottell, Richard (*b.* in or before 1528, *d.* 1593)'.
Gunn, S.J., 'Brandon, Charles, first duke of Suffolk (*c.*1484–1545)'.
Heal, Felicity, 'Allen, Edmund (1510s–1559)'.
Heijting, Willem, 'Mierdman, Steven [Niclaes van Oldenborch] (*c.*1510x12–1559)'.
James, Susan E., 'Katherine [Kateryn, Catherine] [*née* Katherine Parr] (1512–1548)'.
King, John N., 'William Baldwin (d. in or before 1563)'.
Loades, David, 'Proctor, John, (1521?–1584)'.
Löwe, J. Andreas, 'Smyth, Richard (1499/1500–1563)'.
Mears, Natalie, 'Singleton, Hugh (*d.* in or before 1593)'.
Neville-Sington, Pamela, 'Pynson, Richard (*c.*1449–1529/30)'.
Pantzer, K.F., 'Berthelet, Thomas (*d.* 1555)'.
Pettegree, Andrew, 'Wolfe, Reyner (*d.* in or before 1574)'.
Pettegree, Andrew, 'Utenhove, Jan (1516–1566)'.
Pettegree, Andrew, 'Hill, Nicolas [Nikolaos van den Berghe] (*d.* 1555)'.
Pettegree, Andrew, 'Lynne, Walter (*d.* in or before 1571)'.
Pettegree, Andrew, 'Day, John (1521/2–1584)'.
Pollard, A.F., 'Powell, Humphrey (*d.* in or after 1566)', rev. Anita McConnell.
Ryrie, Alec, 'Whitchurch, Edward (d.1562)'.
Ryrie, Alec, 'Brinklow, Henry (*d.* 1545/6)'.
Shrank, Cathy, 'Mardeley, John (*fl.* 1548–1558)'.

Steggle, Matthew, 'Udall, Nicholas (1504–1556)'.
Tedder, H.R., 'Jugge, Richard (c.1514–1577)' rev. Joyce Boro.
Trueman, Carl R., 'Traheron, Bartholomew (c.1510–1558?)'.
Trueman, Carl R., 'Barnes, Robert, (c.1495–1540)'.
Wabuda, Susan, 'Latimer, Hugh (c.1485–1555)'.

Index

a Lasco, Jan   55–56, 84, 174
Acts,
   Six Articles (1539)   37–40
   Uniformity (1549)   18, 45, 54
   Advancement of True Religion
     (1543)   37–39, 41
   Forty-Two Articles (1553)   19
   Repeale of Certaine Statutes (1547)   41–43, 59
   Silencing Disputes on the Eucharist
     (1547)   42–43
   For the putting away of diverse books and
     images (1549)   90–91
Antwerp   8–9, 25, 37, 40, 50, 55, 59, 63–64, 120, 136, 138, 173
Argentine, Richard   186, 249–250

Baldwin, William   102, 187, 248
Bale, John   2, 37, 48–50, 60, 70–72, 83–84, 104, 137, 227, 246, 249
Barlow, William   104
Barnes, Robert   49, 52, 173
Basel   9, 20, 25–26, 37, 81, 120–121, 191, 195
Becke, Edmund   74, 93, 98
Becon, Thomas   37, 46, 48–49, 84, 100, 111, 140, 249
Bergagne, Anthoni-Marie   61, 64
Berne   20
Berthelet, Thomas   3, 30, 79, 120, 130, 158–159, 205–206, 255
bibles   28, 78, 92–99, 112–114, 130, 173–174, 195, 214, 239–241, 245
   censorship   38, 41
   Great Bible   9–11, 38, 41, 85, 87, 92–93, 95–96, 98, 101, 119–120, 125, 129–130, 134, 152, 194
   Coverdale bible   38, 138–141, 156, 210
   Tyndale bible   38, 93, 128, 138, 220
   Taverner bible   93, 112, 214
   small format   43, 96, 98 127–128
   'Matthew' Bible   87, 92–93, 98, 140, 185, 214, 232, 239–241
   Richard Jugge's revision of Tyndale's bible   93, 108–110
   Marian and Elizabethan bibles   95–96
   diglot New Testaments   97–98

black rubric controversy   19
Bocher, Joan   54, 68–69, 74
Bonham, William   94, 226, 234, 236, 238, 240
Bonner, Edmund, bishop of London   18, 38, 58, 61, 84
bookbinding   192–197
   King Edward and Mary binder'   195
   Medallion binder   82, 194–195
book fairs   3, 9, 203
booksellers   39, 181, 198, 200–204, 233, 256
book burnings   38, 61, 66
Book of Common Prayer   18–19, 45, 85–89, 107, 125, 134, 151–152, 155–156, 194, 226
Brandon, Catherine, duchess of
   Suffolk   248–249
Brandon, Henry, duke of Suffolk   82
Brinklow, Henry   52, 217
Bristol   202–203
Bucer, Martin   17n, 21n, 46, 50, 53, 56, 60, 84, 95, 196, 246
Bullinger, Heinrich   2, 16n, 37, 46, 50, 53, 56–58, 74, 80, 82, 184–185, 244–245

Calvin, Jean   2, 20, 37, 46–47, 53, 107, 187, 206, 245
Caly, Robert   60, 62–64
Cambridge   21, 84, 121, 196–197, 202–203, 226, 246
Canterbury   23, 89n, 202–203
Capito, Wolfgang   103
Catechisms   84–86, 88, 91, 100–104, 107, 111–112, 143, 200
Cawood, John   30, 97, 110, 140–141, 160, 201, 205, 207
Caxton, William   8, 120
Cecil, William   43–45, 79, 85, 110–111, 174, 217, 247, 249, 251
Champneys, John   53, 69, 72
Chaucer, Geoffery   124, 149–150, 221, 229, 233–234, 240
churchwardens' accounts   86–87
Cole, Thomas   69, 75
compositors   181–184, 188, 191
Copland, Robert   187–188
Copland, William   73, 148, 160–161, 182, 209, 221–223, 229, 234–235, 238

correctors   183–188
Council of Trent   20
Coverdale, Miles   46, 48–49, 52, 80, 83–84, 200, 235, 251–252. *See also* bibles, Coverdale bible
Cranmer, Thomas, Archbishop of Canterbury   17–19, 21, 56, 68, 71, 83–89, 104, 111, 242
   author   2, 37, 46, 48, 54, 66–67, 72, 81, 83, 106, 143–144, 168, 170–171, 173, 195
   Homilies   18, 85–86, 88–89
   the Bible   18
   canon law   19
   internationalism   21, 80, 172*n*–173
Cromwell, Thomas   78, 200
Crowley, Robert   66, 136, 185–186, 212
Czech   8, 120

Day, John   30–31, 50, 56, 71–72, 74, 86, 91–94, 130, 176, 182, 186, 205, 209–211, 214–217, 248–249, 255
   Eucharist tracts   43
   bible printing   93–94, 96, 98, 108, 130, 214, 221
   patents   100, 110–113
   illustrations   140, 142–144, 152, 154–155
   type   159–160, 191
de Marcourt, Antoine   47, 50, 89
de Worde, Wynkyn   8, 120–121, 163–164, 187
debasement of the coinage   15, 23–24, 199–200
dictionaries   80–81, 220
Dublin   23, 86
Dudley, John, earl of Warwick, duke of Northumberland   15, 54
   recantation   64
   censorship   45, 47–48
   patron   19, 84, 111, 247
duodecimo format   43, 81, 93, 96, 98, 123, 127–128

educational publications   11–13, 81, 238
Edward VI, King of England   3, 31, 76–77, 246
   libraries   82–83, 195, 245, 247
   bible   96–97
   depictions   133–134, 143, 240, 244
Elizabeth I, Queen of England   245, 254
   Religious Settlement (1559)   19
   printing   27, 95, 110–113, 120–121, 138–140, 155, 179–180, 187, 256

English vernacular printing   7, 9, 11, 24, 28–31, 40, 81, 120, 157, 162, 178, 203
Emden   59, 238
Erasmus, Desiderius   37, 47, 50, 226
   Paraphrases   41, 85–86, 88, 91–92, 102, 250–253. *See also* Whitchurch, Edward, *Paraphrases*
Eucharist   18, 42–43, 48, 62, 66, 70, 100

Faques, William   120
Fisher, John, bishop of Rochester   37, 172, 206
Fleet Prison   56, 58, 72
Florio, Michelangelo   46, 55, 84–85
Format,
   book construction   11, 13, 122–125, 127
   production trends   11–13, 118, 123
   format and type   160–162
France   8, 15, 20, 59–60, 157, 173–174, 189, 191–192
Fries, Augustin   50, 55, 244
Frith, John   46, 49, 52, 54, 104, 217
Froschauer, Christopher   80, 92*n*, 98*n*, 125*n*, 127*n*, 168*n*

Gardiner, Stephen, bishop of Winchester   18, 55, 58
   author   59*n*–61, 63–64, 67, 84, 103, 172, 227
Gaultier, Thomas   97, 100, 105–108, 110, 173–174, 195, 221–223, 230, 234, 238
   type   159–160
Geminus, Thomas   121–122, 137, 251
Geneva   20, 47, 173, 245
Germany   8, 20, 69. *See also* Holy Roman Empire
Gilby, Thomas   52
Gilby, Anthony   46, 66
Grafton, Richard   9, 30–31, 88, 143, 176, 182, 205–206, 209–212
   imprisonment (1543)   39
   Printer to Edward, the Prince of Wales (1545)   39
   King's Printer of all books and statutes, acts, proclamations, injunctions and other volumes issued by the king   77–80
   canonical church works   85–89, 91
   bible printing   93, 98, 130

INDEX

Grafton, Richard (*cont.*)
   service books patent 93, 98, 100–102
   illustrations 132–144
   initials 150–156
   type 159–160, 192
grammars 81
Grey, Lady Jane 85, 244
Grynaeus, Simon 80

Hall, Edward 132–135, 143–144
Harte, Henry 53, 69, 71, 75
Hebrew 80–81, 196
Henry VIII, King of England 13, 61, 199
   censorship 37–39, 42–43
   printing 5–9, 11–13, 81, 119–122, 130, 176
   religious refugees 17, 49, 59, 81
Herford, John 55, 74, 98, 103, 121, 127, 225–228, 230
Hill, Nicolas 31, 50, 86, 93–96, 105, 107, 110, 173–174, 176, 182–183, 209, 211
   Illustrations 121–122, 130, 140, 143, 146, 148–149, 214
   type 159–160
   printer for hire 209, 211, 216, 218–221, 224–230, 233–235, 237–241
Hill, William 71–72, 91–94, 96, 142–143, 211–214, 222–223
Holy Roman Empire 8, 23, 25–26, 69
Homilies. See Cranmer, Thomas, Archbishop of Canterbury
Hooper, John, bishop of Worcester and Gloucester 3, 37, 46, 55–58, 60, 74, 83–84, 244–246
House of Lords 19
Huggarde, Myles 62–63, 66

Ipswich 23, 89–90, 186, 196, 199, 203, 206
Ireland 89–90, 100, 102, 226
Italian States 8–9*n*, 23

Joye, George 46, 48–49
Jugge, Richard 50, 93, 98, 100, 105, 108–110, 115, 131, 140–142, 201, 209, 220–221, 235–236, 238, 255
jurisprudence publications 12–13, 27, 30, 79, 112, 238

Kele, Richard 94, 148, 187, 207–209, 213, 216, 221–224, 229–230, 234–238, 240
Kett's rebellion 15, 44, 70

Kingston, John 148
Knox, John 19

Latimer, Hugh 2, 37, 46, 52, 84
Latin books 3, 11–12, 26–27, 29, 41, 64–65, 77–78, 80–81, 84, 95, 97, 101, 111–113, 166–168, 171–173, 175–176, 183, 245
Lawton, John 73
Lesse, Nicholas 228, 248–249
Lever, Thomas 46, 56, 84, 89
literacy rates 22, 51, 90, 178, 199
London 6, 8, 22–24, 198, 202
   economy 24, 198–200
Louvain 59, 61, 63–65, 173–174
Luther, Martin 2, 20, 46, 50, 53–54, 103, 227, 243
   Lutheranism 16, 20
Lynne, Gwalter 100, 103–105, 115, 143, 148, 209, 211, 220, 224, 227–229, 246–248
Lyon 8, 23, 25, 63, 120, 173

Mardeley, John 44, 46, 53–54, 70–71, 213
Marten, William 73
Mary I, Queen of England 32, 62
   printing 59, 65, 97–98, 110, 112–113, 140, 175, 179–180, 207, 256
Mary, Queen of Scots 14
Mayler, John 138–140, 146
medical publications 13, 27*n*
Melanchthon, Philipp 2, 46, 50, 53, 104, 185
Micronius, Martin 46, 55, 84, 113
Mierdman, Steven 31, 55, 100, 138–140, 173, 176, 182–183, 191, 209, 211
   bible printing 93, 95–96, 98, 108, 127–128, 130
   Antwerp & clandestine trade 50, 55, 104, 219
   patent 104–105
   illustrations 138–141
   printer for hire 218–221, 228
More, Thomas 65, 227
Mühlberg, battle of 20
Myddleton, William 142–143, 158, 182, 205–207

Netherlands 8, 20, 157, 173–174, 191
Nicolson, James 138–141 148
Norwich 15, 202–203
Nuremberg 8*n*, 25, 120

Ochino, Bernardino   46, 53, 55, 84, 103, 186, 246
Oecolampadius, Johannes   46, 53, 60, 227, 243
Order of Communion   85–86, 88, 91–92, 94
ordinances and edicts   13, 30, 36–37, 79, 234, 238, 240
Oswen, John   71, 74, 86, 89–90, 98, 100, 102, 115, 202, 205–206
Oxford   21, 61–62, 84, 106, 167, 185, 196–197, 202–203, 246

Paget, William   44, 247
paper   86, 119, 128
    page sizes   122–125
    production   160, 176, 189–190
    presentation   126–127
Paris   8–9, 22–23, 25, 59–61, 63, 120, 138, 163, 173, 189
Parr, Katherine, Queen of England   147, 242, 250–253
patents   39, 72, 78, 80, 88, 90–115
Paul's Cross, St Paul's Churchyard   38, 106, 185
    publishing syndicate   93–94, 124–125, 148–150, 214, 221–223, 225–229, 232–241, 253
    booksellers and book shops   80, 201, 203, 226, 235–236
Petre, William   45, 240n
Petyt, Thomas   94, 148, 201, 213, 234–240
Poland   7, 120
Pole, Reginald   64
Ponet, John   46, 80, 83, 111
Portugal   7, 120
Powell, Humphrey   72, 74, 86, 89–90, 100, 102, 112, 114–115, 189–190, 225, 227
Powell, William   97, 125, 142–143, 146, 154, 158, 160, 182, 205–207, 228
pressmen   182–183, 188
Privy Council   39, 44, 47, 61–62, 68, 97n, 108
proclamations   38–42, 47–49, 70, 81, 97, 104, 194, 240n–241
provincial printing   23, 56, 89–90, 102, 115, 121, 186, 196, 199, 203, 206
provincial booksellers   200–203
Proctor, John   62–63
Pynson, Richard   9, 120–121, 191

Radicalism   14, 53–54, 57, 62, 67–75, 213
    anti-radical publications   74–76
    anabaptism   67, 69
    anti-trinitarianism   67–68
    sacramentarianism   67
Raynald, Thomas   61, 70, 86, 91–94, 96, 142, 148, 211–214, 216, 222–223, 225
Regnault, Francois   9, 138, 200
Rhegius, Urbanus   47, 53, 103, 227, 243
Ridley, Nicholas, bishop of London   58
Rogers, John   185
Rouen   59–60, 63–65
Roy, William   49–50n

Schmalkaldic League   20
Scoloker, Anthony   71–72, 110, 162, 186, 209, 211, 216–217, 249–250
Scotland   14–15, 80, 246
Seres, William   31, 71, 186, 209–211, 214–217, 249
    Eucharist tracts   43
    bible printing   98
    patent   100, 110–112
    illustrations   140, 143–144
sextodecimo format   66, 96, 98, 108, 123, 127–128, 174, 220
Seymour, Anne, duchess of Somerset   246–248, 252–253
Seymour, Edward, duke of Somerset   14–15, 18, 44–45, 68, 80, 195
    author   143, 187, 248
    patron   55, 70, 84, 104, 242, 244–246, 250
Shepherd, Luke   46, 53–54, 71–72
Shrewsbury   202
Singleton, Hugh   213, 223, 225, 227
Smith, Richard   55, 61–62, 64–66, 103, 172, 213
Smyth, Henry   146, 234–237
Spain   8–9, 25
St Paul's Cathedral, *See* Paul's Cross
Sternhold, Thomas   102, 111–112
Stoughton, Robert   71, 169, 248
stranger churches of London   21, 55, 84–85, 100, 103, 105–108, 113, 173–174, 181–182, 248–249
Strasbourg   63, 120
Sutton, Henry   148, 180n
Swiss Confederation   8, 20, 25, 80, 244

INDEX

Tab, Henry   208*n*, 222, 230, 234–236, 238
Tottell, Richard   100, 106, 110, 112–113, 115, 205, 207, 235–236
Toy, Humphrey   213, 226
Toy, Robert   94, 225–226, 234–236
Tracy, Richard   49, 52
Traheron, Bartholomew   81–83
Tunstall, Cuthbert, prince-bishop of Durham   59
Turner, William   49, 52, 74
Type   157–171, 175, 198
  production   190–192
  italic   158, 166–168
  rotunda   158, 166–168
  fraktura   158, 166
  bastarda   158, 162–16
  schwabacher   121, 158, 166
  textura   158, 162, 168
  Greek   80–81, 121, 158, 166, 191
Tylle, William   142, 144–146
Tyndale, William   37, 46, 48–49, 52, 217, 226.
  See also bibles, Tyndale bible

Udall, Nicholas   100, 113–114, 121, 167–169, 251
Utenhove, Jan   46, 55, 84, 107

van der Straten, Derick   50, 136–137
van Parris, George   68, 75
Veale, Abraham   94, 201, 225–227, 234–237, 240
Venice   8–9, 23, 25, 120
Vermigli, Peter Martyr   21*n*, 46, 55–56, 60–61, 80, 84, 113–114, 167–171, 184–185, 246, 251
Vestment controversy   56

Waen, Jan   61, 65
Wales   89, 100, 102, 202
Walley, John   94, 148, 209, 221–222, 224, 226, 230, 234–248
Wentworth, Thomas, first baron   186, 249–250

Wesel   50, 63, 137, 227
Western Rising (Prayer Book Rebellion)   14–15, 44, 88
Whitchurch, Edward   9, 31, 55, 74, 82, 114, 176, 182, 185, 205, 210–212
  Paraphrases   85–89, 91–92, 102, 118. *See also* Erasmus, Desiderius
  bible printing   43, 64, 93, 98, 130
  canonical church works   85–89
  service books patent   100–102
  illustrations and initials   132, 138–140, 143, 146–147, 152–153, 156
  type   159, 192
Wittenberg   8*n*, 25, 37, 120
Wolfe, Reyner   61, 100, 168–173, 175–176, 205–206
  King's Typographer and Bookseller for Latin, Greek and Hebrew   77–78, 80–81, 83, 111
  patent   100, 105–106, 110
  illustrations   143–144, 170
  type   159–160, 166–168, 175, 191
woodcut illustrations   103, 129–156, 162–165, 255
  Great Bible   9, 138, 152
  second-hand trade   136–156
  title borders   109, 133–134, 141–150, 170, 214, 240
  initials   150–156
Worcester   23, 56, 86, 89–90, 196, 199, 202
Wycliffe, John   49–50*n*, 136
Wyer family press   176
Wyer, Robert   162–166, 180*n*, 205–207
Wyer, Richard   71
Wyght, John   94, 148, 213, 222, 234–238, 240

York   201–203

Zurich   16*n*–17, 80
  reformed church   20, 74, 184, 244–245
  printing   37, 50, 55, 63, 184–185
Zwingli, Huldrych   20, 46, 53, 89, 186, 217